The practical guide to

ALLOTMENT GARDENING

Growing Vegetables and Fruit

Step-by-step techniques for cultivating organic produce on your plot all year round

CHRISTINE AND MICK LAVELLE

LORENZ BOOKS

CONTENTS

INTRODUCTION

The aim of this book is to show how anyone can become a successful allotment gardener. Whether you are an experienced gardener or not, an allotment can easily become a productive and absorbing hobby that can involve your whole family. Time spent on an allotment provides a vital link with nature and an opportunity to escape the troubles of modern living. To most people they are places to grow fresh food, but they can also have a value as little green oases or even mini nature reserves.

Above: *Watering is just one example of a task that, while straightforward, must still be done correctly in order to ensure success.*

WHY GROW ON AN ALLOTMENT?

The start of the 21st century has seen a huge rise in the popularity of home-grown foods. Many turn to this because of concerns for their family's wellbeing following successive food scares, although it is arguably the individual empowerment that growing food gives that ultimately proves the biggest draw. Many home-growers also believe that the food they grow is not only inherently healthier, but also tastier and, without a doubt, fresher.

HOW THE BOOK IS ORGANIZED

Growing your own food, although an attractive idea, does require certain skills. This comprehensive book is intended as an essential guide to show you how to do this. It aims to try and demystify this area of gardening, and is structured in a simple, down-to-earth way, with easy-to-follow explanations throughout. The language used is largely non-technical, although the techniques described are based upon sound scientific principles. Explanations of underlying principles are followed by clear advice on how best to lay out, build, plan, plant and maintain plots for home-growing. While ideally suited to beginners, the book should also prove useful for those with more gardening experience who want to expand and transfer their skills to an allotment site.

The text is lavishly supported with illustrations and photographs and, wherever possible, growing techniques and systems are described. Projects are accompanied by straightforward step-by-step instructions showing how jobs should be done, and many important tips and useful 'how-to' guides bring all the ideas to life. Plans and instructions are included to help you to understand how to blend the functionality of the growing space with other needs, such as providing a outdoor play space for children.

WHAT THIS BOOK COVERS

Starting with an explanation of what allotments are, the text outlines the underlying principles and natural cycles that exist both on a global scale and within your own plot. It aims to show how an allotment should ideally work in harmony with nature's rhythms and reveals how you can manage

Below: *In time, your allotment will develop its own character that is as much about you as the plants that you choose to grow there.*

Below: *Planning crops, such as lettuce, is very important if you want to ensure a steady supply through the season.*

Left: *The framework and layout of your allotment is a key aspect of successful growing, and needs careful planning.*

your cropping to take best advantage of these. Understanding the soil is fundamental to creating a successful allotment, and this is described simply and concisely to ensure that you can prepare the ground properly.

Once these basics are explained, the section dealing with planning your crops gives detailed advice on how to assess your own wants and needs so that you can go on to create an effective and workable plan for a yearly cropping schedule. This is followed by a section on how to grow the crops themselves. Practical, effective horticultural practices are combined with simple, commonsense advice on harvesting and storing a range of crops; helpful hints on choosing tools, equipment and materials; and advice on how to decide whether you need structures such as sheds or glasshouses. The importance of environmentally friendly practices features throughout the text, although alternatives are also discussed and compared.

The directory section gives clear descriptions of some of the commoner types of edible crops that you may want to grow, how to grow them, and tips for getting the best from them. Each entry includes information on the pests and diseases that affect the plants, how to harvest and store them, and recommended varieties to try. The importance of keeping your crops healthy is dealt with in detail in the plant health section, while the final chapter, a month-by-month calendar of care, helps you plan your plot for the year and provides an at-a-glance reference.

The book isn't just about the practice of growing crops, however, and considerable emphasis is placed upon getting out there and enjoying time on your plot. Tending plants, rather than being a chore, can easily become a time for you and your family to relax and experience closeness to nature within your own 'safe' space. Whether you see your allotment as an outdoor living space, a wildlife haven or as a place to grow food for your table, the application of careful planning, sound crop selection and tried-and-tested gardening techniques outlined in this book can help you to transform your plot into a highly productive space. Ultimately, an allotment can offer you a healthy place in which to spend time, a great opportunity to meet fellow gardeners and a relaxing and sociable way to garden.

Right: *Sheds provide both storage and shelter from the elements, making them an invaluable addition if you have the space.*

26

ALLOTMENT BASICS

Obtaining an allotment can be a time-consuming process. It helps, however, to know a little about the area, the specific site, the rules and regulations governing the allotment, and what you want to achieve so you can be specific about your requirements. Once you have a plot, you will need to make a number of decisions about what you can do with it and how you are going to set it out. This chapter aims to help you with your planning by providing information about how how to set realistic goals, different layout options, and additional considerations such as permanent structures, keeping livestock and buying tools and equipment.

Left: *The sight of an allotment at the height of the growing season is enticing, but is ultimately the product of much hard work.*

Above: *Flowers such as these sunflowers make a colourful addition to the plot and can be used as cut blooms for the home.*

Above: *Time spent protecting your crops is worthwhile, and means you will reap the rewards later with a bumper harvest.*

Above: *Larger allotments may have room for a glasshouse and shed, but you should always allow space for a composting area.*

THE HISTORY OF ALLOTMENTS

Above: *Allotments have always been a place where generations meet, sharing both time and experiences in a natural setting.*

Allotments and community gardens are a familiar sight in a modern urban setting. They originated as a result of social concerns about the plight of the poor and needy, as well as to provide a source of vital food production during wartime, but for many gardeners today the emphasis has shifted and they now represent a place where city-dwellers can get back to nature and grow tasty and healthy food while mixing with like-minded individuals.

WHAT IS AN ALLOTMENT?

Essentially an allotment is an area or 'parcel' of land allotted to a tenant, who undertakes to tend and cultivate the area, usually in return for a small rent being paid. The word 'allotment' was first coined in England In the late 1500s, under Elizabeth I, as the name for the plots of land attached to tenant cottages that were given as compensation for the loss of common lands. Similar land allocation schemes exist in other countries; they follow a similar framework, although their names can vary. In North America, Australia and New Zealand, for instance, the term 'community garden' is used, whereas across much of Europe they tend to be described as community, family, social or work gardens.

WHY WERE ALLOTMENTS NEEDED?

Since ancient times, people have shared pieces of land around their village in order to eke out an existence by growing crops and grazing livestock. As populations have grown, and particularly as industry and agriculture have developed, the need for increased efficiency has meant that there has been ever more pressure on traditional 'shared' approaches to food production. As a consequence, many common areas have disappeared, and people's link with the land and the food it provides severed.

Land Enclosure, as it came to be called, occurred in many parts of the world during the 18th and 19th centuries. While this did increase efficiency in agriculture and food supply to the burgeoning urban centres, it benefited only a relatively small minority of landowners; the majority of people became disenfranchised and were forced to seek work in the growing urban centres as they lost access to the land. In response to this, certain influential members of the ruling elite of the time made moves to provide land in the form of allotments, principally for the poor and unemployed so that they could grow their own produce.

Over time the popularity of allotments persisted, but it was during the two world wars of the 20th century that they were most appreciated, providing food security during times of shortage. After World War II, however, there was a decline in interest as eating and growing fresh food was eclipsed by the arrival of convenience food, a trend that escalated through the second half of the 20th century. This was reversed only at the very end of the century, as concerns over food quality and a feeling of alienation from nature led to a new demand for allotments, which is as yet unabated.

WHERE DO YOU FIND THEM?

Allotments and community gardens are often concentrated in areas of high-density living, mostly in urban centres, although some are to be found in more rural settings. What they all usually have in common is a group of local residents who no longer have a direct connection to the land. Allotments can be very diverse, often as varied as the surrounding communities of gardeners that use them. Some are nurtured communally and their produce shared among all participants, whereas others contain individual plots for personal use.

Left: *In the mid-20th century allotments fulfilled a vital social need, as successive wars caused food shortages for families.*

Above: *Allotments are typically moderately sized plots, tended by one owner, and contain a range of edible produce.*

Allotments and community gardens can also vary depending upon where in the world they are found. In the UK and the rest of Europe they tend to be characterized by collections of individual plots, each measuring hundreds of square metres. In North America, while community gardens do include the so-called 'victory garden' areas that consist of numerous small plots, they also encompass 'greening projects', which transform man-made communal areas into green spaces that can be used for growing, keeping livestock or simply as pleasant recreation zones.

THE BENFITS OF ALLOTMENTS

In the hectic modern world, allotments can enhance the quality of urban life, providing a meaningful leisure activity and enabling people to try their hand at sowing, growing, cultivating and harvesting vegetables. In addition, they may also be a place where children and adolescents can play, communicate and discover the natural world. Some are used by disadvantaged groups, such as the unemployed, those with disabilities or immigrant families, offering them the chance to meet like-minded individuals and to help build confidence and a sense of communal living.

As most allotments are characterized by either a collective space or numerous land parcels in one place, tenants quickly develop a sense of cohesion and belonging, involving not only the social interaction of gardening but also contributions to growers' associations, competing in shows or events, and the shared responsibility of having to abide by an agreed constitution and bylaws. This involvement entitles people to certain democratic rights within their communities, and with this comes a sense of empowerment and purpose.

Ultimately, then, the exact nature of an allotment or community garden will vary according to its location and the needs of the surrounding community. For the purposes of this book, an allotment will be viewed as a single 'parcel' of land that is accessible for an individual or family, and, while the communal aspects of allotment gardening are extremely important, it is the mechanics of how to actually grow things on the plot that will be the main focus here.

Above: *Community gardens in urban areas enable tenants to experience growing food, despite often having very modest plots.*

Above: *Seeing where vegetables come from helps children to connect more readily with nature in a way that is great fun for them.*

WHY GROW ON AN ALLOTMENT?

An allotment is far more than simply a place in which you can grow your own food. Indeed, many people recognize that having a plot is actually a lifestyle choice. While producing healthy fresh fruit and vegetables may be the central activity, the site also provides opportunities for fresh air and exercise, fun for the whole family and the chance to join an established community of people with similar interests.

FRESH, HEALTHY FOOD

In recent years people have become much more interested in growing their own fruit, vegetables and herbs. In itself, this may not seem particularly remarkable, but it represents a dramatic reversal of the declining trend in this area that marked most of the late 20th century. One of the reasons for the shift was concerns about the quality of food from supermarkets following numerous food 'scares' in the 1980s and 1990s and new information about pesticide residues, both of which raised the profile of organic foods. This, coupled with a growing awareness of food miles and wasteful packaging, meant that many became increasingly sceptical about the food they were buying. A greater public demand for more details about where food came from and how it was grown arose, and with it there was a corresponding surge in grow-your-own tendencies, as this it not only assures the safety and quality of the food, but also cuts out the need for transport and packaging.

The problem for a lot of people, though, is that many modern households do not have gardens, and those that do either don't have enough room to grow crops or they are poorly situated. Allotments are an ideal solution for people in this situation, offering them the chance to grow enough fresh food to feed the whole family in some cases.

An allotment of around 250m^2 (2688ft^2) can produce enough vegetables to keep a family of four or five going for most of the year. Not only that, but clever planning will result in a wonderful array of fresh produce, from expensive delicacies such as artichokes, asparagus or French (green) beans, to traditional staples such as cabbages, carrots and potatoes.

HEALTHY OUTDOOR LIVING

Although food production is usually the prime motivation for most allotment-growers, the lure and benefits of fresh air and gentle exercise are also extremely important. In many ways, an allotment could be likened to an outdoor gym, enabling people to take exercise while being in touch with the natural world around them. All in all, an allotment is good for both mental as well as physical well-being, and has the added bonus of being much cheaper than joining a gym.

An allotment also allows people with little or no land around their own property to have a plot of land 'to call their own.'

Below: *Growing runner beans up a set of bamboo canes will help maximize the space on your allotment.*

Below: *The whole family will enjoy eating the fresh and tasty food they have grown themselves, and the shopping bill will also go down.*

Above: *Allotments offer an absorbing hobby that will provide tasty, fresh produce and help promote a healthy way of living.*

This in itself can be an extremely important motivation, enabling people to gain fulfilment within their leisure time and achieve a sense of ownership and personal space.

SOMETHING THE WHOLE FAMILY CAN DO

Allotments can be a personal, and solitary, hobby, where growers go to escape from it all and spend a little time on their own. Increasingly though, they are places where the whole family will go. Even a modest-sized plot can be a wonderful place to encourage children to learn about nature and growing food. At its most basic level it shows them where food really comes from – that it is grown, involves effort and is not merely a pre-packaged product on a supermarket shelf. It also introduces them to a wider variety of foods than they may otherwise have encountered, and involving them in the whole process, from seed packet to dinner table, can be a great way to get them to eat their five-a-day. The excitement and anticipation involved in growing the food is often the best motivation there is to encourage healthy eating.

HELPING PRESERVE THE ENVIRONMENT

While many of us feel that we would like to help protect the environment, modern living often leaves us feeling helpless in the face of the challenges of reducing our carbon footprints. An allotment is a form of empowerment in this respect, giving you the ability to grow food that limits the use of fertilizers and pesticides, transportation, packaging and waste. A well-managed allotment that takes full advantage of recycling and composting techniques is an environmental benefit in itself, which, if managed properly, can help not just to minimize harm to nature and wildlife, but can even become a mini nature reserve.

A LIFESTYLE CHOICE

Growing food on an allotment will change your life in a variety of ways. At its simplest it will reduce your weekly shopping bill and provide fresher food which almost invariably tastes better than that bought from stores. It is also a great chance to meet new people, often from all walks of life, and share both their and your own experiences. It is perhaps this communal aspect of an allotment that is ultimately the most life-changing benefit and, in many cases, proves the greatest inspiration.

BENEFITS OF GROWING ON AN ALLOTMENT

Below are just a few of the positive benefits that allotment gardening may bring to you, your family and your local area and environment.

- It is a good way to keep fit, in the fresh air, without having to expend very much money.
- Provides an excellent opportunity to make new friends.
- You will produce your own food, which will be tastier and cheaper than that available in most stores.
- Crops can have higher nutrient values than commercially grown ones, as well as inevitably being much fresher.
- The monthly shopping bill should be greatly reduced if you plan the crops carefully so there is something on offer all year.
- Growing your own food gives a sense of achievment and satisfaction that can bolster the spirits.
- It will provide cheap entertainment for all the family and an opportunity for everyone to learn new skills.
- Offers the space for novice and experienced gardeners to expand their horizons and try their hand at growing crops that they may not have room for in their home gardens, as well as potentially being introduced to more exotic species by neighbouring plot holders.
- Children and young people will have a safe space in which to play and learn more about the natural world as well as gaining an understanding of where food comes from.
- An allotment is a community and can help people to feel more involved with their local area.
- The allotment site will provide a habitat for insects, birds and animals, enriching the local environment and helping biodiversity.
- A well-tended allotment is attractive and will improve the look and overall atmosphere, especially in urban areas.
- Compost heaps offer an easy way to reduce household waste, while lateral thinking and recycling of wood and other materials engenders a sense of thriftiness and sustainability.

Above: *Fresh home-grown crops are a major incentive for getting an allotment, but are the result of commitment and hard work.*

OBTAINING AN ALLOTMENT

A well-tended allotment site can be quite a spectacle; one that can excite and inspire you to obtain and tend a plot of your own. While the prospect of the allotment lifestyle is appealing, it is very important that you find out how to apply for one and make certain that you get one that is right for your needs. Remember that an allotment can be a real commitment that will require time and effort for it to be as productive as possible.

FINDING AN ALLOTMENT

Obtaining an allotment is usually a relatively simple process, once you have the details of where to apply and who to contact. Who this is often depends upon the ownership of the site. Allotments and community gardens vary around the world and their ownership might well be influenced by where you live. In Britain for instance, the majority are owned by local authorities and applications are lodged with a local council. Others elsewhere may be owned by private associations or even private landlords, and it is well worth visiting an allotment area near you to familiarize yourself with the site in question and find out more about who you would need to contact.

Some community gardens limit their membership to residents within a particular catchment area or even an individual housing project, and membership may be relatively short term. In other places, however, plots might remain with a particular tenant for years, even decades, meaning that applying for a plot might simply get you on to a waiting list, which can be as much as 20 years! Either way, it will pay for you to do your homework, and you may discover you need to apply to several to stand a chance of getting a site. Contacting local allotment or produce associations can be extremely useful as they will often be able to put you in touch with the right people.

BE REALISTIC ABOUT YOUR OWN ABILITIES

While enthusiasm is an essential prerequisite of allotment gardening, it is essential that you temper this with a degree of realism about what you will be able to achieve. You need to remember that established plots are the product of a sustained level of effort by the tenant. In short, what you get out of a plot will depend upon what you put into it.

The biggest obstacle for many new allotment tenants can be over-ambition. If you are applying for a new plot, you would be well advised to pause for a moment, examine your motives and consider what will be involved in taking it on. Try not to be put off by the difficulties you foresee however, as the object of the exercise is not to stifle your ambition but merely to be objective. Once you have a clear idea of your own capabilities then you are ready to make your application, as you'll be clearer about what sort of plot best suits your needs and can make your application accordingly.

Left: *When you are considering getting an allotment, it is always worth talking to other plot holders first to find out if it is for you. They will be able to tell you how much effort, time and money is really required, as well as providing inspiration and advice.*

Far left: *You may want to consider having a shed on your allotment as a handy place to store your gardening tools and other equipment.*

Right: *You will need certain tools in order to establish and maintain an allotment site, and these should be factored in when calculating the cost of having a plot.*

Below: *Community gardens are a great way of getting to know other people in your area and gaining knowledge and expertise from fellow gardeners.*

CONSIDER THE TIME AN ALLOTMENT WILL NEED

While the idea of time spent on an allotment can be enticing, you need to remember that it is a year-round commitment that will often involve your being there in all weathers. Crops need regular attention and fitting this around the rest of your life can occasionally be a struggle for even the most committed allotment-growers.

The best way to approach this is to remember that a little bit of time as often as other commitments will allow is usually better than sporadic bouts of feverish activity. It isn't something that you can be half-hearted about though: a successful allotment is the product of regular attention and, perhaps most importantly, time devoted to crops just when it is needed.

GO AND TALK TO PLOT HOLDERS

The idea of approaching more experienced plot holders may seem daunting, particularly when you are new to allotment growing. In reality, however, the majority of allotment holders are very friendly and approachable. People that tend plots are essentially gardeners, and as a rule they will enjoy meeting people who share their interest and be more than willing to answer questions and pass on their pearls of horticultural wisdom and encouragement.

Plot owners can usually offer invaluable practical advice about whether the site in question may suit your particular needs, what type the soil is, which crops can be grown there, and the rules and obligations that apply to plot holders and how these affect them. They may also give insider information on whether plots are likely to become vacant for rent. Often they will offer to take you on a tour of their own patch and tell you how they went about creating a productive plot.

Talking and meeting tenants can also be the best way to understand the sense of community that exists on a site, which in turn can bolster your enthusiasm if your application results in your being put on a long waiting list.

WEIGH UP ALL THE POTENTIAL COSTS CAREFULLY

While one of your objectives for growing on an allotment might be for you to save money, you should consider that unless you are lucky enough to inherit a well set out and maintained plot, you may need to invest in some materials in order to make it meet your own needs. Add tools and equipment to this, the cost of seed, fertilizers and a whole host of other sundries such as string, canes, netting etc., and the costs can soon mount up.

The best idea is to plan your plot so that you can set it up gradually, spreading the cost over a period of time, and concentrate on getting the layout right. Don't think that 'throwing money' at projects will guarantee success, and remember that magazines and garden centres are often full of 'must-have' items, which, in truth, you can often do perfectly well without! It is worth investigating local recycling schemes at this point, as you can often get a surprising amount of tools and equipment for free.

Above: *Young or tender crops appreciate some protection from cold nights and a fleece tunnel is one way of giving this.*

UNDERSTANDING YOUR ALLOTMENT

Plants, like all living things, flourish when given the right conditions. Certain plants will only thrive in a hot, sunny and dry garden, for example, while others may need a cool, moist and shady environment to prosper. If you are to have healthy plants, you need to choose those that are best suited to your site and this means understanding exactly what conditions prevail and taking into account a range of environmental factors.

CLIMATE

The climate affects plants in a variety of ways, depending on the plant's location, its stage of maturity, the length of exposure and the intensity of the type of weather. Climate may have a dramatic effect on plant growth and development, especially when extreme weather conditions prevail.

TEMPERATURE

All plant species have their own maximum and minimum temperature tolerances, beyond which the life processes of the plant cease. As a general rule, the maximum temperature that most plants can tolerate is around 35°C (95°F), while the minimum is highly variable. The air and soil temperatures are also crucial in influencing dormancy within plants and this, in turn, largely dictates the length of the growing season.

Air temperature is affected by the degree of energy received from the sun. A sheltered site that benefits from the warming effects of the sun may be used for growing plants that are indigenous to warmer climates.

Soil temperature influences a plant's root development and the rate at which water and nutrients can be absorbed. Sandy soils warm up quicker and earlier in the season than clay soils, mainly because they are relatively free-draining and do not hold as much water. Sites that receive a lot of sun, or with a slight incline towards it, will also warm up quicker than shady ones.

WATER

This is the major constituent of all plants. In most allotments, rainfall is the principal source of water for plants and it can be lost through evaporation or surface run-off, although much of it is soaked up by soil particles. This water may then be absorbed by the root hairs of the plant.

Water may also be held in the air and is referred to as humidity. The amount of water vapour in the atmosphere at any one time is referred to as the relative humidity and is measured as a percentage of the saturation point (100 per cent humidity).

Waterlogging refers to the build-up of water that may occur in badly drained soil with poor structure. The roots of plants that are not adapted to these conditions will suffer and probably die through asphyxiation.

LIGHT LEVELS

Sunlight enables photosynthesis (the method by which plant food is made) to occur. As a result, it is vital to new growth as well as sustaining existing growth. Seasonal changes in light levels may also trigger different stages in the plants' development.

AIR CIRCULATION

Even moderate winds can increase a plant's transpiration rate. However, a light wind can also have beneficial effects, providing relief from extreme heat and cooling the foliage. It will also 'change the air' around the plant, and thus help to alleviate a stagnant atmosphere that could promote disease.

ASSESSING THE CLIMATE

Climatic information for your local area is generally available. Weather forecasts are an obvious source, but long-term records are a good option. From these you can find out about average rainfall, snow, frosty days, wind direction and monthly temperatures.

Left: *Seasonal crops growing on an allotment need watering in dry times, and there is no better source than collected rainwater.*

MICROCLIMATES IN AN ALLOTMENT

Even a small plot can contain a variety of microclimates, ranging from cool, shady corners to hot, dry areas. A proper assessment of the growing conditions allows you to choose the right plants for the right place.

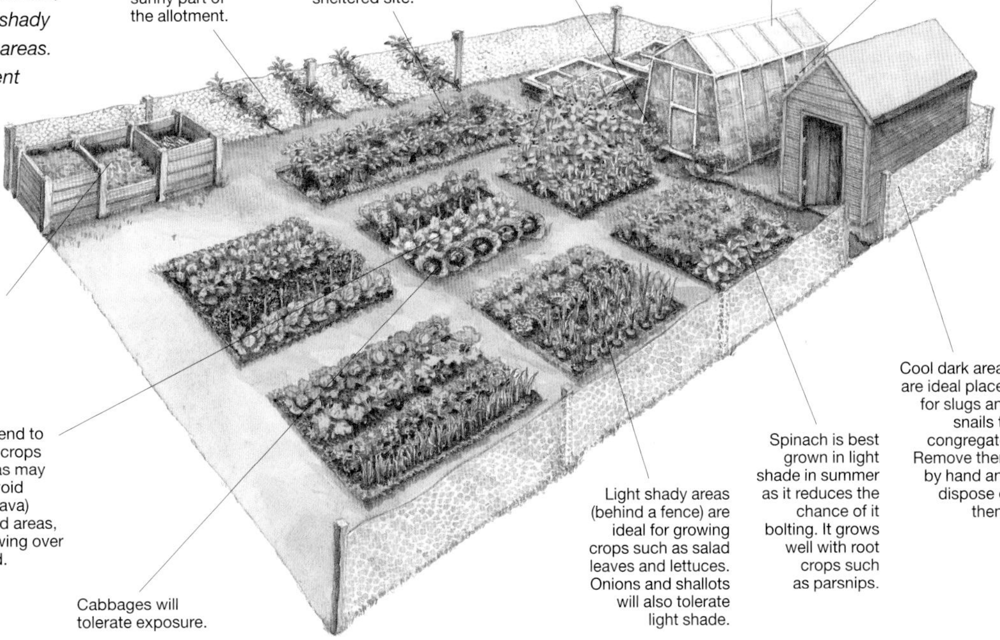

AN ALLOTMENT'S MICROCLIMATE

The prevailing weather conditions in confined or discrete areas are termed the microclimate. For example, there will be a range of environments within a small allotment area that may be very different from those weather conditions prevailing elsewhere in the locality. Observe what is going on in your own plot and keep a careful record of the position and influence of the following features:

Walls, hedges and fences may cause wind turbulence and dryness, depending upon their height and density. They may cause cold air to build up on sloping sites by preventing it from 'draining away' downwards. This can create frost pockets that may have a crucial affect on the type and range of plants that may be grown.

Shadow projections from permanent features, such as buildings, walls, hedges and large trees, may create a range of dense shadows, resulting in dark, dry and often cool conditions that will only suit certain plant species.

Hot spots may occur with aspects that are subject to high and prolonged levels of sunlight. Plants may struggle in the dryness created by such strong sunlight.

Damp areas may be anticipated where the ground is low-lying, especially on very heavy soils. During intense rainfall you should also note the direction of water flow including, where necessary, the route taken by excess surface water, which may in extreme cases be the cause of soil erosion.

Soil type and pH play an important role in the ability of a site to support particular plant species. The relative acidity or alkalinity can affect the availability of certain essential nutrients, leading to either shortage or toxicity in plants not ideally suited to the pH of a soil. It is always better to choose plants suited to the soil type on a plot. Attempts to alter the pH by acidifying or adding lime are rarely satisfactory and neither are long-term solutions.

Existing habitat types on and around the allotment indicate what plants are likely to thrive. Notes should be made on the range of species and the likely wildlife value.

The allotment topography (the shape and aspect of the land) may also affect what you are able to do. If a garden slopes toward the direction of the midday sun, for instance, it will be warmer than a flat site. Sloping or uneven plots have their own problems, particularly if you wish to site a greenhouse.

RIGHT PLANT, RIGHT PLACE

Once you have assessed your allotment environment, you will be able to choose the right plants for your site. Every location has its own unique set of advantages and limitations, and these take time to evaluate, so trial and error is ultimately the most reliable method.

Right: *A rain gauge allows you to assess soil moisture and helps show when crops might need extra water to maintain their growth.*

THE NATURAL CYCLE

All the crops grown in an allotment are entirely dependent upon a range of natural processes. For example, plants produce their own food using carbon dioxide from the air, water from the soil and energy from the sun in a process known as photosynthesis. The energy in this sugar powers all the growth, development and life-giving processes within the plant. Once the natural cycles are understood, you can learn how to work in harmony with nature's rhythms and cycles.

Above: *Plant leaves are remarkable structures because they are the factories in which a plant makes its food.*

WHAT PLANTS NEED

In natural systems, nitrogen, phosphorus and potassium are repeatedly taken up by the plant, used and returned to the soil when the plant dies, drops its leaves or is eaten by an animal. This process is known as nutrient cycling. Plant nutrients are covered in more depth later. For now we need only look at three of the most important natural cycles: water, carbon and nitrogen.

THE WATER CYCLE

The movement and endless recycling of water between the atmosphere, the surface of the land and under the soil is called the water cycle and is driven by the energy of the sun and the force of gravity.

Water vapour in the atmosphere condenses into clouds, then falls as snow, rain, sleet or hail. This water may be taken up by plants, stored in lakes, enter the soil or flow over the surface of the land in streams and rivers. The sun causes water to evaporate back into the atmosphere, or gravity may pull it down through the pores of the soil to be stored as slow-moving ground water.

Water can also return to the atmosphere indirectly through plants' leaves – a process known as transpiration – and this is highest during periods of high temperatures, wind, dry air and sunshine.

THE CARBON CYCLE

All life on earth is based on carbon, and the chemistry of the carbon atom and its derived substances is called organic chemistry. Carbon has many sources, some living and some dead. When carbon is released into the air, the origin is called a source. All living things release some carbon and are sources, but there are other sources too, including volcanoes and activities such as burning wood and fossil fuels.

When carbon becomes part of a living organism, or is locked up in sediments or rocks, it is said to have entered a sink. The balance between carbon that has been liberated from a source and that entering a sink is important for the health of the planet, and has an effect on the global temperature.

THE NITROGEN CYCLE

Nitrogen is used by living organisms to produce a number of complex organic molecules such as amino acids, proteins and nucleic acids, the 'building blocks' of life. The largest store of nitrogen is in the atmosphere, where it exists as a gas. This store is about one million times larger than the total nitrogen contained in living organisms.

Despite its abundance in the atmosphere, plants can only take up nitrogen in two solid forms: ammonium and nitrate. Most plants fulfil their needs using nitrate from the soil. Ammonium is used less frequently because it is toxic in large concentrations. Most ecosystems have nitrogen stored in living and dead organic matter, which re-enters the cycle via decomposition. Decomposers in the soil, such as bacteria and fungi, chemically modify the nitrogen found in this organic matter.

Almost all of the nitrogen found in any terrestrial ecosystem originally came from the atmosphere and is biochemically converted ('fixed') into a useful form within the soil by specialized bacteria. Members of the bean family (legumes) and some other kinds of plants form relationships with nitrogen-fixing bacteria. In exchange for nitrogen, the bacteria receive food from the plants and special root structures (nodules) that provide protection.

Left: *Understanding how nature's cycles work will help you to take best advantage of the local conditions of your allotment.*

NATURAL CYCLES IN A TYPICAL ALLOTMENT

Even a modest-sized allotment plot is a perfect example of what occurs in nature, as elements and nutrients are repeatedly recycled through both the actions of the grower as well as a range of other living creatures. This example shows three main cycles.

In the food chain, insects and fruits are eaten by birds and small mammals, which are in turn eaten by larger species such as hawks and foxes. The carbon and nitrogen cycles show how these elements are processed by plants.

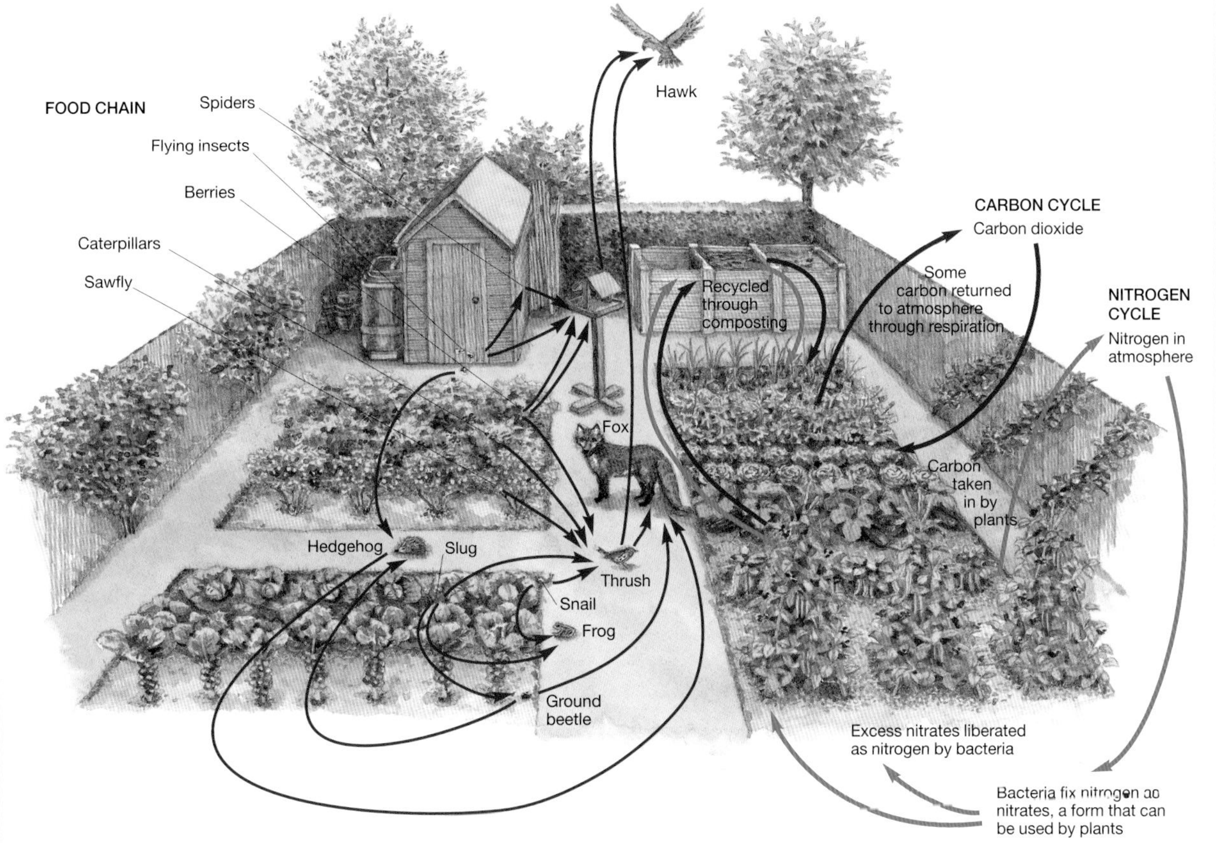

OXYGEN CYCLE

The oxygen cycle describes the movement of oxygen within and between its three main reservoirs – the atmosphere; living things; and rocks, lakes, rivers and oceans. The main driving force for this cycle is plant life and its production of food through photosynthesis. When plants make food they release a lot of oxygen, and it is for this reason alone that the atmosphere on Earth contains around 21 per cent of it. All living things breathe in oxygen and use it to release the energy contained in food. In this way, the carbon cycle and oxygen cycle combine and balance.

Nutrient cycles, then, are a matter of balance, having an important impact upon our daily lives, and learning to work with them can improve the health of your allotment.

WHAT ARE ECOSYSTEMS?

Short for ecological systems, ecosystems are communities of plants and animals that consist of a given habitat (the place where an organism lives) and its community (all the plants and animals that live in it). Any group of living and non-living things interacting with each other (including those found in allotments) can be considered an ecosystem.

The chemical materials that are extracted from the environment and changed into living tissue by plants and animals are continually recycled within the ecosystem. These nutrient cycles are at their most efficient when an ecosystem has a good diversity of species. Such diversity tends to make a community stable and self-perpetuating.

Below: *The presence of animals such as toads on a plot are an indication of a stable and balanced ecosystem.*

PLANNING THE PLOT

The prime objective for most allotment-growers will be food production. A good plot plan will outline not only where the crops will go, but also where you need to put all the other things that will help you to achieve this. The shape and structure of the plot can exert a huge influence over what you can and cannot do, meaning that it is important that you get this right from the outset. You also want to avoid the cost, both in terms of time and money, of having to redo something that isn't right.

Above: *A network of paths are essential for getting around the plot and help define the layout and overall look of the site.*

SET THE DESIGN OBJECTIVES

The real trick of any successful allotment plan is to start by making two lists. The first list should be a wish list, containing all the things you want to do there. While this will include activities such as growing food, flowers or keeping livestock, remember to add things such as a relaxation or safe area for children's play etc., as these too will influence your design. If the list is not already too long, you can add other, desirable, non-essential features that you might like to include if space permits.

The second list will detail all the things that you will need in order to fulfil the activities you have thus far outlined. It should include the materials required as well as the activities it involves, as these may need additional items to be included in the design that you had not given much thought to until now.

Finally, before you draw up your proposed ground plan, you need to compile an inventory of what is already there. On an established plot there may already be a basic structure on the site that can be used or adapted to suit your needs with little additional effort or cost. If you want to start again, removing the previous layout can add to the time and cost of setting up your plot and will need consideration and planning.

TOP PLOT PLANNING TIPS

Include a composting area – recycling green waste is the easiest way to ensure a good supply of organic soil conditioner.

Include paths and access points – make main paths wide enough to get a wheelbarrow down; paths between rows can be smaller.

Consider whether you need permanent storage – a shed is a great addition to the plot, but is there enough space or do you really need one?

Know where the nearest water source is – if you have to walk a long way to fill a watering can, then planting 'thirsty' crops will mean a lot of effort!

Visit 'model gardens' for inspiration – many gardens have model vegetable patches that can be a great inspiration.

Talk to the adjoining plot holders – they know a great deal about the site as a whole and may even know something about the history of your own patch.

Work out how much time you have – if you can't hoe it, don't sow it!

DECIDE THE BASIC LAYOUT

To many, the fact that crops are mostly short term, and as a consequence can be moved around on a regular basis, is part of the essential appeal of an allotment. The yearly planning cycle and changes this regularly brings to the plot make it a dynamic and engaging pastime. While true for the plants however, compost bins, sheds, greenhouses, paths and other structures are necessarily permanent items. This means that you will need to decide where these need to go before you plan where crops will be grown.

You will also need to make early decisions over where certain longer-term crops will be sited. If you want to grow fruit for example, it might need support on wires or trellis, a frame for netting and above all sufficient space. Other crops, such as artichokes, asparagus or rhubarb, require little in the way of structures but are nonetheless permanent, and will require a dedicated space.

Finally, if you want to get around the plot easily, you will need to ensure that you have a network of paths. This is the point when you really start to define how the plot will look and it will give you the chance to apply a bit of creativity. Traditional designs can see the crops laid out in straight rows with

Below: *A composting area is a must for any allotment site. Ideally you will need at least two heaps or bins to ensure a steady supply.*

Below: *Planning your plot in advance is an essential first step to make sure it is both productive and efficient all year round.*

AN ALLOTMENT PLAN

The vegetable beds shown here have been set out on a four-year crop rotation plan.

square or rectangular beds to accommodate this. There is no reason to stick to this if you prefer not to though, and you can always go for a more ornamental look to suit your own needs or personality.

PUTTING IT DOWN ON PAPER

Creating a plan for an allotment is generally quite a simple affair. Start by drawing up a ground plan of what is there already. The drawing should ideally be to scale and should include notes on the direction of the prevailing winds, sunny or shady spots (noting if these change during the day), always bearing in mind that even the sunniest plot may have shady pockets created by fences hedges or trees.

Identifying your soil type is particularly important when planning the crops, and the existing vegetation often gives you all sorts of clues as to what will grow well on your patch. Have a look around your neighbours' plots and see what plants are growing successfully there and talk to them about their experiences. Note the position of water mains and any other nearby features.

Once you have drawn up the sketch plan, you can use this to create the design for your allotment. Use some paper to draw a scale outline plan that shows the plot, complete with any features you intend to keep. Place a sheet of tracing paper over this and sketch on your ideas. Start with the basics, such as where your shed, compost bins or other permanent structures will be. Remember that these will need to be accessible, so draw in pathways accordingly.

Once you have the basic structure of the plot set out, you can begin to look at the rest of your wish list. Start with the most important items and work down the list. Remember to think very carefully about how much space each will realistically need and how much of a particular crop type you are likely to use. How productive a particular variety is should also be borne in mind – some types require a lot of work for little reward. Make sure you separate 'real need' from simple desire when you do this. Cost should also be a consideration here, as there is not much sense in coming up with a complex plan if you don't have enough money to act upon it.

Maintenance is also a key factor during the planning stage. The amount of time, effort and – where some crops are concerned – expertise needed should be thought through before you finalize your plan. The best approach is always to try and fit the maintenance requirements around your own lifestyle and avoid being too ambitious in the early stages.

THE ALLOTMENT FRAMEWORK

Before crops can be planted, the layout of any plot must be defined. Areas earmarked for growing crops, a shed, a composting area or other structure, and the network of paths and boundaries that link it all together must be clearly laid out. Planning which materials will be required, where these will come from and how they will be used is an essential part of the planning process that will pay dividends later if done properly.

Above: *Raised beds are both tidy and easy to maintain, and are a cheap, efficient way to define the framework of your allotment.*

ASSESSING THE SURROUNDINGS

In the vast majority of cases, allotments and community gardens are already set out as part of a planned and orderly framework of individual plots. Each of these will normally have good access – often via a network of paths between individual plots – while the site generally should have a secure boundary, some form of water provision for irrigation, and perhaps other facilities such as storage areas or toilets.

Having said all of this, your own plot, unless you are very fortunate, is unlikely to be structured in the way that you want or need for your own purposes, so you will have to work out a framework that allows you to best use the space. Creating a series of raised beds, for example, may be the first task you need to do.

Before you make any plans for the site, however, establish exactly what will be feasible, given the existing site facilities. Water is usually the most important consideration. If the plot lacks a nearby water source, you may well struggle to grow 'thirsty' plants in dry spells, unless you plan to install water butts or other rainwater capture systems. Equally, any power needed for lights or automated vents on a greenhouse will be difficult to power unless mains electricity is provided. The simplest solution is to work within the site constraints, ideally using simple, reliable technologies whenever and wherever you can.

MAKING A RAISED BED SYSTEM

1 *Start by levelling the area of ground where you intend to position the raised bed. Use a tape measure to set out the dimensions and mark the corners with pegs or short pieces of cane.*

2 *Measure and cut the timber using a sharp carpentry saw. If you are using pre-treated timber, you will need to apply a wood preservative to the cut ends to prevent rot occurring on those surfaces.*

3 *The ends of the sawn wood can be joined by simply nailing them. If the wood is thin or prone to splitting though, a small hole can be drilled and the boards fixed with screws.*

4 *When placing the frame on the prepared ground, check that all sides are level using a spirit level. This will ensure that water does not run over the sides when you water the bed.*

5 *Anchor the corners of the frame using 'pegs' made from small pieces of similar treated timber. Drive these down the inside edge of the frame and nail or screw them in place to secure them.*

6 *Fill the frame with the growing mix. This is normally a mixture of the original topsoil combined with additional compost (soil mix). This ensures that it retains moisture and gives the medium a nutrient boost.*

SELECTING MATERIALS

For most allotment-growers, improving and maintaining the environmental credentials of their plot will be high on the agenda, along with producing high-quality, healthy food. In order to minimize the impact on the wider environment, ensure that the ecological credentials of materials you buy for the allotment are sound. Strive to obtain materials from local sources whenever possible and find out where they come from or how their extraction impacts upon the environment. Timber for posts and fences, mulch material and some types of compost (soil mix) – especially peat-based ones – can all be detrimental to the environment if not carefully sourced.

In addition to the source of the products, it is also worth finding out what chemical treatments the material has undergone during manufacturing. Some timber, for example, is treated with preservative that may leach out into the soil over time. Ask questions before buying.

USING PLANTS TO CREATE A LIVING FRAMEWORK

PLANT SUPPORTS

Any woody plants can be cut down to the ground on a regular basis, and you can collect thin branches in a system called coppicing. On a small site, such as an allotment, limitations on space mean that this must be done every year or two to prevent shrubs from becoming too large.

PLANT SPECIES	CULTIVATION	POTENTIAL USES
Willow *Salix* spp.	Tolerant of wet or heavy soils but very vigorous if not controlled. Usually best cut every year.	Useful for weaving hurdles or making living retaining walls. Can be invasive on small plots; dogwood (*Cornus sanguinea*) is a better choice when space is limited.
Dogwood *Cornus* spp.	Suitable for most soil types. Can sucker aggressively and is usually best cut every year.	After coppicing it produces attractive red, orange or lime green shoots (depending upon the species). Suitable for plant supports or fine weaving work.
Hazel *Corylus avellana*	Suitable for most soils if the drainage is good and the pH is 6.5 or more. May be cut every 2–3 years.	Young straight stems are an excellent choice for wattle work, weaving and bean sticks. Smaller twigs make good pea sticks or bird deterrents.

HEDGES

Low-growing hedges can be used as borders around vegetable beds and are easy to maintain as they can be kept neat by trimming. Do this twice a year, in spring and then again in mid-summer for woody specimens; or once, in spring, for grasses or herbaceous plants.

PLANT SPECIES	CULTIVATION	POTENTIAL USES
Lavender *Lavandula* spp.	Needs a sunny, well-drained position. Prefers alkaline conditions but grows in most soils.	Good for low, informal edges. An excellent companion plant on account of its aromatic foliage. Rich soils promote more leaves but less essential oils.
Rosemary *Rosmarinus officinalis*	Prefers a hot sunny position on slightly alkaline, light, dry soil. Dislikes excessive winter wetness.	Repels carrot fly, making it particularly valuable as an informal edging hedge. Plants are smaller but richer in essential oils when grown on chalky soils.
Miscanthus *Miscanthus* spp.	Grows on most acidic to slightly alkaline soils. Can tolerate drought and occasional wetness.	Can be used to form annual windbreaks. Dry, cut stems can be used as a straw substitute. Choose a dwarf variety such as 'Little Zebra' or 'Little Kitten'.

PATHS

Natural, organic materials used to make paths are more environmentally friendly than hard landscape materials. They often prove more attractive to look at and are much easier to lay than slabs or other hard materials, and generally cost less – an important consideration on a site that you do not own.

PLANT SPECIES	CULTIVATION	POTENTIAL USES
Wood chip	As a rule almost all woody branches can be chipped, provided that they are disease-free.	Excellent material for making paths between beds, it also makes a very effective mulch or soil conditioner if it has been composted for a year or more.
Turf	Grow as a short mown 'lawn'. Make sure that it does not encroach into beds or growing areas.	The easiest way to cover bare earth quickly. It makes good paths but can also be a way of maintaining areas not currently in production until they are needed.

RECYCLED MATERIALS

Wherever possible you should aim to use recycled materials on your plot. The most obvious way to do this is to recycle organic matter such as plant material on a compost heap, although there are other ways that you can use recycled materials that are not produced in your garden. For instance, plastic bottles can be used as mini cloches to protect seedlings and old carpet makes an ideal cover for a compost heap or patch of (as yet) unused ground.

Recycled building materials such as bricks, slabs, timber and railway sleepers often prove extremely useful and can reduce costs considerably, while having environmental benefits.

Gardens that rely heavily upon recycling material produced within their own confines are naturally self-sustaining, and wherever possible you should try to develop this into the framework of the plot. Some external input will always be needed from time to time, but the garden's long-term success will be assured.

LIVING FRAMEWORKS

You can use living material to construct a framework for your allotment. The simplest example of this is probably using grass for stabilizing soil on slopes and pathways, although woody plants are often used to create hedges and delineate boundaries. A little ingenuity and knowledge can provide amazing results. Take a look at the chart above for some simple ideas.

Willow is a prime example of a material that is not only very easy to grow, but can be used in a number of ways. It is fast-growing and roots easily from twigs put into the ground, making it perfect for use as living barriers or even retaining walls for soil. Woven willow (often called wattle) can be used as a building and fencing material.

Below: *Willow is ideal to use as a living framework. It does not rot and is self-sustaining, surviving longer than timber.*

ALLOTMENT STRUCTURES

The excitement of getting a new allotment can, if not tempered by caution, lead to a bout of unabated over-ambition. While structures such as sheds, fruit cages and greenhouses might seem ideal additions to the plot, these can be costly. Before buying or installing any large additions, therefore, consider how much they will get used and whether there are alternatives more suited to your needs, if not your budget. Polythene tunnels and cloches are often perfectly adequate for a small plot.

Above: *A fruit cage is an extremely valuable addition to a plot if you intend growing a lot of fruit, but it takes time and effort to build.*

SHEDS

Although a bonus on an allotment, you will need to check in the rules for your site whether you can have a shed or not. Some sites have a no-shed rule, and even where they are allowed, there are often size restrictions. However, many allotment holders can and do build sheds, and occasionally these are quite elaborate structures that double up as a 'home away from home'.

If you are able to erect a shed, the next thing to do is to decide upon how to go about this. They are often available as kit forms ranging from inexpensive (if often flimsy) wooden designs to those made from metal, plastic or vinyl laminates, although the more adventurous might prefer to build one from scratch.

Below: *A shed is arguably the most useful structure on a plot. Its environmental value can easily be enhanced with a green roof.*

Before you rush into buying or designing a shed, think what you will need it for. Essentially you might only need a small lock-up for tools, equipment and other supplies. Having said this, a warm, dry shelter might prove a welcome respite from a sudden shower, or a place to sit and eat lunch. Whatever you chose, make sure that it is something that you can build – an unfinished shed is no use at all – and within your available budget.

GREENHOUSES

Adding a greenhouse to your allotment helps to increase the amount and range of plants you can grow by extending the season. Not every allotment site will allow them, however, and they can be easy targets for vandalism. There are many designs using a variety of materials and the decision to have one or not will depend upon what use you can make of it. Remember that they need ventilating and unless you can sort out a source of power to enable automation of this, you will need to be able to visit it, usually twice daily, to do this.

If you don't have space or the time to manage a greenhouse, don't despair. Often all that you need are some cloches and perhaps a cold frame in order to gain many of the advantages of a greenhouse.

POLYTHENE TUNNELS

Like greenhouses, polythene tunnels may not be allowed on your allotment, but if they are, they are often a less troublesome alternative to a greenhouse.

Always choose one of the smaller 'domestic tunnels', as these are the ideal size for allotments. Ultimately, a tunnel soon pays for itself, enabling you to protect tender crops and extend the growing season, as well as allowing you to provide a suitable environment to grow more exotic, warmth-loving crops under cover in the summer months.

FRUIT CAGES

Before going ahead with constructing an elaborate cage for your fruit, you should realistically assess how much you need one. Individual bushes or rows of fruit can easily be protected using temporary structures of poles and netting. This is much cheaper than the kits you buy and, unlike a more permanent structure, has the advantage that you can easily remove it once the fruit is harvested so that the birds can get to the plants to pick off any pests.

RELAXATION AND FAMILY

While most allotment tenants take on a plot as a place to grow food, there are many that choose to use the area simply as a recreational space. This may involve growing some crops, perhaps flowers, or in some

cases using the space as a garden away from home. Obviously, the rules of the site will dictate exactly what can and cannot be done on the allotment (ball games are often not allowed, for instance), but even a moderate-sized plot may have potential and could easily encompass a sitting area. If you have a shed, make sure that you keep a couple of folding chairs in it so you can relax and enjoy the rewards of your labours there and then, or simply put your feet up after a bout of strenuous exercise.

Kids generally love being outdoors, and love to join in. They are never too young to be introduced to gardening, and most enjoy having the chance to play and explore for themselves. For this reason an allotment that consists of neatly growing rows of crops, which might seem like heaven to the parents, offers limited scope to children. Of course the idea of making the plot into a miniature playground would probably be a step too far, but you may be able to devote a little area to a sandpit or a patch of earth for them to dig about in and grow crops, so they can enjoy some real 'messy' fun. If space allows, why not build them a little shed or den, complete with child-sized tools and other equipment of their own? It will help keep them interested and involved and will provide entertainment in a healthy environment that is free to visit.

Above: *A greenhouse extends the potential range of crops but will need daily attention.*

Below: *Leave space for a table and chairs to turn your plot into an alfresco dining area.*

KEEPING LIVESTOCK

Once you have got a vegetable patch under way, your thoughts and aspirations may start to turn to the possibilities of keeping livestock. The lure of perfectly fresh free-range eggs or even meat is certainly tempting, but it must be well thought out beforehand. Domestic livestock are a great way of using up surplus vegetables, kitchen scraps and perhaps even weeds, while enriching your allotment with free manure, but they do need good housing and daily attention.

Above: *Bees and other insects play an important role as natural pollinators, and are vital if you intend to grow fruit.*

IS KEEPING LIVESTOCK FOR YOU?

Before you attempt to answer this question, you will need to find out whether livestock is allowed on your allotment or not. Some sites expressly forbid the keeping of any animals, while others allow the keeping of a restricted range, such as chickens, ducks, geese, rabbits and pigeons. Even where livestock is a possibility, you will usually need permission from the site managers. Get this before building housing or cages for the animals. You should also contact neighbouring plot holders to let them know what you intend to do, as being part of a community means that it is important you keep them informed.

LIVESTOCK AND HOLIDAYS

Even the most dedicated allotment gardener will feel the need to get away for a break every now and again. Leaving your precious plants can be bad enough, but animals need even more frequent attention than crops. Any livestock plan should take into account whether there is anyone who will tend to them when you're away. Remember that this is a big commitment as they will need to be there every day. It is also something that people might be nervous about; looking after animals carries a great level of responsibility.

Above: *While wild rabbits are a serious pest, domestic breeds are easily kept, can be fed crop residues, and are loved by children.*

CLEANING AND MAINTENANCE

Aside from the obvious time commitment associated with tending the animals, you might also want to consider the time that will be required to clean out their housing and outdoor pens. Always remember that any livestock needs to be kept hygienically and may encompass a range of health issues relating to both them and you. Many animal diseases can affect humans and personal cleanliness is vital. Time spent with the animals should usually be followed by a shower and this time needs to be factored in, along with everything else.

CLEANING OUT A HEN HOUSE

1 *It is important that you keep a hen house clean and change the bedding regularly to prevent diseases, as well as bad smells, building up. Line the main hen house and any attached nest boxes with newspaper.*

2 *Add a layer of clean softwood shavings or straw. At weekly intervals, remove the newspaper, straw and droppings, and add to the compost heap. Around once a month, scrub any perches using a pressure washer.*

PLANNING AHEAD

While you may feel enthusiastic about the prospect of keeping livestock now, you should always try and envisage how things will be on a year-round basis. After all, short winter days may mean that you would need to be visiting the animals in near or total darkness on many of your visits. If none of this deters you, then the next step will be to set up the site ready for the animals. Always do this before obtaining livestock and preferably get it checked over by an experienced keeper if possible. Forward planning is essential where keeping animals is concerned but, if done properly, can lead to an enduring and productive pastime that will enrich the appeal of your allotment.

POULTRY

Recent concerns over the quality and welfare of commercially produced poultry products has resulted in an upsurge in interest and numbers of allotment-growers wanting to keep birds. Having a few will ensure a fresh supply of eggs or meat, the treatment of which can be kept to higher standards than commercial operations.

Space shouldn't be a problem unless you have a very small plot, although you do need plenty of time to deal with birds. Laying hens need to be visited at least twice a day; in the morning to let them out and in the evening to put them back inside, checking water and food on one or both visits. They will also need a secure house to sleep in, and it's always worth going to visit local suppliers to take a look at poultry equipment before you decide to take the plunge.

RABBITS

These are looked upon by many modern gardeners as either a pet or – if wild ones visit their plots – a pest. Having said this, during the mid-20th century, thrifty home

Far left: *An active beehive means you can add honey to your produce list, although it is important to remember that keeping bees requires some considerable skill and experience.*

Left: *Chickens are surprisingly easy to keep and can prove to be a productive and rewarding aspect of allotment-growing. Always check whether they are allowed on the site before buying any.*

growers kept them for both their meat and their pelts. They are less frequently kept on allotments now, despite being relatively easy to look after, and partial to much of the green waste that arises from crop residues.

BEES

Arguably, the real value of all bees for allotments is the pollination service that they provide. In addition, keeping honey bees does have the advantage that you can harvest a quantity of honey each year. Bees, however, are something that require a level of knowledge to keep, and if you are new to the subject it would be advisable to contact a local beekeeper or beekeeping association to see if they could offer help or even to put a hive on the allotment site.

Although experienced beekeepers may well successfully keep bees on an allotment, beginners should be aware that a lot can go wrong. They can, and do, sting people – meaning that many allotment managers will not allow bees to be kept.

Even if keeping honey bees is not for you, you can encourage native bees by providing these with a home. Many are excellent pollinators and a good number have become rare in recent years. They have the advantage of not needing much in the way of space once the nest box is set up, and as most are sting-less or unlikely to sting, they can prove to be an excellent compromise for the allotment-grower.

MAKING A SOLITARY BEE NEST BOX

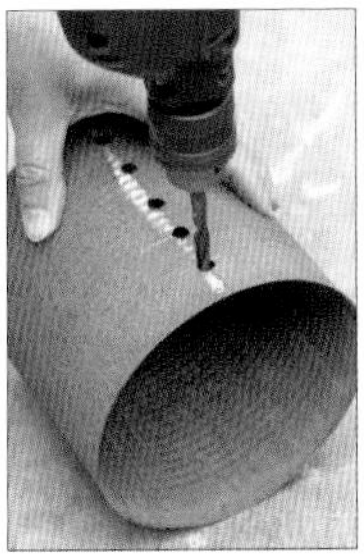

1 *Using an old tin (can) or similar food container, drill a line of holes down one side to provide drainage should any water get inside later. Ensure there are no sharp edges before starting.*

2 *Drill four holes in the tin's base, place it in its final position and fix it to the surface using screws. On surfaces other than wood, mark these points and pre-drill them first.*

3 *Gather a bundle of bamboo canes or other hollow stems that have a range of hole sizes of between 5–10mm (⅕–⅖in) in diameter, discarding any spit or solid ones at this stage.*

4 *Cut the canes or stems cleanly so they are 10mm (⅖in) shorter than the tin, using a fine-toothed saw or a pair of sharp secateurs (pruners), being careful not to split any as you do so.*

5 *Put the canes or stems into the tin and pack them in tightly. Use a hammer to bang the last few in firmly, thereby negating the need for glue and avoiding its associated fumes.*

6 *The best spot for a bee box is a sheltered, sunny spot, preferably at around eye level. As bee numbers increase, you can place more nest boxes out to increase your stock.*

Above: *String lines on spoolers are extremely useful in the allotment, and are used to help form drills and furrows.*

TOOLS AND EQUIPMENT

When you go into any supplier or look at one of their catalogues, there is a seemingly bewildering array of tools on offer, especially if you are new to allotment-growing. Some of these can be used for a variety of tasks, and this versatility makes them indispensible. Others, however, are geared towards highly specific jobs. Once you've purchased your gardening tools, it is important to look after them to keep them in tip-top condition.

CHOOSING TOOLS

Even if you know what items you want to buy, there is still a huge range of types and brands of tools on offer. There are few absolutes when it comes to choosing which tools will be right for you, but it is essential that they will be durable, functional and comfortable to use. Everyone is different in respect of their strength, build and preferences and it is a good idea to test them in the shop for weight and length of handle so that they suit you.

RIGHT TOOL, RIGHT JOB

Having the correct tool for the job makes work easier and faster and will generally give the best results. Digging, for example, will always be much better with a good-quality spade and fork, and these should always be top of your list when it comes to essential tools as they are used most frequently. They need to be comfortable, but this is easy to judge when buying them. The standard size is a 72cm (29in) handle, and the best way to see whether this is right for you is to check whether the top of the handle is around about your hip height. If it is too short, then go for a long-handled one. This is extremely important as using one that is the wrong size for your height can result in back strain. In addition to this, remember that D-handles can be uncomfortable over long periods, but they suit smaller hands better, while a T-handle is much better for larger hands.

Hoes are an essential item for controlling weeds and the best of these are usually forged and have stainless steel heads. Rakes are also indispensable and you should choose one with good solid tines (teeth), mounted on a wooden or metal handle. Finally, a knife, a pair of secateurs (hand pruners), a hand trowel and a wheelbarrow for moving things around the plot should be enough to get you started.

CARE OF TOOLS

Handles of tools often become dirty while you are using them and it is important that you take good care of them in order to extend their useful life. In the case of plastic or other synthetic materials, this usually involves no more than washing them in a little soapy water and drying them thoroughly afterwards. Many hand tools still use wooden handles though, and these can be kept in tip-top condition with boiled linseed oil. This is simply done by applying the oil with a non-linting rag, allowing the wood to fully absorb the first coat before applying any more. When properly and regularly applied, this prevents the wood from drying out and splintering. On a more regular basis, dirty wooden handles are simply cleaned by removing as much of the soil as possible with a stiff brush. Ideally, clean soil off before you finish working on your plot.

If you need to use water on handles treated with linseed the best way to do this is to gently moisten them with a damp cloth, making sure that you don't soak the wood, as this may cause the grain to lift and the handle to swell. Many modern tools are varnished and a quick scrub can be the best option for them, although even these should not be left in for a soak.

If you regularly oil blades or other metal parts then they should remain rust-free. If any rust does accumulate on the blade,

Below: *The side of a shed is an ideal place to neatly and safely store materials such as canes and stakes.*

Below: *Hanging tools up when you have finished with them ensures that you can find them again easily next time.*

remove this with a wire brush and wipe over the cleaned section with an oily rag or brush. Remember that the blades of shears, forks, spades and other tools will soon rust if they are not regularly oiled. If you have bought good-quality tools then it is worth protecting your investment! There is no need to use anything other than general-purpose oil on hand tools but remember that if you have invested in power tools then they may require specialist treatments. Consult the manufacturer's instructions if you are unsure.

SHARPENING TOOLS

Larger blades such as spades and hoes may be sharpened with a fine metal file or, if you have one, a grindstone. Very badly damaged or worn blades may eventually need replacing, if this is an option, or you may have to buy a new tool. If you have any doubts about how to carry out repairs you should consult the manufacturer.

Tools with fine cutting edges, especially knives, secateurs (pruners) and shears, will become blunt with use, and their cutting edges will need regular sharpening. To sharpen blades of knives and secateurs, use a fine sharpening stone prepared with a few drops of general-purpose oil. For a straight-bladed knife, push it forwards and to the side, exerting a little downward pressure. Then turn the knife over and, holding the blade almost flat against the stone, brush it across the surface to take off any rough edges. Use the same method to sharpen secateurs and good-quality forged hoes.

Remember that in very stony and heavy soils, hoes may need sharpening several times per growing season. Sharpen only the outside blade on bypass (parrot-beaked) secateurs and the upper surface of hoes. The job should be finished by wiping the blade with an oily rag.

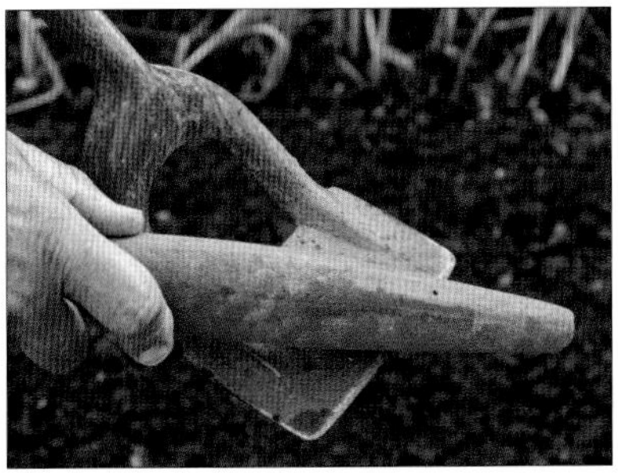

Above: *Sharpening tools will make them more effective and ultimately save you a lot of effort on the allotment.*

ESSENTIAL TOOLS AND EQUIPMENT

	DESCRIPTION AND PURPOSE
Spade	Used to dig or loosen ground or to break up clumps in the soil, a spade has a broad flat blade (called a spit) with a sharp, usually curved, lower edge. The handle should be the same height as your hip.
Fork	A digging fork should have roughly the same dimensions as your spade. It has four strong, sharpened spikes instead of a spit. Forks are used to loosen ground, dig over a plot to lift root vegetables or dig out persistent perennial weed roots.
Swan-necked (English) hoe	The swan-necked hoe is useful for deeper hoeing and cultivating, breaking soil clods and weeding with a chopping action. It is also used to form narrow seed drills with the blade corner, wide seed drills with the whole blade, or drawing up soil ridges around crops.
Dutch hoe	The Dutch hoe's flat, angled, sharp edged blade destroys weeds by cutting them just under the surface. It is particularly useful between rows of young vegetables, ideal for working in fertilizer, and helps maintain a fine, dusty, weed suppressant tilth across patches of bare earth.
Rake	A typical garden rake is a toothed bar fixed transversely to a handle. It is predominantly used for light weeding, loosening, and especially levelling patches of bare soil following cultivation. It can also be used to comb the surface in order to remove stones and debris.
Secateurs	Secateurs or hand pruners are a scissor-like tool, with a 25mm (1in) thick blade that is strong enough to prune hard branches of trees and shrubs. They are available as 'bypass' (two sharp blades that cross each other like scissors), and 'anvil' (one sharp blade cutting on to a flattened base).
Knife	A folding pocket-knife is essential for cutting twine or opening sacks. The ever-popular multi-tool knives often have an assortment of knife blades and other tools.
Hand fork	This hand tool has a pointed, scoop-shaped metal blade and is used for breaking up earth, digging small holes, and especially for planting, weeding, mixing in fertilizer or other additives, and transferring plants to pots.
Dibber (dibble)	Essentially a pointed wooden stick for making holes for planting seeds, seedlings or small bulbs, dibbers come in a variety of designs.
String line	A string that is stretched taut between two pegs or steel pins to make a perfect straight line, this is used to help form drills and furrows for seed sowing. They are easy to make yourself but purpose-made, spooling types are also obtainable.
Seed/planting rule	Essentially a large ruler on to which the correct spacing is marked for planting a range of vegetables or other crops. Some may be notched or marked while others have a hole every 2.5cm (1in) for sowing small seeds.
Watering can	A long nozzled watering can allows water to flow gently and is good for reaching across rows of crops or pots. Ideally, choose one that has handles on both the side and top to ensure easy handling, as well as a detachable spray rose (sprinkler head) for watering seedlings.
Soil riddle	A riddle is usually circular, around 45cm (18in) in diameter, with a rim that holds a steel wire mesh in place. It is typically used to sieve (strain) soil or compost in order to remove stones, twigs, large clods or other debris.
Wheelbarrow	Designed for use by a single person using two handles to the rear, a wheelbarrow is essential for moving bulky or heavy items. One-wheel types are most manoeuvrable in small spaces, on planks or sloping ground, and allow the best control when emptying.
Gloves	Providing a barrier against infection and soil bacteria, gloves are essential for keeping hands safe. Choose a pair that fit snugly on your wrists with no extra room at the fingertips to ensure a good grip. Get tough, pierce-resistant ones for heavy work or impermeable ones if using chemicals.
Twine	Twine is a strong thread or string composed of two or more thin strands or yarns twisted together. A natural fibre that can be composted after use.
Pump sprayer	Sprayers can be used for applying synthetic pesticides, distributing foliar feeds, and misting plants to aid fruit set. Separate sprayers are required for each type of use.

SOIL AND SOIL MANAGEMENT

Soil is the most precious resource in your allotment. Some gardeners inherit well-tended sites, while others may be faced with a rubble-filled mass. However, any soil can be improved through time and effort. If you regard your soil as a living entity, you will see that essential plant nutrients are cycled by a microscopic army of inhabitants and larger worms, insects and grubs. All these creatures need air, moisture and food. Using manure, garden compost and other sources of organic matter is the key to sustaining this soil life and keeping the soil healthy.

Left: *The key to developing a successful allotment plot lies for the most part in the careful management of the soil.*

Above: *A compost heap needs to be turned periodically to ensure all the plant material decomposes properly.*

Above: *Sieving compost is the best way to remove larger pieces that have not fully rotted down. Return these to the heap.*

Above: *Crops that are grown in rows must be rotated on a regular basis in order to avoid soil-borne pests and diseases.*

TYPES OF SOIL

Soil is probably the most important constituent of any allotment site because it is vital for successful plant growth. Understanding your soil and discovering how it can help you to create a healthy, fertile growing environment for your plants should be a priority. The starting point in this process is to look at the different soil types and find out how they affect the plants you can grow. Once you have analyzed the soil in your own site, then you will be able to create a successful allotment.

Above: *All soil types benefit greatly from the addition of organic matter such as this green manure.*

WHAT ARE SOILS MADE OF?

Both natural soils and some potting composts (soil mixes) for container-grown plants usually have five main components. These are mineral particles (the inorganic fraction), organic matter (the remains of living organisms), water (the soil solution), air (which fills the spaces between solid particles that are not filled with water) and living organisms. The proportions of these components vary widely according to the soil type, or the growing medium.

The proportions of water, air and organic matter can be readily changed by soil cultivation and other horticultural practices. A good topsoil will continuously supply plant roots with water, air and nutrients. Subsoil (the largely inert soil layer that lies beneath the thin layer of 'living' topsoil) has less organic matter than topsoil. Plant growth will suffer when the proportions of water and air in the medium are out of balance. Too much air will have the same effect upon plant roots as a drought, whereas too much water causes waterlogging. Growth will also suffer if nutrient levels are too low, too high or if there is an imbalance in supply between different nutrients. In addition, soil that is too compacted for roots to grow will also adversely affect growth.

SAND AND SILT

Soils that are sandy and silty originate from river deposits, windblown sediments or from the erosion of sandstone outcrops. Their general properties are that they do not provide or retain plant nutrients; they are not cohesive and therefore possess a weak structure; and in most cases they are free draining.

Silts, unless well structured, will be waterlogged. Sand, on the other hand, is naturally free draining. The structure and texture of sandy soils means that they are only able to hold a very small reserve of water. Organic matter can improve the available water content but the real trick in avoiding drought-stress lies in ensuring that plants root deeply into the soil. Nutrient shortage can also be a problem on sandy soils, which have a tendency to become acidic over time. Liming and the regular addition of organic matter will help alleviate these problems.

Sandy soils do have the advantage of 'warming up' quickly in spring due to their lower water content and are easier to work early in the year. This means that you can grow a wider range of plants in a sandy soil. Planting or transplanting is also easier in the autumn.

Organic material is broken down very quickly in sandy soils due to good aeration and a temperature that favours rapid bacterial action. Many light soils naturally have less than two per cent organic matter and it is vital that organic matter be added regularly to sustain healthy plant growth.

COMMON TYPES OF SOIL

sand

silt

clay

loam

Sand A free-draining soil that is quick to warm up, but hungry and thirsty.
Silt River deposits can be sticky, but not as sticky as clay. Rich and easy to work.
Clay A heavy soil that is often difficult to work. Slow to warm up, but fairly rich.
Loam A moisture-retentive soil that warms up quickly and works perfectly.

CHOOSING CROPS FOR DIFFERENT SOILS

Soil pH is a measure of acidity. Here are the preferences of some common crops:

Asparagus	6.0–8.0
Basil	5.5–6.5
Beans (runner (green), broad (fava), French (green))	6.0–7.5
Beetroot (beet)	6.0–7.5
Broccoli	6.0–7.0
Brussels sprouts	6.0–7.0
Cabbage	6.0–7.5
Carrot	5.5–7.0
Cauliflower	5.5–7.5
Celery	6.0–7.0
Chicory	5.0–6.8
Courgette (zucchini)	5.5–7.0
Cucumber	5.5–7.0
Garlic	5.5–7.5
Kale	6.0–7.0
Leek	6.0–8.0
Lettuce	6.0–7.0
Marrow (large zucchini)	6.0–7.5
Onion	6.0–7.0
Parsnip	5.5–7.5
Potato	4.5–6.0
Pumpkin	5.5–7.5
Radish	6.0–7.0
Spinach	6.0–7.5
Sweetcorn (corn)	5.5–7.5
Swiss chard	6.0–7.5
Tomato	5.5–7.5
Turnip	5.5–7.0

HAND-TEXTURING METHOD FOR ANALYZING SOIL

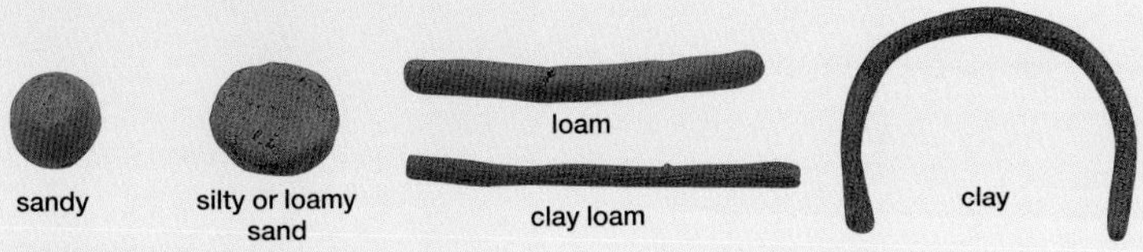

Finding out what type of soil you have is easy and does not require any specialist equipment. This test is ultimately a matter of judgement and will only give you a relative picture of the sort of soil you have. However, it is surprisingly accurate. Simply take a small amount of soil – about a teaspoonful will do – in the palm of your hand. Moisten with a little water (not too much but enough to make it just workable). Once moistened, try to form the soil into one of the shapes shown above.

- Begin by forming a ball. If it stays together, then proceed to the next shape. If it does not form a ball, then you have a sandy soil.
- If you can flatten the ball without it breaking up, then you have a silty sand or a loamy sand.
- If you can roll the flattened ball into a thick sausage shape, then you have a loam.
- A soil that can be rolled into a thin sausage shape is a clay loam.
- If you can bend the soil into a horseshoe or ring shape, then you have a clay soil.

Above: *Most crops grown on allotments prefer a reasonably well-drained soil with a pH of between 6–6.8.*

CLAY

The particles found in clay are extremely small and are able to interact with, and directly affect, the chemistry of the soil. The individual clay particles are so tiny that they are actually bonded together by electrical charges which produce the characteristic plasticity of this type of soil. Clay is both water retentive and rich in nutrients. It has few pore spaces and those that are there have a tendency to become waterlogged, which results in swelling. Shrinkage occurs when clay is dry. As a result, clays heave (swell outward and upward) when wet and crack when dry. They can also be subject to frost action, which causes an increase in tiny, almost microscopic, airspaces (micro pores). Pure clay soils are rare, although some soils may be very rich in clay. They have the potential to be extremely fertile growing mediums if they are well managed.

LOAMS

These are a mixture of sand, silt and clay that results in a blend of the characteristics of each constituent part. They are usually characterized by their clay content. Heavy loams are about 24–30% clay, whereas light loams contain about 12–18% clay. Heavy loams behave and should be treated like clay soils. Light loams should be treated like sandy soils. Medium loams are potentially the ideal mixture, exhibiting the advantages of both heavy and light soils without many of the disadvantages of either.

HUMUS

This is a stable form of partially decomposed plant material that gives topsoil its characteristically dark colour. Humus has a high nutrient-reserve potential (2½ x better than clay), retains water, increases the friability (suitability for cultivation) of heavy soils and its darker colour encourages soils to warm up more rapidly.

SOIL PROFILE

A typical soil profile usually consists of three main elements: an upper layer of dark, fertile topsoil; a middle layer of lighter, infertile subsoil; and a lower layer of bedrock, which ranges from a few to hundreds of metres (yards) deep.

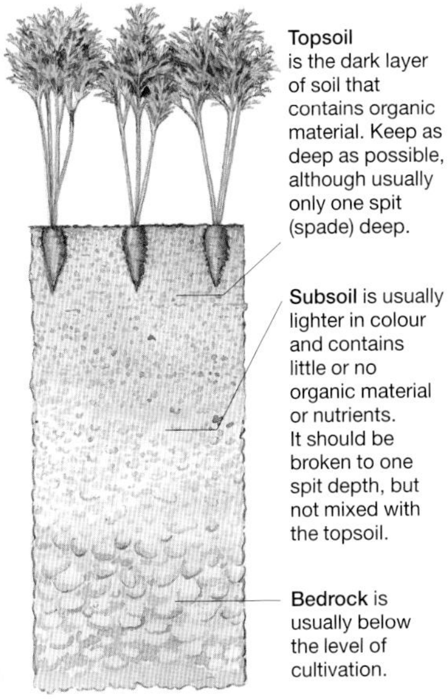

MANAGING YOUR SOIL

Any soil has the potential to be a fertile growing medium in which plants will thrive.

Light/sandy soils

- Maintain levels of organic matter.
- Lime when required. (N.B. It is often easier to select species tolerant of the site conditions in the long term.)
- Fertilize well as light soils are usually infertile. (N.B. Some exotic and native plant species actually thrive under relatively poor nutrient conditions.)
- Irrigate frequently in the first year after planting, less so once deeper roots are established.

Clay soils

- Drainage is essential.
- Maintain lime status.
- Maintain levels of organic matter and fertilize when needed.
- Wise cultivation is needed to conserve winter or summer tilth produced by natural weathering, i.e. cracking due to wetting/drying cycle and breakdown by frost action.

Above: *Even 'difficult' soils can be transformed into a good growing medium by hard work and careful cultivation.*

SOIL STRUCTURE

Soils are made up of mineral and rock particles that give them their natural properties. The character of the mineral fraction cannot be changed but the way that these building blocks are organized within the soil can. Creating and maintaining soil structure is a key aspect of maintaining the fertility of the soil and supporting healthy plant growth on an allotment. Even the most difficult soils can be modified to create a fertile growing medium for plants.

WHAT IS MEANT BY SOIL STRUCTURE?

Soil structure is quite simply the way soils are organized. To use a simple analogy: if we see the soil particles (sand, silt or clay – the mineral fraction) as the building materials – like the bricks and mortar of a house, for instance – then the structure is the architecture. The building materials themselves cannot be altered, but the architecture can vary considerably from home to home. This is the key. It is possible to improve a soil's structure even if the mineral fraction remains unchanged. It is perfectly feasible to have a well-structured clay soil, for instance. It all depends upon how well you manage it.

WHY IS SOIL STRUCTURE IMPORTANT FOR PLANT GROWTH?

In order to survive, plant roots need water, nutrients and air. Plant roots breathe in the soil, taking in oxygen and expelling carbon dioxide. A poorly structured soil may have too little airspace. This can have two negative effects: fresh air (containing oxygen) may not be able to penetrate the soil very easily; and the soil will tend to become waterlogged following rain. Waterlogging will also reduce the air available in the soil.

Below: *A rotavator is a labour-reducing method of breaking up the soil to prepare it for planting. They can often be hired.*

Structure is therefore very important in terms of maintaining the health of plant roots. Plant shoot development is directly linked to root health. A healthy root system ensures healthy shoots and will ultimately result in better growth and crop yields.

HOW DOES SOIL STRUCTURE DEVELOP IN NATURAL SYSTEMS?

Soil structure naturally develops in soils through the effect of weather cycles. Wetting causes soils to swell while drying causes shrinkage. This naturally causes soils to crack. The action of freezing and thawing is also important on clay soils in areas where frosts occur. They form particles known commonly as crumbs. The 'crumb structure' of any soil develops over time and is important in terms of allowing the free passage of water through the soil and air that must be able to move in and out of the soil. In this way soils do not become habitually waterlogged and natural nutrient cycles – oxygen, carbon and nitrogen, for example – are not impeded. Plant roots and soil organisms, such as worms, naturally help to maintain soil structure, as does the natural addition of decaying plant material each autumn.

HOW TO ALTER SOIL STRUCTURE

Humans have learned over time that even an infertile area can be worked – and the structure of the soil improved – by cultivation. This is covered in more detail later but it is essential to understand now that cultivation is a way of rapidly accelerating the natural cycles that promote good structure. Digging and breaking down 'clods' helps to introduce air and creates new pores in the soil. Adding organic matter helps to maintain these pore spaces, retains moisture (in dry soils) and encourages the action of soil-dwelling creatures such as worms. No-dig

Above: *If you need to work on wet soil, work from a plank of wood to ensure the soil is not compacted and its structure destroyed.*

Above: *Dry weather causes soils to crack, which can be a benefit on clay types as it develops their 'crumb structure'.*

Above: *Waterlogging is often the result of poor drainage and can seriously affect plant health as they are deprived of oxygen.*

systems aim to harness this natural cycle more closely, but the goal is the same – a rich, fertile and well-structured soil.

IMPROVING DRAINAGE

Soils that tend to become waterlogged often do so as a result of poor structure and because there is nowhere for the water to go. The vast majority of soils do not actually need (or benefit from) the installation of land drains. Often it is enough to dig over a site because much of the drainage problem may be due to surface compaction. Surface compaction severely reduces the passage of water into the soil and can result in a sticky surface that is prone to 'puddling'.

If you have a sloping site you can dig a 'soak away' drain at the base of the slope and improve the structure of the soil to encourage the rapid dispersal of water following rain. If you have a fairly flat site, then you should consider making a raised bed for growing crops. Raised beds are easier to manage than standard beds and avoid the inconvenience of installing (and maintaining) a drainage system.

IMPROVING SOIL STRUCTURE

1 *One of the best ways to improve the structure of the soil is to add as much organic material as you can, preferably when the soil is dug. For heavy soils, this is best done in the autumn.*

2 *If the soil has already been dug, then well-rotted organic material can be worked into the surface of the soil with a fork. The worms will complete the task of working it down into the soil.*

Above: *A well-prepared soil that is kept free of weeds and dug regularly will result in healthier, more vigorous crops throughout the growing season. A healthier crop will be more resistant to pest and disease attack.*

SOIL CHEMISTRY

While for many of us the word chemistry can be extremely off-putting, the truth of the matter is that everything in life is made up of chemicals. While the pure science of chemistry can be very complex, the chemistry of soil that allotment-growers must master is mercifully simple. A rudimentary knowledge of the chemicals that affect plant growth and how soil chemistry can be controlled and managed is all you need to grow healthy plants in an allotment site.

Above: *You can reduce the acidity of the soil by adding lime some weeks before planting. Test the soil first to see how much is needed.*

OXYGEN

The amount of oxygen in a healthy soil controls the type of life it will support. Nearly all organisms need oxygen to survive. Soils without oxygen are described as anaerobic. Most organisms can survive for short periods under anaerobic conditions, but this causes the accumulation of poisons that can become toxic at high concentrations.

A typical soil has about 50 per cent of its pore space filled by air and 50 per cent by water. Only certain bacteria can remain in anaerobic conditions for long periods of time, although some species of bacteria can readily switch from oxygen-rich to oxygen-poor conditions quickly to adapt to local conditions. Microbes use about 70 per cent of the oxygen in the soil and plant roots use the remaining 30 per cent. Under anaerobic conditions, the efficiency of microbes is poor and decomposition rates are much slower.

WATER

Soil water is vital for all soil life. Without it, microbes cannot grow or remain active and many will go into 'hibernation' until water returns. Fungi, on the other hand, are more resistant to water stress than bacteria. With too much water, oxygen levels drop and the lack of air tends to slow down the nutrient cycles driven by microbes. Water is also the medium by which essential nutrients are able to enter the plant.

SOIL pH

The pH scale is an abbreviated form of 'Potential of Hydrogen'. It is a measure of the degree of acidity or alkalinity of a solution as measured on a scale (pH scale) of 0 to 14. The midpoint of 7.0 on the pH scale represents neutrality. A 'neutral' solution is, therefore, neither acid nor alkaline. Numbers below 7.0 indicate acidity; numbers greater than 7.0 indicate alkalinity.

The level of acidity or alkalinity (pH) of a soil can significantly affect the nutrient availability. Many nutrients become 'unavailable' to plants when the soil is either too acid or too alkaline. Microbial activity in soil is also largely controlled by pH. Fungi tend to predominate in acid soils, bacteria in neutral or alkaline soils.

Soil pH is essentially a measure of the acidity of the soil water, although the soil itself is the deciding factor in respect of what this will be.

Most plants prefer or are tolerant of a specific pH range. Some plants, such as the hydrangea, exhibit a different flower colour depending upon the prevailing pH. Most allotment plants, especially vegetables, thrive within a range of 6–7, which happens to be where the majority of nutrients are available. It is best to maintain this pH in order to optimize the availability of nutrients. Many allotment plants, however, are not too fussy about the pH levels, so if you choose plants carefully, it will not usually be necessary to alter the soil acidity.

ACIDIFYING SOIL

Lowering the pH of a naturally limy soil is difficult because the soil often contains a reserve of calcium that is released immediately upon acidification. Lowering the pH involves the use of flowers of sulphur and is only usually successful over a short period of time.

TAKING A pH TEST

1 *Collect a small sample of soil. Dry it, grind it into a powder and ensure that it is free from stones. Pour the soil into a test tube until it reaches the mark on the side.*

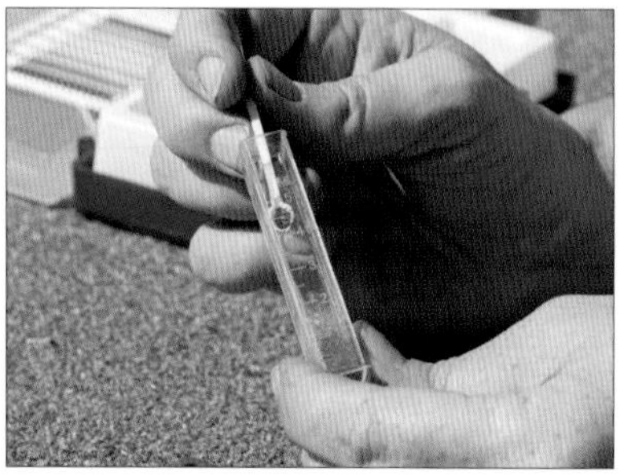

2 *Put a layer of barium sulphate powder into the tube level with the mark. This compound helps the solution to clear rapidly and makes the pH reading clearer.*

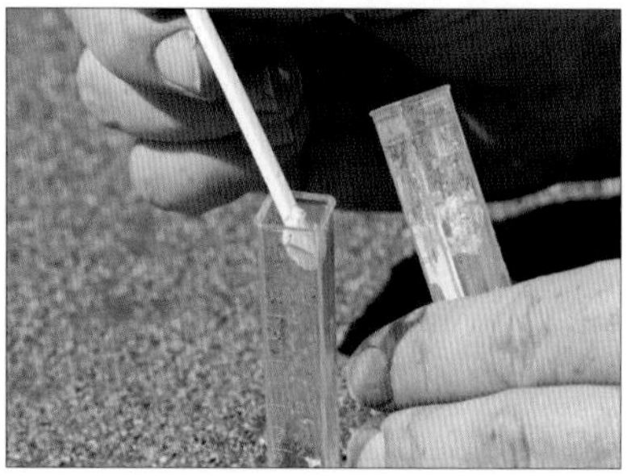

3 *Pour in a little of the indicator solution up to the mark shown on the tube. Be careful not to put in too much because this can make the solution dark and difficult to read.*

TAKING A NUTRIENT TEST

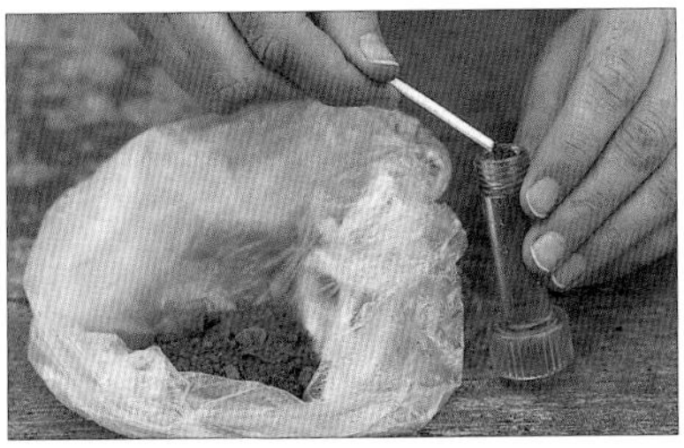

1 *Place a small sample of the soil into the test tube up to the mark on the side.*

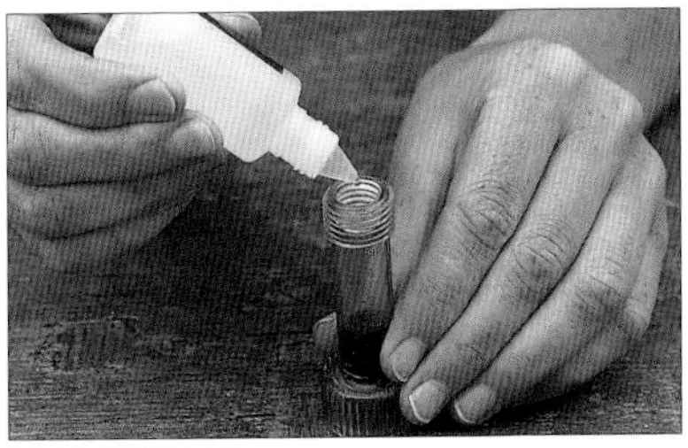

2 *Add a test solution (in this case one for nitrogen) up to the mark on the test tube.*

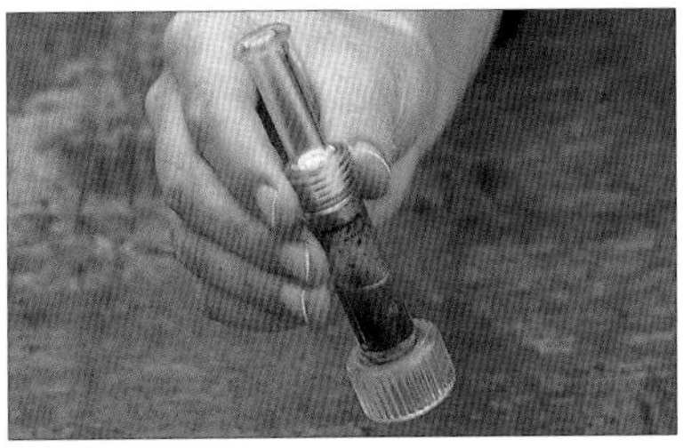

3 *Filter the solution to remove any soil particles and leave just a liquid solution.*

4 *Decant the resulting filtered solution into another clear container in preparation for the final stage of the nutrient test.*

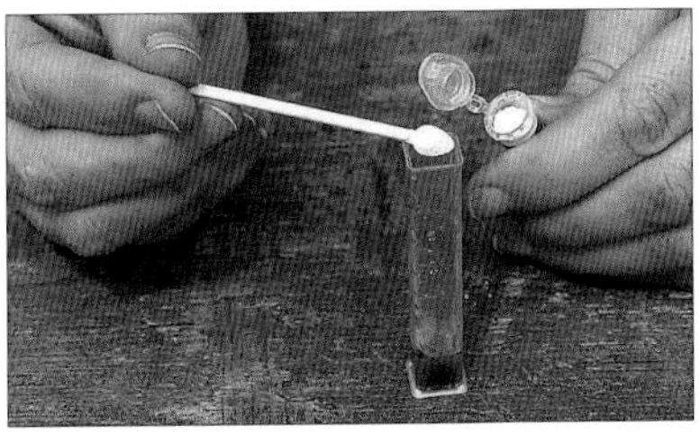

5 *Add a small amount of indicator powder. This will react with the solution and enable a colour reading to be taken.*

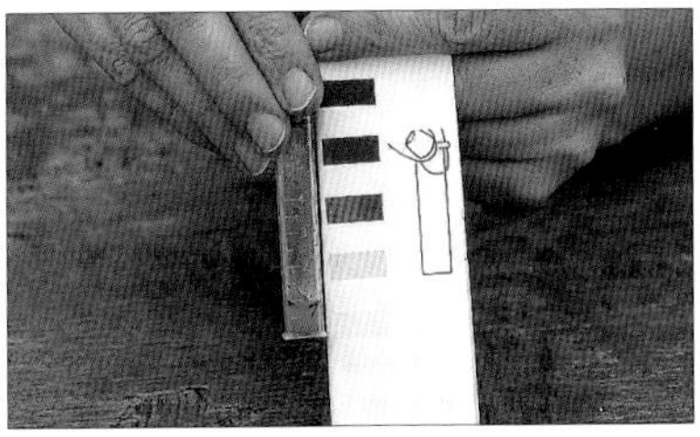

6 *Shake for about 10 seconds and compare with the chart. Here, the low reading indicates that a nitrogen-rich fertilizer will benefit this soil.*

LIMING SOIL

It is generally easier to raise the soil pH than to lower it. Lime neutralizes soil acidity and is commonly applied as ground limestone, chalk or dolomitic limestone (dolodust). Lime requirement cannot be determined from soil pH because it is influenced by soil texture and organic matter content. Clay and humus act as a 'buffer' because of their complex chemistry. If soil is known to be acidic, regular light application is preferable to heavier, more infrequent, doses.

HIGHLY ALKALINE SOILS

Soils that are too alkaline suffer trace element deficiencies of manganese, copper, iron, zinc and boron. Phosphates are also less available, their maximum availability being between pH 6–7. Disease organisms can be more of a problem in calcium-rich soils, as many disease-causing fungal agents prefer alkaline conditions. Some plants, such as potatoes, prefer to grow on acid soils, while others, such as brassicas, thrive in alkaline soils.

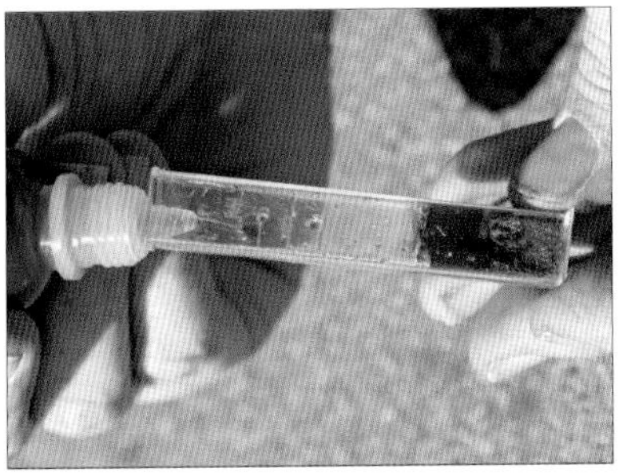

4 *Add distilled water to the mark on the tube and shake the container vigorously for about a minute. Ensure the contents are mixed thoroughly and leave to settle.*

5 *Once sufficiently cleared, compare the colour against those on the chart, choosing the one that most closely matches that of the solution.*

GROWTH RESTRICTIONS IN EXTREMES OF pH

Many vital nutrients that are essential for healthy plant growth become unavailable in extremes of soil pH.

Nitrogen deficiency Most nitrates are released from organic matter and a low soil pH limits the rate of decomposition severely.

Phosphate deficiency Phosphate becomes unavailable outside the 6.5–7.5 pH range. Some plants form relationships with soil-borne fungi that release phosphates in acid conditions.

Trace-element toxicity and deficiency Trace elements, especially aluminium, iron and manganese, are generally more soluble in acidic conditions. Extreme acidity can lead to excessive quantities of trace elements and to plant death. Other trace elements, such as copper, boron and molybdenum, become less available at low soil pH. Molybdenum deficiency affects legumes, which will not grow in acid soils.

CLEARING THE PLOT

Before you can start growing anything you will need to clear the plot of weeds and any other problems. Take time to check what is there already though, as even a plot that was vacated fairly recently can rapidly become overgrown. As well as hiding the soil that lies below, this weedy mass can often conceal useful structures or even perennial crops left by previous tenants. Have a good look at what you have and always take time to talk to the surrounding plot holders to see what they know about the site.

Above: *An overgrown plot, while often daunting at first sight, can contain surprises, which become your first 'windfall' harvest.*

PLANNING AHEAD

Unless you are very fortunate and take over a well-tended plot, the chances are that you will need to clear some or even the entire site. The best way to approach this is to clear a small section at a time. Don't be too ambitious and remember that very overgrown plots might take a year or more to 'tame'. Areas that are not going to be cultivated immediately, but where weeds are more than 15cm (6in) high, will need cutting down though, and the best way of doing this is with a scythe, sickle or – if you have one – a strimmer. On areas with shorter weeds, a rotary mower can be used to keep them in check, until you are able to get around to cultivating them.

Above: *Hand-removal of deep-rooted perennial weeds involves digging out the roots with a garden fork to avoid regrowth.*

USING CHEMICALS

For all but the organic purists, chemicals represent a quick and easy way to control weed growth on the site. Even if you plan to garden without chemicals, applying a systemic herbicide to clear an infestation of deep-rooted perennial weeds can be the only realistic way of getting on top of the problem in the first instance.

If you do decide to use a herbicide spray, however, do so carefully and apply it on a slightly cloudy, preferably cool, still day to remove the chances of it drifting on to neighbouring plots. Always read the manufacturer's instructions and wear suitable clothing, such as gloves and possibly eye protection.

Above: *If areas of ground are to be left unproductive for any length of time, they can be covered over to suppress weeds.*

THE NON-CHEMICAL APPROACH

If chemicals are really out of the question for you then you have to work hard to get on top of an overgrown plot. It is important then that you properly assess just how much time, and indeed energy, you can devote to this. Unless you have an army of helpers or a very small plot it is unwise to try to clear a plot in one go and it will often take several visits, plus a lot of hard work, to clear all the weeds away.

HAND DIGGING

Digging over your patch with a digging fork is an ideal way to both break up the soil and remove weed roots. It can be backbreaking work however, and there is always the risk that you will leave some root fragments behind. Many common perennial weeds spread from even a tiny piece of root, even if this becomes dry and shrivelled, and can come back with a vengeance in the months to come even if you have given the area a thorough digging over.

USING MACHINERY

Using a rotavator (rotary cultivator) may seem like a tempting and time-saving option on a larger plot. If you don't have one they can usually be hired, but although they do make quick work of large areas, unless you have already dealt with perennial weeds (ideally using a herbicide), the roots of these will be chopped up and spread around the plot. In effect, you might simply exacerbate an existing problem in your attempts to save time.

MULCHING AND SMOTHERING

Once an area is clear, it is important that you don't have to go back and clear it again before it is time to plant. Mulches are frequently used to suppress or smother weeds as they emerge from the ground and the most effective way to do this on bare earth is to use some form of matting. Old, rubber-backed carpet is a modern favourite for this, but a whole variety of materials including plastics and other synthetic fabrics will do. Ideally these should be porous to some degree, as an impermeable layer can actually cause a build-up of toxins in the topsoil if left for a protracted period.

SOLARIZATION

Even if you plan to start growing in the newly cultivated ground quite quickly, it may be wise to try and sterilize the soil. Plots used for previous crops may contain potentially damaging soil pests. Ideally, these can be kept in check by crop rotations, but if you are not sure what was grown in the soil recently, this would necessitate a lengthy period where the land was uncultivated.

Solarizing soil is a simple, green solution for sterilizing the area. It involves laying out a clear plastic sheet, which is buried along its edges, in order to trap the light and heat from the sun underneath it. Make sure that the soil is damp before it is covered or the treatment will be less effective. Over a period of several weeks to a few months, the soil temperature beneath the plastic sheet will become high enough to kill many soil pests, disease spores, weed seeds and roots to a depth of up to 20cm (8in). Although it can be a bit fiddly to set up, it is an environmentally friendly way to clear many problems from the soil and is also extremely cheap.

GREEN MANURES

Once you have cleared a patch, the ground should be ready for final cultivation and for you to start to grow crops. If you are not yet ready to plant anything though, the ground must be covered with something to prevent a re-growth of weeds. Although you could use carpet, it may be an idea to make use of the area and sow a green manure crop. These are fast-growing cover crops that will help suppress weed growth simply by preventing light from reaching the ground. Once you are ready to cultivate the plot these can be dug in to help enrich the soil, prior to planting edible crops.

Right: *Even formerly productive plots can very quickly become weedy and overgrown if left untended during the growing season.*

CLEARING WEEDS FROM THE PLOT

1 *Digging out weeds may be one option on an allotment, but if the site is really overgrown, as this one is, then this will necessitate many hours of backbreaking work and you may want to consider another option.*

2 *Using a chemical weedkiller may be the only answer. Ensure that you follow manufacturer's instructions very carefully when using it and wear appropriate protective clothing.*

DIGGING AND CULTIVATION

Every allotment-grower's goal should be a healthy soil to support plant growth and development. Digging is one of the commonest ways to create a rich, fertile and ultimately productive soil. It can be hard work at the outset, particularly on sites not cultivated for some time, but the results – in the form of healthier, more productive plants – are worth it. Quite simply, what you get out of your soil will depend upon what you put into it.

Above: *After a winter exposed to the weather, most soils can be easily broken into a fine tilth with a rake.*

THE BENEFITS OF DIGGING

Winter is the commonest time to dig, but soil can be dug at any time of the year if the conditions are right. Avoid working the soil when it is too dry and impenetrable, or too wet and sticking to your tools and boots. Clay soils may be best dug in mid- to late autumn to allow the action of frost to make the soil more suitable for final cultivation. Lighter soils are best dug in the spring or immediately prior to planting the site. Done properly, digging increases the amount of air space in the soil, which in turn benefits soil-dwelling organisms and plant roots due to the increase in oxygen available. It also lets you add organic matter that will feed these vital denizens of the soil and aid nutrient cycling. Calculate how much organic matter you will need before you start. You should aim to add about 30 per cent of the volume cultivated. A 20m^2 (220ft^2) plot cultivated to one spade's depth will need 2.5 cubic metres (88 cubic feet) of manure or garden compost.

SINGLE DIGGING

This method involves digging down to the depth of one spade (this is called a spit). Single digging suffices on light free-draining soil as long as there is no layer of compacted stones in the topsoil. Much of the procedure is the same as for double digging, but the subsoil is left undisturbed. Mark out the position of the bed. Remove any turf or vegetation from the surface, put to one side and then bury it in the bottom of the bed as you proceed. Work across the bed, digging out a trench that is two spits wide and a single spit deep, and place the soil to one side. Remove stones and perennial weeds as you go. Fork well-rotted manure or compost into the trench. Begin digging a new trench behind the first. Throw the soil forward into the first trench, burying the organic matter. Repeat this process of trenching down the bed until the last trench has been dug. Add organic matter to the base and fill the trench with the soil dug from the first trench.

DOUBLE DIGGING

This is a method for deeply digging the soil, in which the soil is broken up to a depth of approximately 70cm (28in) or more. The method usually involves digging a quantity of soil and setting it aside while aerating and sometimes adding an amendment to the subsoil below, then returning the topsoil. There are several methods of double digging, all of which have their advocates. Two methods for double digging are described here.

First, define the area where the double digging will take place, making an estimate of the area to be dug. Dig a trench, 30cm (12in) wide and a spit deep, across half the width of the bed. Place the excavated soil next to the other half, placing it on to a tarpaulin or similar covering if the surface needs protection.

When the trench is complete, fork the subsoil, rocking it back and forth, to loosen it down to a depth of about 30cm (12in). Then, spread a layer of garden compost

SINGLE DIGGING

Single digging is the simplest method of cultivation. It is well suited to light soils or those soils that have been well worked for a number of years. It simply involves digging and inverting the soil to a single spade's depth, leaving the subsoil below undisturbed.

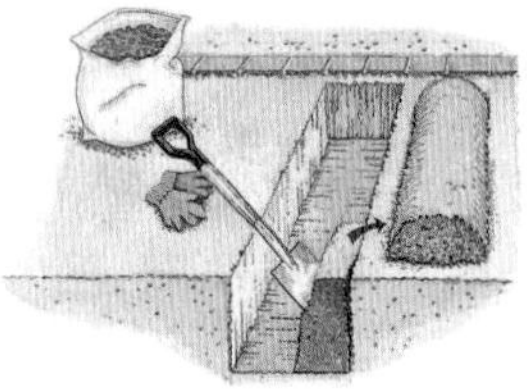

1 *Start by digging a single trench across the width of the plot. Put the soil from the first trench to one side because you will need to use it later in the final trench.*

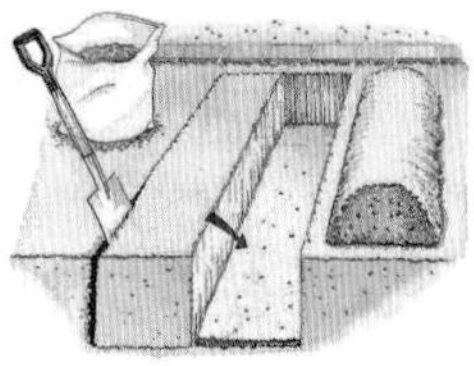

2 *Put a layer of manure in the bottom of the trench. Dig out the next trench and cover over the manure in the first trench with the earth taken from the second trench.*

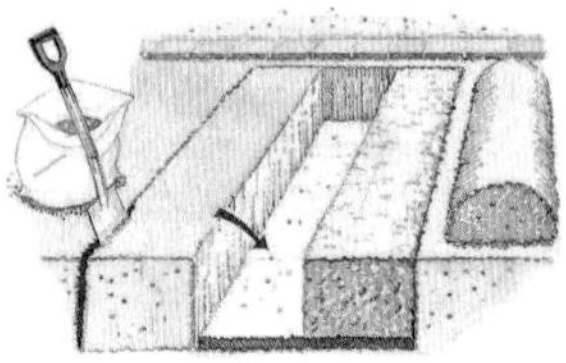

3 *Repeat this process of adding manure to each trench and filling in with earth from the next, breaking up the soil as you go and keeping the surface as even as possible.*

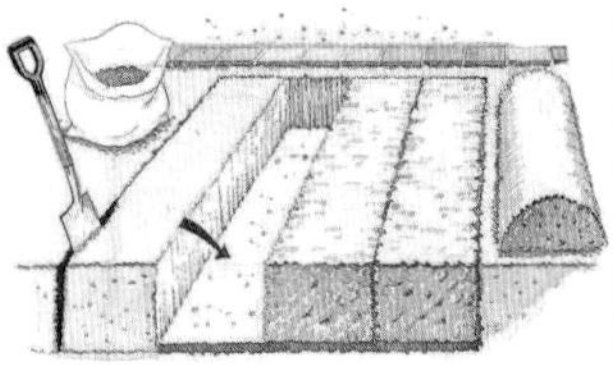

4 *Continue down the length of the plot until you reach the final trench. This should be filled in with the earth taken from the first trench, which was set to one side.*

DOUBLE DIGGING, METHOD ONE

Double digging is a good method for compacted, heavy or poor soils that are in need of rejuvenation. It involves a deep cultivation of both the topsoil and subsoil and is well worth the hard work, producing a wonderful soil in which plants will thrive.

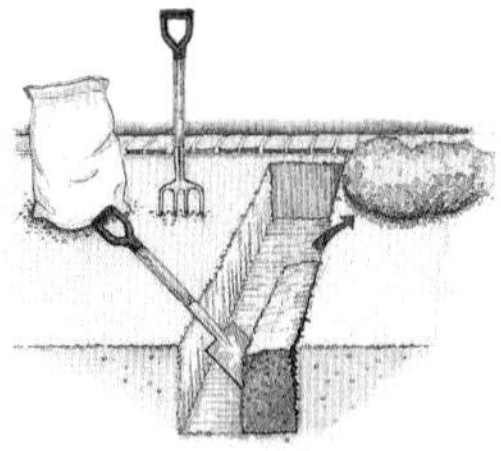

1 *Dig a wide trench, placing the soil to one side so that it can be used later when filling in the final trench.*

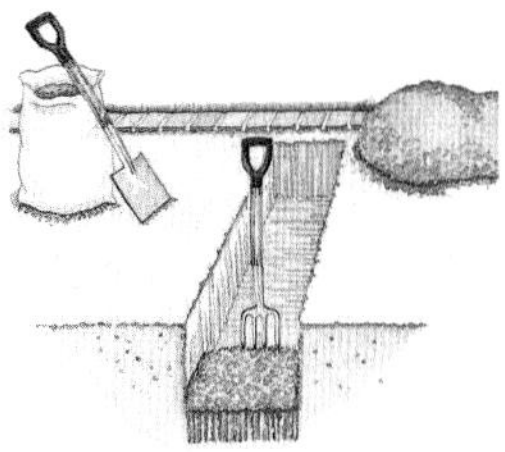

2 *Break up the soil at the bottom of the trench with a fork, adding manure to the soil as you proceed.*

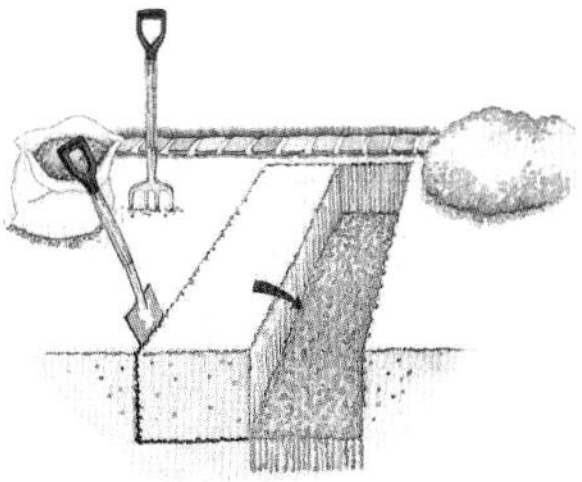

3 *Dig the next trench in the bed, turning the soil over on top of the broken soil in the first trench.*

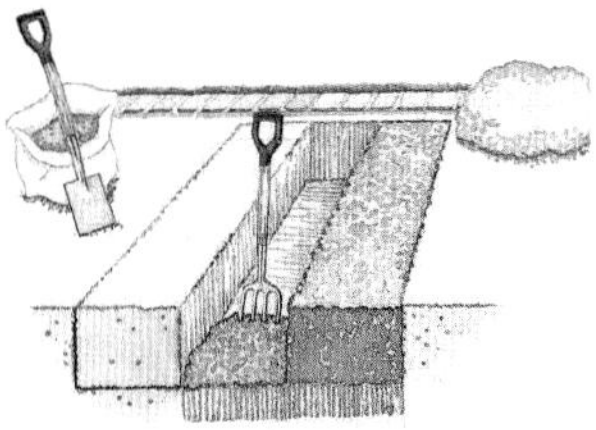

4 *Continue down the plot, ensuring that subsoil from the lower trench is not mixed with topsoil of the upper.*

DOUBLE DIGGING, METHOD TWO

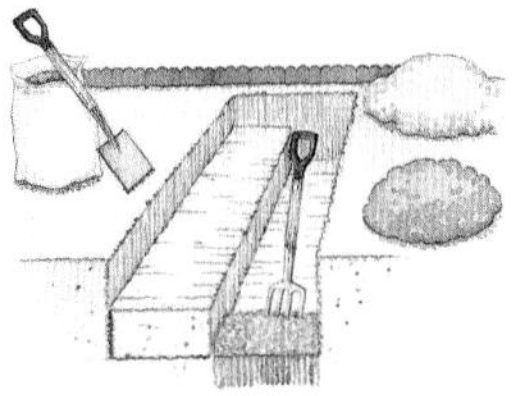

1 *Keeping soil from each level separate, dig the first trench two spits deep and fork over. Dig the second trench one spit deep.*

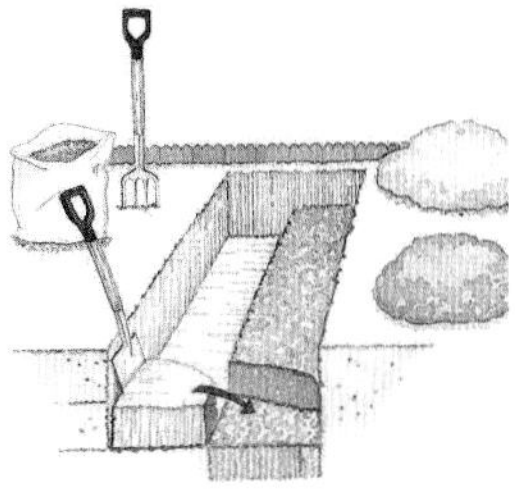

2 *Add organic material to the first double trench and dig the lower spit of the second trench into it.*

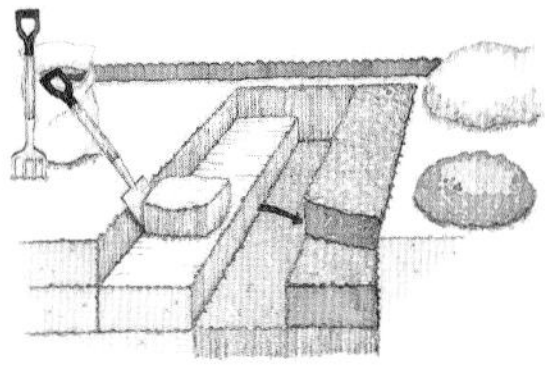

3 *Dig an upper third trench one spit deep, and place the soil on top of that already placed in the first trench.*

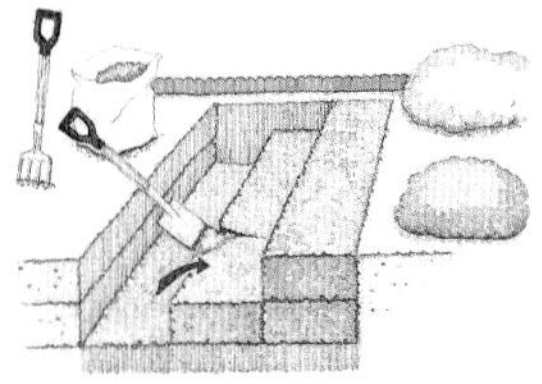

4 *Continue, ensuring that the topsoil and subsoil do not mix. Fill in remaining trenches with soil taken from the first one.*

over the exposed subsoil. Move over one spit's width in the bed, and begin to dig out another trench, moving and inverting the excavated soil into the adjacent trench that was just dug. When you get to the end of the bed replace the soil that was set aside at the outset.

When the digging is finished, level the site prior to planting. More garden compost (approximately 8cm/3in) can be spread over the surface and forked in at this stage.

You do not have to dig the entire plot all at once. Instead, work on small areas, say, one metre (yard) square, whenever you wish. Once you double-dig a bed, it is important not to walk on it. After all, the whole point of double digging is to loosen the topsoil and the subsoil to a sufficient depth so that the roots of the plants can grow unrestricted and water can readily percolate through the soil. Walking on the soil will simply pack it down again.

There is also a second method of digging (shown above) that is less commonly used, which enriches the soil to a greater depth.

SECONDARY CULTIVATION

This normally involves the nourishing of the soil after it has been cultivated by digging and usually entails the addition of some form of organic matter during, or immediately after, its completion. Secondary cultivation also describes light digging used to control weeds or incorporate green manures. The tool generally used for this is a fork. Light forking is often the best method to use in areas with permanent plantings of perennial plants or shrubs.

USING A ROTAVATOR

A rotavator is a useful labour-saving device for breaking down dug clods and creating a fine, free-running 'tilth' that can easily be levelled for planting or seed-bed preparation.

TIPS FOR DIGGING

Digging can be hard work, but simply following the tips given below will help you to avoid strains and injuries.

- Start with a small area, pace yourself and avoid straining your back.
- Use a spade that is right for you and the job. It should be a little higher than hip height when held vertically.
- Do not try to lift more than you can handle. You will dig for longer periods of time by taking smaller amounts.
- As you work, try to establish a rhythm that you can maintain at all times.
- When doing a lot of heavy digging, scrape the blade clean now and then, and, if necessary, use a file to sharpen the end of the spade, following the original bevel of the blade.

SOIL CONDITIONERS

There is quite a range of conditioners available to the allotment-grower for improving the soil. Some are free (if you do not count the time taken in working and transporting them), others are relatively cheap, while those bought by the bag can be quite expensive. The best option is often to begin by using the materials that are closest to hand. Smaller plots or those that are newly established or in poor shape may require soil conditioners to be brought in. This section looks at some of the options.

Above: *A well-conditioned soil will pay dividends in terms of enhanced plant growth and development.*

FARMYARD MANURE

This is usually freely available, although these days it comes increasingly from stables rather than farms. It contains a small amount of nutrients although it usually makes the soil more acidic as it decomposes and should always be well rotted before use. It can also contain lots of weed seeds, which often come from the bedding used for the animals. Occasionally there can be problems if the straw used has been sprayed with pesticides, so always be sure of your source. Farmyard manure is usually cheap or occasionally free for the taking.

Left: *Spent mushroom compost is an ideal material for improving the structure of many types of soil. Its high pH makes it unsuitable as a mulch around acid-loving plants.*

BURYING GREEN WASTE

If you have space, you can simply open a trench in the soil and bury your green waste 20–30cm (8–12in) deep under the soil. It will take perhaps two to three months during the warm season to break down. Avoid planting crops in the soil above until the material has decomposed properly.

Left: *Animal manures can provide both nutrients and valuable organic matter when added to your garden soil.*

LEAF MOULD

Many gardeners believe leaf mould to be the finest addition to any soil. The product itself forms naturally under the closed canopy of forest trees. It is, as the name suggests, the rotted product of fallen leaves. It is not particularly rich in nutrients but it has an extremely good ability to condition a soil and encourages natural nutrient cycles in your soil. It is usually made by the gardeners that wish to use it and is rarely sold on. Anyone who has a ready supply of leaves will find this an easy material to make.

Start by gathering up leaves in the autumn and stack in a chicken-wire cage to prevent them being blown back over the site. Do not add any greens or other materials to the pile. The heap will rot down slowly and be ready for use in one to two years. It can be sited in a dark corner where nothing else will grow, but you must ensure that you keep the pile moist all year round. The wire cage can be removed after two months or so and used again the following autumn. Alternatively, two permanent pits, sited side by side, can be filled (or emptied) in alternate years. Smaller quantities of leaves can be pushed into black plastic sacks with the top closed and with holes pierced by a garden fork around the sides and bottom of the bag to allow some airflow.

SPENT MUSHROOM COMPOST

This is one of the few types of organic matter to have a slightly alkaline effect on the soil. It is a uniform and friable mixture of stable organic materials that is a waste product of the mushroom-growing industry. It is usually quite inexpensive. The composting and growing processes that produce this material bind nutrients to the organic matter, resulting in a substance that holds on to nutrients more readily than fresh or non-composted organic wastes. In addition, the compost has good moisture-holding abilities.

Spent mushroom compost is slightly alkaline, with a pH ranging from 7–8 but generally around 7.3. There are few weed seeds, insects or pathogens because the compost is pasteurized before it is removed from the mushroom house.

BUILDING A LEAF MOULD PIT

1 *Drive in four 1.5m (5ft) posts to form the four corners of a square on the ground. The posts should be spaced about 1m (3ft) apart and there should be just over 1m left above ground once the posts are driven in.*

2 *Attach chicken wire – a 1m (3ft) wide roll is needed for this – to the stakes using 'U'-shaped fencing staples, hammered in firmly. Pull the wire tight across the length of the roll before attaching it to the next post.*

3 *Once the wire has been securely stapled to the posts all the way around, cut it with wire cutters, folding the sharp ends under the attached mesh so that they cannot cut you or snag any clothing.*

4 *Place fallen leaves into the 'pit' until it is full. Firm the leaves lightly in layers as you go, so that the pit is completely packed with leaves but still contains a little air.*

5 *After a year or two, the leaf mould is ready to use. You could build two pits and rotate their use, as a single pit will not be emptied in time to receive leaves the following autumn.*

6 *In order to gain the maximum benefit, you should apply the finished leaf mould to the soil in your allotment in late winter or early spring, when the soil is moist.*

Left: *Beans and other leguminous plants are an important part of a successful allotment vegetable garden, 'fixing' their own nitrogen and so naturally helping to raise levels of soil fertility.*

The addition of spent compost to garden soil can result in a higher pH, increased nutrient-holding capacity and better soil structure. The main disadvantage occurs when the compost is first mixed with soil, as bacteria convert the proteins in the compost to ammonia, which can be toxic to young plants. Try to ensure the source of your compost is an organic mushroom grower.

VEGETABLE INDUSTRIAL WASTE

Some by-products of the food industry, such as spent hop waste and cocoa shells, can be beneficial as soil conditioners in the allotment garden. They are useful in terms of their ability to improve soil structure. However, their smell, which may be described as rancid ale or beer with hops, or sickly cocoa, is often enough to put people off. They are sometimes marketed commercially although they may be available as a local by-product of industry. Whatever product you use, it should be well rotted before it is used as a soil conditioner.

WORM COMPOST

Kitchen waste can be composted with worms both indoors and outdoors, although these two locations have their limitations and advantages.

The materials that are being composted are consumed by the worms and then excreted as worm casts. This process binds the nutrients consumed into a form that can be used by plants and reduces the volume of the original materials. These worm casts are covered with slow-dissolving, semi-permeable mucus that acts as a time-release mechanism for the nutritional content of the worm casts and also gives the finished compost good water-retentive qualities.

Above: *Brandling or tiger worms readily reduce vegetable matter into a useful compost material within a wormery.*

A WORMERY

Worms are an effective way to break down kitchen waste such as vegetable scraps. They will eventually eat their bedding as well as the kitchen waste. The resulting worm casts are a nutrient-rich soil conditioner.

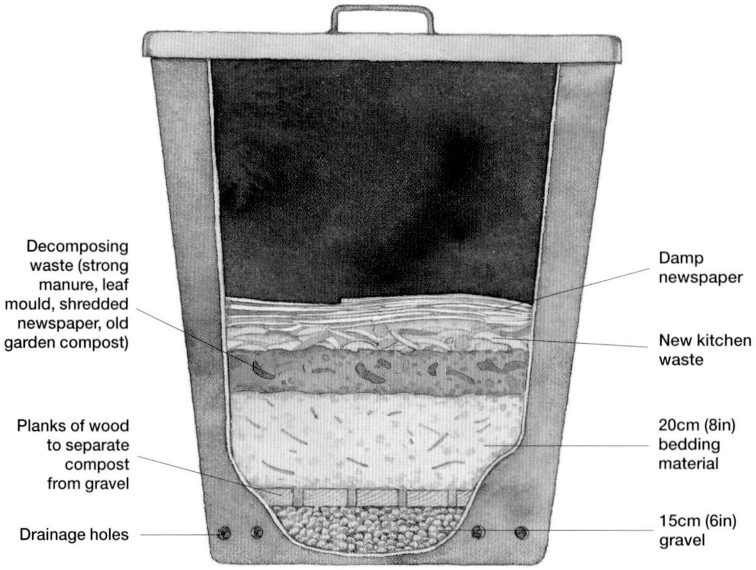

Worm colonies can be built in a similar way to a cold pile compost heap, with materials added as they become available. Excessive heat and frequent pile turning are not needed. Too much heat will actually kill the worms. Alternatively, a purpose-built wormery can be used. Both methods require materials to be placed in a shaded, cool and moist location. The worm colony must not become heated by the microbial action that takes place in normal composting. If the colony does get hot, it may cause the loss of the worms if they do not have cooler areas to which they can escape.

For an indoor worm colony, the wormery (a sealed, ventilated box with a close-fitting lid) is filled with bedding materials (usually damp shredded newspaper or similar) and the worms are added. Vegetable waste from the kitchen is placed on top or a few inches under the bedding where the worms can find and devour it. Eventually, the worms eat their bedding as well as the vegetable scraps. The finished worm castings can be removed and used. New bedding and kitchen scraps are then placed in the container and the worms returned to make a new batch of compost. Many purchased wormeries have the facility to collect the liquid by-product of the worms' activities, which makes an excellent liquid plant food.

It is advisable to check the pH level of the wormery every now and then. Thin, white, thread-like cotton worms are usually an indication that the pH is too low. Adding some calcified seaweed can help to counter this acidity, as can a regular addition of eggshells.

Above: *Leafy crops benefit from the addition of organic matter because it encourages nitrogen-fixing bacteria to do their all-important work in the soil.*

Above: *Organic matter buried under a layer of soil will allow it to break down gradually. A trench 30cm (12in) deep can easily accommodate a layer of well-rotted material 8–10cm (4–5in) thick. This will break down, enriching the soil over time, and is the most commonly used method to add organic matter when digging a plot.*

BENEFITS OF ADDING ORGANIC MATTER

Using organic matter as a mulch or soil conditioner will help to warm up the soil earlier in the spring. This in turn will allow for the earlier planting of some types of plant.

- Organic matter inoculates the soil with vast numbers of beneficial microbes and provides the food source that soil-dwelling microbes need to live. These microbes are able to extract nutrients from the mineral part of the soil and eventually pass the nutrients on to plants.
- Adding organic matter to your soil improves the way in which water interacts with the soil and improves the overall soil structure. All soils can benefit from the regular addition of organic matter.

To sandy soils

- Organic matter acts as a sponge to help retain water that would otherwise drain down below the reach of plant roots. This has the benefit of protecting plants against drought.

To clay soils

- Organic matter helps to increase the air space within the soil, making it drain more quickly. This ensures that the soil does not become waterlogged or dry out into a brick-like substance.

Above: *Even a stack of old car tyres can be recycled and used to make a cheap but effective compost heap.*

MAKING GARDEN COMPOST

Every allotment should have at least one compost heap, where plot and kitchen waste can be broken down by microbes and other soil-dwelling creatures to produce a good medium-fertility soil improver. Making compost is not difficult and is an excellent way to recycle waste. Many growers take great pride in their home-produced compost and all sites can benefit from this sustainable approach to soil improvement.

THE SITE

A position in full sun will give the compost heap additional heat, allowing the contents to decompose more rapidly. If time is not a key factor, partial shade or even full shade will do. Compost is easily made in a freestanding pile in a sunny or partially shaded area in the allotment. Alternatively, a simple structure can be used to contain the pile. A variety of materials can be used to make these structures, including wood, bricks, pallets, a wire cage or even a stack of used tyres. Whichever method you use, you must provide good drainage. An average heap should be around a cubic metre (10 cu. ft). It can be much larger, but any smaller and it will not be as effective.

When adding waste materials to the heap, the items should be as small as you can make them. The more surface area that is exposed, the quicker it will decompose. A chipper or shredder is a big help. Many gardeners are keen advocates of adding a small amount of good topsoil in order to introduce microorganisms that will kick-start the process of decomposition.

Left: *A wall made from a pallet, filled with straw and held in place with chicken wire, allows air to circulate, aiding decomposition.*

Compost heaps in containers can be built up with successive layers of 'green' and 'brown' materials, separating these with thin layers of topsoil.

Sifting the pile is the final stage of the process, with any large pieces of residue being returned back to the new heap.

COMPOST INGREDIENTS

The potential ingredients for your compost heap will be either 'brown' or 'green'. Browns are dry and dead plant materials, such as straw, hay, dry brown weeds, autumn leaves, nutshells, shredded paper, pine needles, tough plant stems and wood chips or sawdust. Because they tend to be dry, browns often need to be moistened before they are put into a compost system.

Greens are fresh (and often green) plant materials, such as green weeds from the plot, fruit and vegetable scraps, green leaves, grass clippings, tea bags, coffee grounds, seaweed, eggshells, fish scraps, green manures and fresh horse manure.

MAKING A HOT PILE COMPOST HEAP

1 *Starting with an empty compost bin, place a layer of 'browns' – straw, old leaves and chipped wood are ideal – in the base of the bin. If the bin is positioned over bare soil, include some fine twiggy material to help to circulate air to the base of the pile.*

2 *Add a layer of brown compost materials, such as autumn leaves, plant stems and wood chips, which should be approximately 15cm (6in) deep, and ensure that it is of an even thickness. The material should be lightly firmed in.*

3 *Add a new layer of 'greens' to the compost bin. Most plant material can be used for this, although you should avoid too much fibrous or woody material such as plant stems. Never include weed seeds if possible.*

Above: *An enclosed compost heap should ideally have one side that opens in order to make it easy to empty the finished material.*

Compared with browns, greens contain more nitrogen. Nitrogen is a critical element in amino acids and proteins, and can be thought of as a protein source for the billions of multiplying microbes.

A good mix of browns and greens is the best nutritional balance for microbes. This mix also improves the aeration and level of water in the pile.

THE 'COLD PILE' METHOD

Make a pile of 'browns', such as autumn leaves, moisten them well and then slowly incorporate 'greens' such as kitchen waste or lawn clippings over the next year (this method can take a full year to finish the compost). If it gets very cold in winter, cover the heap with cardboard or old carpet and peel this back to stir in any greens. In this type of composting, there are never enough high-nitrogen greens to get the pile really hot. Turn the pile a minimum of once a month if you have not recently added any greens, thereby breaking up the decaying mass and making it friable. If you do use this method, be sure you always have at least as many browns as added greens, as too many greens will just create a slimy, smelly mess. Some compost heaps (those with lots of greens added) may reach very high temperatures, some even reaching 70°C (158°F), thereby killing weed seeds. Cold piles, on the other hand, do not and it is best not to add any weed wastes that will contain seeds. If you do, you could risk spreading weed seeds across your allotment in their own growing mix when you come to use the compost.

THE 'HOT PILE' METHOD

Wet the ground under the pile and add twigs or other un-shredded browns to provide some aeration at the base. Layer the rest of your materials, alternating green and brown layers of about 15cm (6in) thickness, and add water as you go. Topsoil can also be added as a 2cm (¾in) layer between each cycle of green and brown materials. Finish the pile with a layer of browns. Cover the pile with a lid or piece of carpet to keep out rain and conserve heat. Check to see that your pile becomes hot within a few days. Turn the pile to decrease composting time. This action allows all the material to be exposed to the hot centre, thereby increasing aeration. Do this once a week in the warmer season, and once a month in cooler periods. The pile's heat should peak every time you turn it, although the peak temperature will be lower with each turn. Always make sure that the pile remains moist, but avoid over-wetting, as this will limit the amount of air circulation and ultimately reduce the speed and efficiency of the process.

COMPOSTING MATERIALS

Many items can be composted into valuable soil conditioners. Whether because of toxins, plant or human diseases or weed problems, some things should never be used.

Good compost materials

Animal manure
Fallen leaves
Grass/lawn clippings
Hay and straw from organic farms
Kitchen waste
Prunings
Sawdust
Shredded browns
Soot and charcoal
Spent hops or cocoa shells
Spent mushroom compost
Weeds and other allotment wastes

What not to compost

Chemically treated wood products
Diseased plants
Human and pet waste
Meat, bones and fatty food wastes
Pernicious weeds

4 *Continue adding greens until you have a layer about 15cm (6in) thick, the same depth as the browns below. Lawn clippings should be placed in layers of about 10cm (4in) or mixed with other green waste to avoid the layer becoming slimy and airless.*

5 *Kitchen refuse, such as vegetable waste, can also be added and is usually classed as a 'green'. You can include a thin layer of soil to add microorganisms before the next layer of 'browns'. Continue layering until the bin is full, then water and cover.*

6 *After two to three months, you should have well-rotted garden compost, which, due to the heat of the pile, will be largely free from weed seeds, pests and diseases. Once the bin has been emptied, it can be refilled in the same way.*

GREEN MANURES

Sometimes referred to as 'cover crops', green manures are plants that are grown to benefit the soil rather than for consumption or display. Green manures replace and hold nutrients, improve the structure of the soil and increase its organic material content. They also smother the soil and so prevent weed growth. Green manures also 'fix' atmospheric nitrogen. They are easy to grow and can be used to improve the soil when manures are not readily available.

Above: *Growing a green manure is an easy and effective way in which to add some organic matter to the soil.*

BENEFITS OF GREEN MANURES

At any time of year, but especially in winter, the soil loses nutrients if it is bare for six weeks or more. Green manures help to counteract this and maintain a more even soil temperature and moisture content. Many green manures grow deep roots to tap resources unavailable to some crops. Others produce a fibrous root system to help build structure in the soil, while many have flowers that attract pollinating insects.

TYPES OF GREEN MANURE

Some green manures are nitrogen-fixers, using bacteria that colonize the nodules on their roots. These microbes take nitrogen out of the air and convert it into a form that plants can use. Green manures are usually divided into two groups: legumes and non-legumes. Leguminous manures include clover, peas, broad (fava) beans and alfalfa. Despite their nitrogen-fixing abilities, legumes have slow autumn growth and add less organic content. They can also be less winter hardy.

Winter rye is the most commonly grown non-leguminous cover crop, but oats, wheat, oilseed rape and buckwheat are also used. Although they do not add nitrogen to the soil, they help maintain levels and have the additional advantage over legumes of growing faster through the autumn, thereby giving better weed suppression. They also tend to break down more slowly than legumes and add more organic matter to the soil. You may wish to use a combination of green manures in order to balance the benefits of the different types.

DEEP-ROOTED GREEN MANURES

The roots of certain green manure 'crops' work through the soil, holding it together as they grow. Once dug in, however, they help to make it crumbly and friable as they rot. Some green manures have very deep roots that reach down into the subsoil and can harvest nutrients that are unavailable to other allotment plants. In this respect they are a form of biological double digging.

PLANTING GREEN MANURES

Winter green manures should be planted early enough to give about four weeks of growth before cold weather stops their growth. Spring or summer crops must be given sufficient time to develop before they are dug in. After preparing the soil, plant large-seeded cover crops in shallow, closely spaced furrows. Smaller seeds can be broadcast over the surface and covered with a light raking, watering if needed until they germinate. Dig the crop in once it is ready, allowing at least three weeks before you intend to plant to give time for the material to rot down. It is best not to allow green manures to go to seed as they all have the potential to become weeds.

Gardens are traditionally dug over and manured in autumn, then left bare over winter. Many nutrients can be lost during this time due to the leaching action of rain. A hardy green manure sown in the autumn can be dug in the following spring, yielding nutrients to a newly sown or planted crop.

USING GREEN MANURES

1 *Sow the seed evenly across the area where you plan to grow the green manure. Either broadcast the seed or sow larger seed thinly in shallow drills and close rows.*

2 *Lightly rake in the seed so that it is covered and will germinate quickly. Water the area thoroughly if there is no rain due or if it does not rain for the following 48 hours.*

3 *Once the seed germinates, allow it to grow a little before digging it into the soil. Never let green manure crops set seed or they will become a weed in later crops on the site.*

TYPES OF GREEN MANURE

GREEN MANURE FOR GROWING OVER WINTER

These species can withstand moderate to hard frost for a long period and can be cut down in the spring, prior to cultivation. The shorter types can also be used as catch (cover) crops around winter vegetables or biennial crops for harvest in the early spring.

GREEN MANURE	SOWING TIME AND METHOD	HEIGHT	WINTER HARDY?	NITROGEN-FIXING ABILITY	TERMS OF GROWTH	DIGGING IN	OTHER NOTES
Alfalfa *Medicago sativa*	Early spring to mid-summer; broadcast at 3g (1/10oz) per square metre (yard).	100–150cm (3–5ft)	Yes	Yes but poor	Perennial. Grow for several months or more than one season.	Any time. Medium effort if young. Hard if left for more than one season.	Very deep rooting. Will grow on most soils. Dislikes acid or waterlogged soils, but drought resistant.
Asilke clover *Trifolium hybridum*	Mid-spring to late summer; broadcast at 3g (1/10oz) per square metre (yard).	30cm (12in)	Yes	Yes	Several months	Any time. Medium effort.	Will withstand wetter soils than other clovers but more prone to drought. Shallow rooted.
Essex or red merviot clover *Trifolium pratense*	Mid-spring to late summer; broadcast at 3g (1/10oz) per square metre (yard).	40cm (16in)	Yes	Yes	Several months	Any time. Easy, little effort.	Prefers good loamy soil. Can be mown or cut several times per season and used for compost.
Grazing rye *Secale cereale*	Late summer to late autumn; broadcast at 30g (1oz) per square metre (yard) or thinly in rows 20cm (8in) apart.	30–60cm (12–24in)	Yes	No	Autumn to spring	Before flowering. Hard work.	Grows in most soils. Keep watered during germination, else yield is poor. Sow thickly to smother weeds.
Phacelia *Phacelia tanacetifolium*	Early spring to early autumn; broadcast at 3g (1/10oz) per square metre (yard) or thinly in rows 20cm (8in) apart.	60–90cm (12–36in)	Yes	No	2 months in summer; 5–6 months over winter	Before flowering. Easy, little effort.	Grows in most soils. Quick to grow in summer. If left, will produce mauve flowers that bees love.
Trefoil *Medicago lupulina*	Early spring to late summer; broadcast at 3g (1/10oz) per square metre (yard).	30–60cm (12–24in)	Yes	Yes	Several months to a year	Any time. Medium effort.	Will grow in most soils but dislikes acid. Can be used for undersowing. Dense foliage.

GREEN MANURE FOR WARM-SEASON GROWING

Plants for use in the spring and summer have to be quick-growing in order to cover the ground and yield benefit within a short period of time. They are generally slightly tender, although lower-growing species can be used as a catch crop around other seasonal crops.

GREEN MANURE	SOWING TIME AND METHOD	HEIGHT	WINTER HARDY?	NITROGEN-FIXING ABILITY	TERMS OF GROWTH	DIGGING IN	OTHER NOTES
Bitter lupin *Lupinus angustifolius*	Early spring to early summer 4cm (1½in) deep; 3cm (1¼in) apart; in rows 15cm (6in) apart.	50cm (20in)	Mild winters	Yes	2–3 months	Before flowering. Easy, little effort.	Prefers light slightly acidic soil. Foliage not very dense. Deep rooted.
Buckwheat *Fagopyrum esculentum*	Early spring to late summer; broadcast at 10g (1/3oz) per square metre (yard) or thinly in shallow rows 20cm (8in) apart.	80cm (32in)	No	No	2–3 months	Before or during flowering. Easy, no effort.	Grows on poor soils. If allowed to flower, attracts hoverflies to aid pollination of crops.
Crimson clover *Trifolium incarnatum*	Early spring to late summer; broadcast at 3g (1/10oz) per square metre (yard).	30–60cm (12–24in)	Mild winters only	Yes	2–3 months or over winter	Before flowering. Medium effort.	Prefers sandy loam soil but will tolerate heavy clay. Large red flowers attract bees.
Fenugreek *Trigonella foenum-graecum*	Early spring to late summer; broadcast at 5g (1/5oz) per square metre (yard) or thinly in 15cm (6in) shallow rows.	30–60cm (12–24in)	Mild winters	No	2–3 months	Any time before flowering. Easy, little effort.	Prefers good drainage but will tolerate heavy or light soil.

Above: *Adding organic matter to the soil surface encourages worms and other organisms that cycle nutrients naturally.*

NO-DIG GARDENING

As the name suggests, no-dig gardening is a method of growing plants without cultivating the ground they occupy. While this may seem unnatural to some confirmed tillers of the soil, it is actually the most natural method available. No-dig gardening mimics the natural cycle; after all, plants have grown on the Earth's surface for over 400 million years without people digging the soil for them. This approach also has the advantage of being less labour-intensive.

ESTABLISHING A NATURAL CYCLE

Essentially no-dig gardening relies upon natural soil processes combined with the action of soil organisms to produce a good soil structure and natural nutrient cycles. There are numerous ways that this can be done, but all rely upon inputs from the top down. A thick top-dressing of organic matter is placed on the surface to be absorbed by the soil itself. Less laborious than digging, the no-dig method does need planning and careful input in order to be successful, although a properly prepared no-dig bed will be every bit as effective as a conventionally cultivated one.

WHAT ARE THE BENEFITS?

Assuming weeds can be controlled, most vegetable crops can be grown with reduced tillage. The key features of a no-dig vegetable-growing system are to keep the soil covered with organic mulch as much of the time as possible and to keep off the soil. The beds are left permanently in place, and there is no cultivation.

Plants grown without tillage use water more efficiently, the water-holding capacity of the soil increases, and water loss from run-off and evaporation is reduced. For crops grown without irrigation in drought-prone soils, this more efficient use of water can translate into higher yields.

In addition, the organic matter in soil and populations of beneficial insects are maintained, as are earthworm populations and microbial activity. Soil and nutrients are less likely to be lost from the ground, less time is required to prepare the soil for planting, and, since there is less bare soil, there will be fewer opportunities for weeds to get established. The mulch of organic matter also helps to keep weeds down.

WHAT ARE THE PROBLEMS?

Potential problems associated with the no-dig method are compaction, flooding and poor drainage. However, if the water-holding capacity of a soil improves, no-till systems may produce higher yields. Soil temperatures under organic mulch can be several degrees lower than bare soil or soil under a plastic mulch. Although the lower temperature can be an advantage, especially in the summer when soil temperatures under plastic can be excessive, it can delay crop development.

Left: *Many allotment gardeners grow crops such as potatoes quite successfully without ever resorting to digging.*

ADVANTAGES AND DISADVANTAGES OF NO-DIG SYSTEMS

Although no-dig beds may require a little longer to establish initially than cultivated plots, they do offer considerable labour-saving benefits to the allotment gardener. They also suffer very few disadvantages when these are weighed against the considerable advantages.

Advantages

- Plants use water more efficiently.
- Better water-holding capacity of the soil.
- Reduced water loss from run-off and evaporation.
- Higher crop yields in areas prone to drought.
- Organic matter in the soil and soil organisms are maintained at higher levels.
- The lower temperature can be an advantage, especially in summer when soil temperatures under plastic can be excessive.
- Soil and nutrients are more easily maintained.
- Less time is required to prepare the soil for planting.
- Fewer weeds become established due to the mulch of organic matter and the lack of bare soil.

Disadvantages

- Soil can become compacted or poorly drained if it is not properly managed.
- Soil temperatures under a mulch can be several degrees lower than bare soil, which can delay the development of crops.

MAKING A NO-DIG BED

A bed system which includes permanent paths is essential if digging is to be eliminated from gardening tasks. Planning the area so that all parts of the bed can be reached from the paths means that you can grow your crops closer together (you do not need to leave extra space for access) and you will be able to harvest more from a smaller area.

Mark out the beds on the ground or build simple raised beds with wooden sides. Alternatively, those wishing to make a more permanent edge could consider a low brick wall. By raising the bed it is possible to create a deep bed of good-quality soil that will warm up more quickly than the surrounding soil. A raised bed also means you do not have to bend down so far to carry out routine tasks and the method is tailor-made for disabled gardeners. Raised edging is also useful for attaching supporting hoops, crop covers and cloches. Edges such as these are also ideal for providing barriers for pests. Devices such as water traps or copper paper are easily attached to them to prevent slugs and snails from entering the bed.

Beds should be no more than 1.2m (4ft) wide and paths at least 30cm (12in) wide with every other path double this width to allow for easy wheelbarrow access. Individual beds should be no longer than 3.5m (12ft), otherwise you will waste a lot of time walking around them. The beds can be of any design, from a simple series of parallel rectangles to a more complex pattern of interlocking shapes. Whatever design you choose, follow the same recommended bed and path widths, remembering that narrow angles and very small beds are more difficult to construct.

Above: *Edging your beds with hoops of bent twigs provides barriers for pests.*

PLANTING POTATOES IN A NO-DIG BED

1 *Place a thick layer of well-rotted manure or garden compost on the bed to be planted. This should be quite deep – at least 15–20cm (6–8in) – as it will quickly decompose during the growing season. Early planting is possible by manuring in winter and covering with plastic sheeting to warm the soil. The potatoes are planted directly into this and may be more closely spaced than those planted in soil, perhaps as close as 30cm (12in) apart.*

2 *Apply a generous mulch of straw once the bed is planted to give cover to the tubers and to suppress weed growth on the manure or compost. Spread a second layer of composted organic material over the straw. Add another layer of straw and composted material. Water the bed well. Once the potato plants begin to emerge, more straw can be laid down on to the bed, as the material put down earlier in the season will begin to compost down.*

3 *As the potato stems grow, mulch heavily in order to ensure that no light reaches the developing tubers. The potato crop will mature at the same rate as potatoes grown in ordinary soil. The no-dig system is possibly the best method for heavy clay soils that are prone to waterlogging. Potatoes grown in this way are also easy to harvest as there is no digging and the potatoes are cleaner once they are ready for harvesting.*

PLANNING THE CROPS

Successful cropping requires an understanding of how crops grow, what they need, when they mature, and the systems and structures you will need to put in place to ensure a good harvest. Each crop has its individual preferences, although many share similar requirements, which means they can readily be grown in the same setting. Knowing the requirements of your fruit and vegetables allows you to choose which ones are right for you, plan an appropriate alloment structure and layout, and work out what needs doing in order to get a successful result.

Left: *Allotment sites can provide a summer spectacle as well as a wealth of fresh, home-grown food for your table.*

Above: *Fruit such as pears and apples grown on an allotment are one of the most welcome delights of autumn.*

Above: *Planting companion flowers on your alloment helps to keep your vegetables healthy by attracting beneficial insects.*

Above: *A greenhouse on the plot not only helps you raise earlier crops but also allows you to greatly increase the range you grow.*

STARTING YOUR PLAN

Taking on an allotment can be quite time-consuming and it is important not to let things slip during the busy times of the year or your crops will suffer and the yield will be lower. Ideally you should get down there as often as possible, but in reality it is best to pace yourself and apply the little and often principle. Choose what you want to grow wisely, according to your needs, tastes and lifestyle, and plan ahead to ensure a steady harvest of useful produce over the course of the year.

Above: *Carefully labelling crops means that you know what is growing where and lends a sense of care and order to your plot.*

MAKE A PERSONAL SCHEDULE

When you take on a new allotment, it is possible that you might be 'making' extra time to get out there. If this is taking you away from other things, it is likely that other matters in your life might become neglected. If there is a chance that time will be an issue, the crops you grow will need to reflect this. An allotment featuring a range of more permanent crops, such as fruit, rhubarb, asparagus or artichokes will prove less time-consuming during the summer months, although it will be less productive on a yearly basis.

It is a good idea is to spend some of the time that you are there taking a look at what other plot-holders are doing. See what crops are successful and what works well for them. Remember that the social angle is often a good way to learn how to get the best from your plot and, as a result, needs to be a part of your schedule.

SET SOME TARGETS

Once you have an idea of how much time you can commit to your allotment, you will need some goals to aim for. While there is no reason not to be ambitious, you need to temper this with a little realism. If your main objective is to grow some fresh vegetables for your kitchen table, then you need to have a harvest by date for the first crop.

Always keep this in mind through the time leading up to this. You could always make a little event of the first crops being cooked; after all, you've worked hard to get to that stage. Don't stop there though, as you'll quickly find targets and achievements to be a great motivator, particularly when you have to go out in chilly winter weather to tend your patch.

DECIDE WHAT TO GROW

A visit to a local seed supplier will usually leave you facing a bewildering array of seed packets. Not only are there many vegetable types but there is also a huge number of varieties for some of them. The descriptions point to bumper harvests of mouth-watering vegetables and it is easy to become confused.

Below: *Cloches and low tunnels can increase the range of early crops that can be grown on an allotment.*

As with any shopping trip, the secret of success when obtaining the right crops is to have a list. Start this by writing down all the things you regularly eat. Chances are, this list will be quite long and will quickly fill up the growing space available to you.

PLANT ACCORDING TO YOUR REQUIREMENTS

Remember that liking something is not the same as wanting to eat a lot of it. Gluts are common on allotments and this is usually because people overestimate how much of one thing they need. In contrast, crops that you are likely to use a lot of can easily run short if you don't plant enough of them.

A quick look around your neighbours' plots will reveal subtle differences in what they are growing. This probably reflects personal tastes on their part and, in time, your plot will be similarly distinguished with your own preferences.

SPREAD YOUR HARVEST OVER THE YEAR

Even if your plot is packed with crops that you will definitely want to eat, the chances are that they could all come at once. If you haven't got somewhere or a way of storing them, this can lead to waste, so it is a good idea to grow several varieties of one crop, choosing a range that matures over a period of time. You can also stagger a few sowings or plantings to spread out the season of each of these, meaning that the food stays on your plot for as long as possible and is always harvested fresh to your table. Sharing and swapping produce with your allotment neighbours is a great way to make the most of each other's gluts, and friends and family will normally welcome free food!

You will also need to learn to fit in with the rhythms of nature. Some crops have a definite season and, although this can be extended artificially using cloches, polythene tunnels, cold frames and greenhouses, there are nonetheless limits as to when it will be available. Remember that this is part of the fun of an allotment; seasonal, tasty, fresh food, that is enjoyed at its best, rather than the same vegetables all year round.

Above: *Careful planning and preparation will be rewarded with a successful allotment packed with your favourite crops.*

Above: *Time spent planning your plot is an essential part of the yearly schedule. Make notes concerning both success and failures.*

DON'T BE AFRAID TO BREAK THE RULES

Probably the best thing about growing your own produce is that you can always experiment with something new. This might be trying to grow a wacky variety or an exotic crop that is more reminiscent of tropical climes, or trying to stretch the season for something well beyond the norm. It can also be an opportunity to try out new techniques in a constrained, controlled environment.

The collective knowledge of the plot-holders around you often outstrips the best books and, what's more, it is specific to your own site. Ask questions, read up on the subject but always make sure that you exercise the basic freedom to just try something new if you want to. If it works, then you will gain a tremendous sense of achievement. If it fails, it doesn't matter. It was fun trying and probably taught you a thing or two along the way without costing you very much other than a little bit of time.

CHOOSING CROP VARIETIES

There is a seemingly endless array of seeds available to the allotment gardener. Each supplier makes claims that their variety is better than all those that went before and any others currently available. Others claim to have older varieties saved from extinction. Personal preference usually dictates the best varieties for you, but an understanding of what you can expect from the seed in a packet can be very useful.

Above: *Onions come in a range of attractive colours and can be grown for their ornamental value as well as for eating.*

WHAT ARE HYBRIDS?

Often when we purchase seed, we respond more readily to the picture on the front of the packet. We may not notice whether it is marked with the terms 'F1' or 'hybrid'. A hybrid is the result of a cross between one variety with pollen from another specific variety. The breeder chooses parent varieties that will produce first generation offspring (F1 hybrids) with known characteristics. The crossing is done in a very controlled manner so that no pollen from another variety is able to pollinate the flowers. As a result, all of the plants that are grown from the hybrid seed will be genetically identical.

Hybrids may be bred to be more widely adapted to environmental stresses such as heat, cold, disease or drought than non-hybrids. They tend to have more uniform characteristics, making crops more predictable in their qualities. They also have 'hybrid vigour' and may grow faster or be more disease-resistant than either of the parents. They may also give better yields than open-pollinated varieties. They will not breed true, however, meaning that seed collected will not produce plants that are the same as the parent (F1 hybrids). For this reason, seed cannot be saved from F1 hybrid plants by the allotment gardener. Seed for hybrid varieties must be purchased year after year from seed companies or nurseries instead, unless you want to take a gamble and grow an array of offspring.

WHAT ARE OPEN-POLLINATED VARIETIES?

Open-pollinated varieties are traditional varieties that have (in some cases) been grown and selected for desirable traits such as taste, yield or disease-resistance for many years. They often grow well in allotment sites as many were originally selected under organic conditions. These plants can mutate and adapt to the local ecosystem, as the seed is often collected and re-used by the allotment gardener.

If a seed packet is labelled 'heirloom', 'open-pollinated' or has no special markings, then it is most likely a standard or traditional variety. The majority of lettuce, bean and pea varieties for domestic use are open-pollinated, while most cabbages, broccoli, tomatoes, cucumbers, melons and Brussels sprouts are hybrids.

Left: *Unusual crop varieties can often be grown from seed that you have collected yourself each year. This is a striking variety of kohl rabi.*

Right: *Allowing a few of your crops to flower will provide you with valuable seed for growing next year's crop.*

Hybrid seeds can dominate the seed market, but open-pollinated varieties are more or less stabilized in their characteristics, remaining fairly consistent and producing seed that will grow into plants that are more or less like the parent plants. They are a little less uniform than hybrids, but the allotment gardener can safely and confidently collect seed and grow plants from them that will be essentially the same as the original plants. Open-pollinated varieties either self-pollinate or are pollinated by wind or insects and they usually produce viable seed.

There have been various claims that open-pollinated varieties do not taste as good as hybrids. It is also claimed that they are smaller and not as uniform and, in many cases, this may be true. However, where matters of taste in varieties are concerned, the only real answer is to try them and see for yourself.

Right: *Old varieties of tomato tend to have varying sizes of tastier fruits. They grow even better among companion flowers.*

WHAT ARE HEIRLOOM VARIETIES?

In the 1970s the European Community brought in regulations to encourage the breeding of new vegetable cultivars and the standardization of older ones. This resulted in a list of approved cultivars being drawn up and it became illegal to sell any cultivar that was not included on this list. It is very expensive to have a single cultivar tested in order to then register it on the list. This meant that many old cultivars were put in grave danger of being lost forever, as the funds to test each variety were not available. It was due to this legislation that the Henry Doubleday Research Association (HDRA), an organic garden organization in England which was established to promote organic issues, founded the Heritage Seed Library (HSL). This seed library ensures that old or 'heirloom varieties' are kept safe for posterity by distributing their seed. Although HDRA grow some of the seeds themselves, they also employ contract growers and seed guardians to make up the bulk of the seeds that are supplied.

Each year a catalogue is sent to HSL members from which they can select up to six varieties free of charge. This distribution set-up overcomes the clause of selling only approved cultivars. This service is also available to members in the United States.

The best heirloom cultivars can be traced back 50 years or longer. Many of these early varieties have been lost already, making those that remain all the more precious. A number of these cultivars have been collected and saved by families and ethnic groups dating back many years. This practice protected the genetic make-up that made each variety successful within a given environment. These base characteristics have become invaluable and the genetic strains of these vegetables are the backbone of modern disease- and drought-resistant hybrids. It is this that makes the collection and preservation of these cultivars so important.

Left: *Many of the heirloom varieties have been selected for the way they perform in local conditions, rather than for crop size, taste or uniformity.*

CROP ROTATION

This is the practice of grouping and growing related plants together and rotating them around different areas of land in a regimented fashion from year to year. Rotating your crops in this way has many advantages, including helping to prevent pest and disease problems from arising in the first place. This method of gardening is fundamental to successful growing. It has been practised for thousands of years and developed into a system that is easy to follow and implement on an allotment.

Above: *The secret to achieving a thriving and healthy vegetable area is to rotate the crops on a regular basis.*

WHY ARE CROPS ROTATED?

Continuous cropping in the same area puts both plants and soil at risk. It not only allows large numbers of soil-borne pests and diseases to build up, but, because crops require the same nutrients from the soil year after year, the practice can deplete nutrient levels. A poor infertile soil produces weak unhealthy plants, which, in turn, will be more prone to pest and disease attacks. All these problems amount to reduced yields and even complete crop failure.

When crops are rotated, the groups are divided up into closely related plants that are prone to similar pests and diseases. For example, carrots, parsnips, beetroot (beets) and potatoes are members of one group and prone to carrot fly, whereas cabbage, kale, broccoli and Brussels sprouts, which are members of another group, can be prone to clubroot and cabbage root fly. If the groups are grown in different areas on a rotational basis, it can help to prevent the establishment of soil-borne pests and diseases.

Combined with regular additions of compost and manure, crop rotation will make the soil richer, replace certain nutrients and help prevent pH imbalances that can result from repeated crops of the same type of vegetable.

Above: *Brassica crops, such as these red cabbages and Brussels sprouts, should be grouped together in your allotment.*

BENEFITS OF CROP ROTATION

There are many benefits to be gained from rotating your crops regularly.

- Prevents the build-up of soil pests and diseases.
- Helps to prevent nutrient depletion from heavy-feeding crops.
- Rotated crops produce higher yields.
- Results in a healthier soil.

MAKING A ROTATIONAL PLAN

The basic rules of crop rotation are simple. If you are planning a four-year crop rotation, the plants you have selected are split up into five groups. Group one contains the legumes (peas and beans); group two contains the brassicas (cabbages, Brussels sprouts, broccoli, kale etc); group three contains the onion family and others (onions, lettuce, garlic, sweetcorn [corn] etc); group four includes root crops (potatoes, parsnips, carrots, beetroot [beets] etc); and finally, group five houses permanent crops such as asparagus and rhubarb.

The vegetable plot is then divided into five sections. The permanent crops are given a specific area and are not moved or included in the rotational cycle. The remaining four groups are allocated an area in which to grow. Every year each group is moved on to the next plot, making it four years before the crops are grown on the same area of land again; hence the term crop rotation.

If space is limited, crops can be grown on a three-year rotation – they are split into three groups and divided up as before, except group three is incorporated into group one.

There is no need to grow each crop in every year of a cycle. Remember that it is the vegetable groups that dictate the cropping cycle according to their soil needs and any associated problems. Rotating the crops helps provide the correct soil requirements for certain crops. For example, cabbages and the rest of the group grow well in soil that has been manured the previous autumn, whereas carrots and other root crops (not including potatoes) do not. Where carrots are to be grown, then the plot will need to be dug deeply in readiness for them.

It is important that you plan where the crops are to be every year, so that you know their position for the following year. A comprehensive cropping plan can help you to maximize the yield on a year-round basis by working out successional sowings and intercropping and catch cropping.

COMMON DIFFICULTIES

When planning the cycle, you may encounter certain problems. Careful planning will show that potatoes often take up more space in a vegetable bed than any other crop and finding enough room to grow them in their allocated area may prove difficult.

If space is proving a problem, consider some of the following strategies. Keep brassicas together as a group and never plant them in the same ground two years running. Keep potatoes together every year; if you have planned a lot of potatoes, move all the other members from group four into group three. Also bear in mind that some root crops, such as potatoes, are manure-friendly, while others, like parsnips, are not. Finally, alternating shallow-rooted plants such as cabbages or lettuce with deep-rooted plants like tomatoes or squash will allow the plants' roots to do much of the soil loosening that would otherwise have to be done by hand.

THREE-YEAR CROP ROTATION

Plot 1 – Peas; broad (fava) beans; French (green) beans; runner (green) beans; bulb onions; leeks; sweetcorn (corn); marrows (large zucchini); squashes and pumpkins; lettuce.

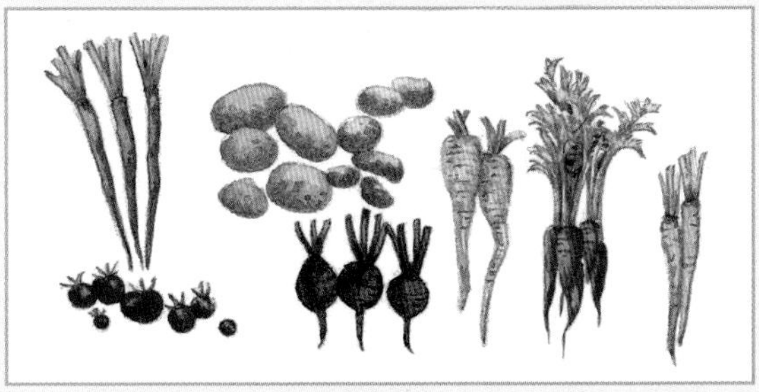

Plot 2 – Potatoes; parsnips; beetroot (beets); carrots; salsify; scorzonera; tomatoes.

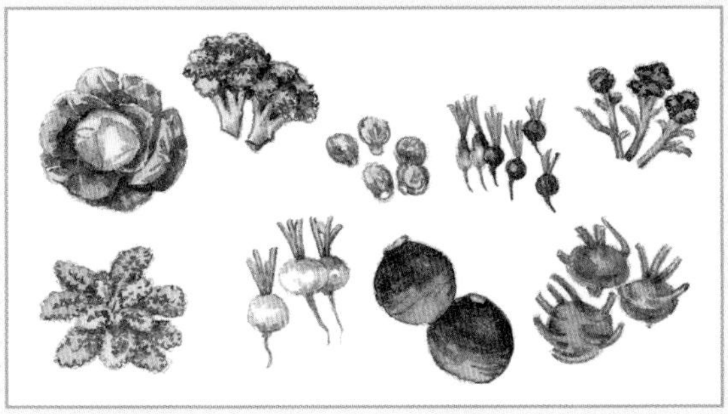

Plot 3 – Cabbages; Brussels sprouts; calabrese (Italian sprouting broccoli); broccoli; kale; swede (rutabaga or yellow turnips); turnips; kohl rabi; radishes.

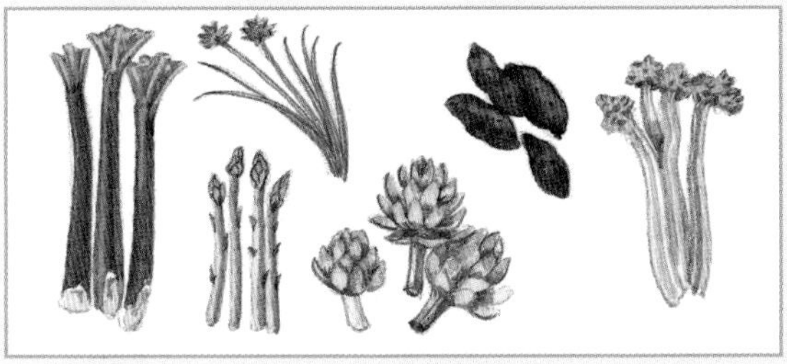

Plot 4 (permanent) – Rhubarb; asparagus; perennial herbs; globe artichokes; Jerusalem artichokes; sea kale.

FOUR-YEAR CROP ROTATION

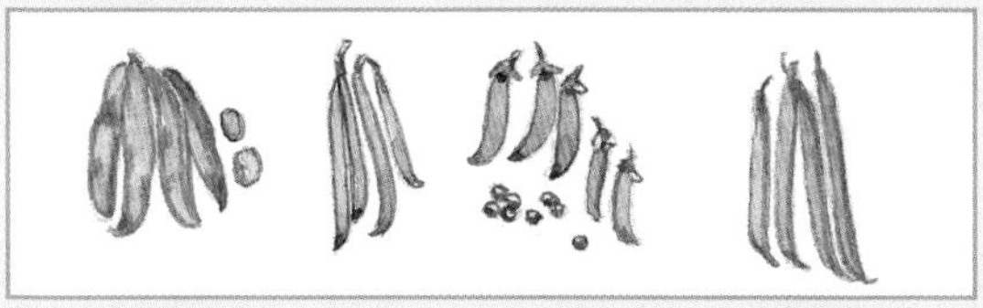

Plot 1 – Peas; broad (fava) beans; French (green) beans; runner (green) beans.

Plot 2 – Cabbages; Brussels sprouts; calabrese (Italian sprouting broccoli); broccoli; kale; radishes; swedes (rutabaga or yellow turnips); turnips; kohl rabi.

Plot 3 – Bulb onions; spring onions (scallions); shallots; leeks; garlic; sweetcorn (corn); marrows (large zucchini), squashes and pumpkins; lettuce.

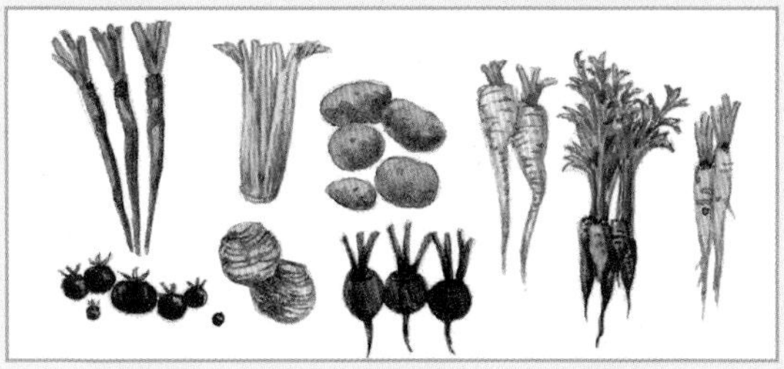

Plot 4 – Potatoes; parsnips; beetroot (beets); carrots; salsify; scorzonera; celery; celeriac (celery root); tomatoes.

Plot 5 (permanent) – Rhubarb; asparagus; perennial herbs; globe artichokes; Jerusalem artichokes; sea kale.

THREE-YEAR CROP ROTATION

Decide on the vegetables you want to grow and divide into the four groups (plots 1–4) shown in the table opposite. Draw a plan to indicate which group of crops goes where, using a different colour for each group. (Remember plot four is for permanent crops.) Move the crops in each group to the next plot the following year.

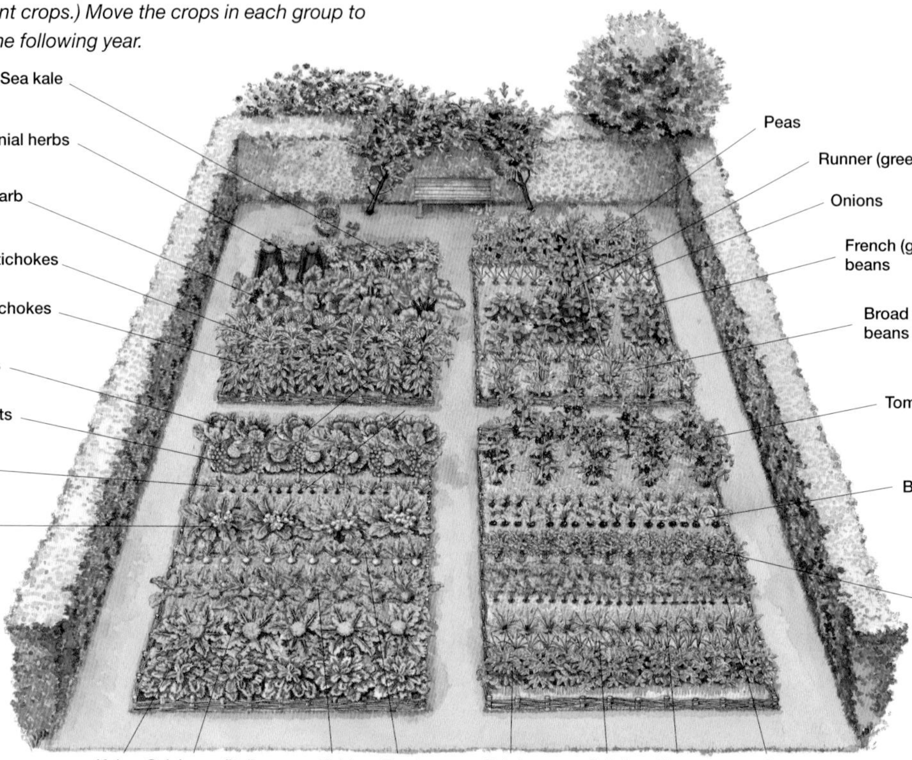

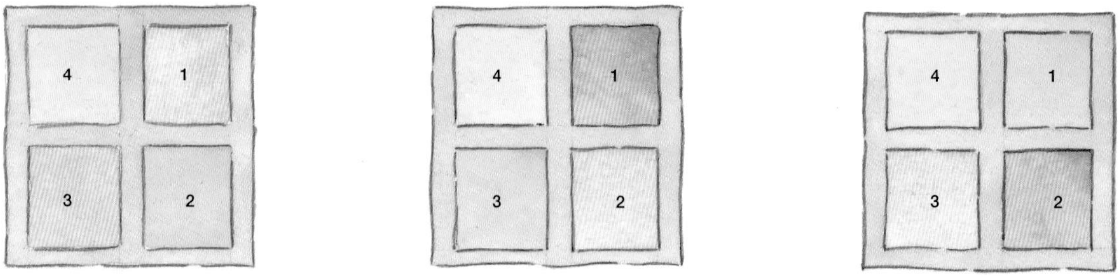

YEAR ONE

YEAR TWO

YEAR THREE

Plot 1
Peas
Broad (fava) beans
French (green) beans
Runner (green) beans
Bulb onions
Leeks
Sweetcorn (corn)
Marrows (large zucchini), squashes and pumpkins
Lettuce

Plot 2
Potatoes
Parsnips
Beetroot (beets)
Carrots
Salsify
Scorzonera
Tomatoes

Plot 3
Cabbages
Brussels sprouts
Calabrese (Italian sprouting broccoli)
Broccoli
Kale
Swede (rutabaga or yellow turnips)
Turnips
Kohl rabi
Radishes

Plot 4
Rhubarb
Asparagus
Perennial herbs
Globe artichokes
Jerusalem artichokes
Sea kale

FOUR-YEAR CROP ROTATION

Divide the vegetables you have decided to grow into the five groups (plots 1–5) shown in the table. Draw a plan to indicate which group of crops goes where, using a different colour for each group. (Remember plot 5 is for the permanent crops.) Next year, move the crops in each group on to the next plot.

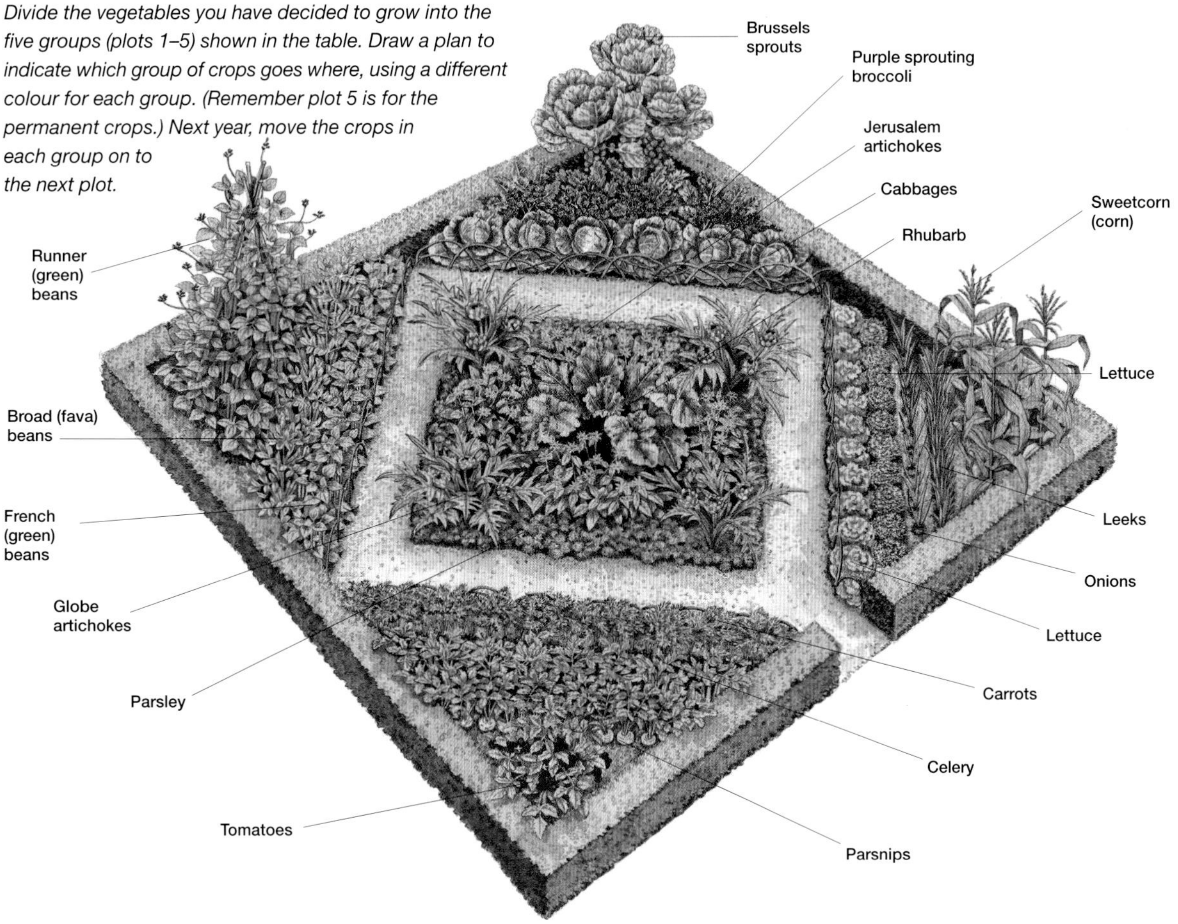

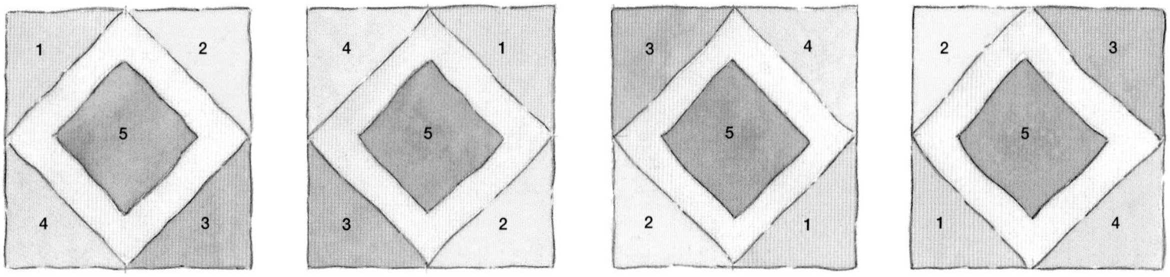

YEAR ONE YEAR TWO YEAR THREE YEAR FOUR

Plot 1
Peas
Broad (fava) beans
French (green) beans
Runner (green) beans

Plot 2
Cabbages
Brussels sprouts
Calabrese (Italian sprouting broccoli)
Broccoli
Kale
Radishes
Swedes (rutabagas or yellow turnips)
Turnips
Kohl rabi

Plot 3
Bulb onions
Spring onions (scallions)
Shallots
Leeks
Garlic
Sweetcorn (corn)
Marrows (large zucchini), squashes and pumpkins
Lettuce

Plot 4
Potatoes
Parsnips
Beetroot (beets)
Carrots
Salsify
Scorzonera
Celery
Celeriac
Tomatoes

Plot 5
Rhubarb
Asparagus
Perennial herbs
Globe artichokes
Jerusalem artichokes
Sea kale

COMPANION PLANTING

Above: *Nasturtiums (*Tropaeolum majus*) have edible leaves and flowers, as well as being a colourful companion plant.*

This is when two or more crops are grown together for the benefit of one or all. The technique creates a colourful landscape, made up of different species, which mirrors nature itself. Plants are grown together for several reasons: for example, they attract beneficial insects and give off odours that may deter or confuse pests. Companion planting is very different from planting large areas of land with only one crop – a monoculture that allows large numbers of pests and diseases to build up rapidly.

HOW COMPANION PLANTING WORKS

Plants have natural affinities with others of their kind. The smell of volatile oils from many plants discourages certain pests, making them excellent companion plants. A good example of this is the well-known relationship between the tomato plant and the French marigold (*Tagetes patula*). The scent of the French marigold is said to deter whitefly from entering the greenhouse and therefore prevents a whitefly attack on the tomato plant.

Plants such as yarrow (*Achillea*) and hyssop (*Hyssopus*) are just a couple of plants from a list of many that attract beneficial insects such as hoverflies. The hoverflies will lay their eggs around these plants and, after hatching, the larval stage of the insect will start to eat adult aphids. So greedy are these larvae that they can eat up to 800 aphids before pupating. Many allotment gardeners grow trays of single-flowered French marigolds to dot around their gardens, both in the vegetable and fruit areas, in order to encourage these eating machines. This is both very effective and quite stunning to look at.

BENEFITS OF COMPANION PLANTING

A mosaic of plants offers many benefits to the allotment, some of which are outlined below.

- Creates a colourful landscape.
- Plants can attract benefical insects.
- Plant odour can deter harmful insects.
- A variety of plants together confuses pests from locating host plants.
- Plants attract birds that prey on pests.
- Flowers attract pollinators.

Certain distinct qualities of a plant have a proven benefit to others, such as fixing nitrogen in the soil. Clover in grass will fix nitrogen, offering the excess nitrogen produced to the surrounding grass which improves the yield. By the same token, others are less suited as partners. It is never wise, for example, to plant two vegetables side by side that attract the same pests, as this effectively doubles the chances of attack. It is advisable to practise crop rotation or use companion planting in between them.

Right: *Companion plants such as the English marigold (*Calendula officinalis*) can provide welcome splashes of colour in the vegetable patch. In addition to this, the pollen of these flowers will attract beneficial hoverflies and parasitic wasps, both of which can help control large numbers of common pests.*

BENEFICIAL COMBINATIONS

There is little scientific evidence of these associations working, but if you talk to any experienced gardener, they will certainly provide plenty of anecdotal evidence. Tomatoes, for instance, like to be grown near basil and parsley plants. This is, of course, useful for cooks as well as gardeners. Separating rows of cabbages, broccoli or other brassicas with rows of onions has always been a popular combination, possibly due to the onion's strong scent confusing cabbage pests. Tomato plants also grow well next to cabbages and seem to deter caterpillars.

Other beneficial combinations include leeks near carrots as they repel carrot flies, while Swiss chard thrives near carrots and beetroot (beets). Never plant carrot and dill close by each other. This makes the carrots woodier and stronger-flavoured, and the dill milder and with weaker stems.

DECORATIVE COMPANION PLANTS

Certain flowers and flowering herbs offer potential benefits for a variety of vegetables. French marigolds (*Tagetes patula*) are cited as a wonder flower by many allotment gardeners and the bright flowers make a colourful companion crop. They deter many pests, and seem to spur growth in roses. They are also said to reduce the number of soil nematodes, while attracting hoverflies and their larvae, which eat aphids. French marigolds are frequently planted with English marigolds (*Calendula officinalis*).

CROPS AND THEIR COMPANION PLANTS

While it is not an exact science, any practitioner of companion planting will tell you that individual crops have their 'preferred companions'. Experience is the best guide, but the list below outlines some plant combinations that work well in most situations.

Apples Chives, foxgloves, wallflowers, nasturtiums, garlic, onions
Apricots Basil, tansy, wormwood
Asparagus Tomatoes, parsley, basil
Beans Carrots, cucumbers, cabbages, lettuce, peas, parsley, cauliflowers, spinach, summer savory
Beans (broad/fava) Potatoes, sweetcorn (corn)
Beans (dwarf) Beetroot (beets), potatoes
Beetroot (beets) Onions, kohl rabi, lettuce, cabbages, dwarf beans
Brussels sprouts Nasturtiums
Cabbages Beans, beetroot, celery, mint, thyme, sage, onions, rosemary, dill, potatoes, chamomile, oregano, hyssop, wormwood, nasturtiums, tansy, coriander (cilantro)
Carrots Peas, radishes, lettuce, chives, sage, onions, leeks
Cauliflowers Celery, beans, tansy, nasturtiums
Celery Tomatoes, dill, beans, leeks, cabbage, cauliflowers
Chives Parsley, apples, carrots, tomatoes
Courgette (zucchini) Nasturtiums
Cucumbers Potatoes (early crop only), beans, celery, lettuce, sweetcorn (corn), Savoy cabbages, sunflowers, nasturtiums
Kohl rabi Beetroot, onions
Garlic Roses, apples, peaches
Grapevines Geraniums, mulberries, hyssop, basil, tansy
Leeks Carrots, celery
Lettuce Carrots, onions, strawberries, beetroot, cabbages, radishes, tagetes
Onions Carrots, beetroot, lettuce, chamomile, kohl rabi, courgettes
Parsnips Peas, potatoes, peppers, beans, radishes, garlic
Peaches Tansy, garlic, basil, wormwood
Peas Potatoes, radishes, carrots, turnips
Potatoes Peas, beans, cabbages, sweetcorn, broad beans, green beans, nasturtium, marigolds, foxgloves, horseradish, aubergines (eggplants)
Pumpkin Sweetcorn
Radishes Lettuces, peas, chervil, nasturtiums
Raspberries Tansy
Spinach Strawberries
Squash Sunflowers
Strawberries Borage, lettuce, spinach, sage, pyrethrum
Sunflowers Squash, cucumbers
Sweetcorn (corn) Broad beans, potatoes, melons, tomatoes, cucumbers, squash, tansy
Tomatoes Asparagus, celery, parsley, basil, carrots, chives, marigolds, foxgloves, garlic, sweetcorn
Turnips Peas, nasturtiums

Left: *Foxgloves (*Digitalis purpureum*) make excellent companion plants for growing under apple trees.*

White alyssum (*Lobularia maritima*), by reseeding frequently, helps to break up the soil and adds to its organic content, while chrysanthemums reduce nematodes, making for healthier soil. Mint almost always works with various types of squashes and brassicas to aid plant growth, although it can become invasive. Tansy (*Tanacetum vulgare*) is said to repel ants, aphids and plant beetles although this, too, can become invasive if not regularly checked.

Chamomile (*Chamaemelum nobile*) is known as the 'plant doctor' by some gardeners because of its alleged ability to encourage other plants to increase their production of essential oil, making plants such as rosemary and lavender taste and smell stronger. Chamomile is easy to grow and looks beautiful anywhere on the allotment, although it should be kept well trimmed to avoid a straggly look. It is also thought that chamomile can help to activate the composting process if it is added to the compost heap.

Lavender (*Lavandula*) is a general insect repellent and makes an excellent small hedge. It is a great addition to the allotment, attracting bees and numerous white and blue butterflies.

Plants that produce berries, such as cotoneaster and the rowan tree (*Sorbus*), will attract birds into the site. Birds, in turn, eat many pests, such as protein-rich aphids, caterpillars and various flies. Thrushes are the unsung heroes of the allotment because they decrease the snail population quite considerably.

Be prepared to experiment before committing to a companion species. Nasturtiums have been cited as an effective aphid control, although many wonder if they do this by attracting all the aphids to themselves. What works in one area may not always work elsewhere and experimentation is the key to success in this interesting yet uncertain area of gardening.

CROPS AND THEIR ANTAGONISTS

Some plants are highly antagonistic to one another. You should always avoid planting the following combinations.

Asparagus Onions and potatoes
Beans Chives, fennel or garlic
Carrots Dill
Cauliflower Tomatoes
Peas Onions, garlic and shallots
Potato Asparagus, pumpkin and summer squash

Above: *Catch cropping in close blocks makes the most of available space and allows more crops to be raised in a season.*

HOW TO GROW VEGETABLES

There are three basic growing techniques that you can use to make the most of your space. These are known as intercropping, catch cropping and successional sowing. By adopting the latter two practices, you will extend the cropping season instead of harvesting all at once. You will also make good use of the available space, therefore increasing yields. All that is needed is careful planning to work out which crops to sow and when.

INTERCROPPING

This vegetable-growing technique increases productivity and also helps to keep the numbers of weeds down. It refers to the practice of planting a fast-growing crop, such as carrots, radishes and lettuce, between main crops that are slower growing. These include vegetables such as cabbages, peas and potatoes.

Intercropping involves harvesting the quicker-growing crop first before the slower-growing one achieves total foliage cover of the soil or shades out the area. A good example of intercropping is to grow a crop of spring onions (scallions) or lettuce between tomatoes. Similarly, spinach or radishes can easily be planted out early between sweetcorn (corn) or, alternatively, radishes can be planted between cabbages.

Intercropping can also be used to increase productivity. It ensures that no space is left unused and makes the most efficient use of light, nutrients and moisture. It will also reduce the amount of weeds in the vegetable patch by maintaining a continuous plant canopy over the soil.

One slight variation on the theme is to combine the benefits of a green manure with a crop. This can be useful in the case of winter crops because the green manure doubles up as a cover crop, protecting the soil from erosion and leaching as well as stabilizing soil temperatures. If a leguminous green manure is planted in late summer or early autumn in a bed along with leafy crops such as Brussels sprouts, it can provide nitrogen throughout the remaining growing season. It will also provide a boost for early crops that will be planted out after the green manure crop has been dug into the soil. While intercropping requires careful planning, it can increase the productivity of even a relatively small vegetable plot.

CATCH CROPPING

This technique is when fast-maturing vegetables, such as radishes and lettuce, are grown in an area of ground that has just been cropped and has a vacancy until the next crop is either sown or planted. The sowing of the catch crops can be done in between the main ones or after harvesting at the end of the season if there is time. It is important to know how long a crop takes to mature when planning catch cropping so that you do not sow anything that takes too long to mature in between the main crops.

Left: *Successional sowing of crops in rows allows the same space in the vegetable plot on the allotment to be kept productive throughout the growing season.*

ADVANTAGES OF INTERCROPPING AND CATCH CROPPING

Making the most of the limited space in your allotment is not only productive, but it also has positive environmental advantages, such as the following.

- Suppresses weed growth in the allotment site.
- Increases the productivity of the vegetable patch.
- Planting green manures enriches the soil with nitrogen.
- Helps to protect against the erosion of the soil.
- Helps prevent leaching.

FAST-GROWING CROPS FOR INTERCROPPING AND CATCH CROPPING

Use all the available space in your allotment by sowing vigorous-growing crops in between rows of the main crops. The list below shows the time it will take for some fast-growing crops to mature.

Carrots	9 to 20 weeks
Endives	7 to 13 weeks
Lettuce	4 to 14 weeks
Radishes	4 to 8 weeks
Rocket (arugula)	3 to 5 weeks
Salad leaves	4 to 14 weeks
Spinach	5 to 10 weeks
Spring onions (scallions)	8 to 10 weeks

SUCCESSIONAL SOWING

This is the practice of sowing the seeds of fast-maturing vegetables at regular intervals several times during the growing season. This practice will ensure that you have a continuous supply of crops such as lettuces, carrots and spinach throughout the season. Successional sowing is also useful where crops are sown directly outdoors early in the season where they may be prone to frost damage. Early crops such as lettuce and radish can be sown under the cover of, for example, a cloche where they will begin to develop earlier than would otherwise be possible. Subsequent sowings outdoors will mature later, thus extending the growing season for harvesting.

Above: *The close spacing of rows and successional sowing of new rows allows the maximum use of space on your plot.*

Gardeners with half plots can use this method by sowing only half a row at a time. This process is repeated a week or so later, with further sowings as often as you like. This way you will have fresh vegetables for several weeks and will avoid a glut.

Above: *Sweetcorn (corn) is a late-maturing crop that can be intercropped with fast-growing, early salad crops. This enables you to make the most of your growing space.*

CROPS SUITABLE FOR SUCCESSIONAL SOWING

Successional sowing can ensure a continuous supply of fresh vegetables, avoiding harvest gluts.

Beetroot (beets)	Spring to summer
Broccoli	Spring to summer
Cabbages	Spring to summer
Carrots	Spring to summer
Endives	Spring to summer
Kohl rabi	Winter to summer
Lettuce	Winter to summer
Parsnips	Winter to spring
Peas	All year round
Potatoes	Spring
Radishes	Winter to summer
Rocket (arugula)	Spring to autumn
Salad leaves	Spring to autumn
Spinach	Spring to summer
Spring onions (scallions)	Spring to autumn
Swedes (rutabagas)	Spring to summer
Swiss chard	Spring to summer
Turnips	Winter to spring

Above: *Herbs are a colourful and useful addition to an allotment and grow quite happily amongst your other crops.*

HOW TO GROW HERBS

Herbs are valued for their culinary, medicinal, decorative and aromatic properties. They come in a diverse range of sizes, shapes and habits, ranging from ground-creeping thyme through to the tall architectural stems of angelica. The choice of herbs is so great that there is always something to offer an allotment-grower who is also interested in cooking aromatic or unusual dishes. Herbs offer a treat for the senses and these fragrant plants are also easy to grow in an allotment.

WHERE TO GROW HERBS

Herbs can be grown in a range of settings, such as custom-designed herb gardens or amongst vegetables, where they can also be used as companion plants. They can also be grown in pots and containers if you want to conserve space, or even in hanging baskets suspended from a shed.

Herbs range from tall showy herbaceous plants such as fennel (*Foeniculum vulgare*) and tansy (*Tanacetum vulgare*) to ground-hugging cushion plants such as thyme (*Thymus vulgaris*). The majority of herbs originate from dry sunny environments and so need sunshine to help them develop their essential oils. It is best to site herbs in an open, sunny spot on the allotment, where they should thrive.

SOIL PREPARATION

Drier sites suit most herbs, and the sunnier and hotter the site the better they will taste. The taste and smell of herbs is usually due to the production of essential oils within the plants. If they are grown in hot conditions, then the concentrations of essential oils will be greater. Growing herbs in very moist rich soils can accelerate their growth, but will result in a milder flavour. They will also look better and flower less than their 'hot-site' counterparts and be easier to harvest.

Herbs are, however, best grown in a soil that is loamy with some added organic matter. The ideal pH is 6.5 to 7.0, which means that herbs can easily be planted among vegetables.

SOWING HERB SEED

Herbs may be sown directly in the soil outdoors, just like vegetables. The preparation of the seedbed and the sowing techniques are exactly the same, and they can easily be interplanted or block planted among other vegetables. Alternatively, herb seeds may be planted under cover, raising them in the same way as early vegetables and then hardening them off before planting out in the allotment. This method is especially useful for more tender, leafy herbs such as basil or coriander (cilantro).

Basil (*Ocimum basilicum*) associates extremely well with outdoor tomatoes. These can be planted out together from an indoor sowing and the crop will be mutually complementary. Indoor sowing can also provide you with herbs that can be cropped earlier in the season than outdoor ones, extending the useful life of your herb patch.

PLANTING HERBS

Herbs can be positioned anywhere in the site as long as it is sunny. They have a range of forms and colours and often make valuable additions to the allotment. Foxgloves (*Digitalis purpureum*), sage (*Salvia officinalis*) and the curry plant (*Helichrysum italicum*) are a few examples of herbs that can be used in annual and herbaceous borders as well as in allotments. Some herbs, such as mint (*Mentha*) and lemon balm (*Melissa officinalis*), can become very invasive if they are not contained in a pot or sunken sink when growing among other plants. Remove the flower-heads from the mint before they have had a chance to seed, as the seed will germinate all over your patch.

Left: *Herbs that you use a lot of can be grown in rows between other crops in order to make the best use of the space available.*

PLANTING THYME

1 *Thyme plants quickly form a low mound, making them an excellent edge for beds and borders. Start by setting out a row in the position you intend planting them.*

2 *Once set out, remove their pots and dig a hole that is at least one and a half times as wide as the roots. Place them in this, refill the hole and firm the soil around them.*

3 *Once you have finished planting, water the plants in using a watering can with a fine rose attachment. Continue watering regularly in the first year.*

PLANTING HERBS IN CONTAINERS

Herbs make excellent subjects for use in pots and containers and these can be placed around sheds and seating areas on allotments, rather than taking up space in beds. Plants in containers dry out quickly, so water them frequently, especially during hot weather. Always plant them in a free-draining potting compost (soil mix) that will not become waterlogged.

There are numerous cultivars of culinary herbs that can be grown on an allotment, and groups of pot-grown herbs can be extremely decorative as well as supplying you with a range of fresh flavourings. Thyme, rosemary, lavender and sage are all good choices to grow in pots and have many uses in the kitchen.

Herb pots require little maintenance, save for watering and the occasional feed during the growing season. Most are rarely long term and are best restarted yearly or every other year. Herbs that are permanently in pots, such as bay trees, will need repotting every year. Spreading subjects such as thyme can be lifted and both top-pruned and root-pruned prior to repotting.

Mint and other spreading herbaceous subjects may need dividing and repotting from time to time. This is done by splitting the crown of the plant into smaller pieces and then repotting one of these back into the container with some fresh potting mix. Dividing in this way is best performed annually for very vigorous herbs.

Harvesting on a regular basis is often enough to control the growth of many potted herb arrangements (where a number are planted in one container), but a light trim may also be necessary from time to time.

Potted herbs may also be grown in the greenhouse to ensure a supply both earlier and later in the season. A series of successional sowings will ensure that you have fresh herbs for most of the year.

Below: *Herbs can be grown very successfully in pots and containers, and make an attractive addition to a seating area.*

Above: *A sunny place provides an ideal location for growing fruit trees, such as this pear, that need warmth and good sunlight.*

HOW TO GROW FRUIT TREES AND BUSHES

Freshly picked fruit from the allotment tastes absolutely delicious. The warm taste of a juicy sweet raspberry or the crisp flavour of a tree-ripened apple would tempt many a gardener into growing their own fruit produce. The tastes can also be quite different from shop-grown produce where storage, handling, packing, transportation and off-the-tree ripening all take their toll on the quality and taste of the fruit.

WHERE CAN FRUIT BE GROWN?

Fruit trees and bushes can be grown wherever there is space on the allotment. Strawberries can be used in hanging baskets or tubs, dwarf apple trees can be planted in containers and a number of fruits, such as cherries, white and red currants and figs, can all be grown against walls. Fruits not only provide produce for the kitchen table but many of them have ornamental qualities and can blend well with other plants in the allotment.

CHOOSING A SITE

The best site for fruit, both indoors and out, is a sunny one. Sunlight is essential, not just for the ripening of the fruit itself but also for flower bud formation and flowering. In addition, fruit trees and bushes often appreciate a sheltered spot where even exotic fruit can be raised. Within the allotment a sheltered sunny wall can provide the ideal place to grow peaches, apricots or figs. If cold winters are a problem, then provide winter protection in the form of a portable frame or, alternatively, grow the plants in a greenhouse. It is worth noting that providing your plants with the ideal conditions for healthy growth will reap its rewards in the end. Not only will you harvest heavier yields, but, more importantly, your plants will be less prone to pest and disease attacks, which is an obvious advantage when growing organically.

Left: *Most fruit bushes will benefit from a generous application of well-rotted manure or compost in the early part of the year.*

SELECTING THE RIGHT PLANTS

Variety selection should not be based purely on hardiness but on personal preference. You may also wish to consider how easy the fruit tree or bush is to grow, fruit size, taste and the time of harvest. Selecting more than one variety can result in having fresh fruit over a longer period as a result of a succession of ripening.

Some fruit trees combine the best qualities of two plants. Grafting utilizes the qualities of the variety as top growth (scion) and other desirable qualities from a rootstock that may be absent from the variety. The scion is the fruiting variety that is budded or grafted on to the rootstock, which is selected for certain characteristics such as dwarfing, nematode insect resistance, soil type, cold hardiness and disease resistance.

The most commonly grown rootstocks for amateur gardeners are the apple semi-dwarfs and dwarfs. Grapes are also grafted on to clonal rootstocks, although they are often supplied on their own roots. Figs, olives and various types of berry are also usually supplied as plants on their own roots.

Dwarf apple trees are very useful in small sites and are eminently suited to container-growing. They produce fruit of the same size, colour and quality as larger standard trees and require the same pruning, nutritional and care regimes as a standard-size tree.

Dwarf trees fruit much sooner after planting and bear less fruit per tree. When harvesting the fruit, you can reach all parts of the tree from the ground without using a ladder and the trees are easier to train and prune on an annual basis. Grafting the desired variety on to special clonal rootstocks 'dwarfs' apples. The most popular dwarfing rootstocks for apple were developed in England and are designated as either EM or M (for East Malling) or MM (for Malling Merton). Dwarfed trees must be pruned annually or size control may be lost. In addition, loss of fruit by frost or pests will also increase growth so necessitating summer pruning.

PLANTING FRUIT TREES AND BUSHES

As with any other type of tree, good ground preparation and careful handling are essential steps to successfully establishing your fruit trees and bushes. The cheapest option when buying fruit trees is to purchase bare-rooted plants. The disadvantage is that they are only available during the dormant season. The most important factor in handling bare-rooted plants is not to let the roots dry out. When you buy trees always check the condition of the roots and packing material. Heel in plants by covering the roots with moist soil in a cool environment outdoors if they are not to be planted immediately.

Dig a hole slightly wider and deeper than the spread and length of the root system, making sure the sides of the hole are not 'glazed' over as this will result in a root girdling. After trimming diseased, dead, broken or extra long roots, place the tree in the hole and spread out the roots. For larger trees, place the stake in the hole and drive it in (remembering to first remove the tree and cover the roots). Place the tree back into

PLANTING A FRUIT TREE

1 *Dig a hole in the ground that is at least half as large again as the roots of the fruit tree. Loosen the sides and the base of the planting hole with a garden fork.*

2 *Remove the pot and check the roots for girdling roots. Tease these out by hand or with a garden fork. Cut out any damaged roots with secateurs (pruners).*

3 *Use a straightedge to make sure that the plant is at the right depth in the hole. Fill around the roots with soil, firm it down and water well.*

4 *Hammer in a stake at an angle of about 60° in order to avoid the roots and place a tie on the tree. Saw off the end of the stake. Nail the tie to the stake to secure it.*

5 *The tree should remain staked for approximately one year. As the diameter of the tree stem increases, loosen the tree tie as required.*

the hole and return the soil, firming in layers of about 30cm (12in) as you go. This avoids large air spaces being left around the roots and ensures that it is set firmly. Trees should be planted at the same depth as they were grown in the nursery. Make sure the bud union (for trees on rootstocks) is about 5–7cm (2–2¾in) above the soil line. Do not place fertilizer in the planting hole as this can be added later. Mulch the newly planted tree with well-rotted manure or compost to suppress weeds.

Container-grown nursery stock can be transplanted at any time of the year. Site preparation is the same as for bare-rooted stock. Make sure that you check the roots as they can become distorted or root bound if they are grown in containers for a long time. Teasing roots out can help avoid root girdling, but the best way to do this is to use field-grown (bare-rooted) stock.

PRUNING NEWLY PLANTED STOCK

Fruit trees must be pruned when they are planted for a number of reasons. If planting bare-rooted stock, the top of the tree must be pruned to counter-balance the loss of the root system which would have been severed in the nursery during lifting. Pruning also forces the growth of laterals from which the future framework of the fruit tree will be selected. Branches that are desirably located can be retained as part of the framework whereas undesirable branches are removed.

FRUIT TREE POLLINATION

Pollination is the transfer of pollen from the male part of the flower to the female part of the flower (the stigma) to allow fruit to set and seeds to develop. Seeds cause the fruit to develop properly.
If both the pollen and stigma are from the same flower or from another flower from the same variety, the process is called self-pollination. Fruit trees that set fruit as the result of self-pollination are called self-fruitful, whereas those relying on pollen from a different variety are called self-unfruitful. The latter needs two varieties near to each other for fruit set to occur. This is called cross-pollination.

Apples Apples generally need two varieties for good fruit set. This can be another apple variety or a crab apple that blooms with the edible crop.
Apricots Self-fruitful
Berries (all types) Self-fruitful
Cherries Sweet cherry is self-unfruitful and needs two varieties for good crop set. Sour cherry varieties are self-fruitful.
European plums Self-fruitful
Figs Self-fruitful
Japanese plums Self-unfruitful as a rule, with the exception of Santa Rosa which will set fruit fairly well without cross-pollination.
Nectarines Self-fruitful
Peaches Self-fruitful with the exception of 'J.H. Hale', which has to be pollinated by another variety.
Pears These always need two varieties to ensure good fruit set.

HOW TO GROW FLOWERS

Cut flowers are a wonderful way to brighten up your home but can be costly if you buy them. For this reason, a cut-flower patch on your allotment is the perfect way to ensure that you have a regular supply of flowers that have not been transported across the world. Even a small patch should be able to accommodate a few plants and most are easy to grow. Where space is limited, they can be slotted in among rows of vegetables or raised as catch crops following an earlier harvest.

Above: *Sunflowers are easy to grow, and their large, showy blooms make excellent cut flowers, or can be left for wildlife.*

WHERE TO GROW FLOWERS

Generally, the majority of cut flowers prefer a sunny spot on well-drained, fertile soil. Ideally this should be sheltered from strong winds that could blow them over or damage the blooms themselves. Annuals, biennials and some bulbs that are short term are well suited for growing in rows and can be rotated yearly as part of your ongoing rotation regime or grown as catch crops and inter-planting. However, shrubs, perennials and some of the bulbs will need a permanent bed, where they can remain for a longer period.

Above: *Flowers make a very colourful addition to the allotment: they can be grown in rows or dotted between other plants.*

SOWING

Annual flowers can either be sown directly into the soil in the case of most hardy types, or in seed trays in spring for more tender (half-hardy) types. Biennials, on the other hand, need sowing between late spring and mid-summer, and will flower the next year. Most shrubby species tend to be slow from seed and it is best to plant pot grown specimens or take cuttings under glass to speed up the process.

PLANTING

As a rule of thumb, bulbs and corms are usually planted in a hole that is two to three times deeper than their width, although this can vary according to the species concerned, so check the packet. Pot-grown plants are planted directly into the ground, ensuring there are no air gaps around the root-ball (roots) and that the compost (soil mix) surface is around 2cm (1in) below the soil level. On light, well-drained land, shrubs and perennial plants are best planted in early winter to allow them to establish quickly in spring before drier conditions arrive.

AFTERCARE

Most annuals and biennials simply need to be kept well watered, especially during periods of drought. Early in the year, they can be fed plenty of nitrogen to encourage strong, vigorous growth, but as soon as

PLANTS FOR CUT FLOWERS

HARDY ANNUALS
Helianthus annuus (Sunflower)
Lathyrus odoratus (Sweet pea)
Nigella damascena (Love in a mist)

BIENNIALS
Erysimum cherii (Wallflower)
Dianthus barbatus (Sweet William)
Papaver nudicaule (Iceland poppy)

HARDY BULBS AND CORMS
Narcissus spp. (Daffodils)
Tulipa spp. (Tulips)
Allium spp. (Ornamental onions)

WINTER AND SPRING SHRUBS
Viburnum x *bodnantense*
Forsythia spp.
Lonicera fragrantissima (Winter honeysuckle)

HALF HARDY ANNUALS
Nicotiana (Tobacco plant)
Zinnia spp.
Cosmos spp.

HERBACEOUS PERENNIALS
Chrysanthemum spp.
Phlox paniculata (Perennial phlox)
Echinacea purpurea (Cone flower)

TENDER BULBS, CORMS AND TUBERS
Gladiolus spp. (Gladioli)
Freesia spp.
Dahlia spp.

SUMMER SHRUBS
Rosa spp. (Rose)
Spirea thunbergii (Baby's breath)
Philadelphus coronarius (Mock orange)

Above: *Gladioli make superb cut flowers, and their upright habit means they are ideal for planting between other plants.*

Above: *If you want to grow flowers for showing, they often need protection, like these dahlias growing under shade nets.*

Above: *Chrysanthemums are herbaceous perennials that inject a welcome splash of colour into any allotment plot.*

Above: *Sweet peas can be raised from seed and yield a profusion of large, bright, fragrant blooms over a long period.*

flower buds appear switch to a high-potassium fertilizer, such as a liquid tomato food, to promote flowering. After flowering, remove annuals and biennials, and cut back any remaining stems on herbaceous perennials. Tender perennials will need to be lifted or covered with a thick layer of mulch in the autumn to protect them from winter cold.

CUTTING FLOWERS

Regularly picking the flowers you grow on the allotment not only ensures a constant supply but also encourages more blooms and prevents them from setting seed. The amount you can harvest will vary, however, and, in the case of shrubs, you would be wise to pick more lightly to avoid stressing the plant. Remember that picking is, after all, a form of pruning, and heavy pruning may cause woody plants to produce a flush of leafy growth with few flowers the following season.

Before you start, make sure your secateurs (hand pruners) or scissors are sharp and clean. Ideally, the best time to cut flowers is during cool weather, with early morning proving ideal as the flowers and stems are arguably at their freshest and filled with water. If this is not possible, then evenings can be almost as good. Once cut, flowers can easily become stressed through lack of water, so the best way to preserve them until you get them home is to place their stems into a bucket of water as soon as they are cut. Make cuts in the stems at a 45° angle, as this will ensure the stem has a bigger cut surface area for water absorption.

When choosing which stems you are going to cut, make sure that flowers such as gladioli, which have more than one bud per stem, have at least one or two buds starting to open. Plants with just one flower per stem, such as sunflowers, should be cut when the flower has almost fully opened. Once the flowers have been cut they will last longer if they are conditioned. This involves putting the stem bases in a clean bucket of cool water, cutting the immersed bases once again, and placing this in a cool, dark place for 12 to 24 hours.

Above: *Warm season crops such as tomatoes can be sown and will crop earlier in a greenhouse than those grown outdoors.*

HOW TO GROW IN A GREENHOUSE

By providing an environment where plants are protected from the elements, in controlled levels of light, shade, temperature and moisture, allotment-growers can either extend the growing season of their favourite crops or even grow plants that otherwise simply would not survive. This warm, protective atmosphere enables you to propagate plants more easily and shelter tender plants from frosts.

WHY GROW IN A GREENHOUSE?

A greenhouse, if used to its full potential, is one of the most valuable additions there is on an allotment, offering the opportunity to grow a much wider range of plants; often making these available much earlier or later in the year. Although cloches and cold frames offer similar benefits at a fraction of the cost, neither gives the same amount of dedicated growing space, and it is this space that ultimately proves important, not least when it gives you the chance to work in warm shelter during the cold gloom of winter. Indeed, the prospect of working in the greenhouse can be a positive enticement on to the plot during the winter months. The fact that you can get inside is also useful as crops are protected the whole time you are working on them, unlike cloches or frames, which remain open all the time you work in them.

WHAT GREENHOUSE IS BEST?

Despite the array of designs available, the simplest constructions are usually more than adequate for an allotment. It is more important that you choose one that is the right size for your plot and your own needs. There is little point in erecting a huge greenhouse if it is only ever half full of crops. Having said that, choosing one that is too cramped might limit its usefulness. For most allotments, a greenhouse that is 2.5 x 5m (8 x 16ft) will provide enough space, and if you really need more space you can always get another greenhouse later.

HOW DOES A GREENHOUSE HELP PLANTS GROW?

Almost all plants like to grow in reasonably warm conditions with most growing best between about 16–24°C (60–76°F). While winter light levels may still be sufficient to help power growth, the low temperatures at that time of the year can severely limit this.

The greenhouse simply raises the temperature by trapping daylight, which heats the air and elevates the temperature to one within several degrees above that on the outside. Of course, these temperatures fall during darkness, but this can be offset by heating the interior. Temperature fluctuations are not all bad news though, and a fall of about 4–6°C (39–43°F) at night is actually preferable for most crops.

TEMPERATURE

Controlling temperature is one of the key aspects of successful greenhouse-growing and you will only be able to do this if you know how it varies throughout the day. Although you can't be in the greenhouse all the time you can take an average temperature reading inside using a special maximum and minimum thermometer. This shows two readings; one is the highest temperature achieved in the last 24 hours, the other represents the lowest. Comparing this to a maximum and minimum thermometer outside the greenhouse can help you see how the interior differs from the prevailing climate and assess if the temperature is fluctuating to extremes.

You should note, however, that more than just the outside temperature influences temperature in a glasshouse, as light levels and ventilation also play a part. Limiting the amount of light during the day by shading will cool the house, as will opening the vents and letting the hot air escape. Heating or insulating the house, on the other hand, and keeping vents shut will maintain temperatures if they fall outside.

Right: *A well-lit, warm greenhouse bench is an ideal place to raise seeds, safe from the ravages of often unpredictable climatic conditions.*

Far right: *A thermometer is vital for enabling you to accurately assess the greenhouse temperature and act accordingly.*

Above: *Even a relatively modest-sized greenhouse can enable you to grow an extended range of crops through the season.*

If night-time temperatures begin to dip, a simple hotbox or burner type heater is usually enough to keep out any night-time chill. These also work by heating the air directly and are used where there is no need to provide heat on a regular basis. During the winter, it is both cheaper and more efficient to insulate a greenhouse by providing additional layers within the structure to trap air. Bubble wrap is a popular method as it is easy to position and allows the transmission of light. In addition to this, careful siting of the greenhouse can help to reduce the chilling or potentially damaging effects of high winds.

LIGHT

Balanced growth requires good glasshouse design and proper planning for the light requirements of the crop. As a general rule, ridged greenhouses should always be orientated with the ridge running east to west to make the best of the available light.

Although natural winter light intensity is often insufficient for certain crops, summer light levels, especially when combined with elevated temperatures, can cause problems. Shading controls temperature and light, and is usually put in place in order to reduce summer temperatures (if excessive) or to protect young plants from intense sunlight.

Right: *Fill watering cans in advance and allow them to warm up, so as to ensure that your plants are not showered in cold water.*

HUMIDITY

Most plants naturally require a humid environment in order to grow healthily and plants grouped together often establish their own small microclimate where the humidity is higher in the immediate vicinity of the plants than elsewhere. Warm air naturally holds much more moisture than cooler air so it is important to increase humidity during the hotter months when it is harder to keep the temperature in protected structures down. Increasing the humidity helps to slow water loss from leaves and may help to prevent wilting or scorch.

Humidity is easily raised by damping down (spraying a hose on hard surfaces, paths or under benches) on hot, dry days. If there are only certain plants, such as young seedlings, that require elevated humidity, then these are best covered with a thin layer of clear plastic.

AIR CIRCULATION

All plants need a constant supply of clean, fresh air around them in order to grow healthily. Outdoors, normal wind movements would supply this, but in a greenhouse you'll need to make provision for it. Ventilators help control excess temperature and air flow. Roof vents should normally occupy the equivalent of 15 per cent of the floor space in order to be fully effective. Side ventilators are also occasionally seen in some greenhouses. If you are away during daylight hours in summer, the time when windows need to be opened on hot days, automatic openers can be used. In winter, windows should be left open as much as possible.

METHODS OF GROWING

Think carefully about how you plan to use your greenhouse and what plants you would like to grow there. Remember also that the true art of greenhouse gardening lies in using every available bit of space. This will involve planning the layout of the growing areas in the greenhouse and making a cropping plan to ensure that you not only use all of the available space, but every 'time space' within the growing calendar.

In open ground Many greenhouse plants will grow well in open soil borders. The soil can be prepared in a similar way to borders outside. Taller crops such as tomatoes are particularly well suited to growing in open borders in the greenhouse, but remember to rotate crops sited in soil to prevent pest or disease build-up.

Above: *Greenhouses are especially prone to disease spread, and any dead or diseased plant material needs to be removed promptly.*

In pots on staging Staging is essentially a shelf or shelves on which plants in pots are arranged, which enables you to work at a comfortable height. It is particularly useful for raising seedlings and propagating plants. The area beneath the staging, which is somewhat shaded, can be used for overwintering dormant plants, as a useful out-of-the-way storage area or to house a water tank.

In grow-bags Grow-bags offer an alternative to open beds where space is limited or no open beds exist. These can be purchased or you can easily make your own by filling large plastic compost bags (about an 80 litre [17.5 gallon] size is ideal) with a mixture of garden compost and a little grit. Each bag will support four tomato plants and an even greater number of smaller plants. They can also be used to raise garden peas or beans.

Climbers and trained plants The growing space available in a greenhouse is not restricted to the floor or staging-height, as the walls and roof can also be used. Ridged houses can be used to raise climbing crops, such as cucumbers or melons, and other climbers such as peas or beans can also be raised under glass during the cooler months.

GREENHOUSE HYGIENE

Practising good hygiene is extremely important for maintaining the health of plants in a greenhouse. Dead leaves and debris left lying about can harbour pests and diseases, as can badly affected plants if they are not removed promptly.

Once a year, clean all surfaces, including glass and glazing bars, thoroughly with a sponge and hot soapy water. This will pay dividends during the growing season by reducing the number of annually recurring pests and diseases.

Above: *Staging enables you to use your greenhouse space efficiently, and allows you to work at a comfortable height.*

WHITENING-OUT GLASS

1 *Make up water soluble greenhouse shading by measuring the correct amount of water into a container.*

2 *Empty the measured contents of the sachet into the water and mix well with a stick to combine thoroughly.*

3 *Paint it on, paying particular attention to surfaces facing the sun. It is waterproof but can be removed when dry with a duster.*

THE GREENHOUSE YEAR

The information shown here is a sample of how a greenhouse can be used to be productive all year round. The essential point is that you should plan what you want to grow, when you want to grow it and of course how much you want to grow. Once you have decided on these factors, it should be a relatively simple matter to make your greenhouse a productive and enjoyable space on your allotment.

MID-WINTER

Sow carrots, onions and lettuces in open borders and interplant with radishes.

Sow early cabbages and cauliflowers in pots

Bring strawberries in from frames.

Wash glass panes and keep conditions on the dry side.

Watch for winter pests and fungal diseases, and regularly remove dead or dying material.

Provide heat as necessary and ventilate during the day.

LATE WINTER

Make further sowings of winter salad crops.

Sow broad (fava) beans.

Pot on early vegetable seedlings.

Keep an eye on ventilation.

Watch for pests and diseases.

Keep conditions on the dry side unless warm.

Pick over plants to remove dead or dying material regularly.

Provide heat as necessary and ventilate during the day when mild conditions allow.

EARLY SPRING

Sow Brussels sprouts seeds in cool houses or frames.

Sow indoor tomato seed.

Prick out seedlings as they develop first sets of true leaves.

Damp down on hot days and ventilate.

Continue to watch for pests and diseases.

Begin to feed plants as growth increases.

Dig, manure and topdress borders ready for planting if not already productive.

MID-SPRING

Sow outdoor tomatoes, celery and celeriac and pot on indoor tomatoes. Sow melons and cucumbers in individual pots.

Harden off early vegetable plants under cloches.

Remove side shoots of early tomatoes; begin feeding as first flower trusses appear.

Damp down at least twice daily when hot and ventilate.

Continue to watch for pests and diseases.

Dig borders and manure if not already done.

LATE SPRING

Plant indoor tomatoes into prepared borders or large pots of loam-based compost (soil mix).

Continue potting on developing cuttings and seedlings.

Pay particular attention to watering as days lengthen.

Provide shade over sensitive crops with shade or glass paint and ventilate well.

Feed plants regularly.

Watch for pests and diseases and control where appropriate.

EARLY SUMMER

Pick tomatoes regularly as they ripen.

Pinch out and tie in melons and cucumbers as they reach their intended size.

Continue potting on cuttings and seedlings of all plants.

Water regularly, twice daily in hot weather and damp down two or three times daily.

Feed plants regularly.

Watch for pests and diseases and control where appropriate.

MID-SUMMER

Continue potting on cuttings and seedlings of all plants.

Hand pollinate melons and cucumbers.

Mist tomatoes overhead and open vents to help flower set.

Feed tomatoes to encourage development of more trusses.

Water and feed plants regularly; damp down two or three times daily.

Watch for pests and diseases and control where appropriate.

LATE SUMMER

Sow seeds of greenhouse winter leaf crops. Continue potting on cuttings and seedlings of all plants.

Remove lower leaves of tomatoes as fruit ripens. Support ripening melons and remove leaves shading fruit.

Harvest cucumbers as they reach the required size.

Water and feed plants regularly; damp down two or three times daily.

Watch for pests and diseases and control where appropriate.

EARLY AUTUMN

Cut melons as they ripen. Clear tomatoes as they finish.

Prepare borders for winter leaf crops.

Gradually decrease watering and damping down, remove shading and provide gentle heat on cold nights.

Continue potting on cuttings and seedlings of all plants.

Gradually cease feeding plants as growth slows and watch for pests and diseases and control where appropriate.

MID-AUTUMN

Plant winter leaf crops, or sow a green manure.

Gradually decrease watering as days shorten and reduce damping down to avoid the risk of fungal infestation.

Pot on any remaining cuttings and seedlings.

Watch for pests and diseases and control where appropriate

Pick over plants to remove dead or dying material regularly. Provide gentle heat on cold nights.

LATE AUTUMN

Keep winter leaf and salad crops clear of weeds.

Lift crowns of rhubarb for forcing.

Keep conditions on the dry side.

Watch for winter pests and diseases as low light levels stress plants. Pick over plants to remove dead or dying material regularly.

Provide heat as necessary and ventilate on mild days. Beware of gales when ventilating.

EARLY SPRING

Keep winter leaf and salad crops clear of weeds.

Sow seed of early onion varieties.

Lift rhubarb and herbs for early forcing and picking.

Keep conditions on the dry side. Watch for winter pests and diseases as low light levels stress plants. Remove dead or dying material regularly.

Provide heat as necessary and ventilate on mild days. Beware of gales when ventilating.

BASIC TECHNIQUES

Growing crops on an allotment, far from being complex or difficult, is largely the application of commonsense horticultural techniques. The practices described here are at the core of successful allotment-growing and while they can take time to master, they are all essentially straightforward. Knowing that you have been responsible for the produce on your plot is not only very satisfying, but also well within the grasp of even novice growers. The following pages are intended to act as an essential how-to guide to this process; from producing new plants, caring for them while they grow and ultimately harvesting and storing them.

Left: *A flourishing plot is the end result of careful planning and preparation as well as regular maintenance.*

Above: *A well-prepared, weed-free plot is the ideal starting point for successful plant growth and development.*

Above: *Both weeds and crop residues can be recycled in the allotment by composting, and then returned to the soil.*

Above: *Growing fruit such as apples on an allotment is satisfying, but it is important that it is stored properly once harvested.*

Above: *Peas planted in straight rows are relatively easy to harvest, so this is a very popular arrangement on allotments.*

WAYS TO GROW DIFFERENT CROPS

When it comes to raising crops on an allotment, there is no one 'correct' way of doing it and there are numerous methods of organizing the layout. Neatly arranged rows of crops are a traditional method, although blocks, raised beds and no-dig systems have become increasingly popular. Each of these has its relative advantages and while some growers favour just one system, others opt for a more eclectic mix.

PLANTING IN ROWS

This is the most traditionally practised and popular form of vegetable-growing. It is an effective method because the spacing of the plants allows the crop to grow without excessive competition. In addition, it is relatively easy to add supports and protection such as cloches to the crops. However, this type of planting does have the disadvantage of needing relatively high maintenance. Due to the large amounts of bare earth left between the rows, the conditions are ideal for weed growth. Rows are spaced according to the optimum growth of the plants and so rows of pumpkins need to be much wider than those for carrots. Setting out rows in this way allows free movement of air along the rows. This results in fewer disease problems which can occur with more closely grown methods such as block plantings.

The rows are quite easily maintained by regular hoeing but can be wasteful of space, particularly in smaller plots. They will produce sizeable vegetables, but this is offset by the actual yield per unit area being smaller than more intensive systems.

BLOCK PLANTING

With this method plants are grown in squares or rectangles rather than in straight rows. Blocks of plants are grown next to each other, for example in dimensions such as five plants by five plants. The numbers of plants grown can be larger or smaller than this. Block plantings use space efficiently, producing many more plants in an area than if grown in rows.

Well-tended soil can support planting that forms a close network of foliage over the soil. The soil will retain moisture extremely well underneath the canopy. It also stops weed seeds from germinating, resulting in a less weedy environment than other growing methods. However, a close canopy of leaves can have disavantages, such as poor air flow and high humidity, which are ideal for attracting diseases such as botrytis. During dry spells watering is essential for the health of the crops. Double check all watering that has been done because water easily runs off the dense cover of the leaves and never reaches much of the root system.

Blocks can be planted and managed at ground level or in slightly raised beds. They suit modestly sized vegetables, such as root and salad crops, which are usually grown in rows. You may have to be inventive with crop protection for early-sown crops, as cloches and low polythene tunnels do not cover the area well. The blocks are edged with permanent paths for easy access to the centre from any side so you need never walk on freshly cultivated soil. As a result, the soil does not get compacted and the closely grouped plants make maintenance and cultivation easier.

Seeding a block involves sowing the furrows thinly along close rows. For example, instead of the usual 30–40cm (12–16in) distance between carrot rows, this can be reduced to 20–25cm (8–10in). Further space savings can result from growing as much as you can vertically, rather than sprawled over the ground. Wire fencing, netting or poles and tepees take up less space than blocks of climbing vegetables. This will also keep the climbing plants dry and free of disease.

FLAT BEDS

As the name suggests, flat beds are constructed at the natural ground level of your allotment. They are the traditional way of cultivating ground for growing vegetables and are most suitable for plots that have good soil. Flat beds will naturally raise the level of the soil, especially where organic matter is added on a regular basis as part of the cultivation regime, but the bed remains effectively at ground level. This form of gardening is relatively labour-intensive because all of the bed is cultivated, with large areas then being used as paths between the vegetables. With raised beds, there are no paths and only the growing areas are dug.

Left: *Planting crops closely in blocks is an efficient use of your space. In addition to this, the practice also helps to suppress weeds and conserves moisture in the soil. This will ensure that the plant is less stressed and growth will be quicker, with less pest and disease damage.*

Above: *Beans trained up poles or a trellis use only a limited amount of space, and help maximize the efficient use of ground.*

RAISED AND EDGED BEDS

These can be freestanding beds or beds with wooden or brick walls constructed several inches above the normal ground level. Raised bed gardens not only look good but they can also help solve many problems associated with soils that are difficult to manage. Problems with soil are often aggravated in urban and suburban settings, where topsoil and vegetation may have been removed or the surface level changed during building work.

Raised beds improve the environment for plants by lifting their roots above poor soil. The growing medium can be amended by the incorporation of manure and/or garden compost. Soil in these beds warms up earlier in the spring, allowing the seed sown to germinate quicker than if it is grown in flat beds. Beds should be located where they will receive full sun and some protection from prevailing winds. Do not site the beds in frost pockets or where air circulation is poor.

Drainage is especially important when growing vegetables. Build the beds so that the crops will not become waterlogged. If the bed contains clay soil, incorporate sand, grit or organic matter to improve drainage. It is a good idea to construct the bed so that it slopes about 2cm (¾in) per metre (yard) of horizontal distance away from any structures, or away from the centre of the bed.

NO-DIG BEDS

As the term suggests, no digging is involved in this method, which is an effective way to retain good soil structure within a vegetable plot. Weeding is kept to a minimum and because the soil is not disturbed it will be alive with worms and other organisms. The bed is made on top of the ground and can be built over existing beds, lawns and even hard or rocky ground. Situate the bed in a sunny area that receives morning sun and has good drainage. It can be any size or shape, depending on your space. Start with a small bed – about 2 x 1.5m (6½ x 5ft) – but with a view to expanding in time.

When preparing the site it is not necessary to pull up the existing site if the soil conditions are good, but if the ground is very poor, compacted, or the drainage is bad, initial digging may be necessary.

Above: *Containers are an ideal way to grow a variety of crops where space is limited. These pots contain courgettes.*

The outside wall of a no-dig bed is formed using logs, old planks, tiles, bricks or stones. Line the bed with a layer of plain wet newspaper, at least 6mm (¼in) thick. This layer should cover the enclosed area completely and overlap slightly, so as to kill off any weeds and stop new ones growing. Spread out a thin layer of hay or straw, ensuring that there are no gaps. Place a layer of good fertilizer, such as chicken manure, 20mm (¾in) thick, on top. Cover with a 20cm (8in) thick layer of loose bedding straw. Follow this with a 2cm (¾in) layer of good organic fertilizer and complete the bed with a top layer of garden compost, about 10cm (4in) thick. Make sure the bed is watered in well. Once it is settled you can plant out seedlings, but not seeds. Sowing seeds can begin when the bed has matured and the soil has become fine and crumbly.

No-dig beds that have been recently created are best for growing crops such as potatoes, lettuce, brassicas and cucurbits, whereas root crops grow better when the bed is mature. No-dig beds are best suited to planting vegetables in small blocks of different varieties rather than in long rows.

Left: *Raised beds provide the ideal solution where the soil on a plot is poor, and have the added benefit of warming up more quickly to allow seed to germinate sooner.*

SOWING IN THE OPEN

There can be nothing more satisfying than sowing seeds and waiting in anticipation for them to germinate. Watching the seedlings grow in your plot, making it come alive with leaves, flowers and insects is a fantastic experience. One of the drawbacks of sowing out in the open is that you are at the mercy of the weather, but you can manipulate your allotment environment by using cloches, small plastic bottles and polythene tunnels to increase your chances of success.

Above: *A dibber is a very helpful tool to use when you are transplanting seeds, seedlings or small bulbs outside.*

SITE REQUIREMENTS

If you are a novice allotment-grower, be assured that sowing seed is easier than you may think. In order to germinate successfully, seeds simply need water, air, a suitable temperature and a place into which they can root in order to support the top growth that will follow. For this reason, good soil preparation is the key to success. Most garden soils are able to supply all the necessary elements and only slight modifications are usually necessary. However, it is important that the ground is prepared in a way that will enable the seed to germinate evenly and grow in a uniform environment. The proper prior preparation of a seedbed can provide the seed with the environment that it needs and has the added bonus of making the task of seed sowing easier.

Preparing a seedbed is simple. Following cultivation, the ground is levelled using a rake, held at a shallow angle, to break down any large clods. The art of levelling is to keep the rake angle shallow and move the high spots over into the low spots with even strokes. Hold the rake firmly at the rear and let the shaft run smoothly through the front hand. All stones and large objects, including organic matter such as twigs or previous crop debris, should be removed by combing them out with the teeth of the rake, while holding the tool in a near vertical position. The soil is then firmed with light treading. A light shuffle across the bed is best. Once firmed, lightly rake the soil again at a shallow angle to produce a light 'fluffy' surface that runs freely through the teeth of the rake. This is the perfect environment for sowing and growing seeds.

SEED REQUIREMENTS

The conditions that seeds require to germinate are easy and straightforward to create. A well-aerated moist soil environment is almost all that the seed needs. Most seeds will germinate quite successfully once the temperature gets above 7°C (45°F). Seeds carry their own food supply that provides them with everything they need for those first crucial days following germination. Once the plant begins to establish and grow, it needs soil-borne nutrients. This means that the soil in which it is growing needs to be of the right fertility for the plant. Poorer soils can benefit from the addition of a base dressing with fish, blood and bone prior to sowing to give the boost that the developing plant needs, although loamier soils need only be properly dug and prepared to support germination.

SOWING SEEDS OUTDOORS

1 *Carefully clear the plot of any previous crop residues or weeds, ensuring that all roots or other plant matter is removed.*

2 *Use a rake to remove any clods or stones. Continue raking until the surface is crumbly and runs easily through the rake's tines.*

3 *Once the soil is fine and crumbly it will need lightly firming to make sure that it has no air pockets, using the flat face of the rake.*

Some seeds can benefit from being soaked for a short period in tepid water just before planting to help them take on the water they need for germination. This is especially true of beetroot (beets), but other large seeds also benefit from this treatment.

SOWING IN ROWS

Seed is usually sown in rows. Using a tightly drawn garden line as a guide, draw the corner of a swan-necked (English) hoe along the line to create a shallow drill of about 1–2cm (⅜–¾in) depth, depending upon the seed's individual requirements. Dry ground can be watered after the drill is made. Sow the seed thinly and mix fine seed with silver sand to make it easier to distribute evenly. Mark the end of each row with a label before moving on to the next.

STATION SOWING

Seeds of larger growing plants, particularly those with seed that is large enough to handle, benefit from station sowing. This involves sowing two or three seeds at intervals that will be the eventual crop spacing. If all three germinate, then the two weaker ones are removed or transplanted to gaps where none has germinated.

WIDE ROWS

Certain seeds, particularly peas and beans, benefit from being planted in wide rows. Two rows are effectively station sown at once, one on each side of a drill that is 15cm (6in) across. The drill is made with the flat of the hoe and after sowing the soil is carefully raked back. Make sure that you do not disturb the seeds from their stations.

Left: *Station sowing is ideal for larger seeds or seedlings that resent disturbance. Use a marked stick to set the spacing of the seed.*

BROADCASTING (BLOCKS)

Broadcasting is an ancient method of seed sowing that was used to sow large areas of crops. It involves a 'broadcasting' action that separates the seed to an even spacing. The easiest way to do this in small vegetable plots is to split the seed into two halves, mixing small seed with fine sand. Scatter the seed carefully, letting it run from your hand in even arcs as you move your arm from side to side. Sow each half of the seed at a 90-degree angle to the other, thereby assuring an even distribution. Gently rake the seed in once sown and lightly water if needed.

PROTECTING SEEDLINGS

Seedbeds, with their fine 'fluffed' earth, act as magnets to birds and animals. Some may take the seed from the ground, but, in truth, most will find it more attractive as a dust bath or litter tray. Once the seedlings emerge, however, some birds find them irresistible. They must be kept out with some form of barrier. One of the easiest methods is to form a low tunnel of chicken wire, supporting this on hoops. For larger areas, a series of stakes in the ground can be covered with netting to keep birds at bay. Sticks with thread or string stretched between them are also effective, but less easily removed for you to tend the crop.

LABELLING

When you sow a row or area of seeds, label it straightaway. Re-usable plastic labels are the best option. Each label should have the name and variety of the plant sown. You may also wish to record the sowing date and if the seed was pre-treated.

4 *Stretch a taut string between two pegs to act as a guide, and use one corner of a swan-necked hoe to form a straight shallow drill.*

5 *Pre-water the drill with a fine rose and leave for a few minutes to ensure that later watering does not dislodge seeds.*

6 *Place a label stating the date and crop name at the row end before sowing seeds according to instructions. Cover lightly.*

SOWING UNDER GLASS

Sowing seed under glass extends the growing season and enables you to raise tender crops that only survive outside in warmer months. It is also ideal for rapidly establishing plants to use as catch crops and as early companion plants. In short, it offers variety and choice for your cropping regimes. Plants raised under glass can be grown on until they reach a size where they are better able to resist pest attack. They can also be planted out at their final spacing, thereby avoiding thinning or gaps in rows.

Above: *A propagator is a useful piece of equipment for raising your seed in ideal growing conditions.*

HEAT REQUIREMENTS

Most seeds have a preferred temperature range within which they will grow. A heated greenhouse will often provide this, although seeds requiring a constant high temperature may need to be grown in a propagator. Such seeds are mercifully rare among vegetables, although cucumbers, tomatoes and (bell) peppers are good examples of crops that will benefit if they are first started off in a propagator.

CHOICE OF CONTAINER

There is a variety of containers that may be used to sow seed under glass. The most common form is the plastic seed tray which has now largely replaced the wooden seed tray. Although more attractive, wooden trays are difficult to keep clean and may harbour plant diseases. Plastic trays can be made of durable polyurethane or sometimes a more flimsy, thin, moulded plastic which is intended for single use. They are available in a variety of sizes, although small 9cm (3½in) pots may be more suitable when you are raising only a few plants.

Modular seed trays are another option. These are made up of individual cells, and a single seed is sown into each one. Seeds that are sown in these trays have the advantage of not suffering any root disturbance when they are planted out in their eventual position. The same is true of some biodegradable pots, which are formed out of paper and coir. These are better (environmentally speaking) than those made from peat, but any recycled material used for these trays is acceptable in the allotment site.

Inventive recycling can also provide an array of useful sowing containers. Re-using plastic cups, vegetable packing trays and any other throw-away items that might otherwise end up on a landfill site are all possibilities worth exploring. Old plastic bottles make good individual propagation cowls for small pots and plastic bags can also be used to cover the tops of pots and trays in order to maintain humidity.

Left: *Many propagators have ventilators on the top in order to aid the flow of fresh air to the seedlings.*

PROPAGATORS

These are, in effect, mini-hothouses that help to keep the seed in a warm, moist, stable environment both above and below the soil line. Expensive propagators involve the use of electric soil-warming cables and some have thermostats to control the soil temperature. Many are designed for use in the greenhouse. Alternatively, instead of buying the whole propagator, you can purchase a heating mat on which the seed trays can stand in order to receive heat at the bottom. This system has the advantage of being mobile and easily moved about from area to area. Another cheaper method is to buy soil-heating cables to bed into sand. The seed trays sit on the bed of heated sand to receive an even supply of bottom heat.

AFTERCARE OF SEEDLINGS

Once seeds begin to germinate they can be moved gradually into a less humid environment. Remove the plastic covers from the trays, or open the propagator vents or lids and, after a few days, remove the lid completely. As soon as the seedlings reach a size at which they can be handled, carefully prick them out into individual pots or larger boxes and trays.

Always handle the seedlings by the leaves, gently lifting each one from beneath, using a dibber (dibble). Never hold them by the stems because this can cause a great

Above: *Modular trays are ideal for planting large seeds and avoid disturbance to roots when planting out or potting on.*

Above: *Individual pots can be used for large seeds. Plant two seeds per pot and remove the weaker seedling.*

SOWING IN TRAYS

1 *Fill a seed tray with seed and cuttings compost (soil mix) that has been thoroughly mixed. Fill the tray to overflowing and do not firm in the compost.*

2 *Using a straight-edged piece of board, level the surface of the seed and cuttings compost by carefully moving the board across the top of the tray.*

3 *Thoroughly water the seed tray and leave to drain for about 20 minutes before sowing the seed. This will ensure that the surface of the compost is moist prior to sowing.*

4 *Larger seed can be placed on the surface of the compost, spaced at regular intervals. Regular spacing in this way will help to prevent overcrowding.*

5 *Once the seed has been sown, use a sieve (strainer) to cover the surface with a fine layer of compost and/or propagation grade vermiculite.*

6 *Do not cover the seeds of plants that require light for germination. Always check the growing requirements of plants before sowing the seed.*

deal of damage to the developing plant. When you prick them out, space them at least 5cm (2in) apart to allow room for subsequent development. Water the transplanted seedlings with a fine upturned rose attached to a watering can that has been filled with water overnight, thus bringing it up to room temperature and not giving the transplants a shock of cold water. Keep the pricked-out seedlings in a greenhouse as a constant temperature will promote healthy growth.

Above: *Watering from below by pouring the water into the base of the seed tray will prevent damage to newly emerging seed.*

HARDENING OFF

Plants that have been raised and grown in a greenhouse cannot be put straight outside once they are a suitable size because their growth will be too soft to withstand the cold. Instead they must be gradually hardened off and acclimatized to outdoor conditions.

The young plants are hardened off by moving them from the greenhouse and into a cold frame, or putting them out under cloches, low polythene tunnels or horticultural fleece. Open up the cloches and cold frames or remove the fleece during the day and replace them at night for a week or two before planting out the seedlings properly or removing the cloches completely. Remove low polythene tunnels after a couple of weeks depending on the weather conditions. If these are severe, leave them in place for longer.

Above: *Growing vegetables in pots under glass can extend the growing season and also provide a colourful greenhouse display.*

Above: *Herbs such as this tricolor sage are ideal for stem tip cuttings, a very easy way to propagate suitable species.*

VEGETATIVE PROPAGATION

Many perennial crops are not well suited to being grown from seed. Using part of a parent plant instead ensures that the offspring (essentially clones) are the same variety as the parent and will produce crops of a known quality, something that cannot be guaranteed with those grown from seed. Vegetative propagation methods include stem tip, hardwood and root cuttings, layering runners, simple division and chip budding.

PROPAGATING NEW PLANTS

While the majority of annual crops are propagated each year from seed, many perennial types are maintained and increased by a method known as 'vegetative propagation'. This simply involves using all or parts of the stems, roots or leaves to grow new plants. The most obvious example of this is arguably the potato, which is almost always raised from tubers. Despite being called 'seed potatoes', these tubers are actually swollen stem tips that would normally over-winter beneath the ground.

The ease of vegetative propagation varies considerably between crops, and in certain cases (most fruit trees for example) stock is almost invariably propagated using a bud or a twig from a tree that produces exceptionally good fruit. When this bud or twig becomes an adult tree, it has the same qualities as the 'mother' tree and is essentially an identical clone of the 'mother' plant. This means that you know exactly what you are getting, something that is not always the case when growing from seed, but the genetically identical stock can sometimes be liable to disease, as it lacks what is termed 'hybrid vigour'.

WHICH PLANT PARTS ARE USED?

Plants may be propagated from many plant parts, and in certain species specialized roots, stems and leaves naturally have a tendency to form new plants, thereby making vegetative propagation easy.
Tubers are underground swollen stems or roots that store food, the best known of which is arguably the potato. While potatoes are stem tubers, dahlias and sweet potatoes are root tubers.
Rhizomes are thick, swollen root-like stems that often send out roots and shoots. Jerusalem artichokes are an example of a crop, mostly propagated yearly from swollen rhizomes.
Stolons are similar to rhizomes, but usually grow above ground level, sprouting from an existing stem, whereas runners arise from a crown bud and creep over the ground. Strawberries are propagated from runners.
Bulbs, such onions and garlic, consist of swollen leaves on a short stem. Onions, although sometimes raised from seed, are mostly grown on from small, under-developed bulbs, called sets. Garlic on the other hand is almost always grown from offsets (cloves) taken from a parent bulb.
Stems are used to propagate many trees and shrubs by encouraging a new root system to be formed on a stem, before or after it has been removed from the parent plant. The two commonest methods used are layering and by stem cuttings. The main difficulty with stem cuttings is keeping the stems alive while they form new roots. Some plant stems root better when the wood is soft and actively growing, while others root best from mature wood.

TAKING STEM TIP CUTTINGS

1 *Take cuttings from the tips of the stems and put them in a plastic bag with a little water. The length of the cuttings will vary, depending on the subject, but take about 10cm (4in).*

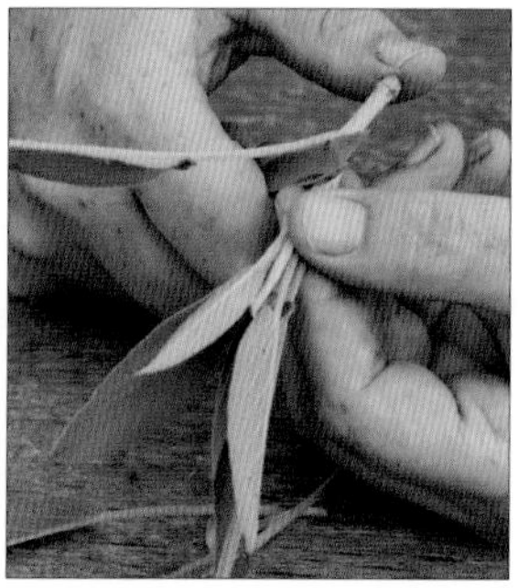

2 *Trim the cuttings to just below a leaf joint and then remove most of the leaves and side shoots, leaving just two at the top. This will help to prevent stem rot.*

3 *Place up to 12 cuttings in a pot of potting mix that is specially formulated for cuttings or a 50:50 mixture of sharp sand and peat substitute such as coir or leaf mould mix.*

4 *Water well, and cover with the cut-off base of a soft-drinks bottle, a perfect substitute for a propagator. A heated propagator will speed up the rooting process. Place several pots in the same unit.*

TAKING HARDWOOD CUTTINGS

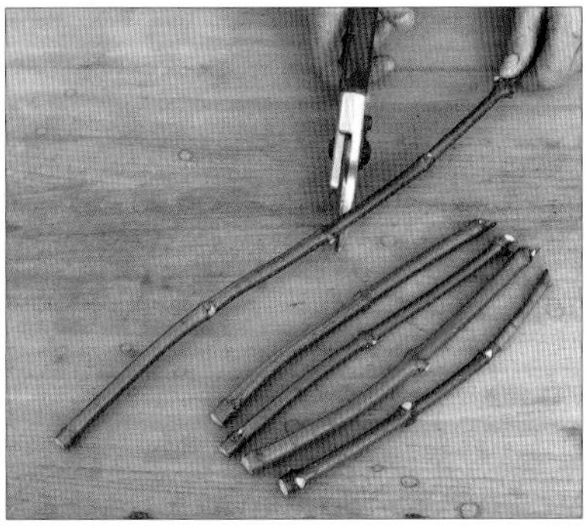

1 *Select healthy, blemish-free pieces of wood about the thickness of a pencil. Cut each of these into sections about 20–25cm (8–10in) long, angling the top cut.*

2 *Stand the cut stems in a jar of water until you are ready to plant them out. Ideally, stand the jar in a cool moist place out of direct sunlight.*

3 *Dig a narrow trench that is deep enough for the cuttings. About 2.5–5cm (1–2in) should emerge above ground. The length of the row will depend on the number of cuttings.*

4 *Loosely fill the trench to about two-thirds full with sharp sand or fine grit. This is essential as it will allow the passage of air around the bases and prevent rotting off. It will also encourage rooting.*

5 *Insert the cuttings about 10–15cm (4–6in) apart, making sure that the angled cut is uppermost. If you place any cuttings in upside down – i.e. with the buds facing downward – rooting will not occur.*

6 *Gently firm the soil, making sure that the cuttings are firm but that the soil surface is not over-compacted. Leave the cuttings for the whole of the growing season before lifting and planting out next winter.*

TAKING ROOT CUTTINGS

1 *Dig up a small section of root from a suitable species with thick fleshy roots. The section must either have a shoot bud or be capable of forming one – in which case the cutting should be taken in the dormant season – if it is to be successful.*

2 *Remove as much of the soil as possible from the root cutting before slicing off the small side roots. Using a sharp knife, remove these as well as dead and damaged portions and any side shoots to leave a section of healthy root.*

3 *Cut the remaining sections of the root into small pieces, approximately 5cm (2in) in length, cutting the bottom end at an angle. Insert the root cutting into propagation potting mix, with the angled end pointing down.*

Cuttings taken from plants that are actively growing are called softwood cuttings. These cuttings are taken from first-year branches that have not yet become woody, with late spring and early summer being the most successful times for this method. Take cuttings 5–10cm (2–4in) long, as larger ones are prone to more rapid water loss. Make cuts slightly below a leaf node (the point where the leaf meets the stem) and remove any leaves on the lower section. Insert them into compost (soil mix), making sure that no leaves are touching each other or the compost. Cover with polythene or place them in a propagator to prevent them from wilting. Remove any cuttings immediately from the tray or pot if they die and pot healthy cuttings up promptly once they recommence growth following rooting. Species suited to this method include vines, figs, peaches, nectarines and plums.

Cuttings taken after the wood is mature are known as hardwood cuttings and these are taken when the plant is dormant. Cuttings can be taken two weeks after leaf fall and before bud burst. Select healthy wood that was produced the previous summer and that is about 'pencil thickness'. Cut it into sections of approximately 15–20cm (6–8in). Several cuttings can be made from the same branch of some shrubs. The basal cuts are made just below a node, and upper cuts slightly above a bud. The upper cut should be slanted so that a cutting is less likely to be inserted into the compost upside down. Bury cuttings vertically in moist sandy topsoil or sand, leaving 2.5–5cm (1–2in) of cutting above ground, and put them in a cool shady place, taking care not to let them freeze. In spring, remove the cuttings from storage and plant them at the same depth in pots or open ground in a sheltered position and in dappled shade. Keep them moist until a root system forms and transplant them the following spring while they are still dormant. Species suited to this method include currants, figs, olives and vines.

Above: *You can very easily make many more strawberry plants from one adult plant by layering the runners, negating the need to buy more plants the following year.*

Above: *Cherries (*Prunus cerasus*) and apples (*Malus sylvestris *var.* domestica*) are among the species that can be propagated successfully by chip budding.*

LAYERING STRAWBERRY RUNNERS

1 *Use a trowel to dig a hole close to a healthy strawberry plant with plenty of runners, making sure that it is large enough to accommodate a small pot.*

2 *Fill the chosen small pot to the brim with seed and cuttings compost (soil mix) and carefully 'sink' this into the hole you made, making sure the rim is just below the soil level.*

3 *The runner will need pegging in place on the surface of the seed and cuttings compost. You can make a peg by cutting a woody branch just below a side shoot to make a small hook.*

4 *Choose a healthy runner, peg it down firmly on the surface of the compost at a leaf-joint and water it in. In a few weeks, it can be detached from the parent, lifted and replanted.*

SIMPLE DIVISION

1 *Water the plant that is to be divided during the previous day. Carefully dig up a clump of the plant using a spade, in this case a Michaelmas daisy (*Aster novi-belgii*).*

2 *Insert two garden forks back-to-back into the plant and lever apart by pushing the handles together. Keep on dividing until the pieces are of the required size.*

3 *The pieces of the plant can then be replanted in the bed, but dig over the soil first, removing any weeds and adding some well-rotted organic material.*

4 *Alternatively, small pieces of the plant can be potted up individually. After watering, place these in a closed cold frame for a few days before hardening off.*

PROPAGATION METHODS

Layering is where a young branch is bent down to the soil and pegged down. The tip is then bent back upward, forming a 'leg', and the bend is covered with soil. Roots will form at the point where the branch bends as the bend interferes with the flow of sap, thereby encouraging root formation. Sap flow can be further reduced by twisting the stem, or cutting a 'tongue' in the lower side of the bark with a sharp knife. The stem will need earthing-up throughout the summer to encourage stem rooting. Species suited to this method include blackberries, blackcurrant and *Corylus* (hazel).

Division is a method usually practised only on herbaceous plants and it involves cutting or breaking up a crown or clump of suckers into segments. Each segment must have a bud and some roots and these are replanted. The clump is carefully dug up and split apart with two spades or forks, or 'chopped' with a shovel or large knife if the clump is firmly massed. Species suited to this method include rhubarb, globe artichoke and many herbs.

Grafting produces a plant in a relatively short period. In addition to this, however, there are other, very specific applications where it is invaluable. Fruit trees that are self-incompatible (unable to self pollinate) for example, can have a piece of a compatible variety grafted on to them in order to assure fruit. Grafting on to a rootstock might also confer a particular growth habit or give added disease resistance, and is often practised by commercial growers as a consequence.

CHIP BUDDING

1 *Select good bud wood that is free from blemishes and obvious damage, pests or diseases. If you are doing this in the summer, then you must first remove the leaves cleanly using a knife.*

2 *Remove the bud from the step using a clean, very sharp, flat-edged knife. Cut out the bud with a thin shaving of the wood below the bark and leave a 'V' shape at the base.*

3 *Prepare the stock plant by cutting a 'church window' shaped notch from the stem that is the same thickness as the chipped bud and leave a small notch cut into the base.*

4 *With clean hands, place the bud into the notch, fitting the 'V'-shaped base into the notch at the base of the 'window cut'. This should be carried out soon after preparing the bud to prevent it from drying out.*

5 *To ensure a successful union of the bud and the stock, make sure that the bud fits snugly, with the edges of the bud-wood in contact with the edge of the 'window' notch.*

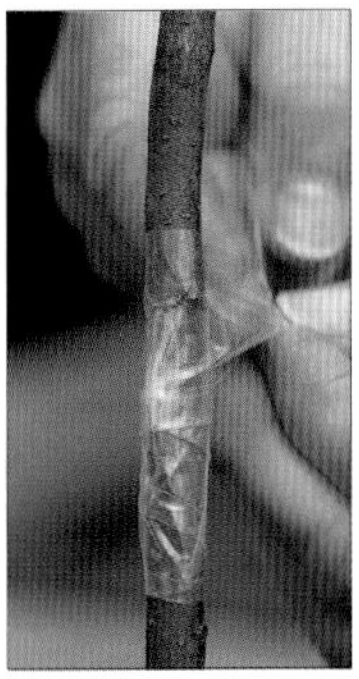

6 *Secure the graft firmly with grafting tape to ensure that the join does not dry out. The graft will usually take in about 4–6 weeks in the summer but winter grafts can take longer.*

CARING FOR NEW PLANTS

Newly propagated plants are at their most vulnerable stage. Even as they begin to establish and grow, young stock remains susceptible to damage for some time to come. The best way to deal with plants, both before and immediately after planting, is to 'toughen them up' over time and this is easily achieved by applying a few simple techniques. Giving young crops a good start in life is a sure-fire way to get a bumper harvest.

Above: *Growing plants from seed is one of the most satisfying ways of producing new stock for the allotment.*

PLANT SPACINGS

All plants need space to develop and flourish. Plants that are growing too closely compete not only for space, but also for light, water and important nutrients. In addition to this competitive stress, they also become prone to a variety of fungal diseases, as the air is not able to move around them. Thinning the seedlings helps to counteract these problems and will result in larger, stronger and healthier plants.

HOW TO THIN SEEDLINGS

Thinning is essentially two processes in one. Firstly, you are removing all the plants that are excess to requirements and at the same time you are selecting the biggest, healthiest and strongest plants that will be retained to form the crop.

Before starting to thin, dry ground must be watered, preferably the night before you intend to thin. A measuring stick, marked with the appropriate crop distance, can be used to show the approximate position of the individual plants. Remove all the plants in between each of the markers, selecting the healthiest plant at or near the mark on the stick. If there are no plants at the marked point, then you can transplant one of the seedlings that is excess to requirements into this position. When you are removing the excess plants, place a finger on the soil at either side of the seedling that is being kept. This protects it from root disturbance. Once you have finished, water the remaining seedlings with a fine rose on a watering can to re-firm the soil around the plants. The seedlings that have been removed can be put on the compost heap.

Avoid thinning using this method on hot dry days or in windy conditions, as the remaining seedlings in the ground may become water-stressed if their roots are disturbed. The alternative, in this case, is to simply snip off the seedlings at ground level with a pair of sharp scissors or secateurs (hand pruners), thereby avoiding root disturbance.

Above: *Rows of seedlings are often too crowded and need to be thinned when the plants are young.*

Left: *Seedlings grown elsewhere in the allotment can be lifted and replanted in their eventual positions. This method is good for crops that need wide spacing.*

THINNING DISTANCES

The following measurements are the distances that need to be left between thinned seedlings.

Beetroot (beets)	7.5–10cm (3–4in)
Broad (fava) beans	23cm (9in)
Carrots	7.5cm (3in)
Dwarf French beans (bush green beans)	20cm (8in)
Florence fennel	25cm (10in)
Kohl rabi	20cm (8in)
Lettuce	23cm (9in)
Parsley	15cm (6in)
Peas	5cm (2in)
Parsnips	15–20cm (6–9in)
Radishes	2.5–5cm (1–2in)
Runner (green) beans	25–30cm (10–12in)
Salsify	15cm (6in)
Scorzonera	15cm (6in)
Spinach	15cm (6in)
Spring onions (scallions)	5cm (2in)
Swedes (rutabaga or yellow turnip)	30cm (12in)
Swiss chard	30cm (12in)
Turnips	15–20cm (6–8in)

TRANSPLANTING SEEDLINGS

1 *Water your row of seedlings at least an hour before transplanting and preferably the night before if no rain has fallen.*

2 *Using a fork to loosen the soil, gently lift the seedlings. Take care to handle them by their leaves and never touch the stems.*

3 *Using a tight line, straight edge or notched planting board, replant the seedlings at the appropriate spacing for that crop.*

4 *Gently water the seedlings immediately after sowing. Never let roots dry out at any stage during transplanting.*

METHODS FOR TRANSPLANTING

The most common way of transplanting seedlings involves planting container-grown plants into open ground. Early vegetable crops can easily be raised in this way. The other method is to raise seedlings in open ground near to where they are to be planted out. Transplanting outdoor seedlings means that a smaller area of the vegetable plot is needed for sowing and, in consequence, a smaller seedbed is required. Transplanting seedlings is a good way of growing plants such as lettuce that are to be used in catch-cropping beds or where plants are to be planted out in no-dig beds.

The ideal time for transplanting outdoor seedlings is during damp overcast weather because this helps to prevent the seedlings' roots drying out. As is the case when thinning the plants, the seedlings will need watering the evening before. It is best to dig up only a few plants at a time, discarding any that are weak, damaged or appear to be sick. Seedlings can be placed in a plastic bag to maintain humidity around them while they are out of the ground.

A garden line can be set out in the vegetable patch in a similar manner to the way in which it is placed for preparing a seed drill. The position of the plants can then be determined using a measuring stick. Use a dibber (dibble) or thin trowel to plant the seedlings, firming lightly around the base before moving on to the next transplant. Once the row is completed, it is important that you water them in.

For catch cropping or planting among other plants, the surrounding crop may well determine the spacings between the transplants, although the procedure remains exactly the same.

COMMON PLANTING DISTANCES

Always allow the correct spacing between crop plants so that they will grow into healthy specimens.

Asparagus	30–38cm (12–15in)
Aubergines (eggplants)	60cm (24in)
Bell peppers	45–60cm (18–24in)
Broccoli	60cm (24in)
Brussels sprouts	50–75cm (20–30in)
Cabbages	30–50cm (12–20in)
Calabrese (Italian sprouting broccoli)	15–23cm (6–9in)
Cauliflowers	50–75cm (20–30in)
Celeriac	30–38cm (12–15in)
Celery	23–30cm (9–12in)
Courgettes (zucchini)	60cm (24in)
Cucumbers	60cm (24in)
Garlic	15cm (6in)
Globe artichokes	75cm (30in)
Jerusalem artichokes	30cm (12in)
Kale	60cm (24in)
Leeks	15cm (6in)
Marrows (large zucchini)	60cm (24in)
Onion sets	10cm (4in)
Potatoes	30–38cm (12–15in)
Pumpkins	90–180cm (3–6ft)
Rhubarb	75–90cm (30–36in)
Runner (green) beans	25–30cm (10–12in)
Sea kale	30cm (12in)
Shallots	15–18cm (6–7in)
Sweetcorn (corn)	30cm (12in)
Tomatoes	60cm (24in)

Right: *A shade box can protect vulnerable seedlings from strong light and heat while they are being acclimatized.*

AVOIDING TRANSPLANT SHOCK

Even if young plants were hardened off, prior to planting out, they will still suffer a certain amount of stress as a result of their move. The degree to which this affects their growth in the long term will of course vary, and depends upon the steps you take to avoid the problem.

It is worth remembering that no matter how carefully you handle them while planting, some, albeit slight damage, is still likely to occur. Roots, stems and leaves can all be affected, and the plant will need to recover from this while it is also dealing with the challenge of establishing itself in its new home. As a rule of thumb, the younger the plant, the more quickly it will re-acclimatize. Having said this though, very young plants are naturally more susceptible to other stresses, meaning that it may well be better to grow them on a little first.

The fact that the plant experiences a change of location can also cause problems at first, although young plants typically recover from this quite quickly. Plants that have been grown in a sheltered location, for example, initially struggle if they are planted in an open situation, even if this is not particularly windy. Equally, plants grown in an open sunny situation would not benefit from being transplanted into a cool, shady place.

The real trick is to ensure that you gradually acclimatize them to their new setting. Plants not used to an open setting may need a little shelter or light shade for a few days as they get used to their new home. Remember, also, that even if they come from a similar location to that which they are planted into, they may well have been growing in close proximity to one another, gaining benefit from the humidity this promotes. Once planted or transplanted, however, they will be at their

Below: *Water young plants carefully, as overwatering can be just as harmful to their development as underwatering.*

Below: *Tender seedlings, such as this pumpkin, require very delicate handling when they are planted out or potted on.*

Below: *If pests, such as rabbits, are a particular problem on the site it may be worth installing fencing.*

PLANTING OUT CONTAINER-GROWN PLANTS

1 *Container-grown plants need careful handling to avoid damaging new growth. Pushing them out rather than pulling the stem will minimize harm.*

2 *Lay them out in their final spacing or positions prior to planting, using a line to keep them straight if you are planting them out in rows.*

3 *Use a trowel to excavate a hole, planting the root-ball (roots) no more than 1cm (½in) below the soil surface, and gently firm the soil around the plant.*

4 *Once the whole row is planted, water the plants using a watering can fitted with a fine rose attachment. Set them back upright and re-firm if needed.*

final spacing and this sudden isolation, whilst beneficial in the longer term, can cause a measure of water stress in those first few days. Be prepared to cover them with some fleece if a sudden cold snap threatens and make sure they get enough water while their roots are establishing.

PROTECTING VULNERABLE STOCK

Some newly planted specimens prove a real magnet for the unwanted attention of pests such as birds or rabbits, and it is important to keep these out. Birds often peck out onion sets for example without eating them, and pigeons can easily shred newly transplanted brassicas. Fortunately, these pests can easily be deterred by covering plants temporarily with netting. If birds and rabbits prove a major problem, however, it may be worth making more permanent fences or cages to protect your crops from outside harm.

Frames or hoops, fixed over the bed, can be used to support various protection according to the season; fleece or polythene in early spring and autumn, netting to keep pests out and shade in the height of summer. If you are going to opt for a more permanent protective structure though, it is a good idea to make sure that it can be moved off, as this will allow you access to maintain and harvest the crop easily and ultimately to cultivate the ground in the following spring. A fixed cage structure over a raised bed, for instance, may mean that you have to bend double to work on the area, making reaching some crops and carrying out tasks such as digging and weeding much more difficult.

WATERING AND FEEDING

Even though you will need to water new plants regularly, especially in hot or very windy weather, be careful not to overdo it. Some vegetables, including most root crops and members of the onion family, need only be watered during their establishment and even then do not like to be too wet. A rose attachment is a good investment as it is a gentle way of watering,

Feeding is also not necessary in the early stages, and in many cases can prove detrimental to young, sensitive roots. As a rule of thumb, if you applied a fertilizer before planting, you probably won't need to apply any more for 2–3 weeks after putting plants in the ground, when the plants show visible signs of growth.

Below: *Birds can affect your crop both when plants are young and when it is ready to be harvested, so you need to be vigilant.*

Above: *This is a sturdy brick cold frame with a soil bed for growing winter and early spring vegetables.*

COLD FRAMES AND CLOCHES

Individual and multiple plant protectors are useful for covering the transplants or seedlings of warm-weather vegetables or flowers that are set out ahead of the normal planting season. These usually take the form of low plastic tunnels, cloches or individual bell jars. The colder the area in which you live, the greater their usefulness because they effectively extend the length of the normal growing season.

COLD FRAMES

These enable you to sow summer flowers and vegetables some weeks before outdoor planting and may even allow for an extra crop within a season. They are relatively inexpensive, simple structures, providing a favourable environment for growing cool-weather crops in the very early spring, the autumn and even into the winter.

Cold frames have no outside energy requirements, relying on the sun as a source of heat. They collect heat when the sun's rays penetrate the light (the top cover) which is made from plastic, glass or fibreglass. The ideal location for a cold frame is facing the direction of the sun with a slight slope to ensure good drainage and maximum solar absorption. A sheltered spot against a wall or hedge is best. Sink the frame into the ground to provide extra protection, using the earth for insulation. Put a walkway to the front and adequate space behind the frame to help when removing the light.

Designs for cold frames vary. For example, some contain barrels that are painted black and filled with water. These absorb heat during the day and release it at night. Some cold frames are built with a very high back and a steep glass slope. Others are insulated very well and may also include movable insulation. A simple method of providing insulation is to use sacks filled with leaves over the top of the frame and bales of straw or hay stacked against the sides at night in order to protect against freezing.

There is no standard-sized cold frame. The inside depth of the frame should be determined by the height of the plants that you plan to grow. Spring annuals, perennial seedlings or low over-wintering stock may need as little as a 30cm (12in) back board and a 20cm (8in) front board. Potted plants may need a 38cm (15in) front board and a 45cm (18in) back board. A standard glass frame light is usually about 1 x 1.8m (3 x 6ft). Do not make the structure too wide for weeding and harvesting; a width of 1.2–1.5m (4–5ft) is convenient to reach across.

Cold frames are useful for hardening-off seedlings that were started indoors or in a greenhouse. This hardening-off period is important because seedlings can suffer serious setbacks if they are moved directly from the warmth and protection of the greenhouse to the outdoors. It is also possible to start cool-weather crops in the cold frame and either grow them to maturity or transplant them in the allotment. Cold frames may also be useful for rooting the cuttings of deciduous and evergreen shrubs and trees, and the softwood cuttings of chrysanthemums, geraniums and fuchsias during the warmer months. Ventilation is most critical in late winter, early spring, and early autumn on clear, sunny days when temperatures may rise above 45°C (113°F). The light should be raised partially to prevent the build-up of extreme temperatures inside the frame. Lower or replace the light early each day in order to conserve some heat for the evening.

In summer, extreme heat and intensive sunlight can damage plants. You can avoid this by shading with a lath (a slatted wooden frame) or old bamboo window blinds. Water plants early so that they dry before dark; this helps to reduce disease problems.

CLOCHES

Traditionally a bell-shaped glass cover, a cloche is a movable structure that serves as a mini-greenhouse. Cloches can be used to protect transplanted tender plants from spring frosts. They also help to warm up the soil for crops sown directly in the soil.

Left: *When the seedlings are fully acclimatized and ready to be planted out, the lights or lids can be left off altogether.*

Above: *A rigid plastic cloche is easy to use. The sections butt up against each other and can be pegged into the soil. End pieces are also available to create a sheltered microclimate.*

Above: *Glass bell jars are simple cloches for covering one plant. They are expensive, but large plastic jars make a good, if not as attractive, alternative.*

The traditional or European cloche is usually built in 60cm (24in) sections that vary in height from 20–60cm (8–24in) and 40–65cm (16–26in) in width. It is made of four panes of glass held together with heavy galvanized wire fittings. It has a handle for ease in carrying and for operating the ventilation system. Several cloches placed end to end make a miniature greenhouse.

Plastic bottles with the bottoms cut out can provide protection for small individual plants. These will last a season or two, but will become brittle over time. Flexible fibreglass sheets held in an inverted 'U'-shape by stiff wire hoops or small wooden stakes can be used to cover rows of plants.

A tunnel-like plant protector can be made with a 1.5m (5ft) strip of plastic or fleece laid over 1.8m (6ft) wire hoops placed 1m (3ft) apart. Elastic tiedowns over the top near each hoop will hold the plastic.

Temporary cloches can also be made by arching black, semi-rigid, plastic piping over the row or bed and sticking it into the ground on each side. Lay clear plastic over the arches. If the beds are enclosed with wood, attach brackets to the inside edges of the boxes or sink short pieces of pipe with a larger inside diameter along the sides to hold the arches. The arches can be used to support fleece or shade cloth to ward off both frost and bright sunlight. When this cloche is no longer needed, simply remove the plastic sheet and pipe ribs and store them until the following season.

THE BOTTLE RADIATOR

In areas prone to late air frosts, this simple method can protect outdoor crops such as bush tomatoes. Fill a glass or plastic bottle with water and place it next to the plant. The sunlight will warm the water in the bottle, which will in turn release a gentle heat at night. This is sufficient to prevent cold shock to the plant and will ensure good growth and cropping. It can also be used in conjunction with a fleece covering to enhance the warming effect.

Far left: *Upturned, clear plastic bottles with the bottoms cut out are ideal for using as mini-cloches, protecting individual plants. This is also an environmentally friendly technique.*

Left: *Old-fashioned cloches are particularly good for decorative sites. However, they are also very expensive and quite fragile.*

Above: *Seasonal crops often require frequent watering, and this is something that all family members can get involved with.*

WATERING

In order to cultivate a successful allotment, it is crucial to recognize the water requirements of different plants. It is of vital importance that you know when and how to provide the right amount of water, as well as how to avoid either drought or waterlogging. Conserving the water in the soil as well as storing and recycling this valuable commodity are of key importance in the vegetable, fruit and herb plot, especially in areas where rainfall is seasonal and droughts are common.

PRINCIPLES OF WATER MANAGEMENT

After rainfall or irrigation, the soil pore spaces are filled with water, the air is displaced and the soil saturated. If the rain or irrigation were to continue, then surface pooling or runoff would occur. Water drains from the soil through the pore system and is replaced to some extent by air. After draining, any remaining water may be lost through evaporation or taken up by the plant and lost through its leaves.

All sands and loamy sands tend to have a low available water capacity. Loams and clay have a medium capacity while very fine sandy loam, silt loams, peats and any soil with a high water table have high available water capacity. Clay soils often have a large amount of water within them, but it is held so tightly that plants are not able to obtain it.

Below: *A watering can is ideal for allotment use, and unless you have mains water is often the only practical method available.*

WATER AND THE PLANT

All plants are largely made of water and it is critical that water levels are maintained if the plant is to grow and develop. Soft fleshy subjects, such as courgettes (zucchini), tomatoes and other vegetables, use large quantities of water, particularly during establishment. Plants with large leaves or with extensive branch systems, such as large apple trees, will remove gallons of water from the soil in the course of a hot sunny day.

WATERWISE GARDENING

Since water supplies are limited, we need to do all we can to conserve soil moisture. As the top layer of soil dries out, the dry soil acts as an insulation to further rapid moisture loss. Take advantage of this by avoiding over-cultivation, particularly during the summer, as this may bring moist soil to the surface to dry out. Always try to maintain a well-structured soil and avoid capping (a hard, partially compacted surface layer) as this can prevent the absorption of rainfall by the soil, leaving puddles that quickly evaporate.

Mulches help to conserve moisture either by holding water or acting as insulation provided that they are deep enough. Keep the soil surface weed-free and provide shelter from drying winds. Maintain drainage, as if this is poor it will lead to limited root growth of the plant and poor soil structure.

Below: *It is vital to get water directly to the roots of plants; here a pipe is used to channel the water straight into the ground.*

STORING AND RECYCLING WATER

Water is a precious resource that is sometimes in short supply. Plants in open ground may acclimatize to the soil conditions, but those growing in pots are more susceptible to drought. Mains water can provide an answer but this can be labour-intensive if only watering cans are allowed on the site.

Storing and recycling household water is a relatively complicated undertaking that is usually best left to specialist contractors. The potential health risks mean that it is not usually wise to store this type of water for any length of time, but it can be used fresh to water non-food plants. You may also find it hard or impossible to transport household water to an allotment site, although you could use large plastic jerry cans if you have a regular supply and can ensure that it will be used fresh.

Rainwater may be a viable alternative and you can collect it on site. The quickest and easiest option is to install water butts to collect water from downspouts from roof drains. This method will rarely provide enough water for your whole plot, but is often plenty to water (or supplement the

MAKING A BOTTLE SEEP TUBE

1 *Plastic bottles can make excellent seep irrigation tubes. Start by making some small holes in the cap and screwing it on tightly.*

2 *Using a knife, sharp pair of scissors or secateurs (pruners), cut the base off the bottle so that it forms an open-ended tube.*

3 *Push or bury the bottle neck firmly into the ground next to the plant and fill the open end with water, re-firming if needed.*

watering of) plants in containers, particularly edible plants such as herbs. Rainwater is naturally acidic and is, therefore, not likely to contain many harmful bacteria. Its acidity also makes it the ideal choice for misting plants under glass on hot days (as it will not mark the leaves with lime) and suits many species sensitive to domestic water additives. Rainwater is also a must for people wishing to grow 'acid-loving' specimens, such as blueberries, in pots.

WATERING PLANTS

In areas where seasonal water shortage is a regular problem, choose drought-tolerant species where possible. Seasonal crops (such as vegetables) tend to suffer the most from drought due to the limited time that they have to develop extensive root systems. If you wish to grow these plants in drier areas, they will need to be watered regularly to survive prolonged dry periods. Perennial fruit and vegetables, on the other hand, may actually become more drought-tolerant if they are watered less. This is because they will have to root deeper to find water. Perennial fruit and vegetables will need to be watered in their first season following planting to ensure their long-term survival.

Remember that applying a good drench on a more occasional basis allows the water to penetrate more deeply and have a better long-term effect because it encourages deeper rooting. Watering little and often can prove detrimental in drier climates by causing surface roots that may become very drought-prone. After the first growing season following planting, they are better able to cope if not watered at all. Applying a mulch at this time is extremely beneficial.

WATERING METHODS

Plants can be watered in many ways, but all generally fall into two categories: hand watering or automatic systems.

Hand watering The commonest 'tool' used for this method is the watering can. Numerous designs exist but they all rely upon a gradual delivery through a spout. A rose ensures that a fine spray is delivered that will not wash away soil or damage plants. Hoses can also be used for hand-watering and many nozzles have been designed to deliver a shower of water rather than a jet.

Seep or drip hoses Generally, not many allotments will allow the use of sprinklers, so resourceful allotment-growers often put together a seep or drip hose system, fed from a watering can. These are essentially 'leaky pipes' that gradually release water into the soil over a large area. Bottle seep tubes provide a more localized solution and are a very cheap and easy way of delivering water just where it is needed at the base of a plant.

Standard hoses can also be used on some sites, and these offer the benefit of gradual delivery over a large area and can be operated manually from a mains water supply. A good watering every few days can be extremely beneficial to most plants, especially if recently planted.

WATERING PROBLEMS

These are usually the result of either too much or too little water being applied to the plant. Both over- and under-watering have similar symptoms because both are related to root death. An over-watered plant's root system begins to die off due to a lack of oxygen. The plant becomes short of water and wilts. Other problems can result from the wetting of foliage. Watering in full sunlight can give plants a scorched appearance, so water in the cool part of the day.

Right: *Water butts are both practical and environmentally friendly and ensure that the water is soft and free of added chemicals.*

FEEDING

In order for plants to grow and sustain their life processes, they require water and air as well as a range of naturally occurring elements. At least 16 different elements are needed by all plants for successful growth and development. Three of these elements – carbon, hydrogen and oxygen – are obtained from the carbon dioxide in the air and from the water and oxygen in the soil. In addition to these, plants also need a selection of other important nutrients, which are described here.

Above: *Foliar sprays are a quick and easy way for the plants to obtain nutrients in a short space of time.*

IMPORTANT PLANT NUTRIENTS

In addition to carbon, hydrogen and oxygen, plants need other important nutrients, which they obtain directly from the soil or compost (soil mix). These nutrients are commonly divided into two groups, depending upon whether they are found in plants in high or low concentrations. When they are found in high concentrations and are needed in large amounts, they are known as macro or major nutrients. There are three of these: nitrogen (N), phosphorus (P) and potassium (K). Every gardener must be fully aware of the functions of the 'essential three'. Nitrogen is basically the shoot and leaf maker and is especially important early in the growing season; phosphorus is used in the formation of roots; and potassium plays a vital role in flower and fruit formation and is also key to hardiness in overwintering plants. Elements that are needed in relatively small amounts are the micro or trace elements, of which there are ten. Among the most important of these are calcium, magnesium and sulphur, although all play a vital role in the growth and development of the plant.

FERTILIZERS

A wide variety of substances can boost nutrient levels. They should be used in addition to composts and manures.

Animal manure Bird manure is an organic source of nitrogen. Use in pellet form, as the fresh substance will burn plant roots.

Bonemeal Promotes strong root growth due to its high phosphate content. When using, always wear latex gloves.

Calcified seaweed This organic fertilizer raises the pH of the soil and adds calcium, like limestone, but also contains magnesium.

Fish, blood and bone A general fertilizer that is normally applied in the spring to promote root and shoot growth.

Ground limestone This raises the pH and supplies calcium where there is a deficiency. It is applied as a powder when it is needed.

Growmore This general-purpose fertilizer is used in spring and summer around the base of shrubs to give them a boost.

Hoof and horn This material gives a slow release of nitrogen where strong growth is needed and is applied in the spring or early summer.

Rock phosphate Used mostly to counter phosphate deficiency and as an alternative to bonemeal.

Seaweed meal Helps to build up humus levels in the soil and is used on a wide range of plants.

Wood ash An excellent source of potassium that can be added directly to the soil or to a compost heap.

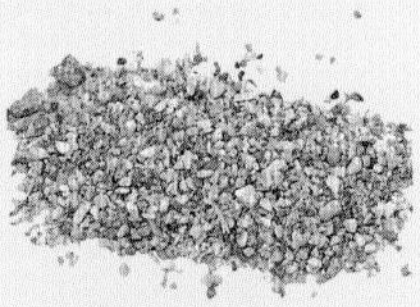

Bonemeal

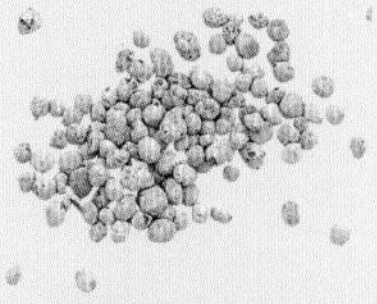

Calcified seaweed

Fish, blood and bone

Hoof and horn

FEEDING PLANTS

Numerous nutrient fertilizers are available. All have their relative advantages, but they should be used only as part of a combined strategy that aims to harness natural nutrient cycles, for example top-dressing the soil with well-rotted organic matter. This is the catalyst to nutrient cycling in the soil as it feeds the vast array of soil organisms that make use of essential plant nutrients. The majority of garden composts do not contain especially large amounts of the major plant nutrients; it is their long-term ability to feed soil life that makes them so valuable.

FURTHER FEEDING

Despite the best intentions, plants can become short of a certain type of nutrient. This is usually avoided by giving the plant a supplement of a 'plant food' that is rich in that particular nutrient. This can be applied as a foliar feed. Foliar feeding involves spraying a fine mist of a low-strength solution of the feed. The exact concentrations vary according to the feed being used, but a rough guide would be to use a quarter strength of that which you would apply as a liquid feed to the soil. The main benefit of foliar feeding is that the nutrient will be taken up quickly. The residue is best washed off after a couple of days. Applying a weak solution of Epsom salts as a foliar or liquid feed is an example of applying such a tonic.

MAKING COMFREY TEA

1 *Cut a large bundle of comfrey leaves from the patch in your allotment. Choose good, green, leafy growth. Remove the leaf and stem, but avoid using the crown.*

2 *Place in a plastic container with holes in the base. Weigh down the leaves. Line a second larger container with a plastic bag and place the first container inside. Tie the bag at the top.*

3 *The thick dark liquid from the decomposing comfrey leaves collects in the bag below. The lower bucket allows this to drip down and stores it until the process is complete.*

4 *Decant the finished liquid into a jam jar for later use. The liquid feed must be diluted before it is applied to plants at a ratio of about 10 parts water to 1 part concentrate.*

LIQUID FEEDS AND TEAS

Compost tea is easy to make. Comfrey is ideal for this, but stinging nettles are also very good. You could also use sheep or goat manure, or finely sifted compost from the heap. Simply fill an old pillowcase or burlap bag with your chosen material (comfrey, nettles, compost or manure) and sink it into a large bucket, dustbin (garbage can) or barrel of water. Cover the container and let it steep for a few days. Remember, the longer you steep, the stronger the tea will be. You may use the final 'brew' as a light liquid feed, and it can also be used as a foliar feeding medium, provided that it is well diluted. Don't throw the plant residue in the bag away as it can be used as a very effective mulch. An alternative method for making the tea is shown above.

Worm colonies in containers also produce a liquid feed that is a tonic for your plants. It should be diluted to a ratio of about 10 parts water to 1 part liquid feed. It is generally high in potassium and phosphorus. Wormeries can be bought on-line.

SYMPTOMS OF DEFICIENCY

Plants exhibit varying symptoms of a nutrient deficiency. General ones are stunted growth, discoloured leaves, including mottling and inter-veinal coloration, and the premature death of leaves or other parts of the plant. Plants may also display twisted or distorted growth as well as poor root growth and development. In many cases, the symptoms are often seen first in the plant's extremities, such as the tips of the shoots, as these are furthest away from the nutrient source. If a plant cannot obtain enough of any nutrient from a soil it will be because there is either little or no nutrient present in the soil, or the nutrient is not 'available' to the plant.

Any element can also be toxic to the plant if it is present in sufficiently high amounts or out of balance with other elements in the growing medium.

OTHER FEEDING METHODS

1 *An alternative method of feeding is to use a good-quality liquid feed. This is most useful for plants that are growing in containers. Add the fertilizer of your choice to one of the waterings, according to the manufacturer's instructions.*

2 *Granular fertilizer can be applied by hand, spreading it over the area covered by the roots below. Follow the manufacturer's instructions. You may wish to protect your hands when applying the fertilizer by wearing a pair of gloves.*

3 *Apply a layer of well-rotted organic material, such as farmyard manure or garden compost, to the surface of the soil around the plant. If the plant is not shallow-rooted, lightly fork the material into the top layer of the soil.*

PLANT NUTRIENTS

The following table highlights the characteristics of the soil nutrients. Symptoms of deficiency may be seen on different parts of the plant at different stages of growth, although it may not always be immediately obvious that a plant is suffering from a nutrient deficiency. Some of the more important symptoms that can be seen on plants are listed below, together with remedies and toxicity causes.

PLANT NUTRIENT	NATURAL ORGANIC SOURCE	PLANTS MOST IN NEED	SOILS MOST IN NEED	SIGNS OF SHORTAGE	HOW TO AVOID SHORTAGE	TOXICITY CAUSE
Major plant nutrients						
Nitrogen (N) The 'leaf maker'	Bird manure, blood and bone, grass clippings	Vegetables grown for their leaves, such as lettuce and spinach	Sandy soils in rainy areas	Stunted growth; small pale green leaves; weak stems	Apply a base dressing before sowing or planting. Top-dress in spring and summer with organic matter.	Excessive use of nitrogen-rich fertilizer
Phosphates (P_2O_5) The 'root maker'	Comfrey, seagrass, horse manure, blood and bone	Young plants, root vegetables, such as carrots, and fruit	Sandy soils	Stunted roots and stems; small leaves with a purplish tinge; low fruit yield	Apply a base dressing of bonemeal. Use fish, blood and bone when top-dressing plants.	Excessive use of fertilizer
Potash (K_2O) The 'flower and fruit maker'	Comfrey, horse manure, seagrass	Fruit, flowers and potatoes	Sandy soils	Leaf edges turn yellow, then brown; low fruit yield; fruit and flowers poorly coloured	Apply a compound organic fertilizer or wood ash as a base dressing or top-dressing.	Excessive use of fertilizer; lack of magnesium
Minor plant nutrients						
Boron (B)	Beetroot (beet) leaves, horse manure, compost, seagrass, untreated sawdust	Root vegetables, top fruit (apples, pears etc.)	Sandy soils	Brown heart (roots); narrow leaves; corky patches on fruit	Top-dress with compost or apply borax in severe cases.	Irrigation water
Calcium (Ca)	Dandelion, lucerne hay, comfrey, horse manure, compost, blood and bone	Fruit, vegetables, flowers	Acid and potash-rich soils	Similar to nitrogen shortage – stunted growth and pale green leaves	Apply lime or use gypsum or calcified seaweed.	High pH causes toxicity for some acid-loving plants
Copper (Cu)	Nettles, yarrow, horse manure, dandelion, chickweed, compost, untreated sawdust	Fruit, vegetables	Sandy soils	Dieback; brown spots on leaves	Top-dress with compost.	Copper-based fungicides
Iron (Fe)	Stinging nettle, compost, dandelion, horse manure, spinach and seaweed	Soft fruit, strawberries and carrots	Chalky soils	Yellowing of younger leaves	Trouble can occur on chalky, peaty, very light and acid soils. Iron shortage in chalky soil is due to lock-up by calcium and hard to avoid.	Rare
Magnesium (Mg)	Grass clippings, seagrass	Tomatoes	Sandy, peaty and potash-rich soils	Yellow or brown patches between veins of older leaves	Apply a mulch of compost or Epsom salts if deficiency is severe.	None
Manganese (Mn)	Chickweed, compost, untreated sawdust	Many crops, especially peas	Chalky soils	Yellowing between the veins of older leaves	Shortage in chalky soils is due to lock-up by calcium (see iron). Acidification for some plants.	None
Molybdenum (Mo)	Cornstalks, compost, grass clippings	Brassicas, such as cabbage	Acid soils	Narrow leaves	Apply lime and top-dress with compost.	None
Sodium (Na)	Seaweed	Root vegetables, fruit	Sandy soils	Very rare except in a few seaside-loving plants	Not usually warranted.	Land reclaimed from sea
Sulphur (S)	Cabbage leaves	All plants	Soils in rural areas	Stunted growth and pale green leaves	A light dusting of flowers of sulphur during the year.	Industrial sites and acid rain
Zinc (Zn)	Horse manure, corn stalks, garden compost, untreated sawdust	Fruit, vegetables	Sandy soils	Dieback	Top-dress with compost.	Leaching from containers

Above: *If you are using a bought fertilizer, always read the label and only apply the recommended dose, to avoid overfeeding.*

Above: *Excessive fertilizer use results in nutrients leaching into watercourses, causing problems such as algal bloom.*

PROBLEMS CAUSED BY OVERFEEDING

While we tend to associate nutrient-related problems with a shortage, applying excessive fertilizer also brings a host of problems, both for your plants and ultimately for the wider environment. Overfeeding plants is, at its most basic level, wasteful. Plants can only take up a certain amount of nutrients, and the majority of any excess is usually lost through leaching (being washed away by water). Leaching of nutrients does not destroy them, however, and while lost to your own plants, the soil water that seeps away from your plot ultimately must go somewhere. This is usually to groundwater (aquifers) or slow-flowing underground rivers, and from these sources it can enter drinking water supplies, surface-flowing rivers or ultimately the sea, causing problems such as eutrophication, which can lead to a reduction in oxygen levels in that water. Although your own contribution to this would of course be very small indeed, it does no good when it is leached away, and is ultimately a form of pollution – one that is easily avoided.

Before leaching of excess nutrient happens however, high concentrations of fertilizer in the soil can cause considerable damage to the roots of your crops. In essence, a high concentration of plant food in the soil starts to reverse the process that roots use to remove water and dissolved nutrient from the soil. The effect is akin to burning the roots and the knock-on effects will be seen through changed growth patterns and an overall loss of condition to the plant.

Leaves and new shoots on your plants are often the first things to show visible signs of overfeeding, and the symptoms are often very similar to drought stress – due to the loss of healthy root – but in young plants can easily be mistaken for lack of nutrients. Indeed, young plants are especially sensitive to overfeeding, particularly in the time following transplanting or planting out.

A simple rule of thumb for spotting the symptoms are: leaves that curl under from the outside margins or hook downward at the tips (as the plant tries to retain moisture), gradually becoming darker green and brittle or glossy, are the commonest sign of overfeeding; discoloration, spotting or mottling of older leaves, accompanied by reduced leaf and shoot size of new growth, on the other hand, are all common signs of underfeeding.

Even if plants are not directly harmed by overfeeding, imbalances to their nutrition can still cause unwanted growth patterns, so it is important to try and get it right. Excessive nitrogen applied to fruiting crops may encourage large amounts of foliage while inhibiting the production of flowers and ultimately fruit. If nitrogen is applied late in the year, plants make excessive 'soft' growth that is less hardy and root crops overfed with nitrogen may become tough, fibrous or poor-tasting.

MAKING LIQUID MANURE

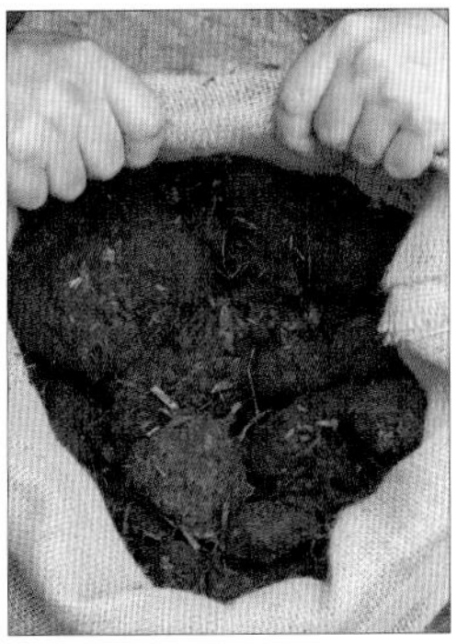

1 *Fill a permeable bag or sack with some fresh animal manure using 1 litre (1½ pints) manure for every 10 litres (2 gallons) of water you intend using.*

2 *Tie the top of the bag with string and submerge the bag in a dustbin (garbage can) filled with water. Leave for 1 month in warm weather or 3 months if cooler.*

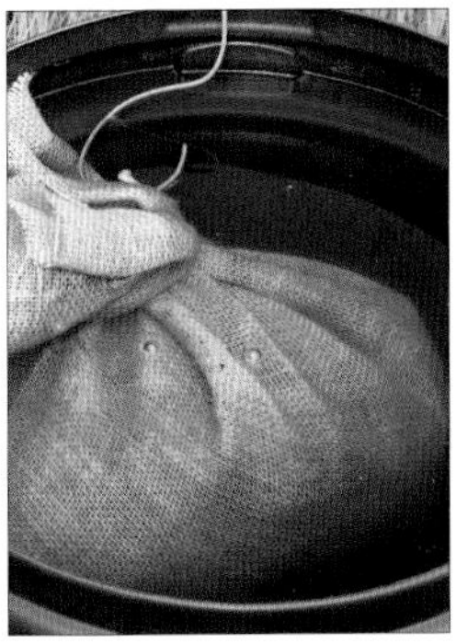

3 *Once the manure has soaked sufficiently, dilute with water in a 2:1 ratio, wearing gloves. Avoid using it directly on crops that will be harvested soon.*

STAKING AND SUPPORT

Above: *Young, straight branches, such as these hazel rods, make an excellent method of support that you can even grow yourself.*

Staking the plants on your allotment not only makes the area look tidier, but it also allows crops to grow and bloom without toppling over, breaking, or smothering smaller plants nearby. It will also save you a considerable amount of space. What is more, staking improves air circulation, meaning that your plants will be less likely to suffer from common fungal diseases. Staking must be done early on in the growing season, preferably when the plant is young, if you want the full benefit from it.

WHICH PLANTS NEED STAKING?

The decision to stake a plant depends largely upon what it is. Low-growing sturdy crops often need no support, whereas taller heavy cropping types, such as tomatoes, usually require robust supports in order to help them carry a full load of fruit. Equally, cut flower species, such as dahlias, can also benefit from a strong stake in order to support heavy flower heads from toppling and breaking the stems, particularly during windy spells or heavy showers. Many fruit trees require staking, either when young or if they are grown as cordons. Soft fruit bushes, especially cane fruits, also benefit considerably from support.

Staking your crops generally results in cleaner produce that is less susceptible to damage, allows more air and sunlight to reach the plants, and makes cultivation and harvesting easier. In addition, it is a more efficient use of space and this, combined with the other advantages, can ultimately mean that you get higher yields from your available space.

Having said this, this 'intensified' approach to your plot can mean that more frequent watering is needed and that extra time is spent preparing the plot and tying in the growing plants. Many allotment-growers believe that this is time well spent, so it is worth trying.

STAKING MATERIALS

There is a wide range of materials that can be used to stake your plants and each of these has their relative merits and drawbacks. Ideally, the best materials are those you have to hand, but if you have to purchase materials then you should think carefully about what you want them to do before spending too much money.

Natural materials such as timber, bamboo, branch-wood or twigs are freely obtainable and, provided that you are careful about their origin, tend to be a renewable resource. The fact that they are natural in origin does mean that they tend to rot and need replacing, sometimes on a yearly basis.

Right: *An excellent way of recycling old materials is to use scrapped scaffold poles and clips to make a robust frame for climbing plants. Nets and wires can be fixed on to the frame to support runner (green) beans, sweet peas and gourds.*

Far right: *Bamboo is traditionally used for staking and support. Bamboo canes are strong, light and durable. If cleaned at the end of the growing season and stored in a dry area, the canes can be used for a few years.*

Above: *Wooden trellises are a lightweight, durable and cheap way to divide the plot, providing an ideal place to support climbers.*

Left: *Although a shed takes up space, using it to support a climber such as this vine makes it a productive area once more.*

There is a range of synthetic materials, including plastics, uPVC, carbon fibre poles, and galvanized or plastic-coated metal. A huge number of brands and designs are available, almost all of which have two things in common: they are durable and, as a consequence of their manufacture, quite costly. Arguably, however, their longevity offsets these initial costs.

STAKING METHODS

Stakes are an ideal way to support individual plants, particularly those with one central stem, such as young trees.

Cages and frames are particularly good for bushier specimens that need all-round support and have the added bonus of cutting out the need for tying. Having said this, the design of some types can make pruning or pinching out side-shoots difficult, resulting in crowded growth inside the cage itself.

Trellises are essentially a lattice-work panel traditionally made of timber, although synthetic substitutes are increasingly common. There are many designs available, some of which can be fixed on to a wall to provide support for climbers, while others can be used as free-standing supports.

Wires may be attached to a wall or fence to provide support for climbing plants in a similar way to a trellis. Wires can also be stretched horizontally between posts or stakes to provide support for plants such as cane fruits, or as a crisscross framework for climbers.

Sticks and twigs are used either as protection for seedlings or support for low-growing plants. Twiggy sticks are often called pea sticks by gardeners, due to their suitability for supporting shorter varieties of peas and beans.

TYING MATERIALS

The way that you attach the plant to a support is arguably just as important as the support itself. Ideally, ties must be flexible and slightly loose to allow the plant room to grow without tearing, ripping or scarring the plant stem. Natural materials such as raffia or twine do of course have the advantage of being biodegradable and if combined with natural supports mean that the whole system is derived from renewable sources.

Synthetic materials are mostly made of coated wire, Velcro, plastic or rubber and there are a numerous 'systems' available. Although some of these can be reused, the majority cannot, and they must be disposed of and not composted.

BASIC PRUNING

The task of pruning can seem a daunting prospect to some gardeners, but there is, in fact, no great mystery surrounding pruning and a few basic rules are all you need to get started in most cases. At its simplest level, pruning should be regarded as a way of introducing some order to your allotment, giving your plants space to grow and look their best, while also controlling them within a set area. The following section provides some basic advice to enable you to prune with confidence.

Above: *Cuts should be made like this one, just above a bud or a pair of buds, but not so close that you risk damaging the buds.*

WHY IS PRUNING NECESSARY?

Pruning is usually carried out to control the growth of stronger subjects that may otherwise damage those of a weaker habit growing alongside; it also ensures plants do not outgrow their allocated space and cause an obstruction. Pruning is also used especially on fruit trees and bushes to train a plant to a specific shape or form; to maintain or improve flowering; and to improve the shape or 'balance' of an individual shrub or tree. Finally, it is used to remove dead, damaged, diseased or pest-infected growth. This last type of pruning is referred to as hygienic pruning and helps maintain plant health and vigour.

Constant pruning, however, is not always necessary for the good cultivation of plants. Once a plant has become established and the initial framework has been formed, pruning is often reduced to a minimum. The major exceptions to this include plants that are pruned annually in order to improve flowering, fruiting or quality of foliage. Apples, peaches and other fruit trees and bushes are regularly pruned to increase the yield of fruit.

SUCCESSFUL PRUNING

There are arguably two hallmarks of good pruning: a well-planned, careful and methodical approach to the work undertaken; and a good knowledge of the requirements of the plants that are to be pruned. The real results may not always be apparent for months and, in the case of trees, for years.

With secateurs (hand pruners), always try to place the thin blade on the trunk/branch side of the cut. This will result in a short stub and will also prevent a layer of damaged cambium tissue being left immediately under the line of the cut, which could lead to disease entering the wound.

Cuts should always be made immediately above a bud or a pair of buds and should be done as cleanly as possible. Use well-maintained secateurs that are regularly sharpened. Make sure that you do not position your blade too close to the bud or the tissue connecting the bud to the main plant body could be damaged and this would affect fruiting. As a guide you should cut 1–3mm ($\frac{1}{16}$–$\frac{1}{8}$in) above a bud to ensure it is not damaged during cutting.

Be careful when using a saw close to a trunk or stem to remove heavier thicker branches. The weight of the branch can sometimes cause splitting and tearing to the main stem wood or bark. Injuries such as these often increase the likelihood of disease affecting the plant.

A simple rule of thumb when deciding what to cut is to remember the 'D's. These are: dead, dying, diseased, displaced or deformed branches. All of these must be

Above: *Long-handled pruners are essentially secateurs on long handles, and will cut through thicker wood and more inacessible shoots compared to secateurs.*

Above: *It is important that you always cut out and remove any dead or diseased wood. For thicker material, you may need to use either secateurs or a saw.*

Above: *Most soft and bush fruit needs to be pruned back once it has been planted. Remove any weak growth completely, then cut back the longer shoots by half.*

PRUNING AUTUMN RASPBERRIES

1 *Autumn raspberries are pruned differently from summer ones. As with all raspberries, during the winter they consist of a mixture of fruited and new canes.*

2 *Regardless of what sort of raspberries they are, the canes should all be cut right down to the ground using secateurs (pruners) and completely removed.*

3 *Once the canes have been cut back, new growth quickly appears. Once the canes are tall enough, they should be tied in to supporting wires.*

removed as the first stage of any pruning work. Then add to this list the 'C's: criss-crossing branches and crowded growth, taking care (arguably the most important 'C'!) all the time to ensure that you avoid removing too much growth. Finally, once you have cleared this material, it is possible to see what further work needs to be done.

Many species have very specific pruning requirements, based largely upon their growth habits, its effect upon cropping and ultimately their tolerance of the treatment. Reading up on the specific requirements of the bush or tree in hand is essential, therefore, if you are going to get the best results, and well worth the time that it takes. Make a few notes in a notebook to help remind you what these are before you start and always be prepared to take a little time when pruning. Acting too hastily can easily spoil the job. Finally, remember that pruning is best viewed intermittently from a distance. You can only cut a branch once, and if you cut the wrong one, you cannot effectively rejoin it. Always check that you know the full extent of a branch and what effect its removal will have, therefore, prior to making the cut.

Above: *Cutting back new growth on a pear or apple tree at just the right time will reduce its vigour and promote the formation of fruiting spurs.*

Above: *It is often necessary to thin out some of the foliage on a fig bush in order to expose the developing fruit to sufficient sunlight to ripen well.*

PRUNING EQUIPMENT

There is a range of tools that can be used for pruning. It is advisable to use the correct tool for a specific task because it will make the process both easier and more efficient.

Pruning knife Using a pruning knife requires both skill and a sharp blade. A blunt knife can easily damage the plant. Cut away from you and keep hands clear of the direction of the cut.

Secateurs (hand pruners) When small branches are to be removed, it is easiest to use secateurs and remove the branch in one go. Secateurs are the commonest type of pruning tool and are best used on twiggy material up to about the width of a pencil.

Loppers Use these on branches up to 2.5cm (1in) thick. Loppers are useful in situations where secateurs may not easily reach, such as in dense tangled shrubs. Loppers should not be used for very thick branches or they may easily be damaged.

Extension loppers Ideal for cutting out-of-reach branches up to 2.5cm (1in) thick. They are a useful tool but they can be tiring to use and require some practice.

Ratchet and snap cut shears These have three times the power of conventional shears. Used for branches up to 4cm (1½in) in diameter.

Narrow curved Grecian saw Use on branches up to 5cm (2in) in diameter where the branches are very crowded. It cuts on a pulling cut, making its use above shoulder height very easy.

Extension saw This is similar to the Grecian pruning saw, but has an extended handle. It is very useful where larger branches need removing from smaller fruiting trees.

Bow saw Used for cutting larger branches. Available in various sizes. It cuts with a pushing cut, making its use above shoulder height tiring.

HARVESTING AND STORING VEGETABLES

There are few hard and fast rules for harvesting your crops, but you need to plan how you intend to do this. When you go out into your allotment, it is tempting to pick only the good vegetables and leave the rest. You should, however, always pick and compost poor or rotten ones as well as harvesting the best of the crop. Diseased or damaged crops can begin to rot and could infect or damage the remaining harvest.

Above: *Onions are an easy crop to store and last for several months provided that you dry and ripen them thoroughly first.*

PLANNING A SUCCESSFUL HARVEST

The key to a successful harvest lies not just in its execution, but in careful advanced planning. If you staggered the sowing or planting of crops, you should ensure that vegetables mature and ripen over a longer period, and this of course has the advantage that you don't need to deal with it all at once. It is also important that you have set plans in motion as to how you intend to store the inevitable excess. Crops stored incorrectly often deteriorate very quickly and can become unusable. Storing fresh produce may also need plenty of space: space that is cool, dry and free from unwelcome visitors such as mice or other pests.

You need to think about storage from the outset then, and have your plans in place ahead of the start of the harvest season for the crops in question. After all, once the harvest begins in earnest, you will find that you have very little time, between gathering the 'fruits' of your labours, preparing it for storage and getting the plot cleared and ready for a new crop.

TIMING YOUR HARVEST

The timing of a harvest will of course vary according to the crop in question. Winter and spring crops such as some brassicas and root crops, can be harvested intermittently throughout the cool season. Other crops only grow in warmer seasons, meaning that the availability of produce is markedly seasonal. In addition to this, some crops are only fit for consumption once they have passed a particular growth stage or fully ripened. For others though, the decision as to when they are ready to be picked fresh from the plot is simply a matter of taste. Some people prefer to pick young less developed beans for instance, whereas others prefer their beans more 'mature.' Salad leaves can be taken as baby leaves, as can squashes and courgettes (zucchini); picking what you need at the time that you need it, meaning that you gather a little and often rather than waiting for a heavy harvest later.

Above: *Harvested marrows and pumpkins can be stored in trays that should be kept in a cool, dark place.*

WHY STORE CROPS?

Whilst it is always preferable to have fresh rather than stored vegetables, this is only really feasible for most crops during their growing season. As the yearly harvest inevitably peaks during late summer times of glut ensue, and there is only so much that can be traded between you and your neighbours. The problem with a large and sudden amount of fresh produce, however, is that it rarely stays that. If left, it quickly goes past its best and in the worst case scenario, rots or otherwise spoils. In addition, harvest times are often followed by shortages. As the summer glut subsides, the autumn pickings gradually become

CLAMP-STORING POTATOES

1 *Clear a patch of ground approximately $1m^2$ (1 sq yd), and dig a trench, 10cm (4in) deep, filling it with clean, dry straw.*

2 *Pile the potatoes into a pyramid shape on top of the straw, the base of which should be no more than 50cm (18in) across.*

3 *Cover the potato pile with a further layer of straw, piling this to around 15cm (6 in) thick over the whole of the pile.*

4 *Dig a trench to improve drainage, and pile 15cm (6in) of soil over the clamp, leaving a straw-filled hole in the middle.*

LIFTING POTATOES

1 *Unless you need new-potatoes, wait until the top growth withers as they continue to grow under the ground until then.*

2 *Use a fork to lift the potatoes, shaking free any soil that is attached to them; leave them to dry on the surface for a couple of hours.*

3 *Once they have dried, brush off any remaining soil and carefully inspect them; avoid storing damaged or blemished ones.*

more meagre and the range of winter produce, whilst each may be individually satisfying, is rather limited to a few of the hardiest crops. Ironically the time between early to late spring often marks what is known as the 'hungry gap', a period between the last of the winter crops and start of the early crops where fresh produce can be scarce. Storing produce helps alleviate this, and means that you get the best all-year-round value possible from your plot.

HOW TO STORE VEGETABLES

When it comes to storing crops, there are several options. Root vegetables and some brassicas can be left in the ground in all but the coldest winters, lifting them as and when they are needed. Some, such as parsnips, actually develop a better taste after they have been subjected to frost and cabbages become all the sweeter in the cooler months. In very cold areas, or if heavy frost threatens, root crops can be lifted and stored in a cool dark place. Brush away as much soil as possible (do not wash them) before laying them on around 1cm (½in) of sand or a layer of newspaper in the bottom of a wooden box, making sure they don't touch each other. Cover the crop with a mixture of sand and a sterile organic substance such as coir, untreated sawdust, fine leaf-mould, fine bark or sterilized soil before adding another layer of roots. Repeat this layering until the box is full to the top and all are covered. Repeat with another box if necessary. Place in a frost-free environment such as a shed or cellar.

Other vegetables can be stored on shelves or in boxes, ensuring that they do not touch each other. Onions and garlic may be kept in open sacks or in strings. Cabbages can be kept in nets, hung in a cool dark place until needed for up to 2–3 months. Other brassicas, such as sprouts, are best kept outside, harvesting them as needed.

FREEZING AND PRESERVING

Vegetables usually need some preparation prior to being frozen to make the process more successful. This is usually done by blanching them for a couple of minutes in order to destroy enzymes that would otherwise cause the vegetables to deteriorate quickly. Blanching also helps to keep the colour, texture and flavour and to retain vitamin C content. The vegetables are mostly prepared as you would normally before being plunged into the boiling water for about 2–3 minutes. They are then removed, drained immediately and plunged into a bowl of iced water to cool them as quickly as possible. Once cooled, they are drained once again, patted-dry on kitchen paper, packed and frozen in single-portion bags. The other option is to cook the vegetables as part of a recipe, then freeze them.

Lastly, a good way to preserve fresh vegetables is to pickle them or make other forms of preserve such as chutneys. As with so many things, the way you choose to store your produce will largely be a matter of taste. The best option is often to try as many methods as you can to maintain the maximum variety through the winter.

CROPS FOR STORING OVER WINTER

Harvest time often brings the problem of a crop glut. Storage can enable you to enjoy this bounty for longer.

Asparagus Best consumed fresh. Cook or blanch before freezing.
Aubergines (eggplants) Cook before freezing.
Beetroot (beets) Shelf storage or pickling.
Bell peppers Blanch before freezing. Pickle or dry.
Broad (fava) beans Freezing or drying.
Brussels sprouts Freezing. Leave on plant until needed.
Cabbages Freezing or shelf storage. Leave in ground in mild conditions.
Carrots Leave in ground in mild conditions. Shelf storage.
Cauliflowers Blanch before freezing. Shelf storage if hung upside down in dark and misted.
Celery Cook before freezing. Limited shelf storage.
Courgettes (zucchini) Cook before freezing. Limited shelf storage.
Dwarf French beans (bush green beans) Freezing.
Garlic In sacks or strung.
Kale Harvest through winter.
Kohl rabi Leave in ground if mild or protected. Medium shelf storage.
Leeks Freezing. Leave in ground in mild conditions. Shelf storage.
Marrows (zucchini) Cook before freezing. Shelf storage.
Onions In sacks or strung.
Parsnips Leave in ground until needed, or late winter.
Peas Freezing or drying on plant.
Potatoes Store in paper sacks once cleaned and dried.
Pumpkins Cook before freezing. Good shelf storage if fully ripe.
Rhubarb Cook before freezing.
Runner (green) beans Freezing.
Shallots In sacks or strung.
Spinach Cook before freezing.
Swedes (rutabaga or yellow turnip) Leave in ground until needed (may go woody by late winter).
Sweetcorn (corn) Freezing or pickling.
Tomatoes Cook before freezing. Pickle.
Turnips Leave in ground until needed.

HARVESTING AND STORING HERBS

Many commonly used culinary herbs such as basil, coriander (cilantro), chives and parsley can be grown successfully outdoors during the summer months. If you are not able to spare growing room on allotment vegetable beds, they are easily grown in pots and can be sited around sheds or seating areas. Herbs are very easily harvested and most of the storage techniques are simple and straightforward.

Above: *Aromatic herbs such as rosemary (*Rosmarinus officinalis*) can be used to flavour bottles of vinegar or olive oil.*

HOW TO HARVEST HERBS

Various parts of herbs, including the leaves, flowers, fruits and seeds, are gathered at different times, depending upon the plant and the part that provides the desirable properties. Annual leafy herbs such as basil (*Ocimum basilicum*) and parsley (*Petroselinum crispum*) should be carefully picked, never taking more than about 10 per cent of the growth in a single picking.

The same is true of perennials such as sage (*Salvia officinalis*), thyme (*Thymus vulgaris*) and rosemary (*Rosmarinus officinalis*) because severe pruning or over-stripping of the leaves will weaken the plant. It is important that you do not remove more than one-third of the growth at any one time. If you harvest carefully, you will get a more vigorous leaf growth that will result in healthier plants.

Above: *The best time to harvest herbs is usually just before they flower. This is when they have their strongest flavour.*

As a general rule, pick herbs just before the plant is about to flower, which is when they have the strongest flavour. Pick the leaves when they are fresh and at their sweetest, selecting blemish-free, upper leaves. Collect the leaves in early morning or late evening, provided they are dry, rather than in bright afternoon sun when the plant's sap is rising. This is when the aroma of herbs is at its strongest and is easily lost if picked during this time of day. Flowers such as borage (*Borago officinalis*) and lavender (*Lavandula angustifolia*), however, are best picked just before they reach full bloom and once they begin to open in the heat of the day.

Rhizomes, such as ginger and turmeric, are collected in autumn, just as the leaves begin to change colour and the maximum amount of nutrition has been stored. Use a fork to gently free the roots from the soil and always avoid 'hand-pulling' them. Choose only the best ones and use a vegetable brush to gently loosen any dirt. If you do need to wash them, do so quickly in cold water and avoid soaking them, as this can result in lost flavour.

Harvesting seeds tends to vary from plant to plant. Some seeds, like those of borage, simply fall to the ground as soon as they are ripe. Thyme seeds are very small and hard to see. Parsley and coriander seeds shake off very easily, and frequently the plants will have sown next year's crop for you before you realize they have gone to seed. One method of harvesting any seed that is difficult to collect is to tie a small paper bag over the flower head when the seeds start to form, ensuring that you can collect the seed without losing any. It would be advisable to use this method for collecting from plants with small seed as they can drop off when ripe or sometimes spring from the plant.

Above: *Herbs can be dried for later use by hanging them in bunches in a dry place out of direct sunlight.*

DRYING HERBS AND FLOWERS

Store herbs in a cool, dry place with minimum exposure to air and sunlight. One of the most popular methods of preserving them for use during the winter months is drying. This method can actually improve the flavour of some herbs, particularly the leaves of bay trees (*Laurus nobilis*). Herbs may be dried in bundles secured with a rubber band or string and hung upside down from a rack in a dry location such as an airing cupboard or shed.

When drying the herbs, the temperature of the area should not exceed 30°C (86°F) because the plants' essential oils will evaporate at or above this temperature. Do not dry your herbs in the kitchen where they will be spoiled by the humidity caused by cooking.

Fresh herbs can also be placed in brown paper bags. Remember to label the bags because it will be hard to distinguish between the herbs once they have dried. Store in a dry, dark, cool place until the herbs inside are dry, shaking the bags occasionally so that the plants dry evenly. Remove any stems and store the dried herbs in airtight jars. Keep the jars away from light to protect the colour and flavour of the herbs. Roots are best chopped into small pieces and dried in an oven. In general, you can expect those that you have grown and dried yourself to last at least two years.

Above: *After herbs have been hung up to dry, separate the seeds from the dry flower heads before storing in tightly sealed jars.*

STORING HERBS

Herbs can also be preserved in other ways, so that you can use them in cooking throughout the year.

Herb salts In a cool oven, spread a layer of ground salt on a sheet of baking parchment. Sprinkle the chopped fresh herbs on top of the salt and bake for 10–20 minutes. When the herbs are dry, let them cool and place in a jar. Chives, oregano, thyme, lemon balm, lemon thyme, parsley, rosemary and basil can all be treated this way.

Puréeing This method involves mixing approximately 60ml (4tbsp) of olive oil with 2 litres (8 cups) fresh basil leaves which have been washed and dried. These are blended in a processor until puréed before being transferred to a jar. Stir each time you use it and top with a thin layer of oil afterwards. The purée should keep for up to one year in a refrigerator.

Freezing herbs Herbs such as dill, fennel, basil and parsley freeze well. The herbs should be cleaned and put into separate, labelled freezer bags. Alternatively, chop the leaves and freeze them with a little water in ice-cube trays. Chop the herbs finely, filling each cube, half with herbs and half with water, before freezing. Transfer the frozen cubes to plastic bags and label. Frozen herbs are best used within six months.

HERBAL INFUSIONS

You can also make a hot infusion of leafy herbs by placing the herb and any fine-quality olive oil in a glass bowl. This is then placed over a pan of gently simmering water and heated gently for about three hours, ensuring that the water in the pan does not dry out. The strained oil, once it has cooled, should be stored in airtight bottles or jars.

A cool infusion of flowery herbs involves using fresh herbs such as chamomile which are ground with a pestle and mortar and packed into a large jar and covered with oil. The sealed jar is then left in a warm, sunny place for two to three weeks and shaken occasionally. It is then strained and placed into airtight jars or bottles where it can be stored for up to a year.

A simple way of creating aromatic olive oil is to simply add a large sprig of your chosen herbs – rosemary and mint are good choices – to a bottle of olive oil. Store the bottle in a cool dark place for about ten days before using.

You can also make you own herbal vinegars by adding fresh herbs such as tarragon or rosemary or cloves of garlic, slices of ginger, chillies or peppercorns and all-spice powder to white vinegar. Crush about a quarter litre volume (1 cup) of loosely packed fresh herbs for each litre of vinegar. If you are using dried herbs, use half the amount of herb stated above. It is important that you use only commercially prepared vinegars, as home-made vinegar may not have a low enough pH to prevent bacterial growth. Place the vinegar in a pot on the stove and heat, but do not boil. Place the herbs in a clean, sterilized jar and slightly crush them. Pour the vinegar over the herbs and cover the jar tightly. Let the herb-vinegar mixture steep in a dark place at room temperature, shaking the jar every couple of days. After a week, strain the vinegar and place in bottles and store for up to six weeks.

DRYING AND FREEZING HERBS

1 *Pick seed just as it is ripening. Place the seeds on a tray or in a paper or muslin (cheesecloth) bag. Leave in a cool, dark place for a few days until the seed is dry.*

2 *Herb seeds that have been dried can be stored in old glass jars with an airtight lid. Store the jars in a cool, dry, dark place and label them for future reference.*

3 *Herbs can be frozen in ice-cube trays. Fill the trays with water after you have added the herbs to make ready-to-use cubes. Herbs can also be packed into freezer bags.*

HARVESTING AND STORING FRUIT

When harvesting your fruits, you will find that there is only so much you can eat fresh or give away. There is always surplus fruit left over and you are faced with the question of what to do with it. Leaving some on the plant to help feed the wildlife at your allotment is a good idea, but storing the rest of the excess fruit using a variety of methods will ensure that you can eat your home-grown produce over a longer period of time.

Above: *Damaged fruits are no good for storing but if left on the plant they will feed a whole host of visiting wildlife.*

HOW TO HARVEST FRUIT

The key to successfully storing fruit begins well before harvesting commences. Your first objective should be to grow fruit that is as healthy as possible because it will be the best for storage. Harvesting immature crops or attempting to save those that are in poor condition – due perhaps to a lack of water or nutrients or to pest and disease damage – can lead to many storage losses.

There are several ways that fruit can be stored and the condition of the picked crop will usually be the deciding factor as to which of these you should use. Top fruit such as apples and pears can often be stored fresh through most of the winter, whereas stone fruits and berries, such as peaches, strawberries and raspberries, must be quickly consumed, turned into a preserve or frozen.

Careful handling, both during and following harvesting, is essential because, from the moment they are harvested (and in many cases well before), crops have no means of repairing any physical damage that they may suffer. Even firm, strong-looking fruit such as apples can easily be bruised, although the damage may well not show up immediately.

As well as good handling, a careful selection of the fruits during harvesting is essential for successful storage. You should inspect the picked fruits and select only those of the best quality for fresh storage. Reject any that have a broken skin or show any sign of pest or disease damage. Do not throw them on the compost heap yet, however, because damaged fruit may well be useful for making preserves such as jellies and jams, or for freezing.

It is also a good idea to leave a small percentage of mature fruit on the plants when you are harvesting to help feed the surrounding bird and insect population.

STORING FRUIT

In general, the storage area for fruit must be frost-free, safe from pests, rainproof and ideally kept at a constant temperature. The long-term storage of any fruit calls for

STORING FRUIT

To store surplus fruit and avoid the risk of rotting, make sure that you use the appropriate method.

Apples, pears and quinces Store in a cool place for up to 12 months, depending on the variety.

All other fruit Eat immediately or freeze. Alternatively, preserve fruit by bottling or making into jam. Fruit can be kept for up to 12 months, depending on the method of preservation that has been used.

Below left: *Pick soft fruits such as strawberries, raspberries and gooseberries carefully to avoid bruising the fruit.*

Below: *Pears can last for up to 12 months, depending upon the variety. Lay them in a recycled box, ensuring that the fruits do not touch and air can circulate around the fruit.*

Above: *Fruit trays, recycled from supermarkets, make ideal storage boxes for surplus fruit. The trays should be kept over winter in a cool, dry place such as a garage or shed.*

Above: *Soft fruit is best placed in small individual containers as it is picked to prevent it being squashed and spoiling. Store in a refrigerator or other cool place.*

cool conditions with adequate ventilation. If you have space, consider having a separate refrigerator for fruit storage, or choose an area with a low temperature that does not go below freezing. A shed or garage can be ideal, in many cases, but even these spaces may need extra insulation if winter weather conditions become especially severe. Some houses have a basement, cellar or unheated room that may be ideally suited for the task. Attics, however, are not recommended for fruit storage because of their wide temperature fluctuations and variable humidity.

It is worthwhile trying out a variety of different storage methods. This can be done by splitting the crop up and then trying out different locations in your home. You will soon find which are the best places to store fruit, and what areas are best for storing a particular kind of fruit.

Ensure that you check the stored fruit regularly, at least weekly, removing any that show signs of decay. Remember the old adage that 'one bad apple spoils the whole barrel'? This can be true for your crop too unless you prevent rots from spreading. The unblemished parts can often still be used for eating or cooking. If lots of fruits begin to rot simultaneously, it could be that the storage conditions are not suitable, the crop has reached its maximum 'shelf-life' or the fruit was not of sufficiently good quality to start with.

FREEZING AND PRESERVING

Storing fruit in the freezer is an excellent way of storing all the surplus crop that has been produced in your plot. Unfortunately, fruit tends to lose its firmness once it has been frozen, although the taste will remain more or less the same. Raspberries, for example, are best used for making pies or flans after they have been frozen and will be of very poor quality if they are eaten raw. Most fruits can be frozen after they have been stewed or puréed; this is true of fruits such as apples and plums.

Fruits such as strawberries and blackcurrants that do not easily submit to long-term storage are excellent candidates for jam-(jelly-) making. This is surprisingly simple to do and there are many recipes available in cookbooks and on the Internet.

Above: *Fermenting is a great way of storing your excess rhubarb and will keep in the fridge for several months unopened.*

Above: *One of the simplest ways of preserving fruit is to freeze it, although once frozen, most fruits are only good for cooking.*

Above: *Bottling fruit in alcohol is an ideal way to preserve soft fruits such as peaches, nectarines and apricots.*

GARDENER'S GUIDE TO VEGETABLES

Allotments can be extremely diverse, bursting with different crop varieties. With so many vegetables now available, a complete inventory would not be possible here. The intention of this directory, therefore, is to deal with some of the commonest mainstays of the average allotment, those that you are most likely to wish to grow. Each is accompanied by notes detailing how to raise and care for them, where and how they like to be grown, the pests and diseases you may encounter, how to harvest and store them, and suggestions of good varieties to try.

Left: *Many vegetable crops are extremely attractive to look at, such as the beautiful crinkly foliage of the kale shown here.*

Above: *Leafy crops are available in a variety of different colours, making a valuable and decorative addition to the vegetable plot.*

Above: *Onions can be obtained in a wide range of different shapes, sizes and colours. They are relatively easy to grow and harvest.*

Above: *The delicate red flowers of runner beans look spectacular trained up poles or arches in the allotment.*

BULB VEGETABLES

ONIONS

Allium cepa

Onions are available in a wide range of shapes, sizes and colours: oval, cylindrical, red, white and golden brown. They are easy to grow and need little care throughout their growing period. By using different growing methods to obtain a fresh supply, and through careful storage, it is possible to achieve an all-year-round supply of home-grown onions.

SOIL

Grow in fertile soil with good drainage. Do not plant in ground that has been freshly manured. Dig and manure the previous autumn. Add compost to the ground to improve the soil structure. Crop rotation can prevent a number of pests and diseases.

ASPECT

Position in an open, sunny site, but sets will tolerate some shade.

PLANTING SETS

The majority of onion sets are planted out in early spring. Plant in rows, with 10cm (4in) between each set and 25cm (10in) between the rows, so that the tip of the bulb peeks above the surface. Firm around the sets to remove any air pockets. To harvest an early crop, plant out Japanese onion sets in early autumn. These will be ready for lifting in mid-summer of the following year.

Above: *The leaves of these onions have been moved over to one side, and the protection from the glass will help ripen the bulbs.*

SOWING SEEDS OUTSIDE

If you have room, sow directly outside in rows in late summer. Sow thinly, so there will be less waste when thinning. The odour, which is exuded when the stems are crushed during thinning, will not be too strong, so there will be less chance of attracting onion fly. Thin out when the soil is moist. The onions will not be ready for harvesting until late summer to autumn of the following year. To stagger the maturing of the onions, sow direct outside in rows in late winter and early spring. This will produce a crop ready to harvest in early autumn. Protection may be given in colder areas.

SOWING SEEDS UNDER GLASS

Sow seeds in trays in mid-winter. Harden off the seedlings in a cold frame and in mid-spring plant out in rows, 10cm (4in) apart, leaving 25cm (10in) between each row.

AFTERCARE

A weed-free area enhances the yield. Hand weeding is preferable to hoeing as hoes can cut into the bulbs. Water the maturing crop only if the season is dry and stop watering after the onions have swollen. Mulching with compost helps to retain moisture in the soil and suppress weed growth.

HARVESTING AND STORAGE

Harvest throughout the growing season. Onions for storing must be fully mature before lifting. When the onions are mature, the leaves start to turn yellow and flop over. Move the foliage to one side to allow maximum sunlight to penetrate, which will aid the maturing process. At this point lift each bulb slightly with a fork, thus preparing the bulb for lifting, which can be done in a dry period two weeks later. Remove all the soil and dry in a sunny place (if left outside bring indoors during wet periods).

PESTS AND DISEASES

The main pest is the onion fly. The maggots eat the bulbs, resulting in yellow drooping leaves. Onion fly usually affects onion seeds rather than sets. Onion eelworm causes swollen and distorted foliage, kills young plants and softens bulbs on older plants. Destroy any affected plants. Onions are also susceptible to neck rot and white rot.

CULTIVATION

SETS

Planting time Early spring; early autumn (overwintering varieties)
Planting distance 10cm (4in)
Planting depth Tips of onions just showing through soil
Distance between rows 25cm (10in)
Harvesting Late summer (most varieties); mid-summer (over-wintering varieties)

SEED

Sowing time Mid-winter (under glass); late summer outside
Sowing distance Sow thinly
Sowing depth 1cm (½in)
Distance between rows 25cm (10in)
Thinning distance 5–10cm (2–4in)
Harvesting Late summer to autumn

VARIETIES

FROM SEED

'Ailsa Craig' An old variety with globe-shaped bulbs and golden skin.
'Hygro F1' A high yielder that stores well. Round-shaped bulb, slim neck and pale-coloured skin.

SETS FOR SPRING PLANTING

'Jet Set' A recent introduction that tastes delicious. Round and smooth skinned. Matures readily.
'Sturon Globe' A large-sized onion with excellent storage qualities.

SETS FOR AUTUMN PLANTING

'Radar' Hardy and early maturing. Mild flavour and a crunchy texture.
'Senshyu' Yellow, flat bulb with a mild flavour.

SPRING ONIONS (SCALLIONS)

Allium cepa

These slender plants with a white or red shank have a small bulbous base, which can be eaten either raw or cooked. Unlike bulb onions, however, spring onions must be eaten fresh. Sow continuously throughout the growing season and harvest eight weeks after sowing.

SOIL

Like most onions, spring onions prefer a light soil, but they will grow in most soils that are rich in organic matter. Crop rotation helps prevent infection from pests and diseases. They can also be grown in tubs or window boxes in a peat-free potting mix.

ASPECT

Spring onions grow best in an open sunny site, but can tolerate some shade.

SOWING

Sow every three weeks from early spring to late summer for a continuous crop from spring through to early autumn. To harvest an early spring crop, sow 'White Lisbon Winter Hardy' or any other hardy variety in late summer or early autumn. This crop will overwinter and be ready for picking in early spring. Sow crops thinly in rows 1cm (½in) deep with 10cm (4in) between each row.

AFTERCARE

Water in dry conditions and weed during the growing season. Protect overwintering spring onions with a cloche in cold weather.

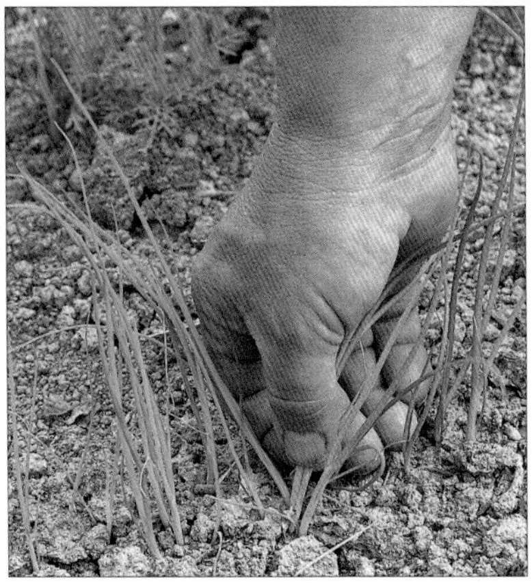

Above: *Thin out congested rows of spring onions. Larger thinnings can be used to add interest to summer salads.*

Left: *Spring onions produce small bulbs that are little more than a slight swelling at the base of the plant. These vegetables can be successionally grown during the spring and summer months and are quick to mature. These are excellent for use in salads and sandwiches.*

Above: *If the spring onions are difficult to lift, water beforehand and use a small fork in order to avoid breaking the stems.*

HARVESTING AND STORAGE

From sowing to harvesting takes around seven to eight weeks. Use a small hand fork to loosen ground before pulling. Thin out the crop when harvesting, taking out every other plant and leaving the remaining plants to grow on.

PESTS AND DISEASES

Onion fly is the main pest, turning the leaves yellow as the bulb is eaten by the maggots, eventually killing the plants. Onion eelworm is another major pest, killing young plants and damaging older plants by softening the bulbs. Destroy affected plants. Diseases such as onion white rot and onion downy mildew can also affect the plant. This is not a severe problem, however, as their lifespan is so short. Move to another growing site if symptoms appear.

CULTIVATION

Sowing time Early spring to early autumn
Sowing distance Thinly, around 1cm (½in)
Sowing depth 1cm (½in)
Distance between rows 10cm (4in)
Thinning distance Sow correctly to avoid thinning, otherwise thin out rows when harvesting
Harvesting 8 weeks after sowing

VARIETIES

'White Lisbon' Excellent variety for successional sowing.
'White Lisbon Winter Hardy' Good for autumn sowing; hardy throughout the winter.

spring onions (scallions)

SHALLOTS

Allium cepa Aggregatum Group

Shallots are very closely related to onions, but they have smaller bulbs with a milder flavour. They usually taste sweeter than onions and the leaves can be used as a substitute for chives in a range of dishes. Shallots will grow clusters of bulbs instead of the single bulb that we are used to with onions. They vary in size and shape. Some varieties are torpedo-shaped, whereas others are rounded, with colours varying from light brown to red.

SOIL

Shallots thrive in a light soil. Plant in ground manured the previous autumn or, if not, add garden compost to the soil before planting. Do not plant in freshly manured soil as this will cause bulb rot.

ASPECT

Grow in an open sunny site, but they will tolerate a little shade.

PLANTING

Higher yields are obtained from planting sets rather than by sowing seeds. Seeds will produce a single bulb for harvesting, whereas sets will cluster up to produce many bulbs per plant. Planting can begin in early winter in mild areas that have a well-drained soil, but, in general, shallot sets are best planted out in late winter or early spring. Plant sets individually, using a dibber (dibble) or trowel, in rows 15cm (6in) apart and with 25cm (10in) between the rows. The tip of the set should be just showing above the surface of the soil.

AFTERCARE

After planting look out for any sets that may have been lifted by the frost and replant. Weed throughout the growing season and water the crop during dry spells.

HARVESTING AND STORAGE

Lift the bulbs in mid-summer, when the leaves have turned yellow, and separate the clusters. Leave the shallot bulbs to dry out on a rack of wire netting. They will be ready to store when the leaves have shrivelled. Remove the dead leaves and any dirt on the bulbs. Store the shallots in a cool, dry place on trays or in netting bags.

PESTS AND DISEASES

Although they are generally trouble free, shallots can occasionally be attacked by the same pests and diseases as onions.

Left: *This is a healthy young crop of shallots with the bulbs beginning to form. They will soon be ready for harvesting.*

CULTIVATION

Planting time Late winter to early spring

Planting distance 15cm (6in)

Planting depth Tips showing through

Distance between rows 25cm (10in)

Harvesting Mid-summer

Left: *Plant shallots using a dibber or a trowel to insert the bulb. Only the tips of the bulbs need to be showing above the surface of the soil.*

Above: *Place harvested shallots on wire racks or trays in order to dry them before putting them into storage.*

Onion fly and onion eelworm attack the leaves and the bulb. Destroy affected crops. Diseases such as neck rot can also be a problem, especially in hot dry summers.

VARIETIES

'Delvad' Stores well and has an excellent flavour.

'Longor' Elegant elongated bulb, with a mild flavour.

'Sante' Large round bulb, high yield.

shallots

LEEKS

Allium porrum

If a range of leek varieties are grown, this traditional winter vegetable can be harvested over a long period of time. The long white shafts have many culinary uses, while the green or blue foliage looks very decorative in the allotment.

SOIL

Grow in a rich fertile soil. Dig thoroughly in autumn, adding well-rotted manure or garden compost. Although leeks prefer moist soil, they perform poorly on waterlogged or compacted soil. Crop rotation discourages diseases such as leek rust.

ASPECT

Require an open sunny position.

SOWING

In early to mid-spring, sow very thinly in rows, 1cm (½in) deep, with 15cm (6in) between the rows. Transplant when the seedlings are 20cm (8in) tall and as thick as a pencil (normally after two to three months). If the soil is dry, water the evening before transplanting to avoid tearing the plants when lifting. Dig out the leeks in batches and transplant out into rows, 30cm (12in) apart, with 15cm (6in) between the plants. Use a dibber (dibble) to make a hole 15cm (6in) deep and drop a single plant into the hole, leaving 5cm (2in) of foliage showing. Do not firm around the base of the plant, but gently water the plant and the soil will settle in around the base.

Above: *Earthing up leeks is essential in order to blanch the stems. You can also plant the leeks in trenches and fill these in.*

Above: *Leeks will stay fresh in the ground for many weeks. Lift when required with a fork as they tend to snap off if pulled.*

AFTERCARE

Earth (hill) up the leeks as they grow, moving the soil up around their stems to blanch them. Keep the rows of leeks weed-free and water the plants if dry, especially when they are young.

HARVESTING AND STORAGE

Leeks will be ready to harvest from early autumn to late spring. Lift the leeks with a fork when needed, as they will keep fresh in the soil for many weeks until they are required. Autumn varieties will not survive winter frosts and therefore need to be harvested before mid-winter.

PESTS AND DISEASES

Leek rust can occur in warm dry weather, causing bright orange pustules to form on the leaves. It often disappears when cooler wetter weather arrives in autumn. Destroy plants if they are severely affected.

Leeks can very occasionally be prone to the same pests and diseases as onions. Destroy any affected plants.

Left: *The green-blue architectural foliage of leeks provides a striking decorative effect in the allotment.*

CULTIVATION

Sowing time Early to mid-spring
Sowing distance Sow very thinly
Sowing depth 1cm (½in)
Distance between sown rows 15cm (6in)
Transplanting time When seedlings reach 20cm (8in)
Planting depth 15cm (6in)
Distance between planted rows 30cm (12in)
Harvesting Early autumn to late spring

VARIETIES

AUTUMN AND MID-SEASON
'King Richard' Good early cropper.
'The Lyon' Thick white stems, with a mild flavour.

WINTER
'Alvito RZ' Resistant to rust and not prone to bolting.
'Giant Winter' Produces well in extremely cold climates.
'Musselburgh' A reliable and versatile favourite.

leeks

GARLIC

Allium sativum

This aromatic bulb is used to season many cooked dishes. Its strong flavour is more prominent in home-grown crops. Garlic does not produce seed, so it must be grown from bulbs, which are available from garden centres or seed merchants. Choose a variety that suits your soil and climate best. Garlic bulbs bought at supermarkets can often fail or produce distorted plants.

SOIL

Garlic grows better in light sandy soils, especially if planting takes place in autumn. It does best in soils manured for the previous crop. Do not plant in freshly manured soil.

ASPECT

Garlic will flourish in an open sunny site.

PLANTING

Plant out in mid- to late autumn if your soil is light and free-draining. Break the bulbs up into individual cloves just before planting. Plant the cloves in rows, using a dibber (dibble) or trowel, to 5cm (2in) below the soil surface. Leave 7.5–10cm (3–4in) between the cloves and 30cm (12in) between the rows. If your soil is heavy and retains water easily, plant out in early to mid-spring. Starting your individual cloves off in pots under glass or in cold frames three to four weeks before planting will benefit the maturing of the crop.

Above: *Wet springs can rot off newly planted garlic bulbs. This can be overcome by starting off the bulbs under glass.*

Left: *The garlic bulbs form below the surface, unlike those of its close relative, the onion, which mainly form above ground.*

AFTERCARE

Weed throughout the growing season and water in spring during dry periods.

HARVESTING AND STORAGE

The leaves will turn yellow when the bulbs are ready for lifting, usually in mid- to late summer. Remove any soil or long roots before spreading the bulbs out on trays or wire staging to dry out. Remove the leaves as well if you are not intending to plait (braid) them later. Store by threading the bulbs on a string or stiff wire, or by tying or plaiting the leaves together. Hang in a cool, frost-free area such as a garage or shed.

PESTS AND DISEASES

Garlic is generally trouble free, although it may be affected by onion white rot and leek rust.

CULTIVATION

Planting time Mid- to late autumn in light soils, early to mid-spring in heavy soils
Planting distance 7.5–10cm (3–4in)
Planting depth 5cm (2in)
Distance between rows 30cm (12in)
Harvesting Mid- to late summer

Above: *Plant bulbs using a dibber or trowel 7.5–10cm (3–4in) apart. Use a line of string to keep the rows straight.*

Right: *Store garlic by threading a stiff piece of wire through the dry neck of the bulbs. You can also tie them together with string.*

VARIETIES

'Long Keeper' Good storage qualities. Often just listed as garlic.
'Printanor' Best planted in early to mid-spring.
'Thermidrome' Suits early planting.

garlic

LEAFY VEGETABLES

SWISS CHARD

Beta vulgaris Cicla Group

Swiss chard is easier to grow than spinach and much less prone to bolting. Swiss chard is also known under the names of chard (rhubarb, red or ruby) and sea kale beet. Spinach beet or perpetual spinach is a type of Swiss chard that is categorized within this section.

SOIL

Swiss chard and perpetual spinach require a soil that is fertile and does not dry out easily. Dig in plenty of well-rotted manure or garden compost in the autumn.

ASPECT

Prefer an open site, but will also tolerate light shade.

SOWING

Sow seeds in late spring 10cm (4in) apart in rows 2.5cm (1in) deep. Keep 38cm (15in) between the rows. When the seedlings have germinated, thin them to a distance of 45cm (18in) for Swiss chard and 38cm (15in) for perpetual spinach.

A sowing can be done in late summer to prolong the season. This crop will harvest until the following summer. Provide winter protection throughout the cold months.

AFTERCARE

Water during dry spells and keep the bed weed-free. Mulching with garden compost will help retain moisture in the soil and suppress weed growth. Remove any flower heads if they appear.

Above: *Swiss chard grown in colder areas benefits from protection in the winter months. Cloches or low tunnels are ideal.*

Left: *Many varieties of Swiss chard produce brightly coloured stems that make for a very decorative display in the vegetable plot.*

Below: *Harvest the crop by cutting off the stems when needed. Cut from the outside inwards to allow the inside to regrow.*

CULTIVATION

SWISS CHARD AND PERPETUAL SPINACH

Sowing time Late spring

Sowing distance Sow 10cm (4in) between the seeds

Sowing depth 2.5cm (1in)

Distance between rows 38cm (15in)

Thinning distance To 45cm/18in (Swiss chard); to 38cm/15in (perpetual spinach)

Harvesting Late summer to spring

HARVESTING AND STORAGE

Harvest when the leaves are small; if they are picked when they have matured the flavour of the leaf will be bitter. Always pick around the outside of the plant, leaving the inner area to regrow. To avoid damage, cut with a sharp knife. Both crops do not store well and are best eaten fresh.

PESTS AND DISEASES

Swiss chard and perpetual spinach are generally trouble free. Slugs are the only major enemy that they might encounter. Spacing plants correctly discourages the overcrowding that causes the humid conditions in which slugs as well as diseases such as downy mildew thrive.

VARIETIES

SWISS CHARD

Often simply listed as Swiss chard.

'Bright Lights' Very ornamental, containing a mixture of red, orange, cream, pink and yellow stems.

'Charlotte' This has an unusual combination of purple leaves and red stems.

'Fordhook Giant' A very attractive variety with large green leaves and white stems.

Perpetual spinach is normally listed simply as perpetual spinach or leaf beet.

KALE

Brassica oleracea Acephala Group

Kale is one of the hardiest vegetables and can withstand wet and poor soil conditions. Coupled with the fact that kale does not have the same problems with pests as cabbages, for example, it is surprising that more people do not grow this delicious winter green. This may be due to the fact that kale has a strong flavour and a bitter taste if it is not cooked properly. Try one of the new cultivars and harvest the young succulent leaves. Many varieties of kale are grown solely for ornamental purposes.

Above: *The foliage of curly kale has a wonderfully textural effect in the allotment vegetable plot.*

SOIL

Kale thrives on fertile well-drained soil and will tolerate poorer soils that other brassicas, such as cabbages and cauliflowers, will not. Dig the soil in autumn, incorporating some well-rotted manure or garden compost. Kale does not grow well in acidic conditions, so you will need to lime the soil after cultivation.

ASPECT

Grow in an open sunny situation.

SOWING

Begin sowing kale thinly in rows in late spring in the open ground. The rows should be 1cm (½in) deep with 20cm (8in) between the rows. When the seedlings have germinated, thin to a distance of 5cm (2in). Lift and transplant the seedlings when they are 13cm (5in) high and plant them in their final location. Water the seedlings the night before lifting in order to make this operation easier. Plant out in rows, with 45–60cm (18–24in) between the plants, depending on the variety grown. Keep a distance of 60cm (24in) between the rows.

AFTERCARE

Weed throughout the growing season and water the kale crop if it is dry, especially in the summer. Mulching with garden compost will help to retain moisture in the soil and also to suppress weed growth.

HARVESTING AND STORAGE

Kale has a long harvesting period, from autumn through to mid-spring. Remove a few leaves from each plant, starting with the crown. This will encourage new succulent side-shoot growth which can be harvested in spring. All growth is best removed with a sharp knife.

PESTS AND DISEASES

Kale is not prone to the worst of the cabbage family pests such as cabbage root fly and club root. However, whitefly, cabbage caterpillar and cabbage aphid can all be troublesome.

Left: *When harvesting kale, select the younger, more succulent leaves. Remove only a few leaves from each plant because this will help the plants to recover and produce more for future harvesting.*

CULTIVATION

Sowing time Late spring
Sowing distance Sow thinly
Sowing depth 1cm (½in)
Distance between sown rows 20cm (8in)
Thinning distance 5cm (2in)
Transplanting time When 13cm (5in) high
Planting distance 45–60cm (18–24in) apart
Distance between planted rows 60cm (24in)
Harvesting Autumn to mid-spring

VARIETIES

'Darkibor F1' Densely curled medium green leaves of uniform habit. Harvest in early winter.
'Nero di Toscano' Extremely dark green leaves that have a blistered appearance. Has a strong peppery taste.

curly kale

CAULIFLOWERS

Brassica oleracea Botrytis Group

The soil requirements and aftercare of cauliflowers are demanding. Failure to provide the right conditions can result in small button-headed plants and low yields. The effort is well rewarded, however, with beautiful white or purple heads (also known as curds) that taste delicious.

SOIL

Cauliflowers need a well-consolidated soil, which is deep, fertile and moisture-retentive, so dig several months before planting, incorporating well-rotted manure or garden compost. Alternatively, plant after a crop of nitrogen-fixing green manure.

ASPECT

Cauliflowers like an open sunny site. It is important to avoid frost pockets if growing winter varieties.

SOWING

Sow the seeds of summer varieties in a cool greenhouse in mid-winter for an early crop. Prick out the seedlings when they are large enough. When they reach 13cm (5in), harden off for a couple of weeks and plant out in cloches in early spring. Plant in rows, 55cm (22in) apart, with 60cm (24in) between the rows. Firm around the plants.

Autumn and winter varieties can be sown outdoors in late spring. Sow thinly in nursery beds before planting in a permanent site. Sow in rows, 1cm (½in) deep, with 20cm (8in) between rows. Thin to 5cm (2in) apart. Transplant seedlings when they are 13cm (5in) tall and bearing 5 to 6 leaves, watering in well and taking care when lifting them. Plant out between 60–70cm (24–28in) apart, depending on the variety, in rows 70cm (28in) apart. Firm in well.

Above: *Protection from the sun is needed for the developing heads. Snap the outside leaves over the heads of the cauliflower.*

Above: *Harvest the firm heads of cauliflower by cutting with a sharp knife just below the first set of leaves.*

AFTERCARE

After planting, mulch the crop with garden compost. Water in dry periods and feed occasionally. Cover with netting or wire mesh in order to protect leaves from birds. In winter, tie up or fold the leaves around the head to protect from rain and frost. Protect from sun in the same way. Use felt or plastic collars around the plants to protect from cabbage root fly.

HARVESTING AND STORAGE

Start harvesting when the heads are small so that not all of the crop is harvested at the same time. When the florets separate or turn brown, they are too mature. Hang upside down in a cool dark shed for up to three weeks; mist the heads now and then.

PESTS AND DISEASES

Susceptible to the same pests and diseases as cabbages.

CULTIVATION

SUMMER CAULIFLOWER
Sowing time Mid-spring (outdoors); mid-winter (under glass)
Sowing distance Sow thinly
Sowing depth 1cm (½in)
Distance between rows 20cm (8in)
Thinning distance 5cm (2in)
Transplanting time Spring (seedlings sown outdoors); early spring (seedlings sown under glass)
Planting distance 55cm (22in)
Distance between planted rows 60cm (24in)
Harvesting Late summer (if sown outdoors); mid-summer (if sown under glass)

AUTUMN CAULIFLOWER
Sowing time Late spring
Sowing distance Sow thinly
Sowing depth 1cm (½in)
Distance between rows 20cm (8in)
Thinning distance 5cm (2in)
Transplanting time Early summer
Planting distance 60cm (24in)
Distance between planted rows 70cm (28in)
Harvesting Autumn

WINTER CAULIFLOWER
Sowing time Late spring
Sowing distance Sow thinly
Sowing depth 1cm (½in)
Distance between rows 20cm (8in)
Thinning distance 5cm (2in)
Transplanting time Summer
Planting distance 70cm (28in)
Distance between planted rows 70cm (28in)
Harvesting Late winter to early spring

VARIETIES

SUMMER
'All the Year Round' A heavy yielder, producing heads all through the summer.
'Idol' This mini cauliflower is ideal for growing in a small site. Good for successional sowing.

AUTUMN
'Stella F1' Suitable for all soil types and less demanding than other varieties. High-quality heads produced.
'Violet Queen' Purple-headed and maturing from late summer to mid-autumn.

WINTER
'Purple Cape' Bears rich purple heads with an excellent flavour. Harvest in early spring.
'Wainfleet' Good frost resistance.

cauliflower

CABBAGES

Brassica oleracea Capitata Group

Cabbages come in a variety of different shapes, colours and sizes. Due to the range of varieties available, it is now possible to harvest this crop fresh all the year round. They are invaluable in winter when there is a limited range of fresh vegetables available. Cabbages can be cooked or eaten raw in salads or coleslaw.

Left: *Cabbages are prone to the fungal disease clubroot. You can reduce the risk of this disease occurring by practising four-year crop rotation. To prevent the spread of clubroot it is best to grow your own plants from seed rather than buying in transplants that may be infected with disease. Purchasing small plants raised in module trays is another safe method to ensure the plants are not infected with clubroot.*

SOIL

Cabbages thrive in firm, well-consolidated soil that is not freshly manured. Therefore, cultivate the land several months prior to planting, adding well-rotted manure or garden compost. Cabbages do best in a soil with a pH of 6.5–7 – if the soil is too acidic, lime after digging and before planting. The fungal disease clubroot thrives in damp acid soil, so improve any drainage problems. Crop rotation helps to prevent an infection.

ASPECT

Likes an open sunny site and will tolerate exposure.

SOWING OUTDOORS

For all varieties, start off by sowing cabbage seeds in a nursery bed. Sow thinly in rows 1cm (½in) deep, with 15cm (6in) between rows. After germination thin out the seedlings in the rows to 8cm (3in) apart to prevent the seedlings becoming weak and spindly. Transplant the young cabbage plants to their permanent position when they are 10cm (4in) tall and have grown 5 or 6 leaves. Water the rows the day before lifting. This will aid lifting and minimize root and stem damage. Apply a general organic fertilizer a week prior to planting for all varieties except spring cabbage. Plant in their final rows, 35cm (14in) apart for spring and summer cabbage and 50cm (20in) for autumn and winter cabbage. Leave 60cm (24in) between the rows for spring and summer cabbages and 65–70cm (26–28in) for autumn and winter varieties. Plant firmly for all varieties. Water thoroughly after planting.

SOWING UNDER GLASS

To grow an early crop of summer cabbage, sow in seed trays, pots or modules in a cool greenhouse in mid-winter. When the

VARIETIES

SPRING

'Flower of Spring' Large pointed heads that are ready in mid-spring.
'Spring Hero F1' Good-sized heads that are ready in late spring to early summer.
'Wintergreen' Spring greens that are ready from late winter or hearting up in late spring.

SUMMER

'Golden Acre' Has lovely round firm heads. Great for cooking or used raw in coleslaw.
'Minicole F1' A white compact type that stores well.
'Stonehead F1' Shows some resistance to mildew and is not prone to splitting. Also stores well.

AUTUMN

'Cuor di Bue' Light green pointed leaves and with plenty of flavour.
'Hardora F1' A red cabbage which produces a good uniform crop. Excellent storage qualities.

WINTER CABBAGE AND SAVOYS

'Best of All' An early maturing Savoy that can be harvested from early to late autumn.
'Christmas Drumhead' An old blue dwarf variety with flat solid hearts.
'January King' Excellent frost resistance, crisp with a sweet flavour.
'Vertus' A Savoy that can withstand severe frosts.

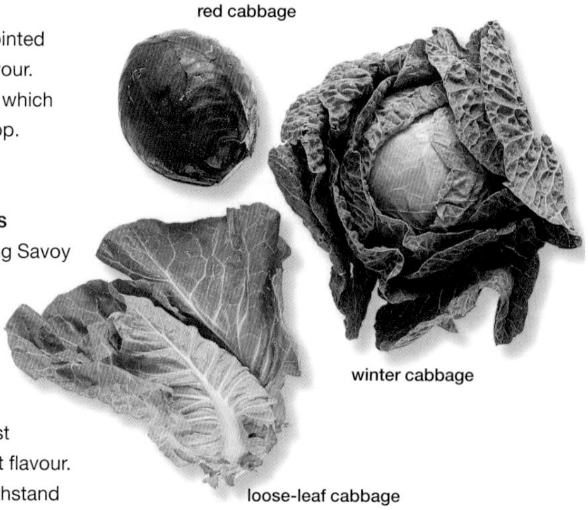

Left: *Blue varieties of cabbage are unusual, but very striking in the vegetable plot.*

Below: *This healthy crop of cabbages is growing well and will soon be ready for harvesting.*

seedlings are large enough, prick out into individual pots or modules. Grow on and harden off before planting outside under cloches in early spring. Follow the same spacing as for transplants (see opposite). Small plants can also be bought from a nursery or garden centre, but always buy from a reputable source as introduced plants may contain clubroot.

AFTERCARE

Water young plants, especially transplants, until established. Keep the beds weed free. Mulch beds with garden compost to help retain moisture and suppress weed growth. If your vegetable patch is prone to attracting cabbage root fly, apply a felt or plastic collar around the base of the cabbage to stop the fly laying its eggs.

HARVESTING AND STORAGE

Cut the hearts when they have become hard and dig up the stalks. Spring cabbage stalks can be left and cut on top with a knife in a cross shape. This will produce another four smaller cabbages.

PESTS AND DISEASES

Cabbage root fly is one of the major pests. Place a collar of felt or plastic around the base of the plant to stop the fly laying its eggs near the plants.

Caterpillars, mainly from the small white butterfly, can munch their way through a considerable amount of leafage. Pick them off by hand or erect a cage around the crop to keep out the adult butterflies. If you see small holes in the young leaves of cabbages it is almost certainly flea beetles. Slugs and snails will also cause damage to the leaves. Protect from pigeons by erecting netting or wire mesh cloches. Cabbages are prone to the soil-borne fungal disease clubroot. The roots of the plant begin to swell and the plants become stunted with all growth severely affected. Destroy any infected plants.

CULTIVATION

SPRING CABBAGE
Sowing time Late summer
Sowing distance Sow thinly
Sowing depth 1cm (½in)
Distance between sown rows 15cm (6in)
Thinning distance 8cm (3in)
Transplanting time When 10cm (4in) tall
Planting distance 35cm (14in)
Distance between planted rows 60cm (24in)
Harvesting Spring

SUMMER CABBAGE
Sowing time Early to mid-spring
Sowing distance Sow thinly
Sowing depth 1cm (½in)
Distance between sown rows 15cm (6in)
Thinning distance 8cm (3in)
Transplanting time When 10cm (4in) tall
Planting distance 35cm (14in)
Distance between planted rows 60cm (24in)
Harvesting Mid-summer onwards

AUTUMN CABBAGE
Sowing time Late spring
Sowing distance Sow thinly
Sowing depth 1cm (½in)
Distance between sown rows 15cm (6in)
Thinning distance 8cm (3in)
Transplanting time When 10cm (4in) tall
Planting distance 50cm (20in)
Distance between planted rows 65–70cm (26–28in)
Harvesting Autumn

WINTER CABBAGE
Sowing time Late spring
Sowing distance Sow thinly
Sowing depth 1cm (½in)
Distance between sown rows 15cm (6in)
Thinning distance 8cm (3in)
Transplanting time When 10cm (4in) tall
Planting distance 50cm (20in)
Distance between planted rows 65–70cm (26–28in)
Harvesting Winter

Left: *Protect young cabbage seedlings from cabbage root fly by placing a felt or plastic collar around the base of the plant.*

BROCCOLI

Brassica oleracea Cymosa Group

Broccoli is also known as purple sprouting broccoli or sprouting broccoli and is closely related to calabrese. The two can be easily confused because calabrese, which has green heads, is often sold in the supermarkets under the name of broccoli. As the common name suggests, most varieties of broccoli have purple heads, but you can also grow varieties with creamy white heads that look rather like small cauliflowers. The harvesting of broccoli fills a period in which there are very few other vegetables maturing.

SOIL

Manure the soil in autumn, as rich soil is required for good growth. Apply a general fertilizer before sowing or alternatively sow a nitrogen-fixing green manure as the previous crop. Broccoli requires a pH of 6.5–7. Lime if necessary to bring the pH up to the recommended level.

ASPECT

Broccoli requires an open sunny position free from strong winds.

Above: *Harvest the shoots of broccoli when they have begun to bud up and before they have come into flower.*

SOWING

During spring sow seeds thinly in rows to a depth of 1cm (½in) with 15cm (6in) between the rows. After germination, thin to 5cm (2in) apart within the rows. When the plants reach 13cm (5in) high, lift them and transplant to their final location. Water the young plants the day before transplanting to soften up the soil, which will make them easier to move. Plant out in rows 60cm (24in) apart with 75cm (30in) between the rows. Plant deeply (with the first leaves sitting on the soil surface) to discourage cabbage root fly and to help stabilize the plant. Firm in well around the base of the plants, again to help stabilize the transplants and to remove any air pockets.

For an early crop, sow broccoli in seed trays or modules under cover from mid- to late spring. Harden off for two weeks in a cold frame before planting out.

AFTERCARE

Keep well watered during dry periods to allow healthy growth throughout the growing season. Mulching the rows with garden compost will help the soil retain moisture and keep weeds in check. Weed the rows throughout the season. Use crop covers of fleece to protect the plants from cabbage root fly in the early stages or protect the plants individually by putting a cabbage root fly mat around each one.

Left: *Purple sprouting broccoli is one of the most colourful and decorative of vegetables for the allotment.*

CULTIVATION
Sowing time Mid-spring
Sowing distance Sow very thinly
Sowing depth 1cm (½in)
Distance between sown rows 15cm (6in)
Thinning distance 5cm (2in)
Transplanting time When 13cm (5in) tall
Planting distance 60cm (24in)
Distance between planted rows 75cm (30in)
Harvesting Late winter to mid-spring

HARVESTING AND STORAGE

Start harvesting in late winter and continue through to mid-spring, depending on the varieties grown. Harvest the shoots before they flower. Cut the shoots when they have begun to bud up and are 15cm (6in) long. Cut the shoots from all around the plant; regular cutting encourages new shoots. Pick off any flowering shoots – if they are left on, the plant will become exhausted and cease to produce new shoots for picking.

PESTS AND DISEASES

Broccoli is prone to the same pests and diseases as cabbages.

VARIETIES
'Purple Sprouting Early' An extremely old variety that matures in early spring.
'Purple Sprouting Late' Ready in mid-spring.
'Rudolf' Large, purple spears appear from early winter.

purple sprouting broccoli

BRUSSELS SPROUTS

Brassica oleracea Gemmifera Group

This hardy vegetable is delicious if cooked correctly. Try growing some of the tasty new F1 hybrids, which freeze very well. If a range of varieties is grown, harvesting can begin in late summer and finish in early spring.

SOIL

Dig the ground and incorporate well-rotted manure or garden compost in autumn. Brussels sprouts do not grow well in acidic soil conditions, so add lime if necessary to bring the pH up to 6.5–7.

ASPECT

Brussels sprouts thrive in an open sunny position that is protected from strong winds.

SOWING

Sow outside in a nursery bed from early to mid-spring. Start by sowing the early varieties and successionally sow mid-season and late varieties in turn. Sow thinly in rows 1cm (½in) deep with 15cm (6in) between rows. After germination, thin out the seedlings to 8cm (3in) apart. Transplant when the seedlings are 13cm (5in) high, watering the previous evening to make lifting easier. Plant in rows, 75cm (30in) apart, with 75cm (30in) between the rows. Firm well to remove any air pockets. You can intercrop between the rows at this early stage. For late-summer picking start the sowing off under glass in late winter. Harden off and plant outside when the young plants are 13cm (5in) high. Use cloches to protect the early stages of growth.

AFTERCARE

Use wire-mesh cloches to deter pigeons. Weed throughout the growing season and water in dry periods. Apply a foliar feed during the summer. Stake any plants if needed and, as early autumn approaches, draw up the soil around the stems to steady the plants against wind. Apply felt or plastic collars around the base of the plants to prevent cabbage root fly from laying its eggs.

CULTIVATION

Sowing time Early to mid-spring
Sowing distance Sow thinly
Sowing depth 1cm (½in)
Distance between sown rows 15cm (6in)
Thinning distance 8cm (3in)
Transplanting time When 13cm (5in) high
Planting distance 75cm (30in)
Distance between planted rows 75cm (30in)
Harvesting Mid-autumn to spring

Left: *As these Brussels sprouts develop, the bottom leaves will turn yellow. Remove these as they do so and compost them.*

HARVESTING AND STORAGE

Start harvesting from the bottom of the plant, picking the sprouts when they are still tight, after the first frosts as this improves flavour. Crop only a few from each plant. Every time the crop is harvested work further up the stem. When all the sprouts have been harvested, cut off the top of the plant and cook as a cabbage.

PESTS AND DISEASES

Prone to the same problems as cabbages. The main problem is clubroot, a soil-borne fungal disease. Destroy infected plants. Small white butterfly caterpillar and aphids may also affect the crop. Remove caterpillars by hand and spray aphids with an insecticidal soap.

Below: *Many gardeners believe that Brussel sprouts are best harvested after the first frost because this improves the flavour.*

VARIETIES

'Braveheart F1' One of the sweetest flavoured sprouts. Matures in early winter to early spring.
'Oliver F1' An extremely early variety, cropping from late summer if sown under glass. Produces large sprouts.
'Trafalgar F1' This will provide sweet sprouts in early winter. It has a good root system.

Brussels sprouts

CALABRESE (ITALIAN SPROUTING BROCCOLI)

Brassica oleracea Italica Group

There is often confusion over the difference between broccoli and calabrese. This occurs because the green spearheads of calabrese are misleadingly sold under the name of broccoli in supermarkets. Calabrese normally has green-headed spears, whereas broccoli has purple or white. Calabrese has a taste similar to asparagus and a succulent texture when it is steamed, rather than boiled.

SOIL

Calabrese grows well in a firm rich soil that has been well manured in the autumn or for a previous crop. It does not mature well in poor soil.

ASPECT

Calabrese thrives best in a sunny location that is sheltered from wind.

SOWING

Calabrese does not transplant well, so sowing directly in rows outside is the best method of growing. Position seeds in groups of two or three in drills 30cm (12in) apart. Rows are best positioned 30cm (12in) apart. After germination, select the strongest seedling and thin out the others.

Above: *Calabrese does not transplant particularly well, and so it is best to sow the seed in situ and then thin out the strongest seedlings after germination.*

AFTERCARE

The young growth of calabrese is susceptible to 'pecking' by pigeons and other birds. Protect the crop by using netting or other barrier methods. Keep the crop well watered throughout the summer. Apply a mulch of garden compost during the growing season in order to help conserve moisture. Regular weeding will also help to do this. Plants that are grown for harvesting towards the end of the season may require staking to stabilize them from autumn winds.

HARVESTING AND STORAGE

Harvest from late summer to mid-autumn depending on variety. Cut the heads (spears) and side shoots while the flower buds are closed. Once the flowers have opened the heads become woody and unpalatable and the production of new ones will cease. Cut the central flower head first to promote the growth of side shoots. Always spread harvesting of the crop, never completely stripping a plant. Cutting of a plant may continue under favourable conditions for up to six weeks.

Left: *Harvest calabrese from late summer to early autumn. Cutting the central flower head first promotes the growth of side shoots.*

PESTS AND DISEASES

Calabrese is prone to the same pests and diseases as cabbages.

CULTIVATION

Sowing time Successional sowing from mid- to early summer
Sowing distance Sow 30cm (12in) apart in groups of two or three; thin to strongest plant later
Sowing depth 1cm (½in)
Distance between rows 30cm (12in)
Harvesting Late summer to mid-autumn

VARIETIES

CALABRESE (ITALIAN SPROUTING BROCCOLI)
'Corvet' Matures 60 days after planting out. Good large heads that produce well after cutting.
'Express Corona' Produces a succession of spears after the main head is cut. Quick to mature.
'Green Comet' A good early cropper with large heads. Little spear production after the main head is cut.
'Green Sprouting' Spears are ready for harvesting in mid-summer; good flavour.
'Italian Sprouting' An excellent flavour with a long cropping season.

ROMANESCO (ROMAN BROCCOLI)
'Romanesco' A large headed variety that is yellow-green in colour. A good substitute for cauliflower.

calabrese (Italian sprouting broccoli)

CHINESE CABBAGE

Brassica rapa var. *pekinensis*

Although this vegetable has been grown in Asia since the 5th century, it is relatively new elsewhere, having arrived in Europe in the 20th century. With its tall erect habit and slender leaves, Chinese cabbage could easily be mistaken for cos (romaine) lettuce. It has a mild flavour and can either be steamed, stir-fried or eaten raw as a salad leaf.

SOIL

Chinese cabbage prefers a fertile soil that retains moisture. Dig in plenty of well-rotted manure or garden compost in the autumn as it performs poorly on denuded soils.

ASPECT

Likes an open position and will tolerate a little shade in summer.

SOWING

It is best to sow in situ because seedlings do not transplant well. Sow in rows 1cm (½in) deep with 10cm (4in) between the seeds and 25cm (10in) between the rows. Once large enough, thin out seedlings to 30cm (12in) apart. If starting off inside, sow into modules or small pots to avoid disturbance during transplanting.

AFTERCARE

Water liberally in dry conditions. Mulch with garden compost to help retain moisture and suppress weed growth.

HARVESTING AND STORAGE

Chinese cabbage is quick growing, maturing 7–10 weeks after sowing. Cut the heads off and leave the stump in the ground to sprout new leaves. Chinese cabbage needs to be eaten fresh.

PESTS AND DISEASES

Older varieties can be prone to bolting; there are a number of varieties on the market that are more resistant to this problem. Slugs, snails and cabbage caterpillars can be a problem. Although Chinese cabbage can be prone to other cabbage pests and diseases, they are not a major problem.

Below: *This young crop of Chinese cabbage is flourishing. The variety is 'Green Rocket F1'.*

CULTIVATION
Sowing time Early to mid-summer
Sowing distance 10cm (4in)
Sowing depth 1cm (½in)
Distance between rows 25cm (10in)
Thinning distance 30cm (12in)
Harvesting Late summer to late autumn

Left: *Chinese cabbage grows very quickly and is ready to harvest in just seven to ten weeks after sowing. Remove the heads and leave the stump in the ground to sprout new leaves. If successional sowing is practised, harvesting can take place until late autumn.*

Above: *The yellow flowers of this Chinese cabbage look very striking against the dark green leaves.*

VARIETIES
'Kasumi' Has a loose habit with extremely good resistance to bolting.
'Jade Pagoda' Extremely tall and thin heads.
'Tip Top' Shows resistance to bolting.

Chinese cabbage

CHICORY

Cichorium intybus

Chicory has a bitter taste that you either love or hate. It is split into three main types: witloof (Belgian chicory), sugarloaf and red chicory (radicchio). Witloof is the traditional forcing type that produces tight leafy heads called chicons. These are produced in winter when the roots are lifted and blanched. Sugarloaf looks rather like a cos (romaine) lettuce, with its large outer leaves encompassing the inner leaves, therefore blanching naturally. Red chicory is self-blanching, but can be forced to produce red and white leaves. They are all a welcome addition to the winter salad bowl.

SOIL

Chicory will grow in most fertile soils. Manure or incorporate garden compost the previous autumn.

ASPECT

Thrives in an open sunny position.

SOWING

Start to sow chicory from spring through to mid-summer, depending on the type grown. Sow thinly in rows to a depth of 1cm (½in). Keep a distance of 30cm (12in) between the rows. Thin to a distance of 15–30cm (6–12in), depending on the variety. For later sowing protect the crop with a cloche.

FORCING CHICORY

To blanch chicory, cut off the leaves in late autumn to just above the level of the soil. Cover the stump with 15cm (6in) of a mixture of compost and grit. The leaves will grow in the darkness under the soil, becoming blanched. Alternatively, lift the chicory roots and plant five in a large pot of free-draining potting mix so the cut tips are just showing. Cut the roots so they fit into the pot. Cover with a pot or a bucket and place inside in a warm dark place. The chicons will be ready to harvest in 2–3 weeks. Cut and re-start the process.

Above: *Red chicory (radicchio) does not need the same care as Belgian or witloof chicory. This variety is 'Alouette'.*

AFTERCARE

Water throughout dry periods and weed during the growing season.

HARVESTING AND STORAGE

Witloof forcing type They will be ready to cut 3–4 weeks after the start of the forcing process. Cut the chicons just above the crown, when the tips of the plants start to show through the potting mix. Leave the roots in, water the compost and a smaller secondary crop may be harvested.

Sugar and red chicory – non-forcing type Cut the chicons when they are 15cm (6in) long. The stumps may shoot again.

Below: *Chicory should be sown in rows from spring to mid-summer. Allow 30cm (12in) between the rows.*

PESTS AND DISEASES

Generally trouble free, although slugs can be a problem in mild, damp weather. Do not plant too close together to allow for maximum air movement. This reduces hot moist conditions that slugs thrive in.

CULTIVATION

Sowing time Spring to mid-summer
Sowing distance Thinly
Sowing depth 1cm (½in)
Distance between rows 30cm (12in)
Thinning distance 15–30cm (6–12in)
Harvesting Autumn into winter

VARIETIES

WITLOOF

'Brussels Witloof' Good for winter forcing.
'Normanto' No soil layer needed when forcing.

SUGARLOAF

'Crystal head' A modern variety that has improved hardiness.
'Sugarloaf' Sweeter than other varieties. Good drought resistance but will only tolerate mild frosts.

RED CHICORY

'Pallar Rossa' Good taste. Green leaves turn dark red. Needs winter protection.
'Rossa di Treviso' Deep red leaves and is non-hearting. Becomes pink and white when it is blanched.

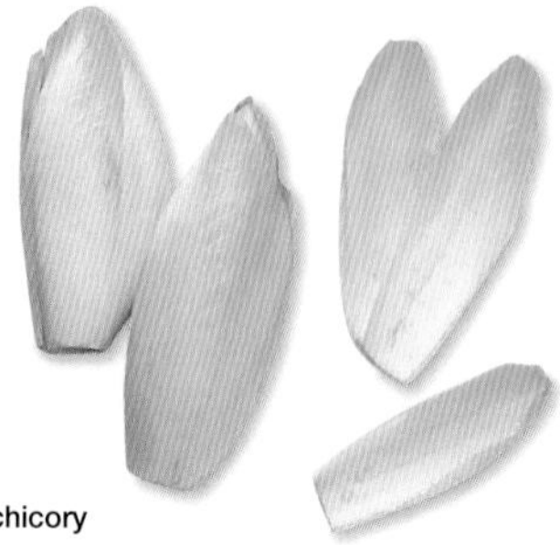

chicory

LETTUCE

Latuca sativa

There are many different types of lettuce to choose from now – cos (romaine), butterhead, crisphead and loose-leaf. These different types come in various shapes, sizes and colours, and are often used in the allotment site. With careful planning, it is possible to crop lettuce nearly all the year round, with the help of a cloche or two.

SOIL

A good quantity of organic matter is needed in the soil, which will help retain moisture. Dig plenty of well-rotted manure or garden compost into the soil in the autumn. Lettuce does not grow well on acidic soil, so lime the area if necessary after digging.

ASPECT

Lettuce likes an open sunny position, but will welcome partial shade if grown in the heat of the summer.

SOWING

EARLY CROP For early crops start by sowing under glass in trays or modules in late winter to early spring. Plant these under cloches to protect against frost.
MAINCROP Start sowing outside from early spring onwards. Sow in rows 1cm (½in) deep with 30cm (12in) between the rows. Thin to 15–30cm (6–12in) apart, depending on the variety grown. Thinnings can be used as transplants for other rows, although this is not usually successful during the hot summer months due to excessive heat.
LATE CROP Late-summer sowings will mature from autumn and early winter. Provide protection for these crops by covering with cloches in mid-autumn. Selected varieties will overwinter under cloches or can be grown under glass.

AFTERCARE

Planted areas need to be weeded throughout the growing season. Keep the crop well watered. It is better to do this in the morning rather than in the evening. The plants will use up the water during the day and the planted area will not be damp in the evening. This will discourage slugs and cause less fungal disease. If slugs are a problem, protect young plants with plastic bottle cloches until well established.

Above: *Many varieties of lettuce are extremely decorative and can be planted out to enhance decorative borders.*

CULTIVATION
Sowing time Late winter (under glass) to early spring onwards
Sowing distance Thinly
Sowing depth 1cm (½in)
Distance between rows 30cm (12in)
Thinning distance15–30cm (6–12in)
Harvesting Early summer onwards

Above: *A hearted lettuce is ready for harvesting when the heart feels firm. If left longer, the plant is likely to bolt.*

HARVESTING AND STORAGE

HEARTED LETTUCE This is ready for cutting when the heart is firm. If left long after this, they are likely to bolt.
LOOSELEAF Pick leaves as needed or cut the whole plant.

PESTS AND DISEASES

Slugs relish lush green vegetation and lettuce is no exception. If slugs are a severe problem, grow on in modules before planting out, as they are less likely to severely damage established plants.

Aphid attacks are common too. Other pest attacks can come from cutworms and root aphids. If the lettuces are planted too close together or are overwatered, fungal diseases such as downy mildew and grey mould may occur. Careful planting and watering can alleviate much of this.

VARIETIES

COS
'Little Gem' Extremely quick maturing. A compact little plant with a sweet flavour.
'Winter Density' Sweet variety that is excellent for overwintering to crop in spring.

BUTTERHEAD
'Avondefiance' Resistant to root aphid and mildew, and slow to bolt.
'Buttercrunch' Dark green in colour with a compact habit.

CRISPHEAD
'Floreal RZ' A firm heart with bubbled leaves. Resistant to bolting and tipburn as well as mildew and root aphid.
'Roxette RZ' An iceberg with a superior flavour. Fast growing, with a solid heart.

LOOSE-LEAF
'Malibu RZ' A vigorous red-leaved lettuce that is resistant to mildew. Uniform in habit.
'Salad Bowl' Green leaves with serrated edges. Harvest for a long period.

SPINACH

Spinacia oleracea

Spinach is a close relative of the beetroot and not the lettuce as might first appear. This crop contains an extremely high iron content, similar to that found in peas. It is a relatively hard crop to grow because it requires a high content of organic matter in the soil and needs copious amounts of water throughout the summer. If the conditions are not ideal, the plants tend to bolt and the crop will be lost. Spinach tastes delicious steamed with fresh crushed garlic or when used in quiches or egg florentine.

SOIL

Incorporate plenty of garden compost or well-rotted manure in the autumn. This will aid moisture retention in the soil during the following summer, which is a must for healthy growth.

ASPECT

Spinach is best grown in light shade in summer, making it a good choice for intercropping. This also reduces the chance of the crop running to seed. Spinach will grow just as well in an open sunny site if the soil remains moist and the area is not too hot.

Above: *This well-maintained vegetable plot includes a thriving crop of spinach. Spinach needs large amounts of water in summer.*

Above: *Spinach is prone to bolting, so choose resistant varieties or site summer crops in light shade to reduce the risk.*

SOWING

Start by sowing in early spring and successional sow until late spring. Sow thinly in rows to a depth of 1cm (½in), with 30cm (12in) between the rows. Apply a general fertilizer prior to sowing. When the seedlings are large enough, thin them to 15cm (6in) apart. They will be ready to harvest in early to late summer.

A crop can be sown in late summer or early autumn. Cover with cloches for protection during the winter. This crop can be harvested over winter and spring.

AFTERCARE

Water throughout dry periods. Weed throughout the growing period. Mulch with garden compost to help retain moisture.

HARVESTING AND STORAGE

Start by harvesting the outer leaves when they have reached a reasonable size; it is possible to remove half of the foliage at any one time. Pick more sparingly with winter varieties. Cut and harvest continually to promote new growth.

PESTS AND DISEASES

The main problem is bolting. This is when the plant grows quickly and starts to flower and set seed, making the crop inedible. This condition is encouraged by hot, dry weather. Site the crop carefully before sowing and choose less prone varieties. Spinach is susceptible to downy mildew, but there are plenty of resistant varieties. Spinach blight can also affect the crop. In both cases destroy infected material.

Above: *When harvesting select young fresh outer leaves. Do not remove more than half the foliage or this will weaken the plant.*

CULTIVATION

Sowing time Successional sow from early spring to late spring
Sowing distance Thinly
Sowing depth 1cm (½in)
Thinning distance 15cm (6in)
Distance between rows 30cm (12in)
Harvesting Early to late summer

VARIETIES

'Avanti RZ' An early maturing variety, suitable for greenhouse production or summer sowings outside. Resistant to powdery mildew.
'Giant Winter' Very hardy and ideal as a winter crop.
'Medinia' A good vigorous summer variety that is slow to bolt and resistant to mildew. A good all-rounder.

spinach

SALAD LEAVES

As salad has become more popular in recent years, alternatives to lettuce are becoming more widely grown. Crops such as endive (*Chichorium endivia*), rocket (arugula; *Eruca vesicaria*) and lamb's lettuce (mache; *Valerianella locusta*) are all delicious salad leaves. Rocket is worth growing as it has a rich spicy flavour. Nowadays many different leaves can be included in one salad bowl, therefore it is not unusual to choose all of the above when preparing a salad. Rocket and lamb's lettuce are mainly grown for winter use when other salad crops are scarce, but can also be grown in the summer.

SOIL

Salad leaves thrive in moisture-retentive soil.

ASPECT

All grow best in cool conditions, so partial shade in summer is ideal. Bolting can occur if the plants get too hot. They are ideal for intercropping.

SOWING

Sow rocket and lamb's lettuce in late summer. Rocket can also be sown through to early autumn. Sow thinly in rows 1cm (½in) deep with 30cm (12in) between the rows. Thin the seedlings when large enough to 15cm (6in) apart for rocket and 10cm (4in) apart for lamb's lettuce. Early sowings can take place for both crops in spring. These will be ready to harvest in summer.

Endives can be sown from spring until late summer. Sow thinly in rows 1cm (½in) deep with 38cm (15in) between the rows. Once the seedlings have germinated, thin out to a distance of 30–35cm (12–14in), depending on the variety. Harvest in summer to winter.

AFTERCARE

Cover with cloches in late autumn or early winter. Water liberally in dry weather. Mulching with garden compost will help to conserve soil moisture as well as suppress weed growth.

HARVESTING AND STORAGE

Individual leaves can be cut off as required. Endives will re-sprout from cut stalks. All salad leaves need to be eaten fresh as they do not store or freeze.

Above: *Broad-leaved endives are more tolerant of cold conditions than the curly-leaved varieties.*

PESTS AND DISEASES

Generally trouble free, although rocket may occasionally be attacked by flea beetles. Slugs and snails may pose a problem for all types of salad leaves.

Right: *Curly-leaved endive can be used in salads or cooked. Unblanched leaves like these are more bitter than blanched ones.*

CULTIVATION

Rocket and lamb's lettuce

Sowing time Spring (early sowing); late summer to early autumn (later sowings)
Sowing distance Thinly
Sowing depth 1cm (½in)
Distance between rows 30cm (12in)
Thinning distance 10–15cm (4–6in)
Harvesting Summer to winter

Endive

Sowing time Spring to late summer
Sowing distance Thinly
Sowing depth 1cm (½in)
Distance between rows 38cm (15in)
Thinning distance 30–35cm (12–14in)
Harvesting Summer to winter

VARIETIES

Endive

'Monaco RZ' A curly-leaved type, with a blanched heart and large green outer leaves.
'Stratego' A broad-leaved type. Compact, slow to bolt and resistant to tip burning.

Rocket

More commonly sold under one of its common names, rucola or salad rocket, rather than varieties.

Lamb's lettuce

Sometimes sold under the common name of corn salad.
'Verte de Cambrai'
An old French variety with a good flavour.

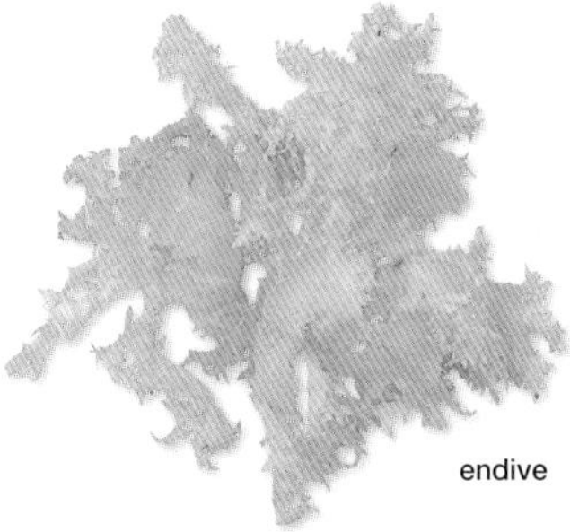

endive

rocket

lamb's lettuce

ROOT CROPS

BEETROOT (BEETS)

Beta vulgaris

For many of us, the word beetroot conjures up a picture of a small, round, red vegetable pickled in a jar. However, this delicious vegetable comes in a range of colours, such as white, yellow, the commonly grown red and a variety with concentric rings of pink and white. Shapes range from round through cylindrical to tapered, depending on the variety grown. Extremely easy to grow, beetroot can be eaten fresh from early summer to mid-autumn. Pickling excess crops will ensure a supply all year round.

SOIL

Grows in most soil types (except acid soils) and thrives on rich moist soils. Adding organic matter to the soil in autumn or early winter will increase water retention, but is only necessary if none was incorporated the previous year. Never sow or plant in newly manured ground. Cylindrical and tapered varieties keep their shape and mature better in sandy soil.

ASPECT

An open sunny site is preferable for growing beetroot. It thrives in seaside locations due to its tolerance to salt, the wild ancestor of beetroot being native to coastal situations.

Above: *Harvesting can begin seven weeks after sowing by pulling the smaller beetroot out. Continue to pull as required.*

Left: *Beetroot grows best in light soils. Growing in raised beds allows you to choose the growing medium best suited to the crops.*

SOWING

Sow the seeds in drills 2.5cm (1in) deep with 20cm (8in) between the rows. Sow 8cm (3in) apart. Some thinning may be required as the seedlings begin to develop. Sow from early spring through until early summer, sowing at two-week intervals. Excess cropping and late sowing can be used for pickling. If earlier crops are desired, then these may be sown under cloches.

AFTERCARE

Thin out seedlings if necessary, leaving the healthiest in situ. Keep any thinnings for the compost heap. Keep the crop weed-free, taking care if using a hoe as they are easily damaged. Beetroot needs a moist soil and should be watered every two weeks in dry periods to avoid 'hardening' of the crop. Consistency in watering is essential as successive wet and dry conditions will make the roots split. Mulching with compost will help the soil retain moisture.

CULTIVATION

Sowing time Early spring through to early summer. Successional sow every two weeks

Sowing distance 8cm (3in) and thin out after germination

Sowing depth 2.5cm (1in)

Distance between rows 20cm (8in)

Harvesting Late autumn to early spring

HARVESTING AND STORAGE

The first crop will be ready to pick about six to seven weeks after sowing. Pull as required, twisting the leaf off rather than cutting. Store autumn-harvested beetroot in boxes, covering the crop with moist peat-substitute or sand. These boxes should then be placed in a cool dry place.

PESTS AND DISEASES

Usually trouble free.

VARIETIES

'Barabietola di Chioggia' Rosy pink skin and white flesh with concentric pink circles.

'Carillon' A cylindrical, long red variety with resistance to bolting.

'Detriot Globe' Good uniform shape and flesh free from rings. Large roots are good for exhibiting.

'Egyptian Turnip Rooted' Early and quick-growing.

'Libero' Good resistance to bolting; fast growing with high yields.

SWEDES (RUTABAGAS OR YELLOW TURNIPS)

Brassica napus

Swedes are very similar to turnips, but their skin is normally yellow and they have a sweeter, milder flavour. Although this vegetable is grouped within root crops, it is botanically a member of the cabbage family. Crop rotation must therefore be planned carefully, grouping swedes in with cabbages because they suffer from the same pests and diseases.

SOIL

Although they will grow on heavy soils, swedes prefer a light soil that contains plenty of organic matter. Dig in the autumn, incorporating plenty of well-rotted manure or garden compost. Adding organic matter increases the moisture retention of the soil in summer, which is essential for good growth.

ASPECT

Thrive in an open sunny location.

SOWING

In late spring to early summer sow thinly in rows 1cm (½in) deep. Keep the rows 40cm (16in) apart. Once the seedlings are large enough, thin out to 25cm (10in) apart.

AFTERCARE

Swedes must be well watered throughout the summer months, otherwise they will turn woody and split. Mulch rows with garden compost to retain moisture in dry periods. Keep well weeded throughout.

HARVESTING AND STORAGE

Harvest from autumn into the winter months. Lift when they are large enough to use – you do not need to wait until they are maximum size. The crop can stay in the soil until spring, lifting only when required. Alternatively, lift and cut off the leaves and store in boxes filled with dry sand. Keep in a cool shed or garage with good air flow.

PESTS AND DISEASES

This crop is prone to the same problems as cabbages. Flea beetles are a frequent pest. To help prevent infestations, prepare the soil well by incorporating plenty of organic matter. Watering the plants regularly in dry periods and mulching will also help. Mildew and clubroot are another common problem. Resistant or tolerant cultivars are available, so choose these if you can.

Above: *Swedes are usually round, but can vary in shape according to the particular variety and growing conditions.*

CULTIVATION
Sowing time Late spring to early summer
Sowing distance Thinly
Sowing depth 1cm (½in)
Distance between rows 40cm (16in)
Thinning distance 25cm (10in)
Harvesting Autumn onwards

Right: *Swedes can be harvested from autumn onwards. You can leave the crop in the soil until spring, lifting it as required. Cut off the leaves, clean off all the soil on the swollen root and store in boxes filled with dry sand. They can also be stored in a vegetable clamp. This is an ideal way of preserving the crop over the winter months.*

VARIETIES
'Acme Purple Top' Medium-sized roots with a good flavour.
'Joan' Good for early sowings. Has a moderate resistance to clubroot and mildew.
'Marian' A fairly new variety with excellent texture and flavour. Moderately resistant to clubroot and mildew.

swedes

KOHL RABI

Brassica oleracea Gongylodes Group

This curious vegetable is a member of the cabbage family. It is the swollen stem, found at the base of the plant, that is eaten. Tasting something like a cross between a cabbage and a turnip, kohl rabi can be eaten raw or cooked. Although not widely grown, it has a number of good qualities. It grows very well on shallow soils and performs well in hot dry weather, whereas its culinary rival, the turnip, needs a firm, fertile soil. The green varieties are used for cropping in summer, while the purple types are mainly grown to harvest in autumn and early winter.

Above: *This extremely healthy crop of kohl rabi has been grown in a free-draining soil in an open sunny position.*

SOIL

Thrives in light soil conditions, but will grow on heavier soils. Dig the soil in the autumn, incorporating well-rotted manure or garden compost if this has not already been done in the previous autumn.

ASPECT

Grow kohl rabi in an open sunny site.

SOWING

Sow the seeds thinly in rows 1cm (½in) deep. Keep 30cm (12in) between the rows. Start sowing under cloches in late winter and outside in early spring. Successionally sow kohl rabi at three-week intervals until late summer. This will provide a fresh supply of tender globes. Thin out the rows when the seedlings are large enough to 15cm (6in) apart.

AFTERCARE

Weed regularly throughout the growing season, taking great care not to damage the shallow roots if you are using a hoe for weeding. Mulching with garden compost will also help to prevent the germination of any weed seedlings. Watering in dry periods will help to prevent the stems of the kohl rabi from splitting, although they are less likely to split than turnips.

HARVESTING AND STORAGE

Pull kohl rabi from the ground when they are about the size of a tennis ball because they tend to become woody if they are left to grow much bigger. Harvest as and when required because they do not store well and tend to shrivel. Later crops will keep in the ground until winter. Cut back the leaves and shorten the roots before taking them indoors to prepare.

Right: *This perfect specimen of kohl rabi has been well-watered throughout any dry periods to prevent the swollen stem from splitting.*

PESTS AND DISEASES

Kohl rabi is prone to the same pests and diseases as cabbages. Flea beetles are the main problem. Symptoms of an attack include small holes in the leaves and stems during the summer months. To avoid an attack, do not let the plants dry out and encourage quick seedling growth.

CULTIVATION

Sowing time Late winter (under cloches); early spring to late summer (outdoors)
Sowing distance Thinly
Sowing depth 1cm (½in)
Distance between rows 30cm (12in)
Thinning distance 15cm (6in)
Harvesting Summer through to early winter

VARIETIES

'Azur Star' Purple-blue bulbs with white flesh. A quick-maturing variety.
'F1 Cindy RZ' An early maturing variety that is slow to bolt. Large white bulbs with strong green foliage.
'Green Delicacy' An extremely old variety. Pale green globes with white flesh.
'Green Vienna' Green-skinned with white flesh. Good for early sowings.
'Purple Vienna' Purple-skinned globes with white flesh. Good for late sowings.
'Rowel' Lovely sweet flesh. Tends not to become woody if picked after it becomes the size of a tennis ball.

kohl rabi

TURNIPS

Brassica oleracea Rapifina Group

Turnips are a very easy crop to grow. Like carrots, home-grown turnips are much tastier than shop-bought specimens. Although the root is normally round, cylindrical root shapes are not uncommon in the early varieties. Turnip roots usually have a white skin that is coloured green, purple or yellow at the top. Inside the root, the flesh colour can vary from white to yellow. Group turnips in with cabbages when planning crop rotation as they are closely related and suffer from the same pests and diseases.

SOIL

Turnips thrive in firm, fertile soil that retains moisture. Dig in the autumn and incorporate plenty of well-rotted manure or garden compost to help retain moisture. If the soil is acidic, lime after digging. Practise crop rotation to avoid soil-borne diseases.

ASPECT

Grow best in a sunny position, but can take some degree of shade.

SOWING

For an early crop, start by sowing under cloches in late winter. Sow direct outside from early spring onwards. Sow thinly in rows 1cm (½in) deep, with 25cm (10in) between the rows for early crops. After germination, thin to 15cm (6in) apart. Successional sowing during spring and summer will ensure a steady supply of turnips. For turnips to be harvested in autumn and winter, sow in late summer. Sow to the same depth, but allow for 30cm (12in) between the rows and thin seedlings to 20cm (8in).

Right: *Harvest early and summer varieties of turnips as soon as they are the size of golf balls for optimum flavour.*

Below: *Do not allow turnips to turn woody. If lifted when young, the crop will not only taste better but be easy to pull.*

AFTERCARE

Regular watering is required, otherwise they run the risk of bolting. Weed throughout the growing season.

HARVESTING AND STORAGE

Pick turnips harvested in summer when they are the size of a golf ball. Varieties for picking in autumn and winter are harvested when required, or lift and store in trays of moist sand and keep in a shed or garage.

PESTS AND DISEASES

Prone to the same pests and diseases as cabbages, mainly flea beetle. Keep watered and prepare soil well to avoid attack. Violet root rot and clubroot are also a problem. Destroy all diseased material. Practise crop rotation to help avoid clubroot.

Left: *Turnips belong to the cabbage family and can suffer from clubroot. Practise crop rotation in order to prevent infection.*

CULTIVATION

Sowing time Late winter (under cloches); early spring and summer (outside)
Sowing distance Thinly
Sowing depth 1cm (½in)
Distance between rows 25–30cm (10–12in)
Thinning distance 15–20cm (6–8in)
Harvesting Summer to winter

VARIETIES

'Golden Ball' A relatively old variety with excellent storage qualities. Round golden roots with tender flesh.
'Market Cross F1' A quick grower. White roots that have an excellent flavour.
'Snowball' Fast maturing and best eaten small; lovely white skin.
'Veitch Red Globe' Roots are two tone, a red top and white bottom. Quick to mature.

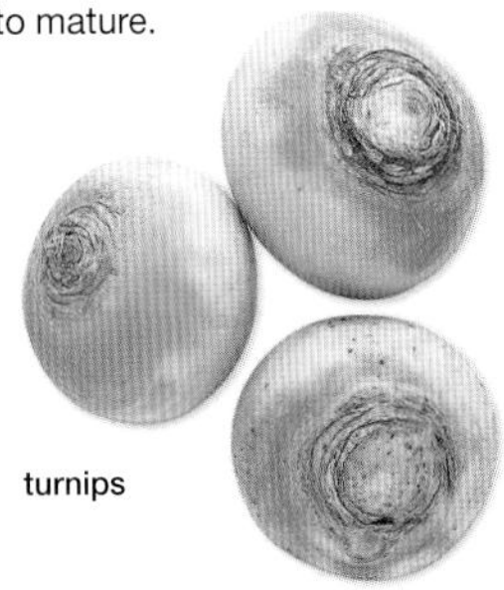

turnips

CARROTS

Daucus carota

If there is a vegetable that tastes incomparably better if it has been grown in your allotment, it must be the carrot. Home-grown carrots have a sweet, juicy flavour compared with the bland, watery taste of those sold in supermarkets. The edible part of the carrot is the root, which is usually orange, although there are also pale yellow and white varieties. Root shapes vary from round to long and tapered. Carrots that are planted within an ornamental area and left in the ground over winter will flower in their second year. The flowers are ideal for attracting beneficial insects into the area.

SOIL

Although carrots will grow in heavy clay soils, they do best on light sandy soils where the drainage is good and root growth is not impaired. The soil should be free of stones and fresh manure, as both will cause the carrot roots to fork. Do not manure the soil in the season before sowing.

ASPECT

Carrots require an open sunny site.

SOWING

Sow outside from early spring, or under cloches from late winter. Sow thinly in rows 1cm (½in) deep with 15–20cm (6–8in) between the rows. Sow successionally until early summer. If your soil is very heavy, use a crowbar to make holes, fill with a compost-and-grit mix and then sow into these holes. Thin the young seedlings to 5–8cm (2–3in) apart. Try to thin on a still evening to avoid attracting carrot fly. Bury the thinnings in the compost heap or wormery to avoid dispersing the smell.

AFTERCARE

Weed the crop regularly, making sure not to disturb the roots or shoots too much. Mulch the crop to help retain moisture and suppress weed growth. It is important to water during dry periods.

HARVESTING AND STORAGE

Start to harvest from late spring onwards, usually seven to eight weeks after sowing. Lift with a fork, especially when the soil is dry. Maincrop carrots can be left in the ground and harvested when required. In colder areas, cover over with straw until harvesting. Alternatively, carrots can be lifted in mid-autumn. After cleaning the roots and trimming the foliage to 1cm (½in), they can be stored in boxes containing a mixture of dry potting mix and sand. The carrots must not touch each other. These will keep until early spring.

PESTS AND DISEASES

The main pest is carrot root fly, which lays its eggs on the plant and can destroy the crop in severe cases. There are several methods to deter the fly from laying eggs. By delaying sowing until early summer, you will miss the first batch of egg laying in late spring. The second batch is in late summer until early autumn. Lift your early summer crop before risk of infestation. Another effective method is to erect a barrier of fleece or fine mesh around the crop. Companion planting can also help. Onions, for example, will mask the smell of carrots. Plant four rows to every row of carrots or plant in a mosaic pattern.

Left: *Plant carrots near onions or chives. This helps mask the smell of the carrots to deter its main pest, the carrot root fly.*

Left: *It is possible to start harvesting carrots from late spring onwards.*

CULTIVATION
Sowing time Early spring (under cloches) and successionally to early summer
Sowing distance Very thinly
Sowing depth 1cm (½in)
Distance between rows 15–20cm (6–8in)
Thinning distance 5–8cm (2–3in)
Harvesting Late spring onwards

VARIETIES

EARLY

'Amsterdam Forcing' Small roots that are ideal for freezing.
'Nantes 2' Matures quickly. Has a lovely sweet flavour.
'Parabel' Small and spherical root that is sweet flavoured.

MAINCROP

'Berlicum' Produces a uniform crop. The roots have good colour and flavour.
'Fly Away F1' Sweet flavour. Bred for carrot fly resistance.
'F1 Magno RZ' Vigorous grower with good colour. Stores well.

JERUSALEM ARTICHOKES

Helianthus tuberosus

The edible parts of the Jerusalem artichoke are the knobbly tubers that grow underground, like the potato. You can boil, fry, bake, roast or stew them. Sample a few from the supermarket before splashing out on a row of them for your vegetable plot. Take care when planning your crop as they are a type of sunflower and can easily reach heights of 3m (10ft). It is advisable to select a variety that has been bred to reach a more manageable size of 1.5m (5ft) if you are gardening in a confined space.

Right: *These Jerusalem artichokes are freshly dug. This variety is 'Fuseau'. Start harvesting the crop in autumn, then lift as and when required over the winter. Clear any remaining tubers from the site in early spring and replant immediately using healthy new tubers.*

SOIL

Grow in any type of soil provided it is not too acid or has prolonged periods of waterlogging. Dig in garden compost or well-rotted manure in autumn. Do not be liberal with this, or too much leafy growth will be produced at the expense of the tubers.

ASPECT

Jerusalem artichokes thrive in full sun, but will also grow well in dappled shade.

PLANTING

If space is limited on the plot it is best to plant one of the compact varieties, otherwise plant tubers bought from a supermarket. Plant at any time from early to late spring. Plant out in rows 40cm (16in) apart. Use a trowel or a dibber (dibble) to plant the tuber 10–13cm (4–5in) deep. Rows need to be 90cm (3ft) apart.

Above: *This healthy row of Jerusalem artichokes has been mulched with a layer of farmyard manure to help retain moisture.*

Left: *Jerusalem artichokes can be lifted when the foliage starts to turn brown in the autumn. Make sure that you remove all of the tubers because any left in the ground will grow the following year.*

AFTERCARE

Earth up the bases of the plants when they are 30cm (12in) high. Water throughout dry periods. Remove flowering heads in the summer months. If the plants are grown on a windy site stake to support tall stems.

HARVESTING AND STORAGE

Lift the tubers when the foliage starts to turn brown in autumn. Cut the stems down before lifting the tubers, taking care to remove all the tubers. Any left in will grow the following year. Lift the tubers throughout autumn and winter when required. If frost is forecast, lift the amount of tubers needed and store in a box of moist sand.

PESTS AND DISEASES

Generally trouble free, although they can be attacked by slugs.

CULTIVATION

Planting time Early to late spring
Planting distance 40cm (16in)
Planting depth 10–13cm (4–5in)
Distance between rows 90cm (3ft)
Harvesting Autumn onwards

VARIETIES

'Dwarf Sunray' Compact habit with ornamental merits. Lovely white skin that does not need peeling.
'Fuseau' Considered the best variety due to the smooth surface of the tuber. This is a compact plant that is suitable for the small allotment.

Jerusalem artichokes

PARSNIPS

Pastinaca sativa

Parsnips are a good vegetable for the inexperienced gardener as they require very little work and are easy to grow. It is the underground swollen root that is eaten. The root looks similar to a carrot but is creamy white in colour and slightly longer. Parsnips taste great used in stir-fries, mashed up with carrot or as an accompaniment to fish or roast meats.

SOIL

Do not grow on freshly manured ground, but on ground that has already been manured for the previous crop. Ideally, the soil needs to be dug over during the winter and be stone-free to produce good-quality parsnips. Compost from your heap may be added to improve the soil structure.

ASPECT

Parsnips like an open sunny site, but will tolerate light shade.

SOWING

It is essential to sow fresh seed every year. Sow in late winter through to late spring in drills 1cm (½in) deep and space seeds 15cm (6in) apart. Alternatively, sow sparingly and thin out at the seedling stage. Rows are spaced 30cm (12in) apart. Germination can be slow, sometimes taking up to three weeks. This allows for intercropping between rows by sowing radish or lettuce.

Above: *It is advisable to sow fresh parsnip seed every year because even one-year-old seed is unlikely to germinate successfully due to reduced viability.*

Left: *Parsnips can be left in the ground and harvested as they are required. The best-tasting parsnips are lifted after the first frost.*

AFTERCARE

Thin out rows of seedlings (where necessary) to 15cm (6in) apart. Throw thinnings on to your compost heap as they do not transplant easily. Water the crop during dry periods, never allowing the soil to dry out. Carry out regular weeding, taking care not to damage the crowns of the new plants.

HARVESTING AND STORAGE

Start harvesting when the foliage starts to die down in mid-autumn. The best-tasting parsnips are lifted after the first frosts. Lift only when required; the remainder can be left in the ground through to late winter. A certain number may also be lifted and stored in a box of moist sand to ensure supplies throughout the winter.

PESTS AND DISEASES

Generally trouble free, but parsnip canker can affect the crop. Do not plant in freshly manured ground. Instead, sow later or use canker-resistant varieties. Acidic soil conditions can also cause canker. Carrot fly and celery fly may attack parsnips.

Above: *Parsnips are hardy plants and so they are best left in the ground until ready for harvesting. Lift with a fork in order to avoid damaging the root.*

CULTIVATION

Sowing time Late winter to late spring
Sowing distance 15cm (6in) or sow sparingly and thin out at seedling stage
Sowing depth 1cm (½in)
Distance between rows 30cm (12in)
Thinning distance 15–20cm (6–8in)
Harvesting Mid-autumn to late winter

VARIETIES

'Avonresister' Resistance to canker.
'Half Long Guernsey' Heavily tapered roots with a sweet flavour.
'Tender & True' Excellent flavour, good resistance to canker.
'White King' A heavy yielding variety with delicious, well-textured roots.

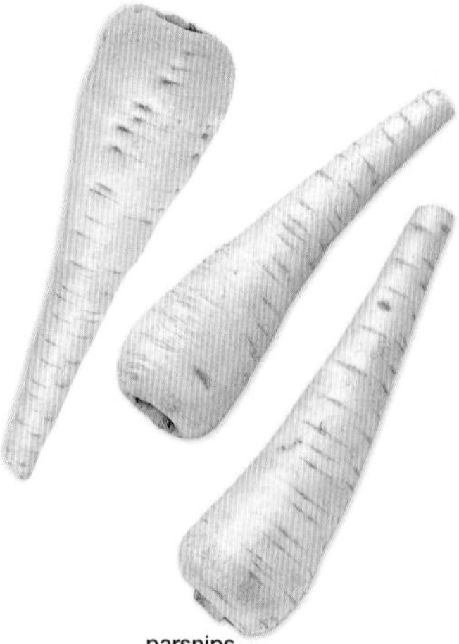

parsnips

RADISHES

Raphanus sativus

This extremely fast-growing vegetable has a wider crop diversity than is commonly known. Along with the familiar round red radish often used in salads, there are also varieties with pink, yellow or white roots. Winter varieties can have roots the size of carrots and other types are grown for their pods. Due to their attractive roots, which sit slightly above the soil, they can be grown among decorative plants in the allotment.

SOIL

Radishes will grow in most soils, but thrive in soil that is rich in organic matter and is moisture retentive. Dig in plenty of garden compost before sowing if the ground was not manured for a previous crop.

ASPECT

Thrive in an open sunny site, but will welcome some dappled shade at the height of summer. This makes radishes ideal for intercropping during this period.

SOWING

Summer crops can be started by sowing outside under cloches in late winter and in early spring. Sow thinly in rows 1cm (½in) deep with 15cm (6in) between the rows. Thin to 2.5cm (1in) apart. Successional sowing will prevent a glut at harvest time. Sow in small rows every two weeks. Sow

Above: *When harvesting radishes, discard any that have become large or old, as they will be too woody and hot to eat.*

winter varieties in mid-summer. They are larger than the maincrop varieties, so the rows should be spaced 25cm (10in) apart and the crop thinned to 15cm (6in) apart.

AFTERCARE

Keep weed-free throughout the season and water in dry periods.

HARVESTING AND STORAGE

Pick radishes before they get too old and woody. Select the larger roots first and leave the rest of the crop to grow. Winter cultivars can be left in the soil with a layer of straw over the top for protection. Harvest

Below: *For small quantities of radishes, it is best to sow short rows every two weeks to obtain a succession of crops.*

CULTIVATION

SUMMER RADISH
Sowing time Late winter (under cloches); early spring onwards (outside)
Sowing distance Thinly
Sowing depth 1cm (½in)
Distance between rows 15cm (6in)
Thinning distance 2.5cm (1in)
Harvesting Late spring onwards

WINTER RADISH
Sowing time Mid-summer
Sowing distance Thinly
Sowing depth 1cm (½in)
Distance between rows 25cm (10in)
Thinning distance 15cm (6in)
Harvesting Autumn onwards

as and when required; otherwise lift the radishes and store them in trays of sand until needed.

PESTS AND DISEASES

Radishes are related to cabbages and are prone to the same pests and diseases. Flea beetle and slugs are normally the main problems. If more problematic pests or diseases take hold, destroy plants and grow in an alternative location.

VARIETIES

'Berosa' Grown for winter use. Grows up to 15cm (6in) long. Ideal for slicing.
'Rondeel RZ' A bright red round radish. Good uniformity.
'Sirri RZ' Excellent root colouring with strong foliage. Stores well.
'Sparkler' A spring variety that has a red base to the root with a white tip.

radishes

POTATOES

Solanum tuberosum

This native of South America is one of the easiest vegetables to grow. Potatoes are split up into two main groups: earlies and maincrop. Earlies are harvested in summer, offering the welcome taste of new potatoes, whereas maincrop potatoes are harvested later and can be stored for use during the winter.

SOIL

Potatoes thrive on sandy soil that is slightly acidic, but will grow almost as well on nearly every other type of soil. However, they grow best on a fertile soil that is rich in nitrogen. Plant in soil that has had organic matter added in the autumn; they should never be planted on freshly manured ground.

ASPECT

A warm sheltered site is best. Always avoid frost pockets, which can damage the foliage of early varieties emerging from the soil.

PURCHASING SEED POTATOES

Seed potatoes are not actually seeds, but swollen tubers from the potato plant. They can be purchased from mid-winter to mid-spring. It is important to purchase certified seed potatoes, as this will ensure a healthy virus-free stock.

CHITTING

Before planting outdoors, place seed potatoes with the seeds' eyes (the dormant buds on the surface) facing upward on a 2.5cm (1in) layer of potting mix in trays or egg boxes. They should be left indoors in light warm conditions to encourage the sprouting of small shoots. This is called chitting. In six weeks the shoots will have grown to 2.5cm (1in), the ideal length to plant. Chitting is essential for earlies but not necessary for maincrop potatoes, although this can still prove beneficial in colder years.

Above: *Before planting out potato tubers, place them in a tray in order to 'chit' them. This is essential for early potatoes.*

Above: *It is only the tubers of the potato plant that are edible. All other parts, such as the leaves and fruits, are poisonous.*

PLANTING

Planting is normally carried out in trenches 10–15cm (4–6in) deep with 30–40cm (12–16in) between the tubers. Keep 45cm (18in) between the rows for first earlies and 65–75cm (26–30in) for second earlies and maincrop varieties. Always plant the seed potatoes with their 'eyes' facing upwards, taking care not to break off the new growth. An alternative to hoeing out the trenches is to plant the potatoes individually (to the same specifications) using a trowel or potato dibber (dibble). Once planted and covered with soil, create a small mound above them.

If you cannot face digging over a vegetable bed, why not try the 'no-dig bed system'? Cover the soil with well-rotted manure or compost and simply place the seed potatoes on top, 30–40cm (12–16in) apart. Cover the seed potatoes with a 10cm (4in) layer of old straw. Alternatively, if you are gardening in a confined space, try planting the seed potatoes in pots. This method can allow people with even the smallest plots to experience home-grown, pesticide-free new potatoes.

Above: *Earth up the potatoes in order to increase yields and prevent light reaching the new potatoes. Light will make them turn green and they will be poisonous.*

AFTERCARE

PROTECTION FROM FROST Cover the young growth with straw or fleece if there is any risk of frost.

EARTHING UP This task is essential if large yields are to be obtained. Earthing up also stops light getting to the new potatoes, which makes them turn green and poisonous. Another benefit of this is

Above: *When harvesting maincrop potatoes, leave them on the surface for an hour or two to let them dry out and to harden the skins.*

that it makes the soil easy to work for crop rotation. Earth up when the foliage is 20cm (8in) tall. Hoe up the earth around the foliage until only a small amount of leaf is still showing at the top. This process is carried out again just before the foliage between the rows joins up.

Watering Potatoes need copious amounts of water throughout their growing period in order to develop plenty of good-sized tubers. It is essential to water heavily in the early stages of development. Watering every 10 days during dry periods is a good guide to follow.

HARVESTING AND STORAGE

Earlies These are ready to lift when the potato plant is flowering – usually towards the end of early summer or the beginning of mid-summer for first earlies, and late summer for second earlies. Harvest the potatoes using a potato fork (with balls on the end of the tines) or a flat-tined fork to reduce damage to the crop.

Maincrop These are harvested in early autumn, 10–14 days after the withered brown foliage has been removed and put on the compost heap. Lift the potatoes on a warm dry day and leave on the surface for several hours to dry out. Store only perfect potatoes in a sack or in trays in a cool, dark, frost-free place. Diseased potatoes do not store well and must be used at once.

PESTS AND DISEASES

The potato's worst enemy is blight. This is particularly bad in wet summers where the weather is hot and humid. The first sign of the disease is brown patches on the leaves. These should be cut off to prevent the spores being washed off into the soil to infect the tubers. Choose resistant varieties if possible. Scab disfigures the tuber by cracking and brown discoloration. Water the crop heavily to help overcome the problem and do not grow on ground that has been recently manured. Potatoes are also damaged by diseases such as violet root rot and blackleg. Slugs, eelworms and cutworms are the worst pests, all of them eating and damaging the tubers.

CULTIVATION

First earlies

Planting time Early spring
Planting distance 30–40cm (12–16in)
Planting depth 10–15cm (4–6in)
Distance between rows 45cm (18in)
Harvesting Early summer

Second earlies and maincrop

Planting time Mid- to late spring
Planting distance 30–40cm (12–16in)
Planting depth 10–15cm (4–6in)
Distance between rows 65–75cm (26–30in)
Harvesting Summer onwards

VARIETIES

First earlies

'Accent' Attractive yellow skin and flesh, high yielding.
'Premiere' Resistant to blight and high resistance to common scab.
'Red Duke of York' Superb texture and flavour.
'Swift' Resistant to golden eelworm and tolerant to blackleg.

Second earlies

'Cosmos' Resistant to blight and common scab.
'Kestrel' Great flavour, ideal for baking. Performs well in drought conditions.
'Marfona' Good for baking, stores well.
'Wilja' Good resistance to disease and drought.

Maincrop

'Cara' Stores well, good blight resistance.
'Désirée' Distinctive flavour and a superb roaster.
'Milva' Good flavour with resistance to blight.
'Valor' Good overall disease resistance together with high eelworm resistance and high resistance to blight.

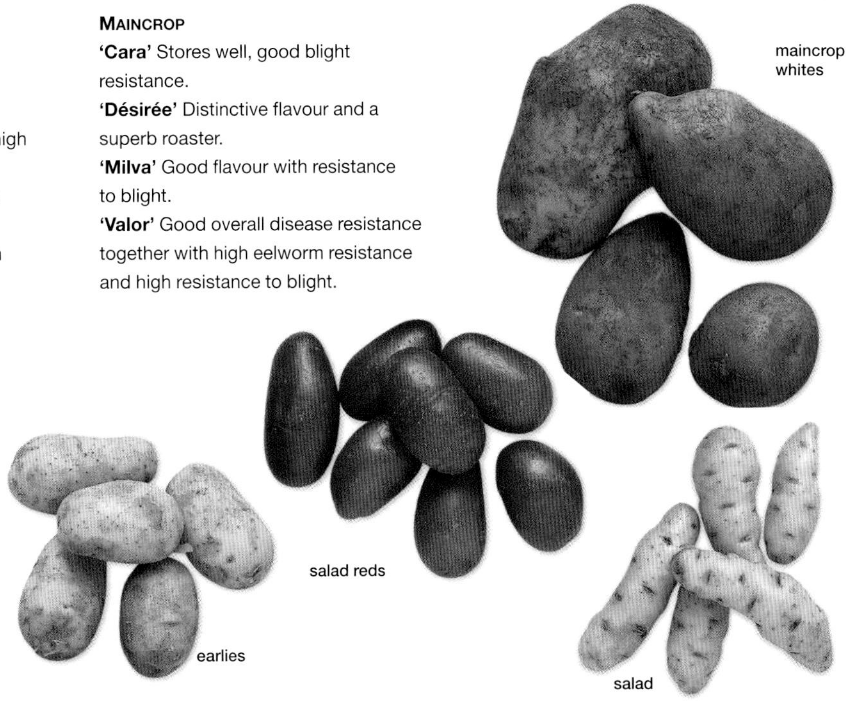

SALSIFY AND SCORZONERA

Tragopogon porrifolius and *Scorzonera hispanica*

These two unusual root vegetables are underused. Salsify is a biennial that has a similar appearance to a skinny parsnip and has a distinctive flavour that has been likened to that of a cross between asparagus and oysters. Scorzonera is a perennial that has black-skinned roots with white flesh and a delicious flavour.

SOIL

Both root crops prefer a light stone-free soil. They do not like freshly manured ground. Ideally, manure should have been added to the ground for the previous crop. Dig deeply in the autumn to ensure good root development, adding garden compost if the soil is poor.

ASPECT

Salsify and scorzonera will thrive in an open sunny site on an allotment.

SOWING

Sow in mid-spring to ensure a long growing season. This will allow for large root development to take place before harvesting. Sow fresh seed every year, as it does not keep well. Sow thinly in rows 1cm (½) deep, with 25cm (10in) between the rows. After germination thin the seedlings to 15cm (6in).

AFTERCARE

An easy vegetable to look after. Keep weed-free. Do this carefully, as roots can be easily damaged by a hoe. Mulching with garden compost will help to keep weeds down. It will also help the soil to retain moisture in dry periods.

HARVESTING AND STORAGE

Both salsify and scorzonera can be harvested from autumn onwards. Like many crops, the taste of both vegetables is enhanced after the first frost. As both crops are hardy they can be left in the ground throughout the winter and lifted when needed. If the roots of scorzonera are not large enough to harvest during the first season they can be left in the ground until the following autumn and winter.

PESTS AND DISEASES

Usually trouble free.

Left: *This crop of salsify has just been harvested. Although salsify can be lifted from autumn onwards, the taste of the vegetables is enhanced if they are harvested after the first frosts.*

Above: *This abundant crop of scorzonera has been harvested in a trug. Some plants are still remaining.*

Left: *Although salsify produces a mass of untidy foliage, it is worth growing just to taste its unusual flavour.*

CULTIVATION
Sowing time Mid-spring
Sowing distance Thinly
Sowing depth 1cm (½in)
Distance between rows 25cm (10in)
Thinning distance 15cm (6in)
Harvesting Autumn and winter

VARIETIES

SALSIFY

'Sandwich Island' An old variety. Very large tapering roots with yellow skin.

SCORZONERA

'Russian Giant' Long black roots. Young leaves can be eaten in salads.

Both crops are often simply listed under salsify (or vegetable oyster) and scorzonera.

PEAS AND BEANS

RUNNER BEANS

Phaseolus coccineus

These climbing plants, known in the US as green beans, are often grown for their lovely red flowers and long green pods, and look wonderful on decorative supports or arches. New varieties offer flower colours in white or mauve. The production of the pods requires pollination by bees.

SOIL

Runner beans thrive in a deep, rich, moisture-retentive soil, but they will grow in relatively poor soil. Manure the previous autumn.

ASPECT

They like an open, sheltered, sunny position. Do not plant in windy areas as this will make pollination difficult and the support structures will be prone to blowing over.

SOWING/PLANTING

Runner beans are half hardy and therefore should not be planted or appear above ground until the risk of frost has gone. For an early start, sow the crop under glass in early spring. The beans are best sown individually in pots and then hardened off to be ready to plant out in early summer. Alternatively, sow directly outside in late spring. Before sowing, build a support for the crop. This is traditionally made up of a double row of canes tied at the top. For a more decorative effect, construct a tepee. Keep 25cm (10in) between each cane. Plant two seeds 50cm (2in) deep per cane and remove the weaker seedling after germination. Dwarf varieties are grown in single rows at 15cm (6in) apart and with 45cm (18in) between the rows. Sow direct or grow under glass for an early start.

Above: *A larger crop of beans will be produced if picked regularly. Select young pods and discard any old stringy ones.*

Above: *Many gardeners sow three beans at the base of each pole – 'one for the crow, one for the slug and one for the kitchen'.*

AFTERCARE

Keep the soil moist at all times, mulching with garden compost to help the soil to retain moisture. After harvesting leave the roots to rot down in the soil as the root nodules contain a valuable source of nitrogen. Turn in the roots when digging the soil during the autumn.

HARVESTING AND STORAGE

Pick the pods when they have reached 20–30cm (8–12in) in length and before they have become stringy and hard. It is important to pick regularly or the plants will stop flowering. Most plants will continue to flower until the first frosts. The only successful method of storage is to freeze any surplus beans.

PESTS AND DISEASES

One of the commonest problems with runner beans is their failure to set pods. This is often the case in periods of hot dry weather. Regular watering will help flowering and pod formation. Mulching will help to retain soil moisture. Pest damage from slugs and snails can pose problems when the plants are young. Diseases such as powdery mildew and chocolate spot may occasionally occur.

CULTIVATION

Sowing time Early spring (under glass); late spring (outside)
Planting out time Early summer
Sowing/planting distance 15–25cm (6–10in)
Sowing depth 5cm (2in)
Distance between rows 45–90cm (18–36in)
Harvesting Late summer until first frosts

VARIETIES

RUNNER BEANS

'Butler' Crops over a long period. Pods are completely stringless and tender.
'Czar-Larg' Long rough pods with white seeds. If left to dry will produce a crop of butter (lima) beans.
'Désirée' A stringless, heavy cropper with a great flavour. Good for freezing.
'Kelvedon Marvel' A good early cropper with short pods.

DWARF RUNNER BEANS

'Arosa RZ' An excellent early heavy cropper. Resistant to common mosaic virus.
'Deuil Fin Precoce' Compact plants that produce purple streaked pods with an excellent flavour.
'Maxi' Grows well in poor soils. A fast-growing variety with pods up to 20cm (8in).

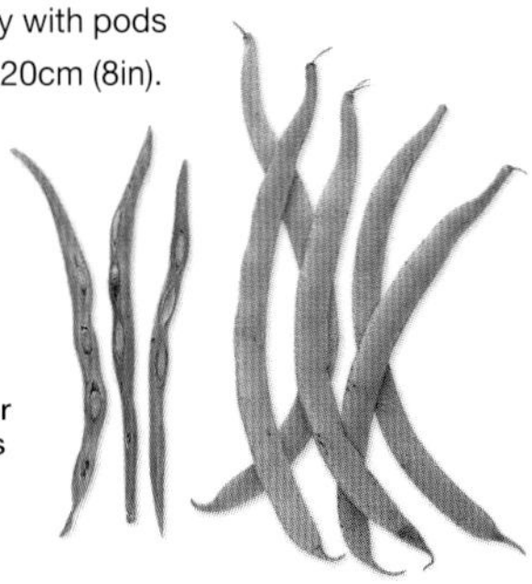

runner beans

FRENCH (GREEN) BEANS

Phaseolus vulgaris

French beans are split into two distinct categories: dwarf and climbing. The dwarf varieties are by far the most popular as they do not take up much room. Both types are frost tender and need to be sown or planted out after any risk of frost has gone. Nowadays, there are many good varieties, which offer colourful pods in yellows and purples to liven up the allotment plot.

SOIL

They thrive in fertile, free-draining soil that has preferably been manured during soil cultivation in the previous autumn.

ASPECT

French beans require an open sunny site.

SOWING

French beans can be sown early under glass in pots in late spring, but they are best sown outdoors in early summer in a single or double row 4cm (1½in) deep with 8cm (3in) between the seeds. Place the rows 45cm (18in) apart. Plant outside in early summer when the threat of frost has passed. Treat climbing varieties in the same way as non-dwarf runner beans.

Below: *The pods of French beans are now found in a variety of colours. This purple pod variety is often grown by allotment-growers wanting something more unusual.*

Above: *Leave the pods that you want to treat as haricot beans until the pods have swollen and turned yellow.*

AFTERCARE

Water regularly when the crop is in flower. Keep the plot weed-free throughout the growing season.

HARVESTING AND STORAGE

Harvest when the seeds are still immature on the plant. Pick regularly to encourage new pods. The beans are best eaten fresh, but they can be frozen. French beans can also be dried and stored in airtight jars and named haricot (navy) beans.

PESTS AND DISEASES

Generally trouble free. Blackfly and fungal diseases can cause problems. Slugs and snails are the main problem, especially at the seedling stage.

CULTIVATION

Sowing time Late spring (under glass); early summer (outdoors)
Sowing/planting distance 8cm/3in (dwarf); 25cm/10in (climbing)
Sowing depth 4cm (1½in)
Distance between rows 45cm/18in (dwarf); 90cm/3ft (climbing)
Harvesting Late summer until first frosts

Above: *Harvesting can begin seven to eight weeks after sowing. It is best to pick while the seeds are still immature.*

VARIETIES

Climbing

'Blue Lake' A heavy-yielding variety that is suitable for freezing. The stringless pods contain small white beans.
'Farba RZ' Pods are round and stringless, growing up to 12cm (5in) long.
'Mantra RZ' A good cropper that produces uniform pods 20cm (8in) long. This variety is resistant to common bean mosaic virus.

Dwarf

'Annabel' A compact variety that is good for growing in pots or grow-bags. A heavy cropper of thin stringless pods.
'The Prince' An early variety. The dwarf-growing flat pod is often used for exhibiting.

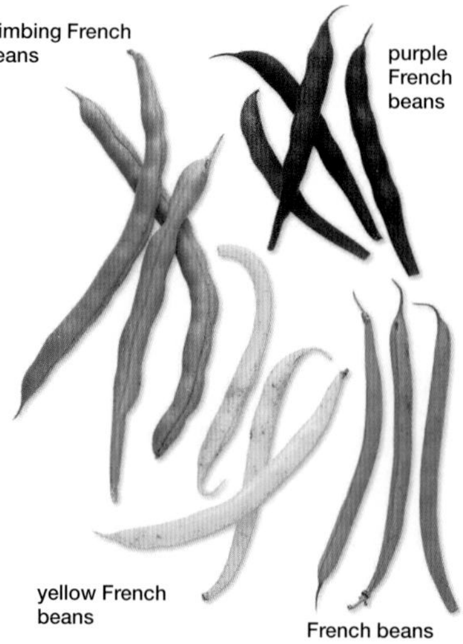

PEAS

Pisum sativum

There is nothing like the taste of freshly picked peas. This is because the moment that a pea is picked its natural sugars start to break down into starch, which affects the flavour. With careful planning and by using a range of varieties, peas can be freshly harvested from late spring until late autumn.

SOIL

Grow peas in a fertile moisture-retentive soil. Dig the soil to a good depth in autumn and incorporate well-rotted manure or garden compost. Do not grow in soil that might get waterlogged, as this will cause basal rotting to the plants.

ASPECT

Peas thrive in an open sunny site, but will withstand light shade.

SOWING

Varieties are categorized as first earlies, which are smooth-skinned, and second earlies and maincrop, which have wrinkled skins. Sow first earlies outside in mid- to late autumn and overwinter the crop under cloches. For a slightly later crop, sow second earlies in late winter to early spring, starting them off under cloches to protect against frost. Maincrop varieties are sown at regular intervals from early spring to mid-summer without protection. Sow in flat-bottomed trenches, 23cm (9in) wide and 5cm (2in) deep. Sow the seed in a double row, 5cm (2in) apart, or in single rows with 60–90cm (24–36in) between trenches or rows.

Below: *Choose old seed varieties if you wish to harvest the crop at intervals, as many modern varieties mature at the same time.*

Above: *Wire netting can support smaller pea varieties, whereas the more decorative hazel sticks are used for larger ones.*

AFTERCARE

Immediately after sowing protect the crop from birds by covering with wire netting, twiggy branches or tie black cotton thread over canes. Provide support, using pea sticks or plastic or wire netting, when the crop reaches 8cm (3in) high. For tall varieties place the supports on either side of the growing stems. Water regularly during dry spells, especially when the crop is in flower. Mulch with garden compost to improve soil-moisture retention.

HARVESTING AND STORAGE

Harvest when the pods are plump but not fully grown, starting from the bottom of the plant and working your way up. Keep picking to encourage production. Mangetouts (snow peas) need to be picked before the pods get tough. Fresh peas freeze well in plastic bags or containers. Dry peas by leaving them on the plant until they rattle about in their pods. Shell peas and store in an airtight container.

PESTS AND DISEASES

Peas are prone to a number of pests and diseases. Pigeons and sparrows can devastate young crops. Netting is the best protection. Mildew can also be a problem. Pea and bean weevil can cause checking of plant growth. The crop may be attacked by pea thrips in hot sunny weather. Silvery patches are seen on the pods and leaves, which will affect the yield. Sow early to avoid major attacks. The white-bodied caterpillar of the pea moth feeds on the peas inside the pods. The adults lay their eggs when the peas are in flower. Sow early or late to avoid the moth's flying period.

CULTIVATION

Sowing time Mid- to late autumn (first earlies); late winter to early spring (second earlies); early spring to mid-summer (maincrop)
Trench width 23cm (9in)
Trench depth 5cm (2in)
Sowing distance in trenches Sow a double row 5cm (2in) apart
Distance between trenches or rows 60–90cm (24–36in)
Harvesting Late spring until late autumn depending on variety

VARIETIES

FIRST EARLIES

'Feltham First' A vigorous grower suitable for autumn sowing.
'Meteor' Compact plants that produce heavy yields.

SECOND EARLIES AND MAINCROP

'Alderman' A tall variety with large pods. A high yielder, but needs support.
'Onward' Large peas with a superb flavour. Crops heavily and has good disease resistance.

MANGETOUT

'Carouby de Mausanne' Purple flowers and large pods. Tastes delicious.
'Oregon Sugar Pod' Superb sweet flavour. Fast growing and tall.

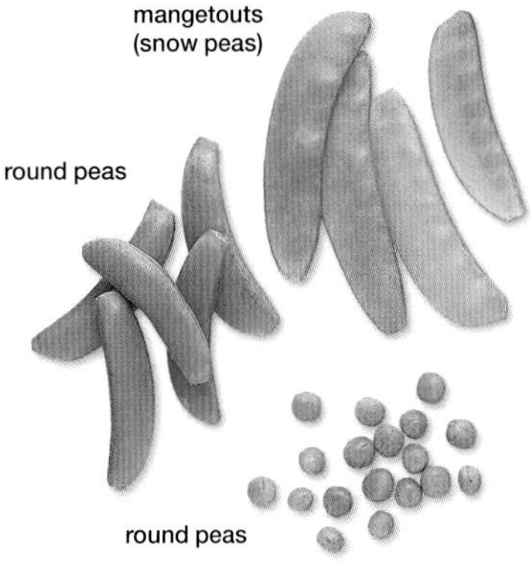

BROAD (FAVA) BEANS

Vicia faba

These are the hardiest and earliest of all the beans grown. Like many vegetables, the fresh or frozen produce that can be purchased from a supermarket does not do its flavour justice. Try growing this crop in your allotment site to experience the true succulent flavour. Varieties can be selected to grow green, white or red seeds.

Left: *To grow a healthy crop of broad beans, choose an open sunny site which is protected from strong winds. As broad beans need plenty of water up until the pods start to swell, mulch the growing crop in spring to aid soil water retention and reduce plant stress in drier periods.*

SOIL

Grow broad beans in heavy soils that are well manured and have good drainage. Dig and incorporate manure during the autumn.

ASPECT

Broad beans thrive in an open sunny site that is sheltered from strong winds. This is essential if you are growing the crop over the winter.

SOWING

Overwintering varieties are sown in late autumn. Other varieties are sown from late winter to late spring. Sow in double rows in a shallow trench, 23cm (9in) wide and 4cm (1½in) deep with 23cm (9in) between the seeds. Alternatively, the crop can be started off under glass in late winter. Sow individually in pots to be planted out in spring.

AFTERCARE

Keep weeds down throughout the growing season. If there is a dry spell, give plenty of water throughout this period until the pods start to swell. Provide support for taller varieties. Place stakes or canes on either side of the crop, 25cm (10in) apart, and run string from stake to stake to support the stems. When the first pods start to form, pinch out the top 8cm (3in) of growth. This will reduce the danger of blackfly attack and aid pod formation.

HARVESTING AND STORAGE

Pick the pods when they have become swollen. Do not allow the pods to be too mature because they will become leathery and tough. Continuous harvesting extends the cropping season. Broad beans are best picked and used fresh. Any surplus beans can be frozen or dried.

PESTS AND DISEASES

The most serious problem is blackfly. Removing the growing tips when the pods are starting to mature will help to deter this problem. The only other major problem is chocolate spot, which can sometimes affect the crop. Avoid autumn sowings if this is a problem and destroy affected material.

Above: *Pinch out the tops of the plants when the first pods have begun to form. This aids pod formation and discourages blackfly.*

Above: *Taller varieties require support. Place canes at regular intervals on each side of the crop, tying string between each pole.*

CULTIVATION

Sowing time Late autumn (overwintering varieties); late winter to early spring (other varieties)
Sowing distance in trenches/ planting distance 23cm (9in)
Sowing depth 4cm (1½in)
Distance between trenches or rows 60cm (24in)
Harvesting Early to late summer

VARIETIES

'Aquaculce Claudia' Extremely hardy variety that is used for overwintering. Long pods containing white beans.
'Futua RZ' Early producer with compact pods. Tolerant of chocolate spot.
'The Sutton' Good compact plant at only 30cm (12in) long.

broad (fava) beans

MARROWS AND SQUASH CROPS

PUMPKINS

Cucurbita maxima

Pumpkins are popular with children because they look so impressive and can be carved out and used as lanterns. The flesh is cooked and makes good soups and pies. They are found in colours such as blue and green as well as the popular yellow-orange. Smaller varieties of pumpkin can be grown that are bred for flavour rather than their eventual size.

SOIL

Deep fertile soil that is rich in humus. Before planting dig out a planting pit 45cm (18in) deep and 60cm (24in) square. Fill half the dug-out pit with well-rotted manure or garden compost and fill back in again.

ASPECT

Plant or sow pumpkins in a sunny position and protect from strong winds.

SOWING

Sowing can begin under glass in late spring at a temperature of 15–18°C (59–64°F). Soak the seeds overnight to speed up germination. Sow the seeds individually in pots. Plant out in early summer in the prepared planting pits after all threat of frost has passed. Plant at distances of 1.8m (6ft) apart. Alternatively, sow directly outside into prepared planting pits 1.8m (6ft) apart in early summer. Keep a distance of 1.8m (6ft) between the rows.

AFTERCARE

To keep the vigorous growth in check, train the stems around the plant, pinning them to the ground with wire pegs. For larger pumpkins, choose one to three good fruits when they are small and remove the rest. Watering needs to take place throughout the growing season. It is advantageous to feed every two weeks during this period. Pinch out the tips of trailing varieties towards the end of the summer. Stop watering and feeding once the fruits are mature.

Above: *Pumpkins take up a lot a space, so careful thought is needed when siting them within the confines of a small allotment.*

HARVESTING AND STORAGE

It is best for the fruits to mature on the plant. Harvest the entire crop before the first frosts, leaving a stem on the fruit of about 5cm (2in) in length. Leave them in a sunny location for about a week for the skins to harden. Pumpkins store well. The popular orange-skinned varieties will store for several weeks, whereas the blue-skinned type will last for up to three months.

PESTS AND DISEASES

Slugs are a problem, especially when the fruits start to grow. Mice can also cause damage. Destroy the plant if it contracts cucumber mosaic virus.

Left: *Harvest pumpkins when they have reached their mature colour. A good indicator is when the stems begin to split.*

CULTIVATION
Sowing time Early spring (under glass); early summer (outdoors)
Planting time Early summer
Sowing and planting distance 1.8m (6ft)
Sowing depth 4cm (1½in)
Distance between rows 1.8m (6ft)
Harvesting Autumn

Above: *Although pumpkins take time and patience to grow, they are ideal plants with which to encourage young gardeners.*

VARIETIES
'Atlantic Giant' Largest pumpkin of all. Stores very well.
'Jack be Little' Produces small fruits that are only 8cm (3in) across. The orange fruits have an excellent taste when stuffed or baked.
'Tom Fox' Medium-sized orange fruits that are great for making pumpkin pie.

pumpkins

SQUASHES

Cucurbita maxima

Squashes are very closely related to marrows (large zucchini) and pumpkins and there is very little difference in their cultivation requirements and culinary preparation. Squashes come in a diverse range of shapes and sizes. The outside flesh colour is also very varied, ranging from almost white to deep orange. They look delightful when used in the allotment, climbing over trelliswork frames and arches.

Squashes can be divided into two main groups: summer and winter types. The difference between the two groups lies in their storage qualities. Summer types will keep for two to three weeks, but are best used fresh from the plant, whereas winter types can still be used fresh but will also keep for long periods in storage.

SOIL

Squashes prefer a soil that is rich in organic matter. Dig over the soil in the autumn, incorporating copious amounts of well-rotted manure or garden compost. This not only enriches the soil with nutrients, but also helps to retain moisture in the soil, which is essential for healthy growth. Mulching with garden compost or straw will also help to prevent water evaporating from the soil.

ASPECT

Squashes thrive in an open sunny site that is protected from strong winds. These conditions are vital for successful growth because they are neither hardy nor robust.

Above: *Squashes undoubtedly have a culinary value, but they are often grown simply for their attractive looks. They look extremely ornamental if they are grown over archways or trellis.*

Left: *The Turk's Turban squash is a distinctive winter squash that will add colour and interest to autumn allotments.*

Above: *If you are growing squashes in a restricted space, cut off the trailing stems two leaves above a fruit. Keep well watered, and feed and mulch regularly.*

SOWING

Squashes can be started off by sowing individually in pots under glass in early spring. Sow individually in modules or fibre pots because they do not like their roots to be disturbed. The temperature needs to be a constant of 18°C (64°F). Harden off and plant outside in early summer, after the risk of frost has passed. They need a lot of room, so leave 1.8m (6ft) between the plants. If you do not have access to a greenhouse, sow directly outside in rows during early summer at a depth of 4cm (1½in). Keep 1.8m (6ft) between each seed and 1.8m (6ft) between rows. It is common to sow two seeds next to each other, removing the weaker seedling after germination to ensure a plant at each station.

Above: *Squash fruits will rot if left to mature on the bare soil or damp grass. Support the fruits with straw to prevent damage.*

AFTERCARE

As the plants grow, train the trailing stems around the plant in a spiral to save space. When training the plants, pin the stems down with wire pegs. Alternatively, the size of the plants can be reduced by cutting off the trailing stems, two leaves above a fruit.

There are numerous varieties of climbing squash available. These can be extremely ornamental, especially when the growth is trained up ornate wire or wooden trellis supports. Keep the crop well watered throughout the growing season and give a high-potash feed every two weeks.

HARVESTING AND STORAGE

Harvest the summer squashes when the skin is tender and they are big enough to eat. Cut off the fruits, leaving 5cm (2in) of stem. Cut winter squashes in the same way if they are to be used fresh, otherwise leave them on the plant and harvest them just before the first frosts. Leave them in a sunny position for one week to harden the skins before storing.

Summer squashes have a relatively short storage life of up to two to three weeks. They are best used fresh from the plant. Winter squashes will keep up to two months if they are kept in a frost-free area. Store the squashes individually by hanging them in nets or boxing them and surrounding them with straw.

PESTS AND DISEASES

Slugs can cause serious damage to crops because they can eat completely through a stem if they are left unchecked. Cucumber mosaic virus is the most serious of the diseases to which squashes are susceptible. The leaves become mottled and the fruit is distorted. Destroy any infected plants. Powdery mildew can cause problems in dry years. This can largely be ignored because the problem is normally not too serious. Keep the soil moist and plant at the correct distances to prevent overcrowding and allow for the free movement of air between the plants. This will help to prevent infections.

CULTIVATION

Sowing time Early spring (under glass); early summer (outdoors)
Planting out time Early summer
Sowing distance 1.8m (6ft)
Sowing depth 4cm (1½in)
Distance between rows 1.8m (6ft)
Harvesting Late summer to early autumn

Left: *Squashes, like pumpkins, are ready to harvest around eight weeks after planting. Squashes are ready to be picked when the stems begin to split, which should take place before the first frosts in autumn. Cut them off with a small stem attached.*

VARIETIES

SUMMER

'Custard Squash' White- and yellow-skinned varieties are available.
'Table Ace' A small, acorn-shaped fruit with dark green skin and orange flesh.
'Tender and True' Ball-shaped fruits with mottled green skin. Bush variety.
'Yellow Crookneck' A bulbous, crooked shape with bumpy yellow skin and sweet flesh. Bush habit.

WINTER

'Pompeon' Shiny dark green flat globe-shaped fruit. Golden flesh. Semi-bush habit.
'Turk's Turban' A good ornamental variety that is also delicious to eat. A trailing variety.
'Vegetable Spaghetti' (also called 'Noodle') Fruits are cylindrical in shape. When boiled, the flesh breaks up into strands that look similar to spaghetti. A trailing variety.

squashes

MARROWS AND COURGETTES (ZUCCHINI)

Cucurbita pepo

Marrows and courgettes are mainly grown for their delightful juicy fruits, although the young leaves, male flowers and small fruits are delicious to eat in summer salads.

SOIL

Marrows and courgettes thrive in soil that is rich in organic matter. To ensure optimum growth, dig in plenty of well-rotted manure or garden compost in the autumn. They grow extremely well on compost heaps.

ASPECT

An open sunny position. They are frost tender, so do not plant out until early summer after the risk of frost has subsided.

SOWING/PLANTING

You can start the crop off in late spring under glass by sowing individually into 9cm (3in) pots. Soak the seeds in water overnight because this will speed up the germination process. Grow on the seedlings and harden them off before planting out in early summer. Alternatively, you can sow direct outside in early summer to a depth of 4cm (1½in). Sow two seeds at a time and then remove the weaker one after germination. Covering with cloches will enhance the germination of the seedlings. Within the rows keep a distance of 90cm (3ft) between each plant for bush varieties and 1.2–1.8m (4–6ft) for trailing varieties. Leave the same distances between each of the rows.

Below: *The male flowers of marrows and courgettes can be eaten – they can be used either raw in salads or cooked.*

Left: *When harvesting marrows, use a sharp knife and cut through the stem 2.5cm (1in) away from the fruit.*

AFTERCARE

Water marrows and courgettes regularly throughout the growing season. Trailing varieties will need to be trimmed in order to prevent them from taking over your vegetable plot.

CULTIVATION

Sowing time Late spring (under glass); early summer (outdoors)
Planting out time Early summer
Sowing/planting distance 90cm/3ft (bush varieties); 1.2–1.8m/4–6ft (trailing varieties)
Sowing depth 4cm (1½in)
Distance between rows 90cm/3ft (bush varieties); 1.2–1.8m/4–6ft (trailing varieties)
Harvesting Mid-summer onwards

HARVESTING AND STORAGE

Courgettes taste delicious when they are young. Harvest them when they are approximately 10cm (4in) long. If left to grow much larger they are classed as a small marrow or they can be left to mature into a fully grown marrow. Harvesting can take place until the first frosts. Courgettes do not store well and are best picked and used fresh. They can be frozen but will lose their firmness. Marrows store well, especially if they are left to mature on the plant. Store in a frost-free place in trays or hanging up in nets.

PESTS AND DISEASES

Cucumber mosaic virus is the most common problem. Destroy affected plants.Slugs love the vegetation. Pick them off by hand or encourage natural predators such as frogs and beetles.

VARIETIES

'All Green Bush' A heavy-yielding variety with mid-green courgettes with a creamy flesh.
'Jemma F1' An attractive variety with bright yellow courgettes. Has a slightly different flavour from normal green varieties.
'Kojac' A hairless and spineless courgette for easy picking. It is a high-yielding variety.
'Nero Milan' This has dark green fruits that are easily picked due to its open habit. A good variety for freezing.

CUCUMBERS

Cucumis sativus

There are two main types of cucumber: greenhouse varieties and outdoor or ridge varieties. Plants for growing under glass are tall climbing ones that bear long, tasty, slender fruits. Outdoor varieties are bushier in habit and produce shorter fruits. Those grown in the open are less prone to pest and disease attacks than when grown under glass. Many of the old outdoor varieties taste inferior compared with the greenhouse types. Choose a new outdoor variety as the taste has improved due to recent breeding.

SOIL

Grow outdoors in a well-drained soil that has been manured the previous autumn. Indoor varieties can be grown in large grow-bags, large pots, soil borders or straw bales.

ASPECT

Outdoor cucumbers are a tender crop, so grow in a sheltered sunny location that is protected from strong winds.

SOWING

Start off indoor varieties under glass from late winter onwards at a temperature of 24°C (75°F). Sow individually in pots. Sow two seeds per pot and then remove the weaker seedling. Cucumbers do not like root disturbance, so plant into their final positions with care.

Sow outdoor (ridge) varieties under glass in late spring or directly outside in early summer. If sown outside, cover with a cloche or bell jar to raise the temperature until after germination. Sow or plant outside, leaving 75cm (30in) between the plants, with the same distance between the rows.

Above: *As the name suggests, greenhouse varieties need to be grown under glass.*

AFTERCARE

Indoor varieties will need supporting with poles and horizontal wires, tying in the climbing stems as they grow. Pinch out the tips when they reach the top of the supports. Tie in the side stems (laterals) along the horizontal wires. Pinch these out two leaves after the development of the first fruit. Greenhouse varieties taste bitter if fertilized, so remove any male flowers. Give a high potash liquid feed when the fruits start to develop. Keep well watered, taking care to water the soil around the plant, but not the plant itself. Misting the plants and watering the paths will help keep the humidity up. Shade the greenhouse with paint or netting to avoid strong sunlight.

Outdoor (ridge) varieties that are grown on the ground will need to be mulched with straw to keep the fruit clean and to stop them rotting. This also raises the soil temperature, helps retain moisture and suppresses weed growth. Pinch out the tips from the main shoots at 6–7 leaves. Mist plants in dry periods to increase humidity and keep well watered. Outdoor varieties need to be pollinated, so it is essential to leave the male flowers on the plant. Give a high potash feed every two weeks when the fruits start to develop.

HARVESTING AND STORAGE

Cut the cucumbers with a knife from the plant before they reach maximum size as this encourages new fruits. Keep harvesting the crop until the first frosts. Cucumbers will keep in the refrigerator for about one week, but otherwise they do not store well.

Left: *Ridge cucumbers are ideally suited for growing outdoors and can be grown just as easily as courgettes.*

CULTIVATION

Sowing time Late winter onwards (under glass); early summer (outdoors)
Planting out time Early summer
Sowing/planting distance 60cm/24in (under glass); 75cm/30in (outdoors)
Sowing depth 2.5cm (1in)
Distance between rows 75cm (30in)
Harvesting Mid-summer onwards

PESTS AND DISEASES

Slugs and snails are a problem. Red spider mite and whitefly attack greenhouse varieties.

VARIETIES

GREENHOUSE

'Conqueror' An extremely old variety that tolerates lower temperatures than normal. Good-sized fruits.
'F1 Cumlaude RZ' A vigorous variety that produces heavy yields. Can be grown in an unheated greenhouse. An all-female variety.
'F1 Deltastar RZ' Delicious fruits that keep well. An all-female variety.

OUTDOOR (RIDGE)

'Bush Champion F1' Good compact variety. Fruits reach up to 25cm (10in). Resistant to cucumber mosaic virus.
'Marketmore' A high-yielding variety. Resistance is shown to cucumber mosaic virus.
'Stimora MIX F1' Can be used for gherkin pickling if harvested at 5cm (2in) or for slicing grown at 10cm (4in).

SHOOT CROPS

CELERY

Apium graveolens

Growing celery using the traditional trench method can be labour-intensive. The young seedlings are planted out in trenches and earthed up, a process that is called blanching. Earthing up makes the harvested stems white, less stringy and longer. The alternative is to grow self-blanching varieties that are planted closely together to carry out the blanching process. Self-blanching types are not as crisp and tasty as the trench type.

Above: *When the stems are 30cm (12in) high a cardboard collar is fitted around the plant to blanch the stems.*

CULTIVATION

TRENCH

Sowing time Early to mid-spring (under glass)

Planting out time Early summer

Planting distance 30cm (12in)

Distance between rows 60cm (24in)

Harvesting Autumn

SELF-BLANCHING

Sowing time Early to mid-spring

Planting out time Early summer

Planting distance in blocks 23cm (9in)

Harvesting Autumn

SOIL

There are two methods of soil preparation: the trench method and that for self-blanching varieties. For trench celery, dig out a trench that is 38cm (15in) wide and 30cm (12in) deep. Put an 8cm (3in) layer of rotted manure at the bottom of this and back fill with soil. This should be done in autumn or winter and allowed to settle before planting. Self-blanching celery is planted out in blocks and not rows. Dig over the soil in the autumn incorporating copious amounts of well-rotted manure or garden compost.

ASPECT

All celery varieties require a sunny site.

SOWING

Trench varieties are best started off under glass in module trays in early spring at a temperature of around 15°C (59°F). Harden off by placing them in cold frames two weeks before planting out in early summer. Plant out in trenched rows 30cm (12in) apart with 60cm (24in) between the rows. Self-blanching celery is started off under glass in the same way. Harden off the plants before planting out in blocks in early summer. Block planting at intervals of 23cm (9in) helps the process of self-blanching.

AFTERCARE

Water thoroughly in dry periods and feed with a liquid feed every two weeks. When trench celery varieties reach 30cm (12in), earth up over part of the stems. Repeat this process at three-week intervals until the soil is up to the lower leaves. An alternative to earthing up is to wrap cardboard around the celery stems when they are 30cm (12in) tall and again three weeks later. For self-blanching celery, place straw around the outside of the block to keep out the light. Green celery varieties do not need straw around the perimeter.

HARVESTING AND STORAGE

Trench celery is ready for harvesting from autumn onwards. Harvest as needed, but remember that the flavour is enhanced by the first frosts. Cover plants in the winter with straw if severe weather is expected. Lift self-blanching celery from autumn by the first frosts. Leave trench varieties in the ground until required, but, in cold regions, lift and store in a frost-free area where the crop will last for weeks. Celery can be frozen, but may turn soft after defrosting, so use only in cooked dishes.

Left: *This form of celery, known as green or American celery, is popular because it does not require blanching.*

PESTS AND DISEASES

Slugs, snails, celery fly and carrot fly can all be a problem, as can diseases such as celery heart rot and celery leaf spot. Destroy affected plants. Irregular watering and feeding can make the celery stalks split.

VARIETIES

TRENCH

'Giant White' Has a good flavour but requires good soil conditions. Stalks are white and tall.

'Solid Pink' An extremely old variety that will stand a number of frosts. Harvest in late autumn to early winter.

SELF-BLANCHING

'Golden Self-Blanching' Yellow dwarf variety with cream stalks, and requires little or no earthing up.

'Tall Utah' Long green stalks that need no earthing up. Harvest in early autumn. Inner stalks self-blanch.

celery

CELERIAC

Apium graveolens var. *rapaceum*

This is a delicious winter vegetable that can be cooked or grated into salads. The part of the vegetable that is eaten looks like a root, but it is, in fact, a swollen stem. It tastes similar to celery but is easier to grow. This vegetable needs a long time to mature, so start it off under glass to allow the maximum growing season available.

Left: *Celeriac is not a true root vegetable. It is, in fact, a swollen stem that forms a hard, round, knobbly base. Harvest the crop around 12 weeks after planting, which can be from around mid-autumn onwards. It is best to finish harvesting before the first frosts.*

SOIL

Celeriac thrives in a fertile soil that retains moisture throughout dry periods. To ensure this, incorporate plenty of well-rotted manure or garden compost when digging over the soil in the autumn.

ASPECT

This crop requires an open sunny location but will tolerate a little shade.

SOWING/PLANTING

Start off under glass in late winter to early spring. Sow in modules or individually in pots and keep them at a temperature of 15° C (59°F). Grow on in this environment until late spring when the young plants need to be moved to a cold frame or cold greenhouse to harden off for 10–14 days before planting out. Plant out 30cm (12in) apart in rows in early summer. Keep 30cm (12in) between each row.

AFTERCARE

Keep well watered throughout dry periods. Mulching with garden compost in early summer will help conserve moisture and suppress weed growth. Remove the side shoots and from mid-summer remove all the lower leaves to expose the crown. Earth up around the stems in early autumn to ensure the swollen stems stay white. Cover the stems with straw in cold areas.

Above: *Earth up the swollen stems in early autumn so that they will remain white before harvesting starts in mid-autumn.*

Left: *Remove any side shoots that may appear, and in mid-summer remove the lower leaves to expose the crown.*

HARVESTING AND STORAGE

Harvesting can begin from mid-autumn onwards. Lift the crop only when it has reached its maximum size. Harvesting can take place right through until early spring. In most cases celeriac can be left in the ground until it is harvested. If the winter weather is too severe, lift the stems, clean them and place in trays with moist sand and store in a frost-free area.

PESTS AND DISEASES

Slugs are more likely to attack young plants than older plants. Celery fly and carrot fly can cause the occasional problem.

CULTIVATION

Sowing time Late winter to spring (under glass)
Planting out time Early summer
Sowing distance 30cm (12in)
Distance between rows 30cm (12in)
Harvesting Mid-autumn onwards

VARIETIES

'Marble Ball' A popular variety with medium-sized globular stems. The swollen stems have a strong flavour. Stores well.
'President RZ' Roots have crisp white flesh. Resistant to hollowness and tolerant of septoria.
'Snow White' A good-flavoured variety with a slightly nutty taste. Produces large white swollen stems.

celeriac

ASPARAGUS

Asparagus officinalis

This perennial crop is a good long-term investment for the allotment. After nursing the crop over the first two years in which no harvesting takes place, the crop will last for 20 years. The delicious tender young shoots (spears) are available from mid-spring to early summer. Asparagus is best picked and eaten fresh. The summer foliage is much prized by florists.

Left: *After harvesting the young asparagus shoots, the crop is left to grow to its full height, thus strengthening itself for producing next year's shoots. If asparagus beetle is a problem, the stems can be cut back in autumn to help keep the population low.*

SOIL

Asparagus thrives in well-drained soil. Before planting or sowing, dig the soil in the autumn and incorporate plenty of well-rotted manure or garden compost. Lime the soil if the pH is acidic.

ASPECT

A well-sheltered, sunny spot to ensure optimum growth.

SOWING/PLANTING

Sowing

Soak the seed overnight before sowing to speed up the germination time. In spring, sow in rows 1cm (½in) deep keeping 30cm (12in) between the rows. Thin to 15cm (6in) between the plants and leave to grow on for one year. Lift the crowns in the following spring and transplant to a permanent site.

Planting

Asparagus plants are sold as crowns during the dormant season and are best planted out in early spring. To plant the crowns, dig out a trench 20cm (8in) deep with a ridge of 8cm (3in) running down the middle. Set out the asparagus in the centre of the ridge, placing the crowns 45cm (18in) apart.

Above: *Harvest the crop when the shoots have reached 15cm (6in). Cut the stems 5cm (2in) below the level of the ground.*

Cover the trenches over with soil to a depth of 8–10cm (3–4in). If more than one row is required, leave a space of 90cm (3ft) apart.

AFTERCARE

Keep the beds clean of weeds throughout the year, but do not use a hoe as this can damage the roots and newly emerging spears. An application of mulch can be given to keep the weeds down and retain soil moisture.

Once the foliage has turned yellow in the autumn, cut back to 5cm (2in) above the soil surface. Draw up a small ridge of soil over the plants before the new shoots emerge in the spring.

HARVESTING AND STORAGE

Newly planted crops will produce their first spears during the growing season, but do not cut any of them. Follow the same practice the second year. Harvesting is carried out in the third growing season in mid-spring to early summer when they have reached a height of 15cm (6in). Cut the spears 5cm (2in) below ground level. Stop cutting in early summer and let the remaining spears develop into foliage. This allows the food reserves to be built up for the following year. Asparagus does not store well and is best eaten fresh.

PESTS AND DISEASES

Asparagus beetle can attack the stems and foliage. This pest likes to overwinter in the foliage. Cutting stems back in autumn can help. New succulent spears are prone to damage by slugs. Violet root rot can cause severe problems. The roots are covered in purple mould and the leaves prematurely turn yellow. In bad cases, destroy plants and make a bed in a new site.

CULTIVATION

Sowing

Sowing time Spring
Sowing distance Thinly
Sowing depth 1cm (½in)
Distance between rows 30cm (12in)
Thinning distance 15cm (6in)
Transplanting time Following spring, same distances as for planting

Planting

Planting time Early spring
Planting distance 45cm (18in)
Planting depth 8–10cm (3–4in)
Distance between rows 90cm (3ft)
Harvesting (from the third year) In late spring for six weeks

VARIETIES

'Cito' A heavy cropper that produces long spears.
'Connover's Colossal' An old variety. Has delicious flavoured spears.
'Franklim F1' Heavy yields of thick spears. A small crop may be harvested in the second year.

asparagus

GLOBE ARTICHOKES

Cynara cardunculus Scolymus Group

This perennial is unusual in that it is the flower that is eaten and not the leaves or the roots, as with most vegetables. After harvesting, the flower bud is boiled or steamed and the various parts are eaten. Globe artichokes do take up a lot of room, so you might consider adding this ornate crop to a herbaceous border if you do not have space in the allotment plot.

SOIL

As this crop will be in the same location for several years, you should prepare the soil to a high standard before planting. Dig deeply in the autumn, incorporating plenty of well-rotted manure or garden compost. Globe artichokes do not grow well on heavy clay as good drainage is essential.

ASPECT

An open sunny site in a sheltered location.

PLANTING/SOWING

Plant offsets of globe artichokes in the spring at 75cm (30in) apart with 90cm (3ft) between the rows. Alternatively, sow seeds thinly in spring in rows 2.5cm (1in) deep with 30cm (12in) between the rows. Thin the seedlings to 15cm (6in) apart ready to transplant the following spring. Plant in the permanent site as above.

Below: *It is easy to see why the globe artichoke is used by garden designers who are looking for architectural form.*

AFTERCARE

Water copiously throughout the growing season and feed every two weeks. Stems can be cut down in autumn and soil drawn around the crown of the plant. Protect the crowns in cold areas by covering with straw or bracken. Lift, divide and replant the crop every 3–4 years. Cultivate and incorporate organic matter to the soil during this process.

CULTIVATION
Planting time Spring
Planting distance 75cm (30in)
Distance between rows 90cm (3ft)
Sowing time Spring
Sowing distance Thinly
Sowing depth 2.5cm (1in)
Distance between rows 30cm (12in)
Thinning distance 15cm (6in)
Transplanting time Following spring
Harvesting Summer of second year onwards

Above left: *Harvest the flower heads of the globe artichokes just before they open and while they are still green.*

Left: *Cut the stems down in autumn and draw the soil around the crown of the plant. The stems can be put on the compost heap.*

HARVESTING AND STORAGE

Begin harvesting in the second year. Cut the flower heads off just before they open and while they are still green. Leave on a stem of 2.5cm (1in) below the head. The heads are best eaten when they are fresh.

PESTS AND DISEASES

Generally trouble free, although they can be affected by blackfly, which is treated by spraying with insecticidal soap.

VARIETIES
'Camus de Bretagne' Large heads with a good flavour. It can be relatively tender compared to other varieties.
'Green Globe' Produces lovely green flower buds. Very popular variety and widely available.
'Purple Globe' Hardier than its green relative but the flavour is inferior.

globe artichokes

SEA KALE

Crambe maritima

This vegetable can be found growing wild along the British coast. It is a favourite among ornamental gardeners who appreciate its architectural structure. Sea kale leaves have to be blanched to make them palatable. The blanched stems are harvested from mid- to late summer. A bed of sea kale will crop well for around seven years before you need to discard it and start again.

SOIL

Thrives in soils that are fertile and free draining, especially sandy or gravelly soil. This crop can grow on heavy soils if grit or gravel is incorporated before planting or if it is grown on raised beds. Dig in plenty of well-rotted manure or garden compost in the autumn.

ASPECT

Requires an open sunny site.

SOWING/PLANTING/THONGS

Sowing Sea kale can be started off by sowing seed in spring, soaking the seed overnight in order to speed up the germination process. Sow thinly outside in rows, 4cm (1½in) deep with 30cm (12in) between the rows. After germination thin the seedlings to 23cm (9in). Let the seedlings grow on and transplant them to their final destination in the following spring.

Planting Plant out sea kale in spring, leaving 45cm (18in) between the plants and the same distance between the rows.

Above: *Sea kale is a favourite with gardeners who let it grow naturally and admire its architectural structure.*

Thongs (root cuttings) Take thongs from existing plants in autumn. The cuttings need to be 1cm (½in) thick and 15cm (6in) in length. Tie these in a bundle and insert the roots vertically into well-drained soil. Make sure that the top of the root is uppermost. It needs to be 5cm (2in) below the soil surface. Alternatively, the cuttings can be placed in large pots of well-drained potting mix. By the following spring they will have sprouted. Plant out the rooted cuttings to the same specifications as for planting.

AFTERCARE

The stems of sea kale are blanched by covering the plants in late winter or early spring with long pots especially made for the job. No light must reach underneath the pots or the stems will turn green and taste bitter.

HARVESTING AND STORAGE

Plants and thongs are harvested in their second year, plants grown from seed one year later. Harvest when the stems are long enough. Remove the cover when all the shoots have been removed. Plants are normally kept for seven years.

Left: *Sea kale can be blanched. This plant has been blanched, but has again been exposed to light.*

CULTIVATION

Sowing

Sowing time Spring
Sowing distance Thinly
Sowing depth 4cm (1½in)
Distance between rows 30cm (12in)
Thinning distance 23cm (9in)
Transplanting time The following spring
Harvesting Summer of second year onwards

Planting

Planting time Spring
Planting distance 45cm (18in)
Distance between rows 45cm (18in)
Harvesting Summer of second year onwards

Thongs

Cutting strucks Autumn
Transplanting time Late spring
Planting distance 45cm (18in)
Distance between rows 45cm (18in)
Harvesting Second summer onwards

Alternatively, discard the plants after harvesting, taking root cuttings for the next crop. Sea kale does not store well and is best eaten fresh from the plant.

PESTS AND DISEASES

The caterpillars of the cabbage white butterfly can feast on the foliage of sea kale. Pick them off by hand if possible. Slugs can also be a nuisance.

VARIETIES

Normally sold under the name of sea kale.

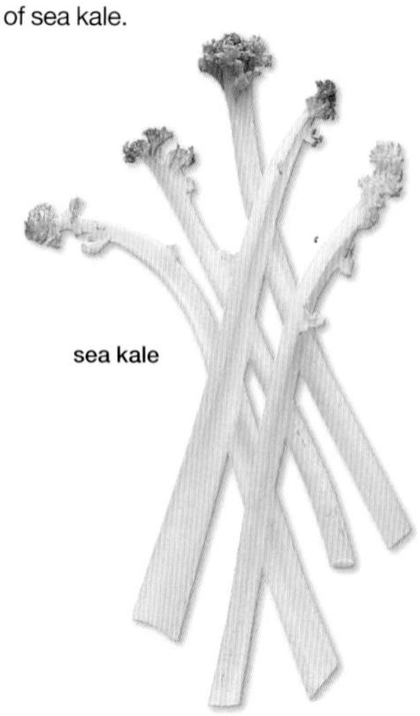

FLORENCE FENNEL

Foeniculum vulgare var. *dulce*

This wonderfully decorative plant is usually grown for its white bulbous base, which tastes strongly of aniseed. It can be eaten raw in salads or braised as a vegetable. Its finely cut bright green foliage means that is makes an unusual and ornamental plant for the allotment. The leaves can also be used as a herb for flavouring dishes.

SOIL

Florence fennel thrives in light well-drained soils. If your soil is too heavy, incorporate grit or gravel before planting or build a raised bed. When digging in the autumn incorporate plenty of well-rotted manure or garden compost. This will increase water retention in the soil.

ASPECT

This crop requires an open sunny site with shelter from the wind.

SOWING

The best time of year to sow is early to mid-summer as crops sown earlier are likely to bolt. Sow thinly in rows 1cm (½in) deep with 45cm (18in) between the rows. After germination thin the seedlings to 23cm (9in) apart. Alternatively, the seeds can be started off under glass, but, as they do not like transplanting, it is best to sow in situ.

AFTERCARE

Water copiously, especially during dry spells. Earth up the soil around the bulbs, as they begin to swell, to around half of their height. Continue to draw up soil as the bulbs expand. This will blanch the bulbs, resulting in a sweeter flavour.

HARVESTING AND STORAGE

Two to three weeks after earthing up check the bulbs. If they have reached the size of a tennis ball they are ready for harvesting. Pull the whole plant up or cut underneath the bulb and leave the root in the soil. This will re-sprout and offer new foliage, which can be used in flower arranging. Fennel does not store well and is best eaten fresh. It will keep for a few days in the refrigerator.

PESTS AND DISEASES

Bolting is the main problem. Do not sow too early or use resistant cultivars such as 'Argo RZ'. Other than that, generally trouble free.

CULTIVATION

Sowing time Early to mid-summer
Sowing distance Thinly
Sowing depth 1cm (½in)
Distance between rows 45cm (18in)
Thinning distance 23cm (9in)
Harvesting Autumn

Above: *When the bulbs begin to swell, draw up the soil around them. This will blanch the bulbs and make them taste sweeter.*

Above: *The secret of growing successfully is to keep the soil moist and weed-free, thus ensuring fast healthy growth.*

Above: *Florence fennel is often planted in flower borders to display its decorative, finely cut foliage.*

VARIETIES

'Argo RZ' Good uniform crop with white bulbs. Resistant to bolting, so good for using as an early crop.
'Romanesco' Lovely dark foliage with white bulbs that have a good aniseed flavour. Sow in late spring to mid-summer.

Florence fennel

RHUBARB

Rheum x hybridum

Although rhubarb is classed as a vegetable, it is mainly used as a fruit. The leaves are extremely poisonous and no part of them should be eaten. Rhubarb looks superb in an allotment and will provide you with a delicious and easy crop over a long period.

SOIL

Rhubarb grows well in soil that is rich in organic matter. Before planting incorporate plenty of well-rotted manure or garden compost into the soil when preparing the site. Remove any perennial weeds as they are difficult to eradicate after the crop has been planted.

ASPECT

A sunny location, away from shade.

SOWING/PLANTING

Sowing Rhubarb can be grown from seed, but the uniformity and quality of the plants cannot be guaranteed. Sow the seeds thinly in rows 2.5cm (1in) deep with 30cm (12in) between the rows. After germination thin out the seedlings to 23cm (9in). The crop is ready to transplant to its final destination during the following winter. Plant to the same specifications as described for planting below.

Above: *A bed of healthy rhubarb is an impressive sight. Rhubarb leaves are poisonous and cannot be eaten.*

Above: *Forcing should only be carried out every other year to prevent weakening the plants. This is a wicker rhubarb forcer.*

Above: *Harvest rhubarb sticks by pulling so that they come out of their 'socket'. Cut off the leaves and put on the compost heap.*

Planting Rhubarb plants can be bought in pots at any good garden centre or nursery. Alternatively, offsets can be divided off established plants during the dormant season. Plant the rhubarb plants that have been bought in pots throughout the spring. Offsets, on the other hand, are planted straight after being split in the winter. Space all the plants 90cm (3ft) apart.

AFTERCARE

Water well during dry periods. Mulch with well-rotted manure or garden compost in the spring and autumn to help retain moisture and suppress weed growth. Plants can be forced into producing shoots early if covered with a bucket or plastic bin in mid-winter. This crop will be ready to pick after six weeks. Do not force the same plants two years running or they will be weakened.

HARVESTING AND STORAGE

The red stems can be harvested from spring to early summer. Pull each stem from the base and it will come away with part of the base. Cut off the leaves and put on to the compost heap. Never strip a plant of all its stems; it is best to leave at least four stems per plant. This enables the plants to recover and produce new growth, allowing the plant to be harvested the following year. Rhubarb will freeze for up to one year.

CULTIVATION

SOWING

Sowing time Spring

Sowing distance Thinly

Sowing depth 2.5cm (1in)

Distance between rows 30cm (12in)

Thinning distance 23cm (9in)

Transplanting time Following winter, plant as below

PLANTING

Planting time Winter (offsets); spring (pots)

Planting distance 90cm (3ft)

Distance between rows 90cm (3ft)

Harvesting From the second year onwards

PESTS AND DISEASES

Sometimes prone to white blister. Cut off and destroy diseased foliage. Otherwise generally trouble free.

VARIETIES

'Champagne Early' Beautiful red stems that are among the first to be harvested.

'Glaskin's Perpetual' Extremely quick growing and lasts for many years. Produces lovely red stems that can be cut in the first year.

'Victoria' A popular variety with thick stems that are ready in late spring.

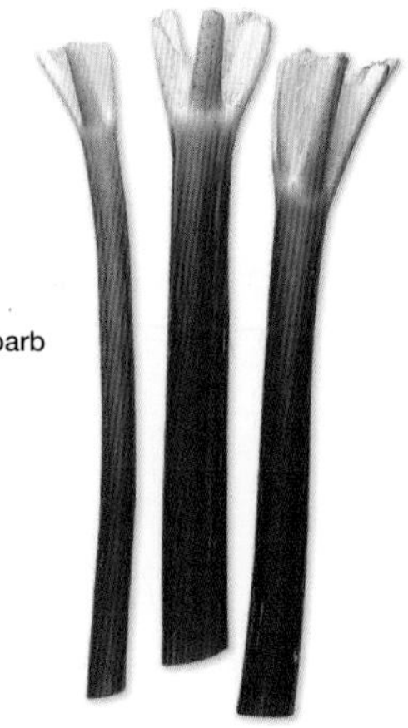

FRUITING VEGETABLES

PEPPERS

Capsicum species

Sweet or bell peppers (*Capsicum annuum* Grossum Group) are commonly used in salads and in many cooked dishes. Sweet peppers do not taste hot like their close relatives, cayenne or tabasco peppers (*Capsicum frutescens*) and chilli peppers (*Capsicum annuum* Longum Group). The plants bear fruits that are green when unripe, turning yellow, red and orange. Cayenne or tabasco peppers are exceptionally hot peppers that need to be used with care.

Chilli peppers are a little less hot than cayenne or tabasco peppers, but are still quite fiery (the seeds, which are the hottest part of the fruit, may be removed).

SOIL

Outdoor crops thrive in a well-drained, fertile soil. Greenhouse types need to be planted up in grow-bags or large pots in peat-free potting mix.

ASPECT

Peppers require a sunny sheltered spot, otherwise they do well in a greenhouse, conservatory or on a vacant windowsill.

SOWING/PLANTING

Sow seeds in trays, modules or individual pots under glass in spring, at a temperature of 18–21°C (65–70°F). If grown in trays, prick out the seedlings into small pots as soon as the seed leaves are large enough to handle.

Peppers have short root systems, so it is essential to pot up the plants gradually until they reach their final pot size of around 23cm (9in). Alternatively, pot up the young pepper plants until they are large enough to plant into grow-bags or soil beds in mid- to late spring.

Plant outdoor peppers outside after hardening off in early summer. Plant in rows 50cm (20in) apart with the same distance between the rows. Peppers can be grown in a vegetable patch, in an ornamental border or in pots on the patio.

AFTERCARE

Keep the crop well watered, feeding once a week with a liquid fertilizer high in potash. Stake and tie the plants as they grow. Good ventilation in the greenhouse is recommended in hot weather.

Left: *Not all peppers are the evenly shaped fruits to which we are accustomed in supermarkets. These red peppers have reached the final stage of ripening.*

CULTIVATION
Sowing time Spring
Planting time Mid- to late spring (under glass); early summer (outside)
Planting distance 50cm (20in)
Distance between rows 50cm (20in)
Harvesting Mid-summer onwards

HARVESTING AND STORAGE

Start to harvest sweet peppers from mid- to late summer. Pick the fruits when they are green, yellow, red, orange or purple. They are best eaten fresh although they will keep for up to two weeks in a refrigerator. Harvest hot or cayenne peppers when they are fully ripe and coloured. Use fresh or store in airtight jars after drying.

PESTS AND DISEASES

Grown under glass they suffer problems such as aphids, red spider mite and whitefly. Damp down the floor and mist the plants to increase humidity and deter red spider mite. Outdoors they may be attacked by aphids.

Above: *Chilli peppers, like sweet peppers, are green when they are unripe, turning yellow and then red when they are ripe.*

VARIETIES

SWEET PEPPERS

'F1 Mandy RZ' Produces large sweet tasting green fruits that turn red when mature. Resistant to mosaic virus.

'Red Skin' An F1 hybrid that produces uniform compact plants suitable for container growing. It has early maturing fruits.

CAYENNE AND CHILLI PEPPERS (HOT PEPPERS)

'Cayenne Large Red' Long, pointed, hot fruits that are produced in abundance.

'Habenero' An extremely hot chilli pepper. The green wrinkled fruits turn light orange when mature.

TOMATOES

Lycopersicon esculentum

Tomatoes are probably the most widely used vegetable for cooking. It is worth growing a few, either in the allotment or in the greenhouse, so that you can experience the sweet juicy flavour offered by home-grown produce. Outdoor varieties look striking dotted among ornamental plants in borders or potagers. However, take care when siting tomato plants because they are closely related to the potato and suffer from several of the same pests and diseases. Include tomatoes on the same crop-rotation programme as potatoes or use grow-bags to prevent the spread of soil-borne pests and diseases.

SOIL

Outdoor tomatoes like humus-rich soil. Dig over in winter, incorporating garden compost into the soil. Plant indoor varieties in grow-bags or pots. If planted in a soil border in a greenhouse, change the soil every year to stop transference of diseases. Add garden compost to improve the soil structure.

ASPECT

Outdoor tomato varieties are tender, so choose a warm sheltered spot that receives plenty of sun.

SOWING/PLANTING

Indoors These varieties can be started off under glass in temperatures of 18°C (65°F) in early to mid-spring. Sow seed in the same way as for outdoor varieties. Plant up into grow-bags, pots or soil borders in mid- to late spring. Plants grown in borders need to be spaced 45cm (18in) apart.
Outdoors These varieties are best sown under glass in gentle heat or an unheated greenhouse in mid-spring. Sow thinly in seed trays if a large number of plants are required or sow individually in pots if only a few plants are needed. Seed sown in trays will need to be pricked out and transplanted into individual pots. Grow on and harden off, ready to plant outside in early summer. Plants need to be planted 45cm (18in) apart for cordon varieties and 60cm (24in) for bush varieties. Keep 75cm (30in) between the rows for both types. Alternatively, tomatoes can be planted into larger pots or grow-bags before being placed outside. Harden off for 10 days before moving outside in early summer.

AFTERCARE

The tomato crop needs to be well watered. Feed every two weeks with a high-potash feed when the fruit begins to swell. If the crop is irregularly watered, causing wet and dry periods, this can cause blossom end rot. Support the crop using canes or suspended strings within the greenhouse and tie in the stems as they grow. Pinch out

Above: *Luscious, bright red tomatoes are a wonderful sight in your allotment, and taste best when eaten straight from the vine.*

the top of the shoots when they reach the end of their supports. Side shoots need to be removed from cordon types.

HARVESTING AND STORAGE

Harvest as they ripen and are fully coloured. A mature fruit is normally deep red in colour. Twist the fruit off the plant to avoid tearing the stem.

Above: *Tomatoes can be grown indoors or outside. Using grow-bags in a greenhouse prevents the spread of soil-borne diseases.*

Above: *Spiral supports are ideal for supporting cordon tomatoes because it saves you from having to tie them in.*

Above: *When you start to see the fruit beginning to ripen, it is time to start feeding the plants with a good organic feed.*

Tomatoes are best eaten straight from the plant. If you have a glut at the end of the season they can be frozen. Only use frozen fruits in cooked dishes as they will lose their firmness. At the end of the season there may be many green tomatoes left on the plants. Sever the plants at the base and hang upside down in a greenhouse or frost-free shed until the tomatoes ripen or put in trays into a drawer to ripen.

PESTS AND DISEASES

Tomatoes are prone to a number of pests and diseases. Aphids, potato cyst eelworm, whitefly and red spider mite are the main pests to which they are susceptible. Tomato blight, grey mould, potato mosaic virus, greenback, tomato leaf mould and scald are the diseases most likely to cause problems. Many of the problems listed here can be solved by undertaking good horticultural practices such as removing dead, decaying and diseased growth from the plants every day. Correct watering and good ventilation will also help to improve the crop.

Right: *Do not throw away the remaining plants at the end of the season. Collect any fruits that are left and hang them upside down under cover to ripen.*

Above: *Remove the side shoots from cordon tomatoes when they are small. Pinch or cut them out with a sharp knife.*

Above: *There is nothing better than to taste the warm sweet flavour of tomatoes harvested from home-grown plants.*

CULTIVATION

Indoor Varieties
Sowing time Early to mid-spring
Planting time Mid- to late spring
Planting/sowing distance 45cm (18in)
Harvesting Summer onwards
Outdoor Varieties
Sowing time Mid-spring (under glass)
Planting out time Early summer
Planting distance 45cm/18in (cordon); 60cm/24in (bush)
Distance between rows 75cm (30in)
Harvesting Late summer onwards

VARIETIES

Greenhouse

'Big Boy F1' Tall plant with large fruits that are good for stuffing and slicing. Nice bright red fruits.
'F1 Aromata RZ' Extremely productive variety with fruits averaging 100g (4oz). Resistance shown to tomato mosaic virus.
'Shirley F1' Popular variety that produces heavy yields. Resistant to fusarium, cladosporium and tomato mosaic virus.
'Super Sweet 100 F1' A tall and strong-growing variety, bearing many small red fruits that are rich in vitamin C.

Outdoor

'Gardeners Delight' Produces small cherry red tomatoes that have a superb sweet flavour. Can be grown under glass or outside.
'Red Alert' A high yielding outdoor variety with small delicious tasting fruits.
'Totem F1' Has a good compact habit. Ideal for pots and window boxes.
'Tumbler' A trailing variety that can be used in hanging baskets and containers. Has lovely, small, red fruits.

AUBERGINES (EGGPLANTS)

Solanum melongena

Not so very long ago, aubergines were a rare sight on the shelves of our supermarkets and shops. Nowadays, they are more widely available and frequently grown by amateur gardeners in the allotment or greenhouse. However, aubergines are tender and in temperate climates are best grown under glass rather than outside where they will struggle to thrive in anything but a hot sunny season. The large, conspicuous, shining fruits range in colour from purple through to white. They taste delicious when they are cooked, stuffed with meat, rice or vegetables, or when used to make ratatouille or moussaka.

Above: *The aubergine is a tropical plant. The most commonly grown varieties produce magnificent purple fruits.*

SOIL

Grow under glass in grow-bags or pots, using a peat-free potting mix. Plants grown outside require a fertile, well-drained soil and should have a general fertilizer applied before planting.

ASPECT

Aubergines thrive in a warm sunny spot that is sheltered from the wind. These conditions are ideally found in a greenhouse, cold frame or in barn cloches.

SOWING

Best conditions for growth are provided under glass. Soak the seeds overnight to improve the germination rate and then sow into individual pots in spring. Ideally the temperature within the greenhouse will be 21–25°C (70–77°F). Once the plants are large enough they can be planted into bigger pots or grow-bags. Aubergines can be hardened off and planted outside if the temperature does not drop below 15°C (59°F). Plant to a distance of 50cm (20in) between plants in a row with the same distance between the rows.

AFTERCARE

Canes and string may be needed to support the plants once they have reached 45–60cm (18–24in). Pinch out the tips of the plants when they reach 38cm (15in) in height in order to encourage fruit formation. Water well throughout the growing season and feed once every two weeks with a high-potash liquid feed.

Left: *Aubergines can be planted up under glass in window boxes or tubs and then moved outside in early summer when the night and day temperatures are warmer.*

CULTIVATION

Sowing time Spring (under glass)
Planting time Mid-spring (under glass); early summer (outside)
Planting distance 50cm (20in)
Distance between rows 50cm (20in)
Harvesting Mid-summer onwards

HARVESTING AND STORAGE

Cut each aubergine fruit from the plant when it is large enough – the flavour quickly deteriorates if they are allowed to become overripe. Harvest under glass from mid-summer and autumn for outside varieties. Aubergines are best used fresh from the allotment although they can keep for up to two weeks once picked.

PESTS AND DISEASES

The usual greenhouse pests affect this crop if grown under glass. Aphids, red spider mite and whitefly are the main pests. Damping the floor down and misting the leaves will increase humidity, which will in turn discourage red spider mite.

VARIETIES

'Black Beauty F1' Produces dark violet coloured fruit that are oval to globe shaped. A very vigorous grower.
'Black Enorma' The largest fruit of all the varieties – up to 675g (1½lb).
'Easter Egg' A novelty fruit that is the colour and size of a large hen's egg. Taste is inferior to the traditional purple varieties.
'Long Purple' An old variety that has deep violet fruits that taste delicious. Not a heavy-yielding type.
'Money Maker' A popular new variety that produces good-sized purple fruits. Crops early.

aubergines (eggplants)

SWEETCORN (CORN)

Zea mays

This giant ornamental crop can reach a height of 1.5m (5ft) and needs a lot of room if it is to be grown in the vegetable plot. Sweetcorn is frost tender and is therefore best started off in the greenhouse and planted out in early summer in order to allow it the maximum growing season.

SOIL

Sweetcorn thrives on a free-draining soil that contains large amounts of organic matter. Dig the ground in the autumn and incorporate plenty of well-rotted manure or garden compost.

ASPECT

Requires a warm sunny location that is sheltered from strong winds.

SOWING

For an early crop, sow seeds under glass in mid-spring. For maximum germination the temperature should be around 13–15°C (55–59°F). Sow individually in pots, grow on and harden off before planting outside in early summer. Seed sown directly outside needs to be sown in late spring through to early summer after the danger of frost has passed. Crop protection is needed in the form of a cloche or cut-up plastic bottle.

CULTIVATION

Sowing time Mid-spring (under glass)
Planting out time Early summer
Sowing time Late spring to early summer (outside)
Sowing/planting distance 30cm (12in)
Sowing depth 2.5cm (1in)
Distance between rows 30cm (12in)
Harvesting Autumn

Sow in blocks, sowing two seeds 2.5cm (1in) deep every 30cm (12in) with 30cm (12in) between the rows. Remove the weaker seedlings after germination. Planting in blocks will ensure efficient wind pollination for the female flowers.

AFTERCARE

If cloche protection has been used to help get the crop off to a good start, remove the cloches when the leaves begin to touch the sides. Keep weeds down around the crop, but do not hoe as it is a shallow rooter. Water well throughout the growing season, especially during dry weather. Add liquid feed every two weeks when the cobs begin to swell.

HARVESTING AND STORAGE

The cobs are ready for harvesting when the tassels on the cobs turn brown. Test the cobs for ripeness. Pull back the sheath hiding the cobs and squeeze one of the seeds. It is ripe if the liquid that oozes out is milky in colour. If the liquid is clear it is unripe. These are best eaten fresh because once they are cut the sugars change to starch. They will also keep well in the freezer.

PESTS AND DISEASES

Can be troubled by smut in hot dry weather. Large galls appear on the cobs, which should be removed and destroyed. Destroy all plants after harvesting. Frit fly maggots can distort the growth of the crop at seedling stage.

Left: *The dying tassel of the female flower hangs from the developing cob. This indicates that it is ready for harvesting.*

Above: *To produce an early crop, start off the sweetcorn in a greenhouse and grow on before planting out in blocks.*

VARIETIES

'Golden Sweet F1' A sweet-tasting variety with bright yellow cobs. It has a high resistance to rust.
'Kelvedon Glory F1' An extremely heavy cropper with a good flavour.
'Minisweet' Produces mini cobs that are harvested at 10cm (4in) long.

GARDENER'S GUIDE TO HERBS

Herbs have been an important part of human culture for thousands of years. Before the advent of modern medicine they were widely used as a cure for many ailments and indeed are still used for medicinal puroposes to this day. Most, however, are now grown for their culinary, cosmetic or simply their ornamental value. They are, like so many allotment plants, quite easily grown, and their value as additions and enhancements to food should guarantee them at least some space on your plot, whether in the ground or grown in pots and containers.

Left: *The leaves of bee-balm (bergamot),* Monarda didyma, *make a refreshing tea and as its names suggests, readily attracts bees.*

Above: *French tarragon (*Artemisia dracunculus*) is a half-hardy perennial whose leaves have an attractive and unique flavour.*

Above: Chives (Allium schoenoprasum*) have pungent hollow stems as well as attractive mauve flowers in summer.*

Above: *Hyssop (*Hyssopus officinalis*), is a small, shrubby herb whose intense, 'mint' aroma is most intense on flowering tips.*

CHIVES

Allium schoenoprasum

Chives are bulbous herbaceous perennials that can grow to a height of 70cm (28in) or more. Smooth, slim, hollow, green leaves are produced in thick tufts. Small white bulbs appear in clumps on the base of the plant below the surface of the soil. Rose-purple or mauve flowers are carried on leafless stalks, making this an attractive herb for the allotment. Garlic chives (*A. tuberosum*) are slightly smaller, growing to 50cm (20in), and their main storage tissue is a rhizome rather than a bulb. The leaves are similar to chives but are flat instead of hollow and the flowers are white. They are one of the kitchen herbs that few gardeners would want to be without.

SOIL AND ASPECT

Chives need a well-drained, fertile soil with a pH of 6–7. They are equally at home in full sun or partial shade, although shade can produce stragglier plants and fewer flowers. Nitrogen is important and a regular application of composted manure is also recommended.

PROPAGATION

Chives can be grown as an annual or a perennial. Space plants 10cm (4in) apart in rows 30cm (12in) apart. They grow better if cut down to 10cm (4in) in summer. Chives are readily propagated from seed, which can be sown under glass in early spring and transplanted or sown directly outdoors. Germination takes 10–14 days. Several cuttings can be obtained each year but the number may be limited by rust disease as the season progresses.

HARVESTING AND STORAGE

The leaves are cut as needed. Although best used fresh, they can be frozen or dried. *A. tuberosum* is sometimes blanched to soften the leaves before eating.

CULINARY USES

The fresh and dried leaves can be used in a variety of dishes. The bulbs can be pickled and the flowers can be used fresh or dried.

CULTIVATION
Sowing time Early spring (under glass); spring (outside)
Planting out time Spring
Thinning and planting distance 10cm (4in)
Distance between rows 30cm (12in)
Harvesting Any time the plant is in growth
Storage Frozen or dried

Above: *The pretty flowers of chives make a tasty and colourful addition to summer salads as well as to the allotment.*

DILL

Anethum graveolens

This annual, with its round, erect stem, grows 30–60cm (12–24in) tall and has finely divided, thread-like, blue-green leaves. The flowers are yellow and, although the fruit is commonly called a 'seed', it is actually a dry half-fruit. This herb exists as two general types: the familiar garden dill (*A. graveolens*), which is known as American or European dill, and Indian or Japanese dill (*A. sowa*). European dill is the most common type and is grown in temperate and subtropical countries around the world. There are a number of different varieties of *A. graveolens*, each with their own fragrance or growth properties.

SOIL AND ASPECT

Dill is adaptable to many soils, but a slightly acidic soil (with a pH of 5.6–6.5) and good drainage is preferred. Germination can be poor in drought-prone, sandy soils or on clays where surface capping is a problem. Position dill in full sun.

Dill can be grown outdoors or in a greenhouse. It can be invasive if it is allowed to go to seed.

PROPAGATION

Sow seed in spring to early summer in shallow drills 3–5mm (⅛–¼in) deep. Germination takes approximately 7–14 days; successional sowing can provide a season-long supply. Thin to 23cm (9in).

HARVESTING AND STORAGE

Harvest the dill leaves or cut back the entire plant once it reaches approximately 30cm (12in) in height. Harvest the seed when it begins to turn brown.

CULINARY USES

Fresh dill leaves are used in a wide range of dishes such as soups and salads. The seed can be used in the preparation of pickles and condiments. The immature or mature seed-heads are also used whole in pickles.

Right: *The tall stems and graceful feathery leaves of dill make this herb a decorative addition to the allotment.*

CULTIVATION
Sowing time Spring to early summer
Sowing depth 3–5mm (⅛–¼in)
Thinning and planting distance 23cm (9in)
Harvesting As required (leaves); when it begins to turn brown (seed)
Storage Dried (leaves and seed)

ANGELICA

Angelica archangelica

Angelica can be grown as an aromatic biennial or a short-lived perennial (for about four years). It grows to 1.5–2.4m (5–8ft) tall. It has upright, ridged, hollow stems and large bright green leaves. The small, white or greenish flowers are borne in summer.

SOIL AND ASPECT

Prefers moist, fertile soil in partial shade and will grow in a wide range of pH from 4.5–7.3.

PROPAGATION

Propagate by seed or root division. Seeds germinate in 21–28 days. The viability of seed decreases quickly so fresh seed is best. It can be sown directly outdoors in the summer or started indoors and planted out later. Space plants 30cm (12in) apart in a row with 60–90cm (24–36in) between rows. Angelica may live up three years before flowering.

CULTIVATION
Sowing time Late summer
Sowing depth 1cm (½in)
Thinning and planting distance 30cm (12in)
Distance between rows 60–90cm (24–36in)
Harvesting Until flowering (leaves); while young (stems); when ripe (seed); early autumn (roots)
Storage Dried (leaves); crystallized (stems); dried (seed)

HARVESTING AND STORAGE

Pick angelica leaves before flowering takes place, and use fresh or dried. Cut the stems while young for crystallizing and storage. The seeds should be picked when ripe and dried. Harvest the roots in early autumn and dry them at 38–60°C (100–140°F).

CULINARY USES

Stems can be steamed and eaten like a vegetable or candied. Dried leaves can be made into a tea and fresh leaves added to salads, soups or stews.

Above: *Although less commonly used than it once was, angelica still makes a striking plant in the allotment and is well worth growing for its culinary uses.*

CHERVIL

Anthriscus cerefolium

This tall, hardy biennial plant is often best grown as an annual. Chervil reaches a height of 30–60cm (12–24in). It has large white flower heads. The delicately cut leaves make it an attractive addition to allotment garden. Although it is more often grown as an ornamental plant, many people use the seed to make herb teas and crystallize the young stems. The leaves can also be used to flavour fish dishes and fruit desserts.

SOIL AND ASPECT

Chervil should be grown in a well-drained, fertile soil with a good organic content and a pH of 6–7. The plants do best in full sun or partial shade. Growing chervil in an open, hot, sunny site may result in the plants going to seed quickly if not kept well watered.

PROPAGATION

Chervil seed should be sown in a sunny position in the spring and then again in early summer. Sow the seed in drills 1cm (½in) deep. A successional sowing every three to four weeks will extend the life of this crop. The seedlings should be thinned or transplanted to 20cm (8in) apart.

CULTIVATION
Sowing time Spring to early summer
Sowing depth 1cm (½in)
Thinning and planting distance 20cm (8in)
Harvesting Late spring onwards
Storage Dried

HARVESTING AND STORAGE

If you wish to use fresh chervil, pick the tips of the stems once a month. If the leaves are to be used dry, then harvest them just before the blossoms open and dry them on trays in a warm room or cool oven.

CULINARY USES

Chervil leaves are used as a condiment and in salads and have a characteristic flavour that is reminiscent of both aniseed and parsley. Chervil combines well with parsley and chives.

Above: *The delicately cut leaves and tall growth habit of chervil make it a pretty addition to an allotment site.*

HORSERADISH

Armoracia rusticana

This rather large plant has leaves that are reminiscent of a dock (*Rumex*) and is used as a herb and a vegetable. The plant has a strong taste and is consequently used only in relatively small quantities. Horseradish is easy to grow and the main problem may be preventing it from spreading too much.

SOIL AND ASPECT

Thrives in any light rich soil, although it will prosper in most soils, particularly those that have been well prepared. If you intend to lift plants completely that are growing on lighter soils then you must remove all the roots to prevent dense regeneration of deep-rooted horseradish plants all over the allotment. Contain plants by planting in a plastic bucket with lots of small holes punched in the bottom. Horseradish is usually best given its own growing area and is not recommended for growing among rows of other crops.

PROPAGATION

Mature horseradish plants are divided and clumps or root sections are planted out in the autumn or spring. You will probably find that one plant is enough but if more are needed they should be planted 30cm (12in) apart.

HARVESTING AND STORAGE

Horseradish is best harvested as it is needed throughout the growing season. For winter use, the roots can be lifted and stored in trays of moist sand for up to two months. The leaves are best harvested when young.

CULINARY USES

The roots are the principal harvest from this plant. They can be simply peeled and grated for use in salads or mixed with other ingredients to make a sauce. Horseradish greens can also be diced and used in various dishes.

Right: *Horseradish is a large and vigorous plant that needs careful placing in the allotment if it is not to take over.*

CULTIVATION
Planting time Autumn or spring
Planting distance 30cm (12in)
Harvesting As required (roots); while young (leaves)
Storage In trays of sand (roots)

FRENCH TARRAGON

Artemisia dracunculus 'Sativa'

This is a half-hardy perennial plant that grows up to 60cm (24in) tall. Tarragon will need winter protection in colder areas or annual replacement. The closely related Russian tarragon (*A. dracunculus dracunculoides*) has a more bitter taste, but is considerably hardier and often grown as a substitute for French tarragon in colder areas. The taste of Russian tarragon improves with age.

SOIL AND ASPECT

Tarragon grows in any well-cultivated soil. The less hardy French tarragon may be best 'plunged' into the ground for the summer growing season and lifted before the winter cold sets in. Divide frequently (every two to three years) or the plant will become root-bound. You should overwinter some plants indoors even in mild areas.

PROPAGATION

French tarragon cannot be grown from seed and so plants will need to be purchased. Once established, clumps can be divided in order to increase stock. The hardier Russian tarragon can be grown successfully from seed and can be raised in pans or shallow drills outside. Both types should be planted out in spring at a distance of 30cm (12in).

HARVESTING AND STORAGE

Harvest tarragon in early summer for steeping in vinegar. For drying, harvest in mid-summer. Harvest fresh tarragon by picking off leaves or tips of branches with multiple leaves.

CULINARY USES

The leaves are widely used for flavouring and seasoning and it is an essential ingredient in French cooking. The French sometimes refer to it as *herbe au dragon*, due to its reputed ability to cure snake bites. It is often used in various sauces, such as tartare and white sauce, and for making herb vinegar.

CULTIVATION
Sowing and planting time Spring
Sowing depth 1cm (½in)
Thinning and planting distance 30cm (12in)
Harvesting Early summer (fresh); mid-summer (for drying)
Storage Dried or frozen

Above: *Tarragon is an excellent plant for allotments, but it must be protected in winter in cool areas.*

BORAGE

Borago officinalis

Borage is an annual that grows to 45–60cm (18–24in) high. The fresh leaves and the sky-blue flowers have a spicy, cucumber-like taste and an onion-like smell. The plant attracts bees and is also a useful companion plant for tomatoes. It is very attractive and worth including in the allotment.

SOIL AND ASPECT

Borage thrives in average and poor dry soils (pH between 5–8). The plants usually do best in full sun, although they will grow in partial shade. To encourage leaf growth, supply rich moist soil, but if flowers are the object, restrict the use of fertilizer and make sure that the plants get plenty of sun. Borage is difficult to transplant once it is actively growing because of its tap root. Transplantation should therefore be done at the seedling stage. Ideal for container culture, borage can be planted in a large tub with smaller herbs around the edge.

PROPAGATION

Sow the seeds 1cm (½in) deep in the spring to early summer. The seeds will germinate in about 7–14 days. Thin or transplant the seedlings so that they are approximately 30cm (12in) apart.

HARVESTING AND STORAGE

The fresh leaves of borage are best, but they can also be dried. Harvest leaves for drying as the plant begins to flower. Dry the leaves quickly, ensuring good air circulation and with no overlapping of leaves. The flowers can be frozen in ice cubes for summer drinks.

CULINARY USES

Borage is primarily used in herb teas but the young leaves or peeled stems can also be chopped and used in salads or boiled as a pot-herb. The flowers make a colourful addition to salads and summer drinks and can also be candied.

Right: *Borage flowers can be used dried in potpourri, but leave on some of the flowers so that you can collect the seed.*

CULTIVATION
Sowing time Spring to early summer
Sowing depth 1cm (½in)
Thinning and planting distance 30cm (12in)
Harvesting Any time (flowers); when young (leaves)
Storage Frozen in ice cubes or crystallized (flowers); dried (leaves)

CARAWAY

Carum carvi

Caraway has aromatic, feathery, finely cut leaves and a thick, tapering root. During the second year, tiny white or pink flowers and reddish brown, crescent-shaped fruits develop. Caraway plants generally grow 75–150cm (30–60in) high when they are in flower. This biennial herb has a variety of uses but is mostly grown for its small aromatic fruit. The leaves can also be used.

SOIL AND ASPECT

Caraway should be grown in full sun in fertile, well-drained soil with a pH of 7.5. It will tolerate most soil types but seed germination can be poor on clay if the soil surface is prone to capping. Caraway needs a position that it can occupy for two seasons, as it will not produce seed until the second. A dressing of garden compost or well-rotted manure should be applied in the first year before planting with an additional mulching in the second year. It will tolerate light frost.

PROPAGATION

Sow seed 1cm (½in) deep in late spring to late summer in rows 40–50cm (16–20in) apart. Germination takes about 10–14 days. Thin to 15cm (6in) between plants. To grow caraway as a root crop, thin to 20cm (8in) apart. Caraway will easily self-seed around the allotment if a few of the flower heads are left.

HARVESTING AND STORAGE

Harvest the seeds when they are ripe and before the first seeds fall. Harvest the roots in the autumn of the second year. Harvest the leaves when young. The seed can be dried and then stored.

CULINARY USES

Caraway seeds can be used in a number of different dishes, while the shoots and leaves can be added to vegetable dishes and salads. The roots, which are like a small, thin parsnip, are sometimes eaten as a vegetable.

Right: *Caraway produces pretty white or pink flowers before seeding and dying in the second year.*

CULTIVATION
Sowing time Late spring to late summer
Sowing depth 1cm (½in)
Thinning and planting distance 15cm/6in (leaf crop); 20cm/8in (root crop)
Distance between rows 40–50cm (16–20in)
Harvesting While young (leaves); when ripe (seed); autumn of second year (roots)
Storage Dried (seeds)

CORIANDER (CILANTRO)

Coriandrum sativum

This hardy annual, which is a member of the parsley family, grows to 60–90cm (24–36in) in height and occasionally survives into a second year. Its erect slender stems are branching and bright green. The small pink, pale blue or white flowers are borne in compound umbels. The seeds are used as a condiment and as a component of beverages.

SOIL AND ASPECT

Coriander grows on most soils, but it does demand a sunny situation. If the plant is to be raised for its leaves, then a rich, free-draining soil with good organic content is recommended. For seed, the soil can be less nitrogen-rich and must be in full sun.

PROPAGATION

Coriander is best sown fresh each season, but it will self-sow in a favourable situation. Plants can also be raised from seed in a greenhouse during the colder winter months for a year-round supply of leaves. Alternatively, the seed is sown outside in autumn or spring in shallow 1cm (½in) drills. Germination can be slow, but once the plants emerge they should be thinned to about 15cm (6in). Plants that are grown for their leaves will benefit from successional sowings every three to four weeks throughout the summer.

HARVESTING AND STORAGE

Coriander seed is usually ready for harvesting just as the seeds are ripe and before they drop. The leaves are gathered when young throughout the summer. The seeds can be stored if they are dried and the leaves can be dried or frozen.

CULINARY USES

The dried powdered seeds are used as a flavouring in dishes such as curries. The aromatic leaves can be used dried or fresh.

Right: *The young succulent leaves of coriander are ideal for both cooking and for use in summer salads.*

CULTIVATION
Sowing time Autumn or spring
Sowing depth 1cm (½in)
Thinning and planting distance 15cm (6in)
Harvesting When ripe (seed); while young (leaves)
Storage Dried (seed); dried or frozen (leaves)

FENNEL

Foeniculum vulgare

Fennel is widely used as a culinary herb. It is a biennial or perennial plant that will grow as an annual if it is not protected. Fennel reaches 1–1.5m (3–5ft) in height. The roots, stalks and leaves are all edible, with the spice coming from the dried seeds. The tiny yellow flowers and finely cut leaves, which can be bronze in some varieties, make it a highly decorative plant for the allotment.

SOIL AND ASPECT

Thrives in a sunny position and a well-drained, rich soil though it will do quite well in poorer conditions. Applying a mulch of well-rotted compost will favour the development of the leafy growth, whereas a poorer site will encourage flowering. Fennel resembles dill, with which it can cross-pollinate, so keep these two apart.

PROPAGATION

Fennel can be grown from seed that is station sown in the spring at intervals of 45cm (18in) in 1cm (½in) drills, although one or two plants are usually sufficient. Can become invasive if allowed to self-seed.

CULTIVATION
Sowing time Spring
Sowing depth 1cm (½in)
Thinning and planting distance 45cm (18in)
Harvesting Before seeds ripen (flower heads); while young (leaves); when ripe (seeds)
Storage Dried (seed); frozen (leaves)

HARVESTING AND STORAGE

The flower heads are collected before the seeds ripen and the seeds are threshed or bashed out when completely dried. The leaves are collected fresh when young and used as needed. They can also be frozen for use during the winter.

CULINARY USES

Fennel leaves are used in salads and sauces and the seeds can be used in sausages and cakes.

Above: *All parts of the fennel plant are edible, making this both a useful and handsome allotment plant.*

HYSSOP

Hyssopus officinalis

Hyssop is a shrubby perennial that grows up to 1.2m (4ft) high. It is used as a pot herb and as an ornamental addition to the edible landscape or allotment. It is particularly useful for creating low hedges for marking boundaries.

CULTIVATION
Sowing time Spring
Sowing depth 1cm (½in)
Thinning and planting distance 30cm (12in)
Planting and transplanting time Spring
Harvesting Any time
Storage Dried

SOIL AND ASPECT

Hyssop thrives in a sunny position in free-draining soil. Wet soils will considerably reduce the life of the plant. A light mulching of rotted garden compost and dried blood in spring will promote good leafy growth. The plant will benefit from regular trimming, which will also provide the new leafy growth that is most suited to culinary use.

PROPAGATION

Despite being a shrubby perennial, hyssop is not particularly long lived, especially on heavier, wet soils, and may need replacing every three to four years. It can easily be raised from seed, either sown in a seedbed and transplanted or sown directly where it is needed. Sow seed in spring in 1cm (½in) drills, thinning to about 30cm (12in). Purchased plants and those raised from cuttings taken in early summer are also planted out at the same distance in spring.

HARVESTING AND STORAGE

Hyssop leaves can be harvested as required and may be dried for later use.

CULINARY USES

Hyssop is used to flavour various liqueurs, including Chartreuse. The leaves, which have a rather bitter taste, are used sparingly to counter fatty dishes.

Above: *The shrubby nature of hyssop makes it ideal for use as an ornamental low hedge in a potager.*

BAY

Laurus nobilis

A hardy evergreen tree or shrub that grows widely in the Mediterranean region. In warm areas bay can grow as tall as 18m (60ft). Inconspicuous white flowers appear in clusters in late spring. Bay can be grown in cooler locations but it must be sited in a sheltered spot and may only make a relatively small tree. Alternatively, bay trees make good pot specimens for a patio and can be overwintered in a cool greenhouse for use in culinary dishes. The leaves are best used when they are fresh or within a few days of picking.

CULTIVATION
Planting time Spring
Planting distance 1.2m (4ft) or more
Harvesting Any time
Storage Dried

SOIL AND ASPECT

Bay trees appreciate a moist, rich but free-draining soil, although they are surprisingly tolerant of poor conditions, especially if sited in a hot sunny position.

PROPAGATION

Take semi-ripe cuttings from the current season's shoots in mid- to late summer. Purchased plants and those raised from cuttings can be planted out in spring at a distance of 1.2m (4ft) or more.

HARVESTING AND STORAGE

Bay leaves can be harvested at any time; the mature leaves have the best flavour. The leaves can also be dried and stored in an air-tight container.

CULINARY USES

Bay is a very popular culinary herb, with one or two leaves at a time being included in a large number of dishes. The leaves are widely used in bouquets garnis or added to soups, sauces or stews. Bay leaf is often included as a pickling spice. It is settling to the stomach and has a tonic effect, stimulating the appetite and the secretion of digestive juices.

Above: *Bay makes a highly decorative specimen shrub for a warm area in an allotment or a cool conservatory.*

LOVAGE

Levisticum officinale

Lovage is a hardy perennial with ribbed stalks similar to celery and hollow stems that divide into branches near the top. Yellow flowers, about 3cm (1¼in) across, are borne in summer. The leaves have a strong taste, whereas the roots have a nutty flavour. Lovage is very robust and can grow as tall as 2m (6½ft) and spread to form a clump several yards wide.

SOIL AND ASPECT

Lovage prefers a well-drained soil rich in organic matter with a pH of 6–7.5. It can tolerate heavy clay soil, but grows best in a more loamy soil.

PROPAGATION

Lovage is easily propagated in autumn by seed, which can be slow to germinate (about 10–28 days), or by root division. Plant seed in rows in autumn at a depth of 1cm (½in) and thin to 60cm (24in). However, as it is such a vigorous plant, you may only want one plant. If more are required, then plant them 60cm (24in) apart in spring. Lovage is hardy but mulching assists winter survival.

HARVESTING AND STORAGE

Leaves are usually harvested twice a season starting in the second year, although large specimens will support a limited harvest continually through the season. The stems are cut in spring and the roots are dug in the autumn of the third year and can be used fresh or dried. Seeds can be harvested in late autumn or when ripe and dried for use.

CULINARY USES

Use the fresh leaves in salads, soups, stews, stir-fries and potato dishes and the seeds whole or ground in cakes, biscuits, sauces, pickles or salad dressings or with meats. Use the dried root as a condiment and cook the grated fresh root as a vegetable. The fresh root can also be used raw in salads, in herbal teas or preserved in honey.

Right: *Lovage is a splendid architectural plant, but it must be prevented from spreading too much.*

CULTIVATION

Sowing time Autumn
Sowing depth 1cm (½in)
Planting time Spring
Thinning and planting distance 60cm (24in)
Harvesting Any time (leaves); when ripe (seed); from autumn of third year (roots); spring (stems)
Storage Dried (leaves and seed)

LEMON BALM

Melissa officinalis

This herbaceous perennial has lemon-scented leaves and clusters of small, white or yellowish, tubular flowers. It grows to a height of 1.5m (5ft) and can be invasive if not regularly cut back to prevent self-seeding. The foliage is a welcome addition to the allotment and is best sited near to a path so that the fragrance is released when brushed against. Bees are attracted by the scent.

SOIL AND ASPECT

The ideal soil for lemon balm is moist but well drained and with a pH of 4.5–7.5. It will grow in sun or partial shade but should not be planted in very dry conditions.

Apply a good dressing of composted manure and a fertilizer such as fish, blood and bone annually to encourage good leafy growth. It is an attractive plant for the first part of the year but can become straggly. It is best cut back to stimulate new, fresh and attractive growth. Cutting back also prevents self-seeding around the allotment.

PROPAGATION

Propagate from seeds, root divisions or stem cuttings. The seeds can be planted directly outside in 1cm (½in) drills in the spring or started off in a greenhouse in late winter. The plants should be thinned to 30–45cm (12–18in) apart.

HARVESTING AND STORAGE

Plants should be cut as flowering begins by cutting off the top growth, leaving a 5cm (2in) stubble for regrowth. Lemon balm can be susceptible to frost and so mulching is recommended if hard frost is likely. The leaves can be dried and then stored for later use.

CULINARY USES

The fresh leaves give a lovely lemon flavour to salads, vegetable dishes, chicken dishes, poultry stuffing and drinks. The dried leaves can be used to make herbal tea and are also added to potpourri and herb pillows.

Right: *Lemon balm is beautifully scented but, like all members of the mint family, it can spread rapidly.*

CULTIVATION

Sowing time Winter (indoors); spring (outside)
Sowing depth 1cm (½in)
Thinning and planting distance 30–45cm (12–18in)
Harvesting When the leaves are still fresh-looking
Storage Dried

MINT

Mentha

Mint is an aromatic herb, with square, erect stems and flowers in the leaf axils. It is an invasive perennial or annual. Most mints grow to about 30–90cm (12–36in) in height. Spearmint (*M. spicata*) leaves are green, slightly crinkled and almost hairless with a very pungent lemony mint aroma and bitter taste. Peppermint (*M.* × *piperita*) has flat, smooth, shiny, pointed green leaves and reddish-lilac to purple flowers. Peppermint and spearmint spread rapidly by stolons and rhizomes and can become a weed problem.

SOIL AND ASPECT

A well-drained, fertile soil with a pH of 5–7 in full sun is preferred, although mints will prosper in a wide range of soil types in sun or partial shade. Mint can become invasive and it is a good idea to plant it in a below-ground container in most situations. Plants can suffer from mildew and rusts and a wilt disease caused by the soil fungus verticillium. Despite this, they have a tendency to spread rampantly through borders if left unchecked. Where mint is regularly cut back, apply a nitrogen- rich fertilizer such as dried blood or pelleted poultry manure and top-dress with well-rotted compost.

PROPAGATION

Mints are usually propagated from cuttings of stems, stolons and root divisions. Plant out propagated or purchased plants in spring, 30cm (12in) apart.

HARVESTING AND STORAGE

Mint can be harvested twice a season, leaving a stubble of at least 10cm (4in), although it is more usually collected as needed, picking the leaves when they are young and fresh. Cutting back stimulates new growth that is perfect for picking. The leaves can be dried or frozen.

CULINARY USES

Mint leaves are added to beverages, jellies, soups, stews, sauces, vinegar and used to flavour meats such as lamb.

CULTIVATION
Planting time Spring
Planting distance 30cm (12in)
Harvesting While leaves are young
Storage Dried or frozen

Above: *Mint is a must for the allotment but take care not to let it spread unchecked in open ground.*

BERGAMOT

Monarda didyma

Bergamot is not widely used as a culinary herb today, but its whorled flower heads make it worthy of inclusion in the allotment. There are various colours to choose from, including bright red. The leaves release an aromatic fragrance when they are brushed against, which makes weeding among these herbs an absolute pleasure.

SOIL AND ASPECT

Bergamot thrives in a rich, moist soil. Soils with a tendency to dry out will quickly kill the plant unless watered. The plants are best replanted in a fresh patch every three years or so and clumps benefit from a light mulching of well-rotted garden compost after a dressing of fish, blood and bone or similar general-purpose fertilizer. *M. didyma* can spread by means of flat stems near the surface, resulting in it needing to be divided and re-situated every two to three years or so. It is also prone to mildew. Other species are much less prone to mildew (and also grow and flower much better) in a moist soil, or at least in a place where they do not get too dry in summer.

PROPAGATION

Bergamot can be raised by division, cuttings or by seed in spring. The seed can be sown in spring in rows at a depth of 1cm (½in), but plants tend to look better in drifts or clumps. In either case the plants should be spaced about 45cm (18in) apart.

HARVESTING AND STORAGE

The leaves should be harvested when they are still young. The flowers can also be picked as they are just opening and both can be dried and then stored.

CULINARY USES

The leaves of bergamot dry well and can be used to make a herbal tea. This is not the same as the bergamot in Earl Grey, which is a tropical citrus. Both the leaves and flowers can be used.

Right: *Garden bergamot is most commonly grown for its pretty looks, rather than for using in the kitchen.*

CULTIVATION
Sowing time Spring
Sowing depth 1cm (½in)
Planting time Spring
Thinning and planting distance 45cm (18in)
Harvesting While young (leaves); as they are opening (flowers)
Storage Dried

SWEET CICELY

Myrrhis odorata

Sweet cicely, an early-summer-flowering perennial, is something of a rarity these days and usually only grown by devotees. It is reminiscent of cow parsley and the seed-heads produced later in the summer are quite attractive in their own right. The leaves are a pretty mottled green, and are large and fairly deeply cut. It grows to a height of 60–90cm (24–36in) and can become invasive when it likes the conditions. Sweet cicely is a good choice for including in a wild allotment plot.

SOIL AND ASPECT

Sweet cicely likes a moist humus-rich soil and, unusually for a herb, will thrive in shade. It is perfectly at home at the base of a hedgerow and provides a pretty effect in late spring and early summer. Like many of its close relatives, the individual plants are short-lived, but it self-seeds prolifically and must be prevented from becoming a weed in an allotment.

PROPAGATION

Sweet cicely can be slow to germinate and difficult to transplant, so it is best sown in situ using freshly ripened seed. Sow seed in autumn in drills 1cm (½in) deep. The seedlings should be thinned to 60cm (24in). Plants should have their seed removed before it gets the chance to self-seed.

HARVESTING AND STORAGE

The leaves of sweet cicely are harvested from spring to early summer, and can be dried. The seeds taste of aniseed only when they are still greenish, so collect them when they are still unripe. The seeds have no taste if they are completely black.

CULINARY USES

Sweet cicely has a mild aniseed flavour that can be used to counter the acidity of sharp-tasting fruit. It was used as a sweetening agent for stewed soft fruits and rhubarb. The leaves make an attractive garnish.

Right: *Sweet cicely is something of a rarity but it is ideally suited to the allotment. It can be used in potpourri.*

CULTIVATION
Sowing time Autumn
Sowing depth 1cm (½in)
Thinning and planting distance 60cm (24in)
Harvesting Spring to early summer (leaves); unripe, when green (seed)
Storage Dried (leaves and seed)

BASIL

Ocimum

The height, leaf colour, flower colour, and growth habit of basil can vary a great deal depending on the variety. Sweet basil (*Ocimum basilicum*) has smooth, bright green leaves and small, white flowers. It can grow 60–90cm (24–36in) high and has an erect and branched habit. Cinnamon basil (*O. basilicum* 'Cinnamon') has a similar habit but is smaller, growing only 30–40cm (12–16in) tall. This type has smaller, purplish leaves, pink flower spikes and an anise-cinnamon-like odour. Lemon basil (*O.* × *citriodorum*) has a growth habit resembling cinnamon basil but has smooth, bright green leaves and small white flowers. Purple basil (*O. basilicum* var. *purpurascens*) is noted for its strongly scented purple leaves.

SOIL AND ASPECT

Basil requires a minimum temperature of 10–15°C (50–59°F) and pH of 5–8 in order to thrive. The growing area should be in full sun with light, fertile, well-drained soil. The application of garden compost or well-rotted manure can aid growth. Avoid applying too much nitrogen, as this will decrease the essential oils in the growing tissue, resulting in weak-flavoured leaf and stem tissue. Keep well watered. Basil is a good companion plant for tomatoes.

PROPAGATION

For an early supply, sow seeds in plug trays in a greenhouse and transplant outside in warm weather. Seed can be sown outdoors in 1cm (½in) drills in the late spring, provided that the soil is kept moist. Thin or plant out at 20–23cm (8–9in) intervals.

HARVESTING AND STORAGE

Pick frequently to avoid the development of woody stems. Regular picking is advised as the leaves become bitter if the plant is allowed to flower. Take care when harvesting as the leaves bruise easily.

CULINARY USES

The fresh or dried leaves are used in tomato dishes, pasta sauces, vegetables and soups. Basil is useful in Mediterranean dishes and is always best used fresh.

CULTIVATION
Sowing time Late spring
Sowing depth 1cm (½in)
Thinning and planting distance 20–22cm (8–9in)
Harvesting Any time
Storage Dried or frozen

Above: *Basil combines well with tomatoes both as a companion plant in the allotment and as an ingredient in cooking.*

SWEET MARJORAM AND OREGANO

Origanum majorana, O. vulgare

Sweet marjoram grows to a height of 30cm (12in) and makes a good companion plant for aubergines (eggplants), pumpkins and courgettes (zucchini). Oregano can grow to a height of 60cm (24in) and is generally hardier than marjoram. It is a sprawling herb and, unlike sweet marjoram, is not suited for growing indoors. Oregano makes a good companion plant for cauliflower, but should not be planted with broccoli or cabbage. Many plants are classified as oregano and their flavour depends on where they are cultivated. In general, the hotter the sun, the stronger the flavour.

SOIL AND ASPECT

Sweet marjoram and oregano thrive in full sun and prefer a light, fairly rich, well-drained, slightly alkaline soil, with a pH of 7–8. Poorer soils result in a more pungent taste and can stimulate early flowering. As it is not entirely hardy, pot up sweet marjoram in autumn and overwinter indoors or sow seed each year.

PROPAGATION

Sweet marjoram is easily grown from seed sown in spring in 1cm (½in) drills or by cuttings taken in summer. Thin or plant out at 30cm (12in) intervals. In cooler areas, marjoram can be overwintered indoors in pots. Oregano can be grown from seed sown similarly to that of marjoram or by taking stem cuttings or root divisions. The seed can be slow to germinate and the resulting plants may not be true to the parent plant, or may even be flavourless, making vegetative propagation the preferred option.

HARVESTING AND STORAGE

Harvest and dry the leaves before flowering occurs. Dry by tying the stems together and hanging in a warm, dry, well-ventilated place. Both herbs can also be frozen.

CULINARY USES

These flavourful herbs are used in many dishes, especially in Italian recipes.

CULTIVATION
Sowing time Spring
Sowing depth 1cm (½in)
Dividing time Spring
Thinning and planting distance 30cm (12in)
Harvesting While young
Storage Dried or frozen

Above: *Marjoram is a good companion plant for pumpkins, courgettes and aubergines as well as a culinary herb.*

PARSLEY

Petroselinum crispum

Although it is a biennial plant, parsley, which grows up to 45cm (18in), can only be cropped in the first year and is usually grown as an annual. In its first year, it develops plenty of leaves, on fairly long stems that come from the crown of the plant. In the second year, the plant produces only a couple of leaves and a long bloom stalk that will self-sow if you allow it. Parsley is one of the most popular and versatile culinary herbs and can be grown indoors or outdoors. It makes an excellent subject for a container or as an edging to paths. There are two forms: curly-leaved parsley (*P. crispum*) and French or flat-leaved parsley (*P. crispum neapolitanum*).

SOIL AND ASPECT

Parsley does best in a sunny spot, but will also prosper in light shade. It should be grown in a moist fertile soil and benefits from the addition of well-rotted garden compost or manure and a nitrogen-rich fertilizer such as dried blood or pelleted chicken manure. Keep well watered in long hot, dry spells.

PROPAGATION

The seeds should be soaked in water and then sown either under cover or outside in 1cm (½in) drills. Thin or plant out at 20–25cm (8–10in) intervals. A spring sowing will provide leaves through summer while a second sowing in late summer will provide winter leaves. These will need protection with a cloche.

HARVEST

Young leaves should be snipped just above ground level as needed. The harvested leaves can be dried or frozen for later use.

CULINARY USES

The leaves and stem are used to flavour and garnish a wide variety of dishes. Curly-leaved forms have a subtle flavour whereas the flat-leaved types have a stronger taste.

Right: *Parsley is one of the most popular and versatile herbs for use in the kitchen. It also looks decorative in the allotment.*

CULTIVATION
Sowing time Spring or late summer
Sowing depth 1cm (½in)
Thinning and planting distance 20–25cm (8–10in)
Harvesting Any time
Storage Dried or frozen

ROSEMARY

Rosmarinus officinalis

This greatly valued herb, which is native to southern Europe, grows up to 1.2m (4ft) tall. As well as a being a useful culinary herb, rosemary is also a beautiful, drought-resistant plant that can be used in landscaping. It has attractive blue flowers that are a good source of nectar for bees. There are two basic types: the trailing or prostrate type and a bush type that will, in time, become large enough to be considered a shrub. Prostrate rosemary makes an excellent groundcover plant.

SOIL AND ASPECT

Rosemary thrives in a well-drained soil in a sunny position. It is slightly tender and will suffer if it is planted in a wet soil during the cold winter months. It is an excellent plant for use in coastal areas. Rosemary is a plant that actually thrives on neglect and will die if you fertilize or water it too much or plant it in very rich soil.

PROPAGATION

Rosemary is best bought as an established plant or raised from cuttings. Plant out in the eventual position in spring to late summer. One plant is usually enough for most culinary requirements, but, if you do want to grow more than this, space the plants 75cm (30in) apart.

HARVESTING AND STORAGE

Harvest the young, tender stems and leaves, taking off no more than one-third of the plant at one time. For drying, harvest just before the plant flowers. After drying, the leaves can be stored for later use.

CULINARY USES

Rosemary leaves can be used for making tea, in sauces or for flavouring many meat (especially lamb) and vegetable dishes. It may also be used in herb breads and is excellent for including in potpourri. It can be used either fresh or dried.

Right: *Rosemary, which is native to southern Europe, will thrive in coastal areas or is ideal for growing in a dry, sunny spot.*

CULTIVATION
Planting time Spring to late summer
Planting distance 75cm (30in)
Harvesting Any time
Storage Dried

SAGE

Salvia officinalis

Sage is a long-lived, hardy, shrubby perennial with grey, felted leaves. It can reach 80cm (32in) in height. It has a distinctive flavour that combines well with a variety of meats and vegetables. Sage is an excellent specimen for use in the allotment. There are coloured-leaved forms, including deep purple and bright yellow, as well as the culinary grey-leaved form. The spikes of blue-purple flowers appear in late spring and will attract bees and other beneficial insects.

SOIL AND ASPECT

Sage is very easy to grow in the right conditions. It prefers full sun and a reasonably fertile, well-drained soil that does not get too dry. The main problem with sage is to keep it under control. Pinch small plants to make them branch, then let them grow to harvesting size and avoid letting the stems get so tall that they lie down or you will end up with a twisted, woody tangle in a couple of years.

PROPAGATION

Sage is best grown from cuttings taken in early to mid-summer or purchased as young plants. They can also be raised from seed. Seeds require 20 days at 20°C (68°F) for germination to take place and are best raised under cover. Sow seed in trays or shallow pans or under cloches in spring in 1cm (½in) deep drills. Plants should be thinned out, transplanted or planted 60cm (24in) apart in their required position.

HARVESTING AND STORAGE

Sage is best harvested when it is just starting to flower and used either fresh or dried. Harvest after the dew dries in the morning, cutting the stems so that there are one or two leaves remaining at the bottom. Air-drying sage will result in a leathery rather than a crisp product that should be stored in airtight jars. Chop or rub the leaves into a powder when you need to use them.

CULINARY USES

The leaves are used to flavour soups, stews, stuffings, sausages and roast meats, as well as to make tea. The coloured leaf forms taste the same as the grey-leaved ones.

CULTIVATION
Sowing time Spring
Sowing depth 1cm (½in)
Cuttings Taken early to mid-summer
Thinning and planting distance 60cm (24in)
Harvesting Any time
Storage Dried

Above: *The pungent leaves of sage are ready for harvesting when the handsome flowers appear.*

SAVORY

Satureja

Summer savory (*S. hortensis*) is an annual that grows to about 45cm (18in). It has a less tidy appearance than winter savory (*S. montana*). Winter savory is a perennial that also grows to about 45cm (18in) high, but is much hardier in cultivation. It can be treated in the same way as common thyme, which it closely resembles, although it is slightly more compact, with darker leaves and white flowers. Like thyme, winter savory makes a good edging plant for a vegetable plot and will benefit from a light pruning in spring to keep it compact. Both winter and summer savory can be grown successfully in containers.

SOIL AND ASPECT

Both types of savory are Mediterranean herbs that need a warm sunny site with free-draining soil. In colder areas winter savory may need some form of winter protection.

PROPAGATION

Summer savory is an annual that needs reasonably warm, damp conditions for germination, but only a little water thereafter. Both types of savory grow well from seed that should not be sown too deeply. They are best station sown at 30cm (12in) intervals in mid-spring in 1cm (½in) drills. Thin to 30cm (12in).

HARVESTING AND STORAGE

You can gather the young stem tips early in the season but when the plant begins to flower, harvest the entire plant and then dry. The dried leaves can be stored for later use.

CULINARY USES

Although these are among the oldest of herbs, they are not widely grown or used today. Summer savory is sometimes called the bean herb because it goes so well with green beans and is used in a range of bean dishes. Both types of savory have a spicy, peppery flavour and are used to flavour fresh garden beans, vinegar, soups, stuffings and rice.

CULTIVATION
Sowing time Mid-spring
Sowing depth 1cm (½in)
Thinning distance 30cm (12in)
Harvesting Before flowering (stem tips); on flowering (whole plant)
Storage Dried

Above: *Savory thrives in warm, sunny conditions and provides a spicy addition to many dishes.*

THYME

Thymus vulgaris

Thyme is a perennial plant that reaches 30–45cm (12–18in) in height. It can be grown indoors or outdoors and in sun or partial shade. There is a very wide range of thymes that can be grown in the herb plot. Most are similar in terms of their culinary value, although the broad-leaved forms have a slightly stronger flavour. The wide range of colours available makes them excellent subjects for ornamental plantings and edible landscaping.

SOIL AND ASPECT

Thyme likes a sunny situation and a well-drained soil. It is not particular about the soil type and will even grow in poor 'gravelly' soils. Thymes are excellent plants for edging borders and can be grown in containers and between the cracks in the paving in patios. They are durable and will even withstand being walked on. They can get straggly after a few years, although a light trimming will help maintain a good habit.

PROPAGATION

Thyme can be grown from seed in spring, although this does not allow for the propagation of particular forms or varieties. Seeds require 25 days at about 16°C (61°F) for germination and are best raised under cover and transplanted out later. Plants can also be raised vegetatively from cuttings or layers taken in early to mid-summer. Plants should be spaced at 30cm (12in) intervals.

HARVESTING AND STORAGE

Nip off leafy stem ends and flowers as and when they are needed when the plants are at the full-flowering stage.These can be used fresh or dried by hanging a bunch in a warm place. They can also be frozen.

CULINARY USES

The leaves can be used with meats, soups, sauces and egg dishes. Thyme improves digestion, destroys intestinal parasites and is a good antiseptic and tonic. Its leaves can be used as a condiment and a tea.

Right: *Despite the wide range of cultivated thymes that are available, most have similar uses in the kitchen.*

CULTIVATION
Sowing time Spring
Cuttings or layers Early to mid-summer
Thinning and planting distance 30cm (12in)
Harvesting Any time
Storage Dried or frozen

GARDENER'S GUIDE TO FRUIT AND NUTS

Almost every allotment will have space for some fruit and, indeed, would not be complete without it. Summer and autumn are the main time for harvesting the majority of crops, and there is nothing that truly compares to the taste of fresh, sun-ripened fruit that has been raised on your own plot. Of course, there are many types of fruit and nuts, not all of which can be grown on an allotment. This gardener's guide concentrates on some of the more common types that you are likely to encounter, and particularly those that are most likely to be successfully grown on an allotment.

Left: *Harvesting fresh fruit that you have grown yourself is one of the greatest pleasures a gardener can experience.*

Above: *Ripening on the plant gives better sweetness and higher vitamin content than most shop bought fruit.*

Above: *Mouth-watering bunches of perfectly ripened fruit such as red currants provide colour during the summer.*

Above: *One of the delights of the allotment is the blossom that precedes the fruit. This is bramble blossom.*

COBNUTS AND FILBERTS

Corylus avellana and *C. maxima*

Both of these nuts are derived from two European species of corylus. The cobnuts are *Corylus avellana*; the filberts are *C. maxima*. The origin of cultivars is confusing and so both are often grouped together. Cobnuts and filberts are largely self-sterile, and are pollinated by compatible varieties grown nearby. There are numerous selections of cobnuts and filberts, many of which are the product of crossbreeding between the two.

OBTAINING PLANTS

Because of the need for cross-pollination, varieties do not come true from seed, and bushes are propagated by layering the 'wands' (self-coppicing suckers that grow from the base) or by grafts.

SOIL AND PREFERRED ASPECT

Both cobnuts and filberts will grow on almost any soil that is well drained, but grow best on a loamy soil with a pH of 7.5–8. They tolerate shade, although a sunny position will generally yield a heavier crop. They need a relatively sheltered position as the flowers that appear in mid- to late winter can be susceptible to wind damage.

CULTIVATION

The bushes are generally planted 4.5–5m (15–16ft) apart, although this can be closer and a number of varieties can be grown in one area. The useful life of each bush is long, with bushes well over 100 years old still able to crop well. Fine sunny days with a light breeze at pollination time favour a good crop. Both cobnuts and filberts benefit from a good mulching in autumn. Keep the ground clean by hoeing regularly in the summer.

PRUNING

Both cobnuts and filberts are best grown as bushes or small trees with a 1m (3ft) tall stem and six or seven main branches. Each branch or wand is pruned to a height of about 2m (6½ft) to allow the maximum amount of light to reach all parts of the bush (essential for nut production) and keep the crop within picking reach. Prune from early winter to mid-spring, preferably to coincide with flowering and thereby aid pollination.

HARVESTING AND STORAGE

Cobnuts and filberts are best enjoyed fresh. Shake from the branches from around early to mid-autumn, repeating this at intervals.

PESTS AND DISEASES

Though relatively trouble free, one important pest is the nut weevil (*Balaninus nucum*). Weevil-infested nuts can be separated by placing them in cold storage for a few days, which induces the weevil grub to emerge. Squirrels and other nut-loving mammals can also be a problem.

Above: *Cobnuts and filberts are easy to grow on most soils but sunny positions ensure the best crops.*

PRUNING AN ESTABLISHED COBNUT TREE

Late summer *Established trees should be pruned in late summer. Strong lateral growths are broken off by hand to about six to eight leaves from the base and left to hang.*

Late winter *Cut back all the broken growths to three or four buds. Never prune back laterals carrying female flowers but remove crowded growths and suckers.*

VARIETIES

COBNUTS

'Kentish Cob' A moderately vigorous, upright grower with large nuts of good flavour. Better pollination is achieved when two different varieties are planted.

'Pearson's Prolific' A compact variety with small to medium nuts of good flavour. Best pollination is achieved when two different varieties are planted.

'Purpurea' Red catkins and purple leaves and small nuts of good flavour.

FILBERTS

'Barcelona' A popular variety needing moist soil and shade in hot climates. Pollinated by any filbert except 'Ennis'.

'Butler' Needs moist soil and shade in hot climates. Pollinate by any other filbert. A pollinator for 'Barcelona' and 'Ennis' with a crop of large nuts.

'Duchilly' A fine-flavoured, long nut. Needs moist soil and afternoon shade. Pollinate by any other filbert.

'Ennis' The largest nut and the heaviest crops in early autumn. Needs good soil moisture and afternoon shade. Pollinate by 'Daviana' or 'Butler'.

cobnuts

MELONS

Cucumis melo

Melons are popular with gardeners who have plenty of space to accommodate their spreading vines. They must be grown in a greenhouse or cold frame in cooler climates. Cantaloupes (muskmelons) do not tolerate cool temperatures or transplant very well, so wait until the soil is warm before planting seeds. Of the different types of melon available, cantaloupes are reputed to have the sweetest flavour, whereas honeydew melons store especially well.

OBTAINING PLANTS

Melons are grown annually from seed, which is sown from early to mid-spring, under glass in cooler areas. The seeds are sown about 1cm (½in) deep in pairs in a 7cm (2¾in) pot and the weaker one is thinned if both germinate. They can be potted on if outdoor conditions delay planting out. Greenhouse melons should be planted into their final position as soon as possible.

SOIL AND PREFERRED ASPECT

Melons can be grown outside in sheltered locations, but do better under cover in cooler areas. Melons require a fertile, well-drained soil that is not too rich and has a pH of 6.5–7. This should be cleared about three to four weeks before planting and the planting pit prepared. Each pit should measure 30 x 30 x 30cm (12 x 12 x 12in).

Above: *Melon vines are vigorous growers that must be restricted in order to ensure good-sized fruit.*

Place a good spade-full of well-rotted manure in the base before backfilling. Water the pit well and cover with plastic to warm up the soil in readiness for planting.

CULTIVATION

Seedlings are best planted out when they have developed four leaves and all danger of frost has passed. They should be planted with about 2–3cm (¾–1¼in) of the pot soil above ground level as a precaution against soft collar rot. Do not firm the soil but water each plant, keeping water off the stem. Plant the melons at 1–1.2m (3–4ft) intervals and place cloches and light shading over them for 7–10 days until they are established.

Melons should be stopped at the fourth or fifth leaf to encourage the production of side shoots. The four strongest side shoots should be kept and the rest removed after two to three weeks. Plants growing in cold frames should be trained into an 'X'-shape. Cantaloupes can also be grown on a trellis, but the fruit must be supported with a sling. Control the vigorous vines by pinching out the growing terminals once the melon crop has set. After this, pinch out all other lateral growths and flowers as they appear. Thinning may be necessary, particularly in areas with a shorter growing season. Bees are necessary for pollination and plants growing under cover may need pollinating by hand. One male flower should be sufficient for about four female flowers. Female flowers are easily recognized by the small embryonic fruit immediately behind them. Regular feeding and watering will aid the development of the crop. A good compost tea is especially useful for this.

HARVESTING AND STORAGE

The fruits are mature when there is a characteristic melon scent and circular cracking appears near to the stalk. When lifted they should part easily from the stalk. Melons do not store for more than a few days and are best eaten straightaway.

PESTS AND DISEASES

Melons are prey to relatively few diseases but a couple can be serious. Powdery mildew can be a problem as can soft collar rot if the stems are allowed to get wet. Verticillium wilt is a serious threat and affected plants should be removed. Many newer hybrid varieties are resistant to major diseases. Pests are generally less troublesome, red spider mite being the only potentially serious one in greenhouses and warmer areas.

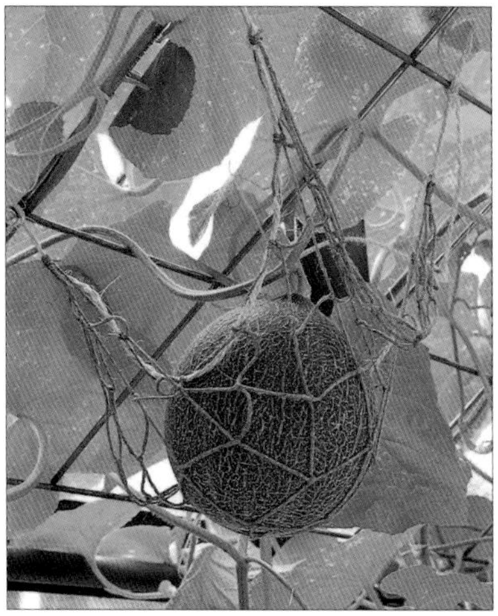

Above: *Melons can be trained to grow as greenhouse climbers, provided that the fruit is supported in a sling.*

VARIETIES

'Hero of Lockinge' Large fruits of a good flavour with a golden, fine-textured flesh. Good for forcing in cold frames.

'Ogen' Small fruits with a good flavour are borne on this early cropping variety. A good plant for cooler areas.

'Superlative' Large, almost round, green fruits with scarlet flesh. A good variety for greenhouses or cloche culture.

'Sweetheart' Medium-sized fruits with firm salmon-pink flesh. A hybrid variety suitable for colder areas.

QUINCE

Cydonia oblonga

The true quince is a low, deciduous, thornless tree with a crooked growth habit. It will reach a height and spread of about 3.5m (12ft), and can even grow to 5m (16ft) or more on a fertile soil. Quinces need little attention once established, and begin to yield apple- or pear-shaped fruits after four or five years. Fruit grown in cooler areas is too acidic to be eaten fresh (although it can be used to make jellies and preserves). It may be sweeter if grown in warmer regions.

OBTAINING PLANTS

Quince is a difficult tree to raise and maintain in the first year and it is best to buy a specimen that has already been raised and shaped for a couple of years in a specialist nursery. It has a crooked shape at first and it is advisable to support the tree for the first few years following planting until it is fully established and has the strength needed to support the crown. Plant bare-rooted trees in the winter dormant season and container-grown stock at any time, provided that it is kept properly watered.

SOIL AND PREFERRED ASPECT

Quinces will succeed in most soils but grow best in a deep, light, fertile and moisture-retentive soil. They do well near water but are equally at home in an open sunny site in warmer areas. They are hardy in most areas but warmth is required to ripen the fruit.

CULTIVATION

In cooler locations quinces need some protection, the ideal position being a sunny corner where two walls meet, with the tree trained as a fan. Prepare the ground well

Above: *Quince is an unusual fruit tree in that it is quite easily grown in a warm part of the allotment.*

prior to planting by digging over the whole area, removing all perennial weeds and applying a base dressing of compound fertilizer such as hoof and horn. Drive in the supporting stake first, before the tree is planted and tied on to it. Space bush trees about 3.5m (12ft) apart and standard trees about 6m (20ft) apart. Apply a dressing of general-purpose fertilizer such as fish, blood and bone in late winter and mulch with a generous layer of well-rotted manure or compost. Keep the area around the tree base free of weeds for a diameter of about 1m (3ft) throughout the growing season.

PRUNING

The aim of any pruning is to achieve a goblet-shaped tree with an open (but not barren) centre. Cut back the previous season's growth by about half in winter for the first three or four years, making the cut to an outward-facing bud. Cut back side shoots to two or three buds if competing with the leader or crowding the centre, but leave all others. After four years, little pruning is required except to tidy up the plant or remove dead, diseased or badly placed branches. Remove any suckers or branches growing from the main stem below the crown.

HARVESTING AND STORAGE

Leave the fruits on the tree for as long as possible so that they can develop their full flavour, but remove before any heavy frosts. The fruits usually ripen in mid- to late autumn.

Left: *Growing a quince against a warm, sunny wall will help the fruit to develop its full flavour.*

VARIETIES

'Champion' Large, round, yellow fruits with a delicate flavour. The tree is extremely productive and begins fruiting when quite young.

'Lusitanica' Pear-shaped, yellow fruits with a down-covered skin that are juicy and good for cooking. The tree is very vigorous but tender and best suited to warmer areas.

'Maliformis' Apple-shaped fruits of a rich golden colour. It is very productive and well suited to cooler climates.

'Meech's Prolific' This variety has fairly large, pear-shaped fruits of a rich golden colour. It is a vigorous grower that crops early.

quinces

Store like apples for about a month before use, keeping them separate from other fruits because they are strongly aromatic.

PESTS AND DISEASES

Quince suffers generally from the same pests as apples. Likely diseases include leaf blight and brown rot of the fruit.

PRUNING A STANDARD QUINCE

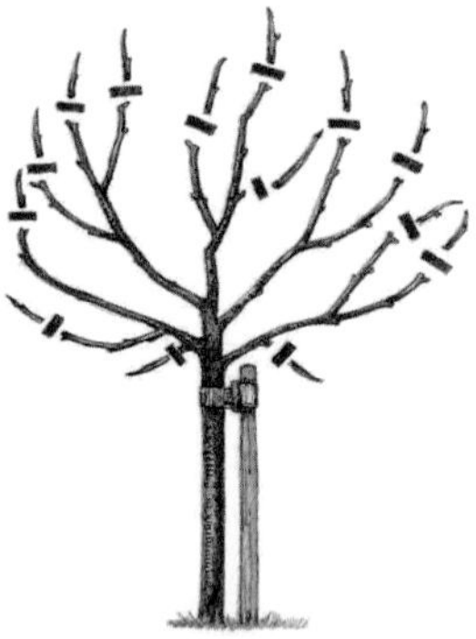

Winter *Establish a strong branch framework immediately after planting. Each winter after this, cut back the leaders of the main branches by about one-third of the previous summer's growth. Make all of the cuts above an outward-facing bud and remove any weak or badly placed branches.*

FIGS

Ficus carica

Figs are deciduous trees from the Mediterranean areas of Europe and the Middle East. They grow mainly in warmer regions but can be grown in temperate areas. Figs grown in cooler areas set fruit without needing to be fertilized, so only one plant needs to be grown.

OBTAINING PLANTS

Figs are usually bought from a specialist nursery, although they can be raised quite easily from cuttings taken in summer.

SOIL AND PREFERRED ASPECT

Figs are tolerant of a wide range of well-drained soils and need full sun. Excavate a pit and place paving slabs around the sides, letting them protrude about 2–3cm (¾–1¼in) above the soil. This restricts the fig's root run and ensures good cropping. Tightly pack bricks or other inert rubble into the bottom. Wall-trained figs need a box of about 2 x 0.6m (6½ x 2ft), whereas freestanding trees need a box that is 1 x 1m (3 x 3ft). Both boxes should be 50–60cm (20–30in) deep. Figs in cooler regions need the protection of a sunny wall and are best grown as a fan.

CULTIVATION

Feed figs in spring using a compound fertilizer such as fish, blood and bone.

Above: *Young embryo figs that form in the first year will only fully ripen in the following season.*

Apply a light mulch of well-rotted manure or compost. Root-restricted figs need regular feeding throughout the growing season with compost tea or worm liquid. Water root-restricted figs, as they can quickly become stressed after even a short period of hot or dry weather. Protect outdoor trees in winter in cooler areas by thatching them with bracken or draping with horticultural fleece. Figs grown in a greenhouse are treated in a similar way to outdoor fans.

PRUNING

The pruning of figs in cooler temperate areas differs to that of warmer climates. In cool regions, the fig bears two crops per year but only one ripens. The fruit that is harvested forms at the top of the previous season's growth and extends back about 15–30cm (6–12in). These are carried over the winter as embryo fruits and ripen the following year. Any figs that form on the current season's growth will not ripen before the autumn and should be removed.

Fan-trained figs are formed in the same manner as for a peach or sour cherry. Established fans should have about half of their developing shoots tipped back in mid-summer. In mid-winter, half of these shoots that carry fruit are pruned back to 2.5cm (1in) to encourage new growth next year. The remaining pruning involves maintaining an open framework.

Where conditions allow for the growth of freestanding trees, these require little pruning save to maintain an open framework and health and vigour.

VARIETIES

'Bourjasotte Grise' One of the sweetest and richly flavoured varieties, with rounded, medium to large fruits. Grow under glass in cooler areas.

'Brown Turkey' A hardy variety with large, oval fruits in late summer or early autumn.

'Brunswick' A hardy variety with very large oval fruits in late summer.

'White Marseilles' A hardy, reliable cropper with large, pear-shaped fruits from late summer to early autumn.

figs

HARVESTING AND STORAGE

Ripe figs are soft to the touch and hang downwards. Slight splitting of the skin and drops of nectar dripping from the eye are also signs that they are ripe. Figs are best eaten fresh.

PESTS AND DISEASES

Figs are generally trouble free although older specimens can become infested with coral spot fungus. Figs grown under glass can suffer from pests such as red spider mite, scale and mealy bugs.

PRUNING AN ESTABLISHED FAN-TRAINED FIG TREE

Mid-summer *Pinch out the growing tips of about half of the young shoots that are carried on the main framework branches. You should do this towards the end of mid-summer. As the shoots develop, tie them to the wires.*

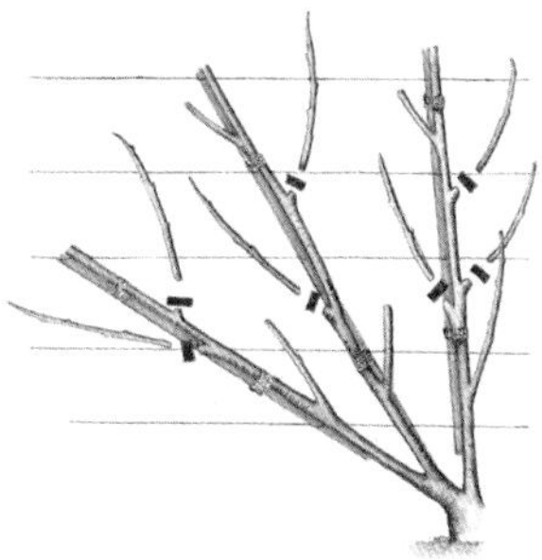

Late autumn *Prune back half the shoots that carried fruits to about 2.5cm (1in) to encourage new growth from the base. Tie in the other shoots, parallel with the wall, about 23–30cm (9–12in) apart, removing any surplus ones.*

STRAWBERRIES

Fragaria × ananassa

Strawberries are a popular fruit and also dependable for home production. The management of this crop is easier than that of tree fruits and even a small allotment site can yield a good crop of this delicious summer fruit.

OBTAINING PLANTS

While some strawberry varieties can be raised from seed, it is more common to buy plants. To be sure that your plants are true-to-type, vigorous and virus-free, purchase them from a reputable nursery. Always try to get registered virus-free plants as these can yield 50–75 per cent more fruit than ordinary stock plants. It is generally not advisable to transplant strawberries out of an old bed because diseases may be introduced.

SOIL AND PREFERRED ASPECT

Strawberries thrive on sandy loam soil, but will produce adequately on heavier soils provided they are well drained. A sloping site ensures good surface water drainage. The ideal soil pH is slightly acidic at between 6.0 and 6.5. The soil should contain adequate organic matter: compost or manure is best dug in at the beginning of the season before planting. Alternatively, a green manure can be grown and dug in. When preparing strawberry plants for planting, never allow them to dry out. Cover the roots with moist peat moss or cloth, and keep the plants shaded at all times. Strawberries begin blooming in spring and can be subject to frost injury, so select a site that has good air movement. Avoid low-lying frost pockets and remember that slopes facing the sun warm up faster in spring and stimulate earlier flowering, but can actually increase the danger of frost injury. In very frost-prone areas, a less sunny slope that delays blooming until after the seasonal danger of frost has passed can be to your advantage.

Above: *Strawberries are so named because straw is placed under the ripening berries to keep them clean and stop them from rotting.*

CULTIVATION

The goal during the first summer of growth after the spring planting is to establish healthy plants as early in the season as possible. In early summer, the parent plant sends out runners once it is established. Frequent, shallow cultivation between the rows, hand pulling of weeds and mulching with 5cm (2in) of hay, straw, or coarse sawdust two or three weeks after planting will greatly reduce the number of weeds.

Apply a fertilizer that is rich in potassium in late summer at the time flower buds are initiated for the next spring's fruit as this will help harden the plants for the coming winter.

Protect the crowns of plants during very cold periods in winter. Do not apply mulch too early in autumn as it can increase crown rot and prevent the plants from completely going dormant, making them more subject to winter injury. Suitable mulches include newspapers, coarse sawdust, straw, hay or any loose mulch that does not compact.

Strawberry fruit is 90 per cent water and any moisture-stress during development will reduce yield. Always ensure that the crop is well watered while cropping.

HARVESTING AND STORAGE

Harvest when the berries are fully ripe. White areas indicate immaturity. Allowing the berry to reach full colour on the plant increases the sugar content and the size of the berry. Pick the berries with the stem and cap attached to allow the fruit to keep for a longer period. Berries that have their caps removed or are injured quickly go off.

The first harvest can occur about 30 days after the first bloom. Check every other day for ripe fruit. Place in shallow containers to minimize injury and chill promptly.

PESTS AND DISEASES

To avoid diseases, do not plant where tomatoes, potatoes, peppers or aubergines (eggplants) have been grown, or back into a site where strawberries have been grown in the last two years. Protect the fruit from birds with netting.

Above: *The developing fruit trusses can be protected from muddy splashes or soil borne rots with a mulch of straw.*

Above: *Removing the leaves and straw mulch after fruiting will prevent the build-up and spread of diseases.*

VARIETIES

'Baron Solemacher' Main cropper with a superb flavour and will tolerate a little shade. Tiny dark red fruits.

'Cambridge Favourite' Produces large red fruits that are mild in flavour. A good heavy cropper.

'Royal Sovereign' An early variety that has a superb flavour. Susceptible to pests and diseases.

'Trellisa' Really good-flavoured medium-sized fruit. Good variety for strawberry barrels.

strawberries

WALNUTS

Juglans regia

The common, or English, walnut is, in fact, native to southern Europe and Asia. The related eastern black walnut is commonly grown in eastern and central USA and is hardier and larger. It also yields a high-quality wood, although the fruit is not as good as the common walnut. Both become relatively large trees and are therefore best grown in larger plots. Walnuts are best grown from a known variety that will yield good-quality nuts. The variety chosen will depend entirely upon personal taste, although most will not begin cropping for five to ten years.

OBTAINING PLANTS

Walnuts are almost always bought in from specialist fruit nurseries and, although they can be grown from seed, it is better to raise a variety if good-quality nuts are needed. The trees are planted in the same manner as all other fruit trees and can be purchased as bare-rooted stock or container-grown trees. Bare-rooted is generally the best option for the long-term health of the plant and these should be planted in the dormant winter season.

For fruiting purposes, you should try to get a three- or four-year-old grafted standard or half-standard tree of a known variety. If you wish to plant more than one tree, allow a space of at least 14m (50ft) between them.

Above: *The familiar walnuts are enclosed in a thick husk, which must be removed immediately after harvesting.*

SOIL AND PREFERRED ASPECT

Walnuts grow best in a deep, fertile and well-drained soil. The ideal soil is a deep heavy loam over limestone, with a pH of 7.5–8. Soils that are less alkaline than this will need a dressing of lime at least two months prior to planting. Thoroughly cultivate the ground at the same time, removing all perennial weeds and adding well-rotted compost and a base dressing of fertilizer such as hoof and horn. Choose an open position with shelter from spring frosts to protect young growth and flowers early in the season as temperatures that dip just below freezing may kill the female (nut-generating) flowers.

CULTIVATION

Walnuts are usually grown as standard trees with a strong central leader and can ultimately reach 20m (66ft) or more. The trees can be slow to crop initially, taking five to ten years before they begin cropping.

VARIETIES

'Bijou' This rather tall tree yields large nuts with a good flavour, rough skins and thin shells. The nuts ripen in mid- to late autumn. The nuts tend to lose flavour in storage.

'Cornet du Perogord' The nuts of this variety have a good flavour and are medium to large with a hard shell. The tree is late flowering although the nuts ripen in mid- to late autumn.

'Franquette' The large oval nuts of this tree have a good sweet flavour and moderately thick shells. The tree is late flowering although the nuts ripen in mid- to late autumn. The tree is vigorous and spreading.

'Mayette' The large, round, tapering nuts of this variety have a delicate flavour that is reminiscent of hazelnuts. It is a vigorous, spreading tree and is late-flowering with nuts that ripen in late autumn.

walnuts

Despite this they are relatively trouble free and make a fine specimen tree where space allows them to develop fully.

PRUNING

Once the crown of the tree has formed, very little pruning is needed, save to cut out dead, diseased or badly positioned branches. Walnuts can suffer from extensive rot if they are pruned excessively. Any pruning is best done in late summer.

HARVESTING AND STORAGE

Walnuts should be picked up off the ground as soon as they have fallen, and de-husked as soon as possible. They should be scrubbed to remove all the fibres and spread out in a warm place to dry. Walnuts can be stored with alternate layers of equal parts of sawdust and salt for up to six months in a cool, dry, frost-free place.

PESTS AND DISEASES

Walnuts rarely suffer from serious pests and diseases, although honey fungus can cause serious damage and rapid death.

PRUNING AN ESTABLISHED WALNUT STANDARD

Walnuts naturally form quite large trees that do not respond well to excessive pruning. They do not require a lot of work once they have become established. Early formative pruning can be useful and should be limited to removing the lower lateral branches and encouraging a good-shaped head (crown) above a straight stem. Walnuts require little pruning once the head has been formed. Summer is the best time to remove any congestion caused by excessive side growths, but this should only be carried out if and when it is required.

APPLES

Malus domestica

There are currently numerous projects being undertaken worldwide to assess which varieties are best for allotment culture. With such a wide choice of apples, this is a complex undertaking and the best advice is to grow a variety that is suited to your climate and taste. You may wish to consider those that are immune or quite resistant to apple scab. Others seem to be resistant to fireblight. If you choose a non-disease-resistant apple, you will have a very wide range of choice, but you will need to put more effort into controlling pests and diseases.

OBTAINING PLANTS

Propagation of apple trees is usually carried out by grafting a known variety on to a rootstock. This allows the grower to get the particular type of fruit that they want and the rootstock may confer other advantages such as disease resistance or dwarfing of the tree. It is possible to raise trees from seed but the results can be variable at best and at worst disappointing. This does not mean that a chance seedling would not produce a fine-tasting apple, but most gardeners opt for the known variety and purchase stock for their allotments.

SOIL AND PREFERRED ASPECT

Apples are hardy in any open, sunny site, provided that it is not too exposed to strong winds. Apples tolerate a broad range of soils but thrive in a clay loam. They prefer a neutral to slightly alkaline soil that is rich, free-draining but moisture-retentive. Treat each newly planted tree with a general-purpose fertilizer such as fish, blood and bone and mulch with well-rotted organic matter to help the soil to retain moisture.

Above: *Apples, restricted for growing in rows by hard pruning, will still yield large amounts of fruit.*

ROOTSTOCKS

The rootstock on an apple tree affects the size and rate of growth of the tree.

M27 An extreme dwarfing stock (bush, dwarf pyramid, cordon)
M9 Dwarfing stock (bush, dwarf pyramid, cordon)
M26 Semi-dwarfing stock (bush, dwarf pyramid, cordon)
MM106 Semi-dwarfing stock (bush, spindle bush, cordon, fan, espalier)
M7 Semi-dwarfing stock (bush, spindle bush, cordon, fan, espalier)
M4 Semi-vigorous stock (bush, spindle bush)
MM4 Vigorous stock (standard)
M2 Vigorous stock (standard)
MM111 Vigorous stock (half-standard, standard, large bush, large fans, large espaliers)
M25 Vigorous stock (standard)
MM109 Vigorous stock (standard)
M1 Vigorous stock (standard)

CULTIVATION

Apply mulch at regular intervals as the old mulch gradually breaks down. Keep the trees well watered in dry climates. Every spring, feed each tree with a general-purpose fertilizer. Some varieties only bear well every second year, with light crops every other year. Prevent this by thinning excess fruit in good years to give the tree strength for the following year. A light fall of apples is natural due to poor pollination. Excess fruit drop could be a sign of boron or magnesium deficiency or insufficient moisture.

PRUNING

Flower buds and fruit develop on the tips of the branches or on short two-year-old spurs along the branches. Train apples early in their life to the desired framework.

PRUNING APPLES

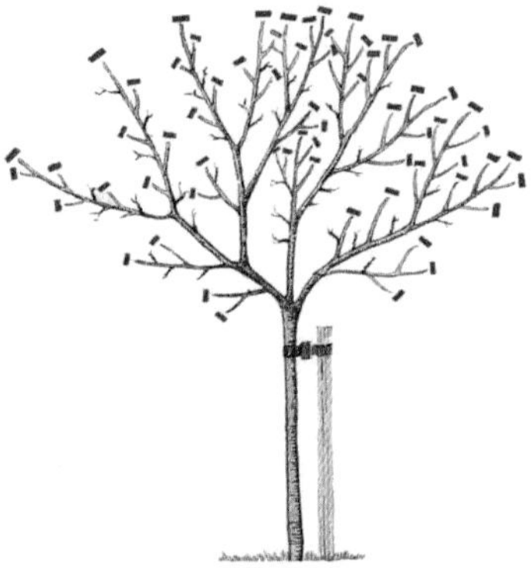

Spur pruning an apple bush tree *After planting, cut back the leader to about 75cm (30in) above the ground. Leave any side shoots that appear just below this cut and remove any others lower down. The following year, reduce all new growth by about half. This will form the basic framework. Subsequent pruning is restricted to reducing the length of new growth by about a third and removing overcrowded growth.*

Planting and pruning an apple cordon *These are planted as feather maidens at 45° to the wirework. All side shoots are cut back to three buds on planting. Subsequent summer pruning (far right) consists of cutting back any new side shoots to three leaves and new growth on existing side shoots to one leaf. Winter pruning (right) consists of thinning out any of the older spurs if they have become congested.*

Left: *Growing apples as cordons is the ideal space-saving method if you only have a small site and wish to grow some fruit.*

As trees mature, pruning mainly involves removing crowded branches. Annual pruning encourages new growth shoots and continual fruiting spur development. Large vegetative growth may indicate too heavy pruning. A large crop of small fruit indicates too little pruning.

POLLINATION USING CRAB APPLES

All apple varieties, whether they are cooking apples or dessert types, need pollination with another apple variety. This involves planting two trees near to each other. A good way to make sure that most varieties will be pollinated is to use a crab apple with a long flowering period. There are many of these and two of the best varieties for this purpose are listed below. Alternatively, you can purchase trees that have two (or more) varieties grafted on to the one rootstock.

***Malus* 'John Downie'** has a long flowering period and thus pollinates most other apples. It is good for wildlife and very attractive, bearing bright red fruit.

***Malus* x *zumi* var. *calocarpa* 'Golden Hornet'** is a spreading tree that has dark green leaves, white flowers and abundant golden-yellow apples. It is an excellent pollinator.

HARVESTING AND STORAGE

Harvest the fruit when fully matured and well coloured, according to the variety that you are growing.

PESTS AND DISEASES

If you are putting in trees for the first time, consider planting disease-resistant cultivars. Many new varieties will go a long way towards solving disease problems before they start.

Common diseases include apple scab, which shows as rough spots on fruits and leaves. Powdery mildew appears as a whitish powder on foliage. Both these diseases can be avoided by planting resistant cultivars or using sulphur spray in spring and summer. Fireblight is another problem, causing withering of branch tips, then entire branches, and sometimes, whole trees. Plant resistant cultivars and prune out infected wood. Codling moths create large tunnels to the core of the apples. Wrap tree trunks in corrugated cardboard to trap larvae that have left the fruits and are looking for a place to pupate. You can also use sticky pheromone traps to attract male codling moths.

To avoid some of these diseases, follow commonsense techniques. Prune trees for good air circulation, which lessens fungal problems, and clean up fallen apples.

VARIETIES

'Braeburn' Large, green fruit with a red blush. Ripens very late but keeps well. Partly self-fertile although it will not pollinate with 'Fuji'. Developed in New Zealand from 'Granny Smith'.

'Cox Orange Pippin' An award-winning apple for taste that keeps up to three months. The fruit is multi-purpose. The tree is less ornamental than some apple trees. It prefers cold winters and requires pruning.

'Fuji' Round to flat apple with a very sweet yellow-orange flesh. Skin colour is red if given enough sunlight and cool temperatures. One of the best sweet eating apples. Stores well.

'Gala' Small- to medium-sized, conic-shaped red apple with excellent flavour and keeping qualities. Possibly the best variety for the early season although it will not cross-pollinate 'Golden Delicious'.

'Golden Delicious' Conic-shaped apple with a long stem, yellow to green skin, yellow flesh, and russet dots. Sweet, juicy, fine-textured. Stores well but susceptible to bitter pit and bruising. Erratic in self-fertility.

'Granny Smith' Round, green to yellow-skinned apple that is quite firm, has crisp flesh and keeps very well. If harvested early, it is green and tart, while later harvested fruit is yellow-coloured and sweet.

'Jonagold' The skin is yellow with red stripes; the flesh is sweet and mild and usually used fresh or baked. 'Jonagold' ripens in mid-autumn and keeps about three months. The tree is vigorous and productive but susceptible to mildew and scab. Its pollen is sterile, so it needs a pollinator although it will not return the favour.

apples

PEARS

Pyrus communis

Pears are among the easiest of the tree fruits to produce because their fertility requirements are not high. They are adapted to a wide range of climates and soils and pest problems are less than for other tree fruits. There are many varieties of pear. Asian and European pears can pollinate each other, but Asian pears often finish blooming by the time Europeans get started. For cross-pollination between pear species, avoid teaming early bloomers among the Asians, such as 'Seuri' and 'Yali', with late bloomers among the Europeans, such as 'Comice' and 'Ubileen'.

OBTAINING PLANTS

Pears can be grown from seed, but you cannot guarantee the quality of the resulting fruit. It is better to purchase known stock from a recognized nursery.

SOIL AND PREFERRED ASPECT

Pears are hardy in any open, sunny site, provided that it is not too exposed to strong winds. They can grow in most soils, but a moderately rich, well-draining soil that is neutral or slightly alkaline is usually best. Very rich soils will stimulate rapid leafy growth that can be disease susceptible and there is therefore no need to add lots of organic matter unless the soil is very poor or excessively free draining.

ROOTSTOCKS

As with apples, the rootstock on which a pear tree grows affects the size and rate of growth of the tree.

Quince C Moderately dwarfing stock (bush, cordon, dwarf pyramid, espalier or fan)
Quince A Semi-vigorous stock (bush, cordon, dwarf pyramid, espalier or fan)
Pear Vigorous stock (standard, half-standard)

Right: *Most pears are ready for picking by the autumn, but they must be fully ripened off the tree. Pick when green and hard.*

CULTIVATION

European pears Pears, like most other fruit trees, are grown by grafting the variety on to a rootstock. Seedlings of European pears (often from Bartlett pears) are usually used for rootstocks. Plant standard-sized trees about 5–8m (16–26ft) apart and dwarf trees about 3–4.5m (10–15ft) apart. Some varieties of pear always need cross-pollination, while others are reliably self-fertile.

Asian pears These are slightly less cold hardy than European types and may suffer tissue damage at temperatures below -20°C (-4°F). Most Asian pears also bloom slightly earlier than their European counterparts and may lose some blooms or buds to freezing in areas that are prone to late frosts. Growing Asian pears is similar to growing European types, but not identical. Asian pears tend to set too heavy a fruit crop, which requires hand thinning of young fruits soon after bloom to ensure a good crop. If heavy-bearing Asian pear varieties are not properly thinned, then the fruit size and quality will suffer.

PRUNING PEARS

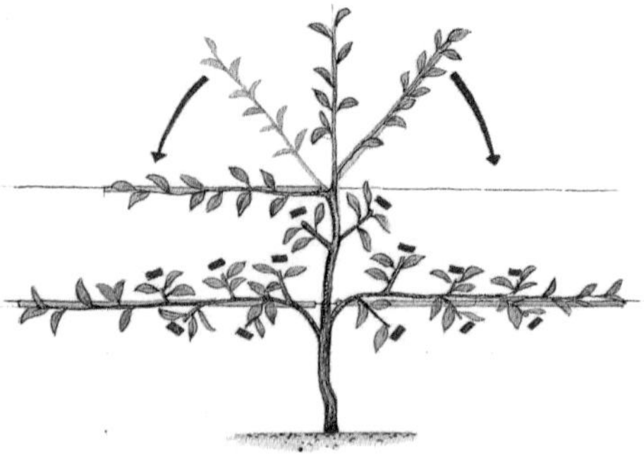

Pruning an espaliered pear *After planting, cut back to two buds above the bottom wire. In the first summer, tie the central growth to a vertical cane and the next two shoots to canes at 45°. Cut back all other shoots to two leaves. In autumn, lower the two side shoots to the horizontal and tie the cane to the bottom wire. In winter, cut back the leader to two buds above the second wire and repeat the above until the espalier covers all the wires. When established, cut back all new shoots to three leaves each summer.*

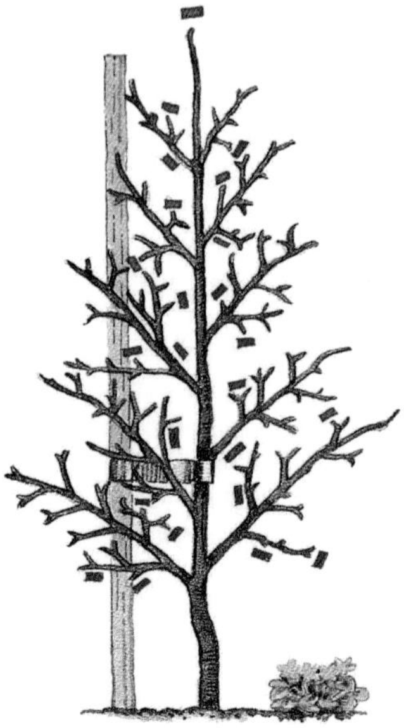

Pruning a dwarf pyramid pear *After planting a pear that you want to grow as a dwarf pyramid, cut back the leader by about a third. Cut back the side shoots to about 15cm (6in). In the first summer, cut back the new growth on the main side shoots to about five leaves and on the secondary shoots to three leaves. Thereafter, cut back new growth on the main stems to five leaves and reduce other new growth to one leaf. During the winter, thin out any congested spurs.*

PRUNING

Pruning pears is generally similar to that of apple trees and involves cutting off unnecessary branches so that light can reach all parts of the tree. Pear trees are also best kept quite low to make it easier to pick the fruit.

HARVESTING AND STORAGE

Bartlett pears ripen in summer, but most other varieties ripen later, usually in early autumn. European pears ripen to perfection only when they are removed from the tree and so are picked while they are still green and hard. The fruit will ripen in a cool place where the temperature does not exceed 24°C (75°F). Asian pears will ripen on the tree and do not have to be picked and then cured like European ones. Pick them once they colour up, when they should be sweet.

PESTS AND DISEASES

Pears have most of the same pest and disease problems as apples, but usually to a lesser degree. One problem that can cause serious damage is fireblight. This is greatly favoured by young, succulent tissues and it is better to try and limit the rate of growth to avoid this. Never try to compensate for rapid growth rates by pruning, as this will only stimulate the production of more susceptible soft tissue growth. Using less compost than for apples, never using manure, not applying large amounts of fertilizer and avoiding growing clovers and other legumes around the tree will ultimately yield better results.

Choosing fireblight-resistant pear cultivars is also a good start, but cultural controls are the best way to limit the spread of this disease. As a group, it is probably accurate to say that Asian pears are slightly more resistant to fireblight than European types. Once fireblight infection has occurred, there is no spray or other treatment (beyond quickly cutting out newly infected limbs) that will minimize damage. If cutting during the growing season, all blighted twigs, branches and cankers should be removed at least 10cm (4in) below the last point of visible infection, and burned. After each cut, the secateurs (hand pruners) should be sterilized. During winter, pruning out of fireblight-infected wood can proceed without sterilization.

The codling moth is probably the most important direct pest of the fruit. Capsid bugs and other 'true' bugs will also feed on pears. Early feeding damage may result in a puckering or dimpling. Mid- and late-season feeding often leads to the development of 'stone cells' beneath the feeding site. The best way to deal with insect pests is to encourage natural predators such as lacewings.

Above: *Pear trees can be trained into a variety of decorative shapes such as this elegant fan on wires.*

VARIETIES

EUROPEAN PEARS

'Bartlett' Ripens mid-season but stores poorly. Blooms early and so needs an early companion variety for pollination. Fruit tolerates intense sun better than average.
'Beth' An excellent, English-bred, self-fertile dessert pear that fruits in mid-autumn. A high-yielding and regular cropper, with white flesh that has a melting texture and excellent flavour. Will commence fruiting from early in its life.
'Comice' Juicy, yellow fruit with good flesh that ripens in mid-autumn, but will keep till mid-winter. Resists fireblight. Best in mild winters. Blooms very late, so not a reliable pollinator for early-blooming varieties.
'Conference' The large, yellow fruit is juicy and sweet, ripening in mid-autumn and keeping till mid-winter. Blooms early and will cross-pollinate with most Asian pears.
'Ubileen' An early ripener (but not bloomer), usually picked in mid-summer and ripening in late summer. The large fruit is yellow with a red blush and a buttery texture. This variety is quite disease resistant.

ASIAN PEARS

'Chojura' A late-blooming variety that has russeted fruit, with slightly astringent skin, which ripens in early autumn and keeps well.
'Seuri' This productive, fireblight-resistant and cold-hardy variety has very large orange fruit that ripens in mid-autumn and does not keep well. This variety blooms very early and is best planted with another early bloomer such as 'Yali'. It will not reliably pollinate any European pear.
'Shinsui' This variety forms a vigorous, upright tree with russeted fruit that is small, juicy and sweet.
'Yali' A hardy variety with deep red autumn foliage. The fruit is classically pear-shaped, yellow and ripens in mid-autumn. This early-blooming variety is a reliable pollinator only for 'Seuri' and other early-blooming varieties (not Europeans) and needs a fairly long cold season.

pears

APRICOTS

Prunus armeniaca

Apricots originally come from warm climates so will need a sunny sheltered spot in cooler regions. In temperate climates, they are best grown as fans against a sunny wall or in a greenhouse, although they can be grown as dwarf pyramid trees in warmer areas.

Left: *Apricots make fine specimens when trained as fans. Canes and wires help to maintain the shape. Grow on a sunny wall in a sheltered location to enable the fruit to ripen and for heathy growth.*

OBTAINING PLANTS

Apricots are propagated by budding them on to rootstocks. Most apricot plants are obtained as bought plants from specialist nurseries. Trees are usually planted during the dormant winter period. Only plant freestanding bush trees in warmer areas where the early flowers will not be damaged by early spring frosts.

SOIL AND PREFERRED ASPECT

Apricots require a moisture-retentive, friable and well-drained soil, rarely prospering in a stiff clay or heavy loam, and a sunny, sheltered site. A pH of 6–6.5 is desirable.

CULTIVATION

Water regularly in the first season and subsequently in dry spells as mature trees may wilt badly. Saturate greenhouse soils in late winter and mulch with well-rotted organic material. Protect the blossom of outdoor specimens from frost by draping horticultural fleece over the trees at night and removing it by day to allow pollinating insects to work. It may be necessary to assist pollination in cooler areas and under glass by hand.

If the fruit set is heavy, then the crop may need thinning. This is done first at 'pea-size' to one fruitlet per cluster, then again after stoning, and when the natural drop is over. Test for stoning by pressing a pin into a few fruitlets. The final spacing of fruit should be about 8–15cm (3¼–6in) apart.

Plants up to fruiting age should be fed in early spring with a general-purpose fertilizer such as fish, blood and bone to encourage growth. Once they reach fruiting age, mulch annually with well-rotted farmyard manure.

PRUNING

Fruit forms on both young wood and old spurs and so it is best to maintain a proportion of each. Shorten the leaders annually by one-third and tie in one healthy shoot per 25cm (10in) of main branch, removing ill-placed and upright growing shoots. Pinch back the rest to four leaves from early summer onwards. Prune fan-trained specimens every year.

ROOTSTOCK

The rootstock will affect the size and rate of growth of the tree.

St Julien A Semi-vigorous stock (bush, fan)
Brompton A Vigorous stock (bush)

HARVESTING AND STORAGE

Leave to ripen on the tree to develop their flavour. The fruit is ripe when it comes away easily by lifting it with a twisting motion.

PESTS AND DISEASES

The main diseases are silver leaf, bacterial canker and brown rot diseases. Aphids, wasps and flies are the main pests.

PRUNING AN ESTABLISHED APRICOT FAN

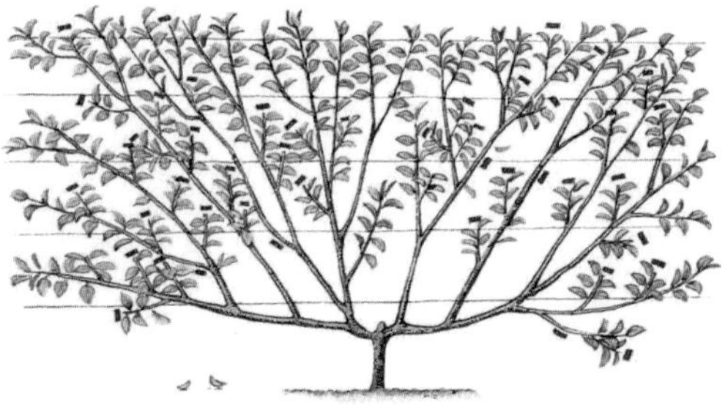

Once the fan has been established, the object of subsequent pruning is to maintain the shape. Cut out any shoots that are pointing in the wrong direction, especially those that point towards or away from the wall. Thin new shoots, leaving one every 15cm (6in). Prune the remaining shoots to five leaves in the spring and then again, after fruiting, back to three leaves.

VARIETIES

'Alfred' Produces fruit of a good flavour that is orange with a pink flush. Fruit ripens in mid- to late summer. A vigorous tree that flowers early and tends to crop biennially.

'Breda' This variety has fruit that is medium to large and orange with a dark red flush. It ripens against a wall in late summer or early autumn in the open. Heavy cropping, but tends to be short-lived.

'Moorpark' An extremely popular variety that has large fruit of a rich, sweet flavour. It is a regular cropper that ripens in late summer. A moderately vigorous plant that is prone to dieback.

apricots

PLUMS

Prunus domestica and *P. salicina*

Plums are divided into two categories: the European plum, *Prunus domestica*, and the Japanese plum, *P. salicina*. European plums are usually self-fertile, but cross-pollination will ensure a better crop. Japanese plums are mostly self-infertile. There are many suitable cultivars but the most popular are the ones that provide fruit until late in the growing season.

OBTAINING PLANTS

Plums are almost always obtained as bought plants from specialist nurseries. There is no truly satisfactory dwarfing rootstock for plums, although trees are sometimes grown on rootstocks described as 'semi-dwarf'. Even these would be too large for a small plot, as a bush-type tree requires a spacing of 4–5m (13–16ft).

SOIL AND PREFERRED ASPECT

Plums need a well-drained soil, with plenty of organic material to hold moisture in the growing season, and a pH of 6.0– 6.5. An acid soil can be limed, but do not plant in an alkaline soil. Trees in thin soils over chalk often suffer from lime-induced iron deficiency. Grow fan-trained plums against a sunny wall.

Above: *While this cluster of plums growing against a sunny wall looks very appetizing, it could have been thinned earlier to ensure larger fruit.*

CULTIVATION

Plant plums between late autumn and early spring. Stake and mulch with well-rotted manure. An established plum needs plenty of nitrogen but, until good crops are being carried, it is usually sufficient to mulch with rotted manure or compost in spring. When crops are being borne, supplement the yearly mulch with a dressing of pelleted chicken manure.

PRUNING

Plums are not very amenable to training, and are seldom satisfactory as cordons or espaliers. They may, however, be grown as fans for wall-training or with the support of posts and horizontal wires. Root-pruning will probably be necessary every five years to restrain growth and maintain fruiting.

Plums may also be grown as semi-dwarf pyramids on a St Julien A rootstock. Such a tree requires a spacing of 3.5m (12ft).

HARVESTING AND STORAGE

Leave on the tree until ripe, then handle carefully. Pick when a bloom appears on the skin for cooking or preserves.

PESTS AND DISEASES

The main problems are aphids, red spider mite, plum sawfly, wasps and birds, as well as rust, silver leaf and bacterial canker.

ROOTSTOCK

The rootstock chosen for a plum tree affects the size and rate of growth.

Pixy Dwarfing stock (bush, pyramid)
Damas C Moderately vigorous stock
St Julien A Semi-vigorous stock (bush, fan, pyramid)
Brompton A Vigorous stock (half-standard, standard)
Myrobalan B Vigorous stock (half-standard, standard)

PRUNING AN ESTABLISHED PLUM FAN

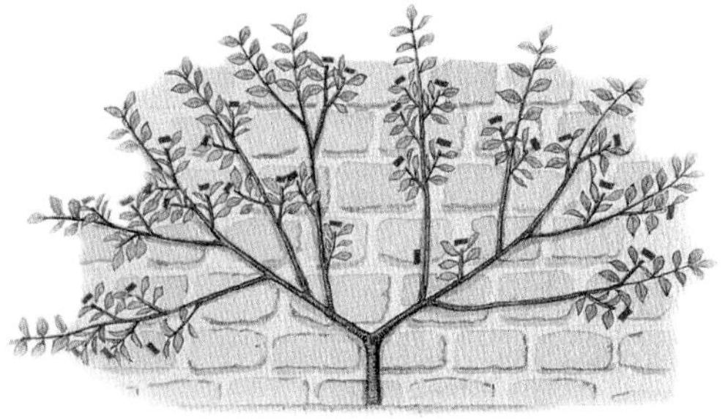

Pruning a plum fan in spring and summer
The main aim when pruning a plum fan is to maintain the fan shape. In spring (above left), cut out any new side shoots that are pointing to or away from the wall. If necessary, reduce the number of new shoots to about one every 15cm (6in). In summer (below left), cut back all new shoots to about six leaves, leaving any that are needed to fill in gaps in the framework. In autumn, after cropping, further cut back the shoots to three leaves.

VARIETIES

'Czar' A reliable bearer of juicy, blue-black fruit with yellow-green flesh in late summer. A fairly compact tree, hardy and usually frost-resistant. Succeeds in shade and fully self-fertile.
'Merryweather' A self-fertile damson, with large, blue-black fruit. Fruits well into the autumn.
'Victoria' Pale red, oval fruits with a greeny-yellow flesh. It can be a heavy cropper on a reasonably frost-free site and is fully self-fertile, bearing fruit in late summer to early autumn.

red plums

yellow plums

PEACHES AND NECTARINES

Prunus persica and *P. persica nectarina*

Peaches and nectarines are identical in all their cultivation requirements, although peaches are slightly hardier and more reliable in cooler areas. They both originate in warm climates and so need a sunny, sheltered spot. For this reason, they are best grown as fans against a sunny wall or in a greenhouse.

Both peaches and nectarines are self-fertile, so only one plant need be grown if space is limited. They do not fruit until their fourth year of growing but will live for about 30 years once established.

OBTAINING PLANTS

Both peaches and nectarines are grown from stock bought from specialist nurseries. They are normally planted during their dormant phase in winter. They are not particularly vigorous, and dwarfing rootstocks are not essential. If you intend growing peaches or nectarines as a fan, use a plant that is grafted on to St Julien A or Brompton A rootstock. If a very small bush is required for container growing, use a plant on Pixy rootstock.

SOIL AND PREFERRED ASPECT

Peaches and nectarines require very fertile, deep, well-drained loam, with a pH of 6.5–7.0. Full sun is essential if the bushes are to prosper. Only plant freestanding bush trees in warmer areas where early flowers will not be damaged by early spring frosts. If these are a problem, grow as a fan against a sunny wall for protection.

Above: *Peaches, grown as fans, are both a decorative and productive way to cover a large sunny wall.*

ROOTSTOCKS

The rootstock will affect the size and rate of growth of the tree.

Pixy Dwarfing stock (small bush)
St Julien A Semi-vigorous stock (bush, fan)
Brompton A Vigorous stock (bush)

CULTIVATION

Plants that have not reached fruiting age should be fed in early spring with a general-purpose fertilizer such as fish, blood and bone to encourage growth. Once they reach fruiting age, mulch annually with well-rotted farmyard manure. Protect the flowers from frost in the early part of the year with a horticultural fleece drape, ensuring that this is removed during the day to allow access for pollinating insects (smaller plants can be hand pollinated using a small sable brush). Never allow plants to become drought stressed once fruit has set, particularly when plants are growing against a sunny wall.

PRUNING

Like other stone fruit, never prune in the winter due to the risk of infection from silver leaf and bacterial canker. Prune freestanding trees in early spring by removing dead or diseased wood, crossing branches that can cause damage by rubbing and overcrowded branches. Prune fan-trained bushes every year. They are pruned by a renewal method in a similar way to that used for fan-trained cherries.

HARVESTING AND STORAGE

Allow to ripen fully before harvesting. The fruit is ripe when it comes away from the tree easily. Store for a few days once picked. Preserve for later use as freezing destroys much of the fruit's texture.

PESTS AND DISEASES

Both peaches and nectarines are prone to the same ailments. Common diseases include peach leaf curl, silver leaf, bacterial canker and mildew. Pests are only an occasional problem, the most serious ones being aphids and red spider mites. Scale insects can be a problem in the greenhouse.

PRUNING AN ESTABLISHED PEACH BUSH TREE

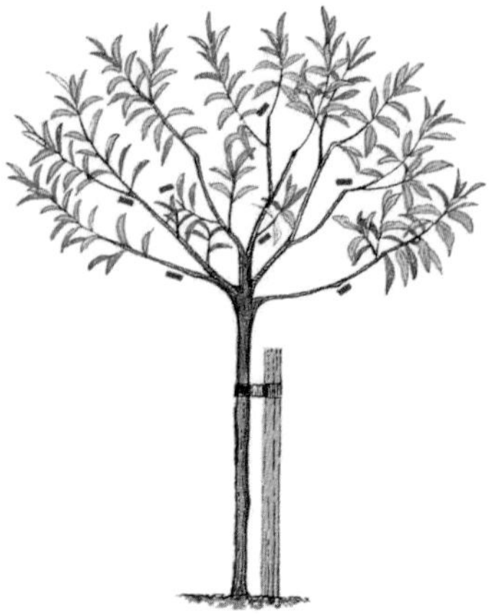

Not a great deal of pruning is required for a peach bush tree. In spring, cut back some of the older barren wood as far as a replacement new shoot. Also remove any awkwardly placed branches and keep the bush open and airy. Avoid making large cuts, as this is likely to allow canker to infect the tree.

VARIETIES

Peaches

'Amsden June' Produces fruit with a good flavour. Ripens in mid-summer. Grow under glass or in the open.
'Peregrine' Large, round, crimson fruit with an excellent flavour. Crops well, ripening in late summer. Is suitable for growing in the open in warmer areas.

Nectarines

'Early Rivers' Large yellow fruits with a rich flavour. Ripens in mid-summer.
'Lord Napier' Large yellow-orange fruits with a rich flavour. Ripens in late summer.

CHERRIES

Prunus species

There are two main groups of cherry that are cultivated for their fruit: the sweet or dessert cherry (*Prunus avium*) and the acid or sour cherry (*Prunus cerasus*). The sweet is the type eaten as a raw dessert fruit, whereas the acid is usually cooked.

OBTAINING PLANTS

Named varieties are propagated on to rootstocks by budding in mid- or late summer or by grafting in early spring. There is currently no dwarfing rootstock available and a mature sweet cherry tree may grow up to 10m (33ft) in height. Bush Morello (acid) trees, on the other hand, rarely reach a height of 5m (16ft). Many varieties can be grown as fan-trained specimens.

SOIL AND PREFERRED ASPECT

Grow in a deep, very fertile, well-drained loam with a pH of 6.0–7.0. Sweet cherries need full sun, but acid cherries prefer light shade and can be trained as fans against a wall receiving little sun.

CULTIVATION

Plant at any time from mid-autumn to early spring. Mulch trees annually with manure or compost and feed fan-trained specimens regularly with a liquid feed.

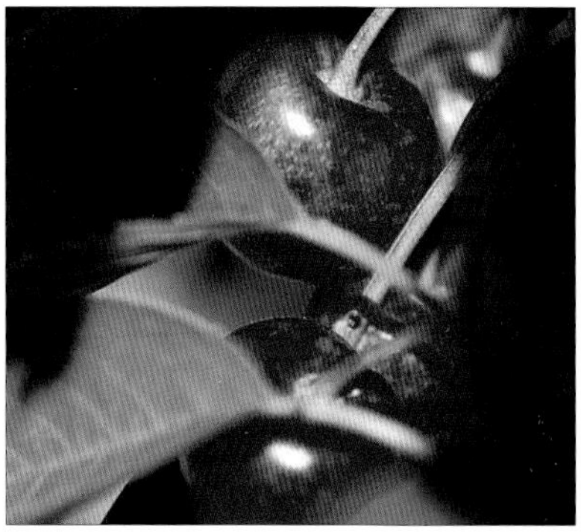

Above: *Few fruits can rival fresh juicy cherries that have been ripened to perfection on the bush.*

PRUNING

Standard and bush trees need little pruning. Maintain an open, balanced habit and remove dead, crossing and rubbing branches. Sour cherries fruit on shoots formed the previous season. For fan training, after the basic fan of branches has been built up, annually replaced side growths are tied in parallel to the permanent branches. The replacement shoots are selected during late spring through to late summer.

HARVESTING AND STORAGE

Leave to ripen on the tree for as long as possible. Sweet cherries are best eaten at once but acid cherries can be stored for a few days. Freeze or preserve to store for longer.

SWEET CHERRY POLLINATION GROUPS

Cherries fruit best if grown near to another variety from the same group that flowers at the same time. This is not necessary for self-pollinating varieties such as 'Morello' or 'Stella'. Flowering period: (e) early; (m) mid-season; (l) late.

Group 1 'Early Rivers' (e), 'Bedford Prolific' (e), 'Knight's Early Black' (e), 'Roundel Heart' (m)
Group 2 'Bigarreau de Schrecken' (e), 'Waterloo' (e), 'Merton Favourite' (e), 'Frogmore Early' (m), 'Merton Bigarreau' (m), 'Merton Bounty' (m)
Group 3 'Bigarreau Napoleon' (m), 'Emperor Francis' (m)
Group 4 'Merton Premier' (m), 'Amber Heart' (m)
Group 5 'Merton Heart' (e), 'Governor Wood' (m)
Group 6 'Bradbourne Black' (l), 'Geante de Hedelfingen' (l)
Universal Donors 'Noir de Guben' (e); 'Merton Glory' (m), 'Bigarreau Gaucher' (l)

PESTS AND DISEASES

Bacterial canker and silver leaf, both of which are spread by pruning. The main pests are birds, blackfly (aphids) and winter moths.

PRUNING ESTABLISHED CHERRY TREES

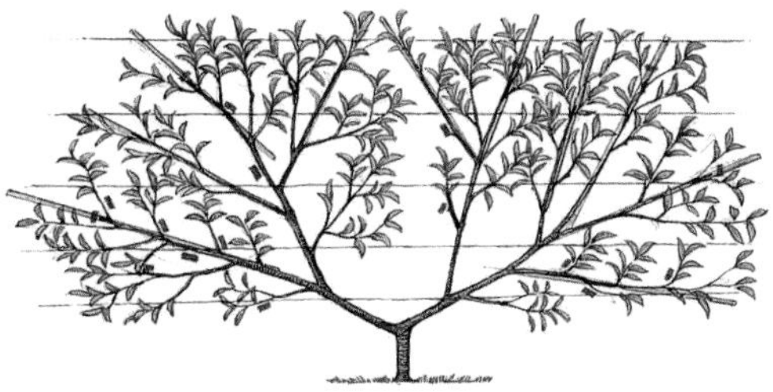

Sour cherry fan *Once established, there are two purposes to pruning a cherry fan: to keep the fan shape and to ensure that there is a constant supply of new wood. To keep the shape completely, remove any shoots that are pointing in the wrong direction. For renewal, cut back in summer all shoots that have fruited, preferably as far back as the next new shoot. Tie these new shoots to the cane and wire framework.*

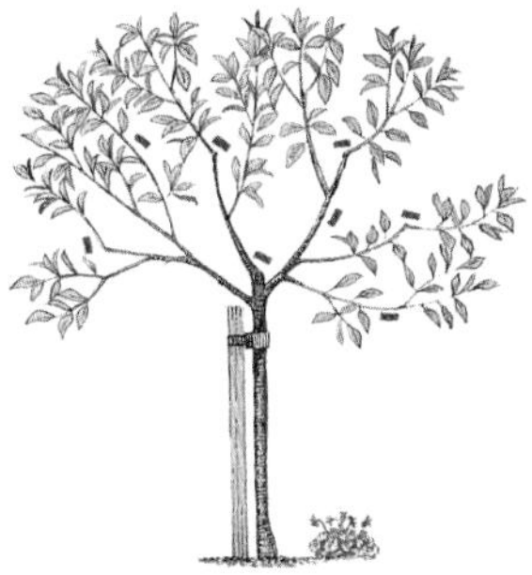

Sour cherry bush or tree *Once established, bush and full-sized sour cherry trees need little pruning other than to remove a third of the old fruiting wood, cutting back to a new growth. You should also remove any branches that are crossing.*

VARIETIES

Dessert

'Bradbourne Black' A large, rich, dark crimson cherry that ripens in mid-summer and is a heavy cropper.
'Kentish Red' A bush of medium vigour that ripens in mid- to late summer. Good on a non-sunny wall. Fruits have a good resistance to bacterial canker.
'Stella' A vigorous variety with large, dark red fruits. A heavy-yielding variety that is also self-compatible.

Acid

'Morello' Juicy fruit with a bitter-sweet flavour when ripe. Crops regularly and is moderately vigorous, ripening in summer to early autumn.

cherries

BLACKCURRANTS

Ribes nigrum

Blackcurrants need a lot of space but are worth growing, as they are extremely high in vitamin C. Aside from this they are one of the true pleasures of summer and more than compensate for their space demands. They also have the advantage of being self-fertile, which means that you only need to grow one bush in order to get a good crop.

Above: *Blackcurrants should be picked as whole trusses complete with the stalks to prevent damage.*

VARIETIES

'Ben Connan' This early-season variety has large fruit and is mildew resistant.
'Ben Lomond' A vigorous, upright grower with large fruit that is freely borne in mid- to late season.
'Ben Sarek' A small compact bush that is highly productive in the mid-season and may suit container culture or the smaller allotment plot.
'Ben Tirran' This late-season variety bears large berries and is mildew resistant.

blackcurrants

OBTAINING PLANTS

Blackcurrants can be propagated quite easily from hardwood cuttings during the dormant season. Choose healthy, blemish-free branches from the previous season's growth that are about 15–20cm (6–8in) long and about the thickness of a pencil. These will make good plants in about three years. More usually, however, plants are bought in.

SOIL AND PREFERRED ASPECT

Blackcurrants are heavy feeders that need a deep, fertile and well-drained soil. It is well worth while taking the time to prepare the soil properly prior to planting. The ideal soil pH is 6.5 and the site should be sheltered and sunny. Blackcurrants will tolerate light shade but the amount of fruit produced will be less.

CULTIVATION

Bare-rooted stock is planted in late autumn or early winter, whereas container-grown stock can be planted out at any time of the year. Plants should be spaced 1.8m (6ft) apart with 2m (6½ft) between rows.

Blackcurrants grow as stooled bushes, which means that they send up new shoots from below ground level. When planting, set the plant 5cm (2in) lower in the ground than it was when grown in the nursery or pot, as this will encourage the formation of new shoots. Ensure that you cut back all the shoots to ground level after planting.

Blackcurrants have a high nitrogen requirement and need feeding with about 100g (4oz) fish, blood and bone or a similar compound fertilizer in spring. They benefit from a mulch of well-rotted manure or garden compost and, if growth seems poor, give a further feed in early summer.

PRUNING

Blackcurrants are always grown as freestanding bushes, so no support or training is needed. They produce fruit on wood made the previous year, which means that in the first year, little or no pruning will be needed, save removing dead, diseased or damaged branches. The second and subsequent years' pruning involves cutting the fruited wood back to ground level to encourage further strong growth. This is done in late summer after fruiting and, as the bushes get older, you may find that fewer shoots are produced from below ground level. If this happens, prune out all the old wood as low as possible just above a young shoot.

It is best to work on a three-year cycle, in the third year cutting out the first year's wood, in the fourth year cutting out the second year's growth, etc. This keeps the bush with a set of branches that will fruit and a set that will fruit the following year.

PRUNING A BLACKCURRANT BUSH

After planting, cut blackcurrant bushes back to a single bud above the ground. The following winter, remove any weak or misplaced growth. Subsequent pruning should take place after fruiting and consists of cutting out up to a third of two-year-old or older wood in order to stimulate new growth. Also remove any weak or misplaced stems.

HARVESTING AND STORAGE

Pick the fruits as clumps when they are ripe. Some gardeners prefer to cut out the whole branch for convenience because this also prunes the bush at the same time. Blackcurrants are practically impossible to store fresh and are best eaten straightaway. They can be frozen or preserved as jelly.

PESTS AND DISEASES

Commonly encountered diseases include mildew, botrytis, leaf spot and reversion disease. The more commonly encountered pests are aphids, sawfly, big bud mite and birds. Provide netting in order to protect against marauding birds.

RED AND WHITE CURRANTS

Ribes rubrum

Red and white currants are relatively easy to grow, even tolerating a little light shade. They can be grown as a bush or trained on walls. Currants fruit on wood that is one year old or off spurs on very old wood. The limited range of varieties belies their versatility as a culinary fruit.

OBTAINING PLANTS

Currants are usually bought in or raised from hardwood cuttings taken during the dormant period.

SOIL AND PREFERRED ASPECT

Grow in a deep, fertile and well-drained soil that has had well-rotted garden compost or manure worked in. The pH of the soil should be kept at about 6.5 to maintain healthy growth. The site should be sheltered and sunny to ensure the best cropping. Currants flower in early spring, so may need some form of protection against frost.

CULTIVATION

Plant bare-rooted stock in autumn or early winter and plants raised in containers at any time. Allow 1.8m (6ft) between plants and 2m (6½ft) between rows. When planting, set the plant at the same level as it was in the nursery or pot. Single cordons should be planted so that the arms are 30cm (12in) apart, double cordons 60cm (24in) apart and triple cordons 90cm (36in) apart.

All varieties of currant are self-fertile, making them ideal for even the smallest of sites. They require a lot of potassium to flourish and will need feeding each spring. A browning on the leaf margins indicates a potassium deficiency, best countered with a liquid foliar feed of seaweed extract.

VARIETIES

RED CURRANT

'Red Lake'
Long trusses of large red berries in mid-summer. An excellent cropping variety.

red currants

WHITE CURRANT

'White Versailles'
A large currant in mid-summer. Excellent variety for making jams.

white currants

Above: *Red currants should only be picked when the fruit is fully ripe and has turned completely red.*

Above: *Red and white currants, grown here as cordons, are tied to lateral wires that are attached to a boundary fence.*

PRUNING

Freestanding bushes need training to produce a strong cup-shaped bush. Prune the bush in the summer, immediately after harvesting. Reduce the side shoots to five leaves and when the main stems have reached the desired height, treat these in the same way.

Train cordon-grown currants upwards rather than at an angle by pruning the main arms in winter. Cut back the leading shoot, leaving two-thirds of the last season's growth. The following summer, prune after harvesting by cutting any side shoots back to 7cm (2¾in) and any secondary shoots back to 2.5cm (1in).

PRUNING CURRANTS

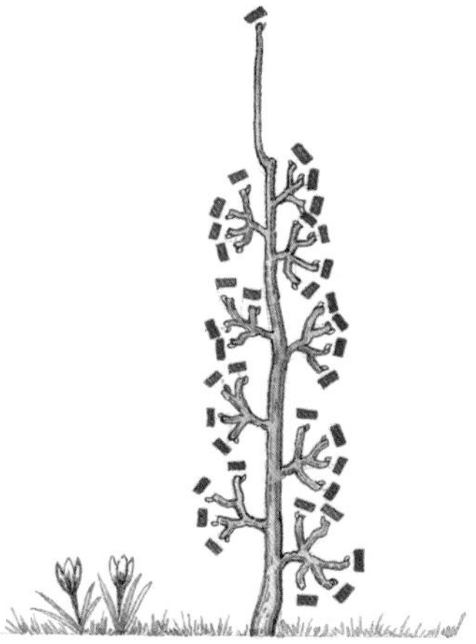

Pruning a red or white currant cordon *On planting, cut back the leader by half of its new growth and the side shoots to one bud. Thereafter, cut back the side shoots every summer to five leaves and, in winter, further reduce these to one bud.*

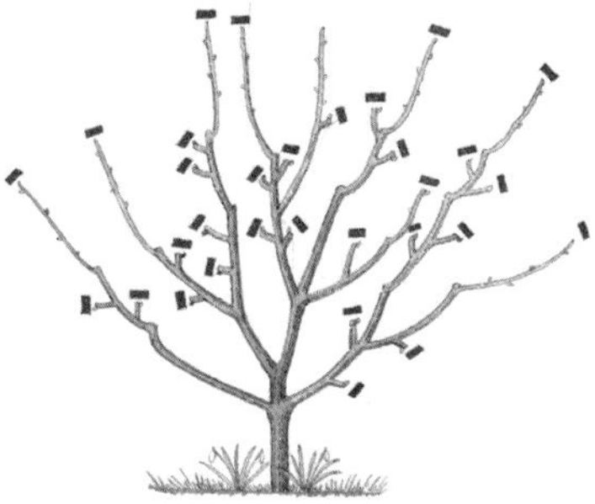

Pruning a red or white currant bush *After planting, cut back each shoot by about half. Subsequent pruning involves ensuring that the plant becomes an open bush. Cut back all new growth on the main shoots and reduce the new growth on all side shoots to one bud.*

HARVESTING AND STORAGE

Pick the sprigs of fruit whole when ripe. Eat straightaway, preserve as jelly or freeze.

PESTS AND DISEASES

Currants are generally trouble free if grown in good soil and well fed. Common diseases include mildew and leaf spot, while pests include aphids, sawfly and birds.

GOOSEBERRIES

Ribes uva-crispum

Gooseberries are one of the earliest soft fruits of the year. The traditional method of growing was as a bush but modern techniques include single, double and triple cordons. Cordons can take up as little as 15cm (6in) of growing space. All varieties are self-fertile, so only one plant can be grown if space is at a premium.

OBTAINING PLANTS

Gooseberry plants should be bought from a reputable supplier.

SOIL AND PREFERRED ASPECT

Gooseberries do best in a soil with a pH of 6.5 in a sunny, sheltered site. Fork over a wide area to break up the soil and remove weeds before digging the planting hole. Add garden compost or rotted manure to the soil at the base of the pit, along with about 50g (1¾oz) of fish, blood and bone or a similar general-purpose fertilizer.

CULTIVATION

Plant bare-rooted stock in autumn or early winter and container-grown plants at any time. Gooseberries are grown on a 'leg' or stem, so cut back all the side shoots before planting. Spread out the roots of bare-rooted bushes in the hole and cover with well-conditioned soil. Firm the soil around the roots. With container-grown bushes, keep the surface of the roots level with the surrounding soil. Wearing latex gloves, apply two handfuls of bonemeal to the soil when filling in and mulch with a well-rotted manure or compost. Plant bushes 1.2–1.8m (4–6ft) apart in rows, depending on the vigour of the variety. Allow a spacing of around 2m (6½ft) between each row. Plant single cordons 30cm (12in) apart, double cordons 60cm (24in) apart and triple cordons 90cm (36in) apart, allowing 1.2m (4ft) between rows.

Keep well watered until established, and cover the soil around them with a 5–7.5cm (2–3in) thick mulch of compost or bark.

Freestanding bushes need no support. Cordons require wires, either attached to the fence or to posts. Gooseberries need high levels of potassium and feeding with a general-purpose fertilizer in spring as well as mulching with well-rotted manure or compost. If growth is poor, feed again in early summer. Browning of the leaves indicates a potash deficiency; apply a liquid foliar feed of seaweed extract. Cover the fruits with fleece to protect against frost.

Above: *Start picking gooseberries before the first berries are fully ripe in order to give the remainder an opportunity to ripen.*

PRUNING

Prune freestanding bushes after harvesting by reducing side shoots to five leaves. Treat the main stems in the same way when they reach their required height and cut out any damaged, dead or overcrowded stems. Prune cordons after harvesting by cutting any side shoots to 7cm (2¾in) and any secondary shoots to 2.5cm (1in).

HARVESTING AND STORAGE

Start picking heavy crops before they are fully ripe to allow remaining berries to ripen. Use the unripe berries in cooking. Eat straightaway, freeze or preserve.

PESTS AND DISEASES

Mildew and leaf spot are common. Pests are usually limited to aphids, sawfly and birds. Protect against birds with netting.

Left: *Gooseberries make excellent cordons. Train them up canes that are supported by lateral wires.*

PRUNING A GOOSEBERRY

The basic aim when pruning gooseberries is to create an open framework. Establish a framework, first of all, by removing the basal shoots and cutting back the main shoots by about half in their first and second years. After this, cut back the new growth on the leaders in winter by about half and reduce the side shoots from these to two buds. Remove any damaged wood and any branches that cross or rub. Remove suckers and basal growth. In summer, prune the side shoots back to five leaves, but leave the main stems uncut.

VARIETIES

'Careless' Large green-skinned fruits ripening to white in summer. A reliable and heavy-yielding variety.
'Keepsake' Excellent flavoured fruits that are green-white in colour, transparent and slightly hairy. Can be picked early for cooking.
'Lancashire Lad' This bush produces large, dark red, oblong, hairy fruits that are extremely juicy. It has some resistance to mildew.
'Leveller' A fertile soil is required to ensure heavy cropping. This variety produces large, oval, yellow-green fruits with a slightly hairy skin and an excellent flavour.

gooseberries

RASPBERRIES

Rubus idaeus

Raspberries are unique because their roots and crowns are perennial, while their stems or canes are biennial. During the first growing season, the shoots of summer-bearing raspberries are strictly vegetative (non-fruiting). The following year, these canes flower, produce fruit, and then die. Autumn-bearing raspberries, on the other hand, produce fruit in the autumn at the tips of the current season's growth.

OBTAINING PLANTS

Raspberry bushes are almost always bought plants, although it is possible to raise them from seed. Existing bushes can be divided in winter and are usually available in late winter as bare-rooted plants in bundles.

SOIL AND PREFERRED ASPECT

Raspberries require an open sunny site, although they tolerate slight shade, and prefer a deep, well-drained but moisture-retentive soil with a pH of around 6.0. They suffer iron deficiency above a pH of 7.0.

CULTIVATION

Raspberries, whether bare-rooted or container-grown, should be planted out in late autumn or early winter. Plant them a little deeper than they were in the pot or nursery and space 45cm (18in) apart with 1.8m (6ft) between rows. Cut the canes to 15cm (6in) above ground and water thoroughly after planting. Winter-planted specimens will commence growth in the spring and produce tall canes. Raspberries need little or no feeding once they have been planted. Mulch, applied in the spring, will usually supply their nutrient needs.

Above: *Wires fixed to a sturdy wooden framework support this flourishing double row of raspberries.*

PRUNING

AUTUMN-BEARING RASPBERRIES

In early spring, prune back all canes to ground level and maintain the plants in a 30–60cm (12–24in) wide 'hedgerow'. No summer pruning is necessary.

SUMMER-BEARING RASPBERRIES

In early or mid-spring, remove all weak, diseased and damaged canes at ground level. Leave the most vigorous canes, those about 1cm (½in) in diameter when measured 90cm (3ft) from the ground. Space the remaining canes about 15cm (6in) apart and cut back the tips to live tissue if any have died back in winter. Maintain plants in a 30–60cm (12–24in) wide 'hedgerow' and remove old fruiting canes at the soil surface after the last harvest of the summer, as this encourages the growth of new shoots the following year.

VARIETIES

EARLY AND MID-SEASON VARIETIES

'Glen Clova' Small- to medium-sized fruits that have a mild flavour. It is a heavy cropper with strong growth.

'Malling Jewel' Sweet-tasting, medium to large, red fruits.

'Malling Promise' Full-flavoured large red berries. A heavy yielding variety that is a vigorous grower.

AUTUMN FRUITING VARIETIES

'Fallgold' Produces yellow sweet-tasting fruits on vigorous canes. Ripens in early autumn.

'Heritage' Mild-flavoured round red berries. A prolific producer that requires a sunny location.

'Zeva' Dark red fruits that are prone to crumbling. A less vigorous variety that ripens in early autumn.

raspberries

HARVESTING AND STORAGE

Raspberries should be picked early in the morning before it gets too hot. They can be eaten fresh, preserved or frozen.

PESTS AND DISEASES

The main diseases that commonly affect raspberries are botrytis (fruit rot), mildew, late leaf rust (*Puccianiastrum americanum*) and *Phytophthora* (root rot) on wet sites. They may be affected by a number of pests including aphids, raspberry beetle, two-spotted spider mite, Japanese beetle, tarnished plant bug, cane borers and clipper beetle. Netting may also be needed as protection against bird damage.

GROWING RASPBERRIES ON POSTS AND WIRES

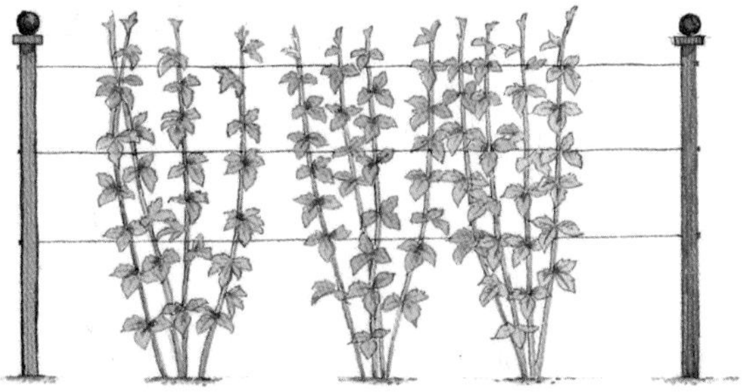

It is essential that raspberries have a strong supporting system of posts and wires. The plants should be set at 45cm (18in) intervals. Each year, new raspberry canes will be thrown up. When fruiting has finished on the old canes, cut these out and tie the new canes to the wires in their place. This sequence should be followed every year. Raspberry plants put out suckers which can quickly become established in the gangways between the rows. These should be dug up as soon as they appear. Pick raspberries regularly when firm and ripe, pulling them off gently.

BLACKBERRIES

Rubus fruticosus

Wild blackberries are gathered in late summer and early autumn in many areas. Growing blackberries offers the promise of high-quality fruit as well as ease of harvesting. The fruit of home-cultivated blackberries is usually much larger and often sweeter. Thornless varieties will make picking much easier.

OBTAINING PLANTS

Blackberries are usually propagated in late winter or early spring by planting root cuttings from healthy plants. Root cuttings should be 10–15cm (4–6in) long and about 1cm (½in) thick. Plant these cuttings 60cm (24in) apart in rows spaced 3m (10ft) apart for a 'hedgerow'. The root cuttings are best placed about 2–5cm (¾–2in) deep. Prepare the soil first by adding plenty of well-rotted compost and a generous base dressing of general-purpose fertilizer such as fish, blood and bone. Add more fertilizer about one month after planting and again in early to mid-summer.

SOIL AND PREFERRED ASPECT

Blackberries are hardy in any open, sunny site, provided that it is not too exposed to strong winds. They grow on a wide range of soil types. A soil pH of 6.0–6.5 is best, but blackberries will grow in soils ranging from a pH 4.5–7.5. A deep, fine, sandy loam is ideal, but blackberries grow well in heavier soils if they are well drained.

Above: *Blackberries often fruit over a long season, starting in late summer and lasting until late autumn.*

CULTIVATION

Canes from erect blackberries will be semi-erect or almost trailing in the first growing season. They should be kept in the row area as they will produce fruit the next year.

PRUNING

Blackberry canes are biennial. Vegetative canes develop the first year, bear fruit the second year, and die after fruiting. New canes produced in the second and later years will be erect and should be cut to a height of 1–1.2m (3–4ft) in mid-summer to encourage lateral branching. Prune hedgerows to a width of about 1–1.2m (3–4ft).

HARVESTING AND STORAGE

Blackberries need to be harvested when fully ripe, as they will not ripen after harvesting. Harvested fruit should not be allowed to sit in the sun and needs to be chilled as soon after harvesting as possible. Most blackberry varieties do not freeze particularly well and are best eaten fresh. Alternatively, they can be made into jelly or stewed before freezing.

PESTS AND DISEASES

While most blackberries are trouble free, spur blight, mildew, botrytis and cane spot are occasional disease problems. Pests are also mercifully few but can include wasps, aphids and raspberry beetle. Birds also love this summer treat and the plants may need protection with netting during their fruiting period.

VARIETIES

'Himalayan Giant' Sharp-flavoured blackberry that is a heavy cropper. Vigorous growth in stems and strong thorns.

'Oregon Thornless' A cut-leaved, thorn-free form of the blackberry. Berries are small, mild and sweet, ripening in early autumn.

'Smoothstem' Large shiny fruits that are rather sharp in taste. Enjoys a sunny location.

blackberries

METHODS OF TRAINING BLACKBERRIES

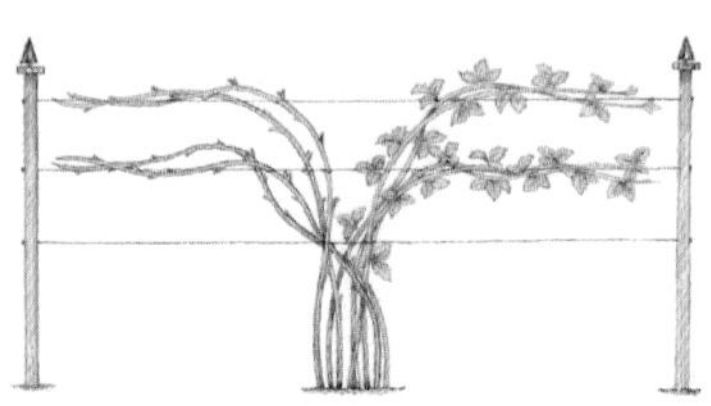

Alternate bay *One way in which you can train blackberries is to tie all the new growth to one side of the wirework. After fruiting, remove the previous year's growth from the other side and then use this for the next year's new growth. Repeat the same process each year.*

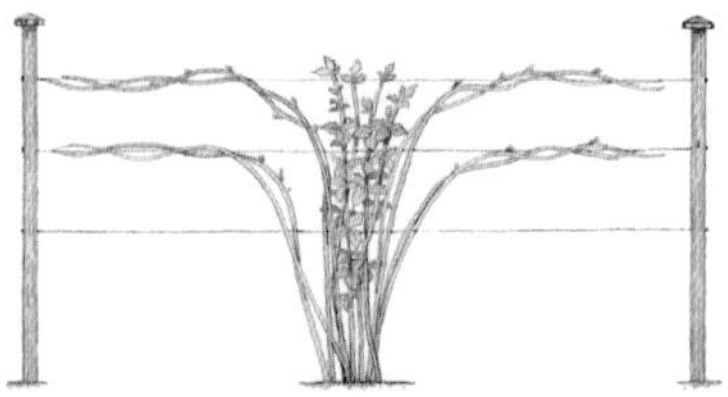

Rope training *A second way to train blackberries is to temporarily tie in all the new growth vertically to the wirework and along the top wire. Tie the current fruiting canes in groups horizontally. Remove these after fruiting and tie the new growth into their place.*

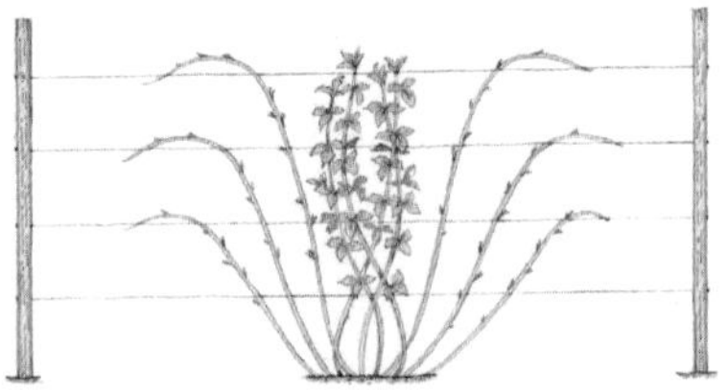

Fan training *Temporarily tie the new canes vertically and along the top wire, while tying in the fruiting canes singly along the wires. Any excess canes should be removed. After fruiting, take these blackberry canes out and tie the new growth in their place.*

BLUEBERRIES

Vaccinium corymbosum and *V. ashei*

Blueberries are divided into two main groups: lowland blueberries (*Vaccinium ashei*), which include the whinberries or bilberries, and the better known blueberries (*V. corymbosum*). Despite some differences between the plants, the berries are essentially the same. Highland blueberries are self-pollinating, but set more fruit if they are grown with other varieties. Bilberries need another variety for successful pollination so at least two bushes of different varieties will have to be grown. The varieties listed in the panel are derived from *V. corymbosum* and will set fruit with their own pollen. For maximum crops at least two varieties should be planted together.

Above: *Pick blueberries when they are ripe – approximately ten days after they turn blue – and use them immediately.*

VARIETIES

'Berkeley' Very large light blue berries with a good flavour are produced on this shrub of moderate vigour.
'Bluecrop' This fast growing variety produces big clusters of large light blue berries. A consistently heavy cropper. It is an upright vigorous spreading bush.
'Earliblue' Similar to Bluecrop but the berries ripen earlier.
'Rancocas' This variety produces small fruits over a long period and maintains a shapely habit.

blueberries

OBTAINING PLANTS

Blueberries can either be propagated from cuttings taken in spring or purchased as plants in containers or as bare-rooted plants. Take 10–15cm (4–6in) softwood cuttings in late spring from the tips of the current season's growth. Alternatively, hardwood cuttings are taken during the dormant season after sufficient chilling has occurred, usually in mid- to late winter.

SOIL AND PREFERRED ASPECT

Blueberries are hardy in any open, sunny site, provided that it is not too exposed to strong winds. They need a very acidic soil, with a pH of 5.0–5.5. The soil should be consistently moist but never waterlogged. It should not be too rich in nutrients prior to planting.

CULTIVATION

Before planting, cut plants back to a height of 15–30cm (6–12in) or remove at least 50 per cent of the top, including all flower buds. Do not allow newly set plants to flower and fruit the first year.

Set the plants at the same depth they grew in the nursery or 1cm (½in) deeper and mulch with a well-rotted manure or compost.

Blueberries are grown as freestanding bushes, so no support or training is needed. They are not heavy feeders, but an annual application of about 100g (4oz) of fish, blood and bone and an annual mulch in late winter will ensure good growth. Blueberries require from 2.5–5cm (1–2in) of water per week. Newly established plants have the most critical water needs and can be damaged by either over- or under-watering. Short periods (one to three weeks) without rain can stress blueberry plants severely. Irrigation during dry periods is required for them to establish properly.

Bilberries require cross-pollination between different varieties for good fruit set and two or more varieties should be planted close by each other. Highland blueberries are self-fertile, but planting with other varieties may increase fruit set and size. Insects, especially wild bees and honeybees, are necessary to pollinate blueberries. For this reason, efforts to attract these insects into your allotment plot will be rewarded by a good fruit set.

PRUNING AN ESTABLISHED BLUEBERRY BUSH

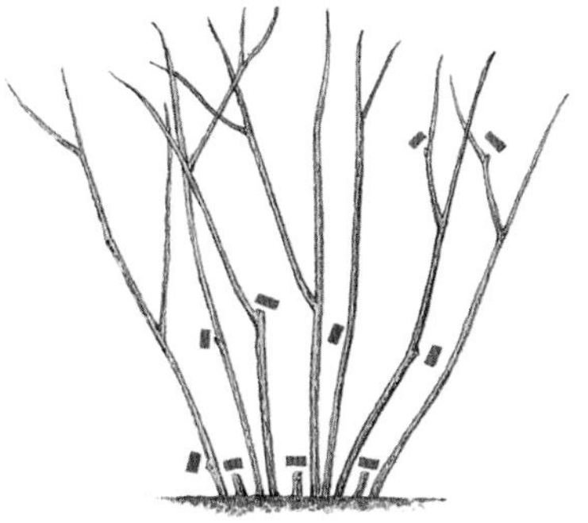

Blueberries fruit on older wood, so no pruning is needed for several years. Thereafter, cut out any weak or misplaced shoots as well as the old wood that has ceased fruiting in order to stimulate new growth.

PRUNING

In the first few years after planting blueberries, remove the tips of the branches in autumn. As the bush gets larger, cut out any old, weak or damaged growth and ensure a free air supply by allowing about 15cm (6in) between each branch.

Prune bilberries immediately after harvesting because this permits shoot regrowth and flower bud formation before plants become dormant.

HARVESTING AND STORAGE

Blueberries should be picked when they are ripe, approximately ten days after they have turned blue. They are best used immediately as they do not store well, but can be stewed and then frozen.

PESTS AND DISEASES

Bilberries are generally more resistant to both pests and diseases than Highland blueberries. Where diseases do occur they are mainly limited to mildew and botrytis, while pests are usually restricted to an occasional outbreak of aphids. Birds are a more common problem and the bushes may need netting to protect against them.

CRANBERRIES

Vaccinium macrocarpon, *V. trilobum* and *V. vitis-idaea*

True cranberries (*V. macrocarpon*) grow in low-lying bogs. Many cranberry varieties exist, most of which are wild selections and not the product of breeding programmes. They are generally only available in the USA and are mostly grown as a commercial crop. The easiest of the three to grow is the highbush cranberry (*V. trilobum*), a deciduous shrub that grows up to 3m (10ft) high. Highbush cranberries require no special soil conditions and tend to be grown from the species and not varieties. Lingonberries (*V. vitis-idaea*) are relatives of cranberries that are grown in many Scandinavian countries and can only be cultivated in cooler locations. There are only a few lingonberry varieties available.

Above: *Cranberries should be harvested fresh from the plant once they redden but are still firm to the touch.*

VARIETIES

CRANBERRIES

'Early Black' This early-season selection has small deep red berries.
'Howes' This is a late-season selection that has small red berries.
'Stevens' This selection is a mid-season cropper with large red berries.

LINGONBERRIES

'Regal' Developed from seed collected in Finland, 'Regal', like 'Sussi', was selected for its superior fruit size.
'Sussi' (patented – Balsgård, Sweden) was the first lingonberry to be selected and named for its exceptionally good crops of larger-than-average fruit.

cranberries

OBTAINING PLANTS

Cranberries and lingonberries are propagated from cuttings and are available from a few specialist growers. The highbush cranberry can be propagated by hardwood and softwood cuttings, layering, crown division and by seed.

SOIL AND PREFERRED ASPECT

Cranberries grown in open soil will need a certain amount of soil modification. They need an acidic soil, ideally with a pH of 4–5, and should be grown in full sun. If your soil is sandy remove topsoil to a depth of 20cm (8in) and add a heavy-duty plastic liner. Pierce the liner and add about one-tenth of the volume of the excavated soil with well-rotted, but acidic, compost. Wearing latex gloves, mix in about 50g (1¾oz) of bonemeal, rock phosphate and dried blood per square metre (yard). Wet the planting mix thoroughly before planting.

If your soil is clay or silty, dig out an area 20cm (8in) deep and add the compost without a plastic liner, adding fertilizer and watering as above.

The highbush cranberry is tolerant of a wide variety of soil types, but it will do best where the soil is consistently moist and well-drained.

CULTIVATION

Cranberries can be planted in mid- to late autumn or in mid- to late spring. Highbush cranberries are best planted in late autumn or early spring. The growing mix needs to be moist to the touch, but does not need to be saturated. Apply a general-purpose fertilizer such as fish, blood and bone in the early summer of each year.

Weed the cranberry bed regularly during the summer. Mulch the plants with pine needles or leaves in late autumn in order to protect against the drying effects of winter winds.

PRUNING

Once the cranberry bed is established, pruning is restricted to the removal of excess runner growth and older uprights as needed. Lingonberries rarely need pruning.

Pruning of a highbush cranberry should also be kept to a minimum and light renewal pruning should be all that is needed.

HARVESTING AND STORAGE

You can harvest berries of all types by hand when they turn red. Pick before a hard frost or protect them with covers.

PESTS AND DISEASES

Cranberries and lingonberries have few insect predators or diseases in domestic settings. Highbush cranberries will occasionally suffer from bacterial leaf spot, powdery mildew, shoot blight, plant bugs or thrips.

CUTTING BACK CRANBERRIES

Cranberries have no specific pruning requirements, and any pruning should be restricted to the removal of excess runners and older uprights only as and when this is needed. Use a pair of sharp shears to cut off any semi-erect or wispy stems in early spring, and top-dress with 50g (1oz) fish, blood and bone per square metre (yard) in order to encourage new growth. Be vigilant in removing weeds from the base of the plants.

GRAPES

Vitis vinifera

In high and low latitudes, where hot summers cannot be guaranteed, grapes are usually grown in a greenhouse. Modern breeding practices have yielded a few varieties that can be grown outdoors in these regions but these are really only suitable for wine-making.

OBTAINING PLANTS

Vines can be propagated from cuttings, commonly referred to as 'vine eyes'. These cuttings should be 30cm (12in) long and inserted to half their length in good soil in late autumn to early winter. Plant out rooted cuttings in autumn or early winter of the following season. Prune the young plant to within 30cm (12in) from its base. Mulch with well-rotted manure or compost.

SOIL AND PREFERRED ASPECT

Despite being hardy, in cooler places vines can only be grown in a sheltered position that remains warm and sunny while the fruit is ripening. They thrive on a poor soil as long as it contains plenty of organic matter. The pH of the soil should be around 6.5–7.0. Soils should be free draining but not prone to drought, especially in the fruiting season.

Above: *Grape vines, grown over an arch or pergola, provide an ideal decorative and shade-giving feature for a small site.*

CULTIVATION

Grow outdoors in favourable areas, preferably given the protection of a warm wall. Mulch annually in spring with well-rotted manure or compost and, if growth seems poor, feed with fish, blood and bone.

VARIETIES

OUTDOOR VARIETIES

'Cascade' The black grapes from this hardy variety have a good flavour and are held in small bunches. They ripen in mid-autumn, and are resistant to mildew.

'Chasselas d'Or' This vine produces white grapes of excellent flavour for dessert or wine. The berries are medium and round in long bunches and ripen in mid-autumn. Only suitable for growing against a wall.

'Siegerrebe' Produces white grapes of a very good flavour that are well suited to wine-making. This heavy cropping variety ripens in late summer and is moderately vigorous. It does not grow well on alkaline soils.

'Trebbiano' A good-flavoured white variety with oval fruits in very large bunches. This vine is vigorous and heavy-cropping, and ripens very late.

white grapes

black grapes

PRUNING ESTABLISHED GRAPES

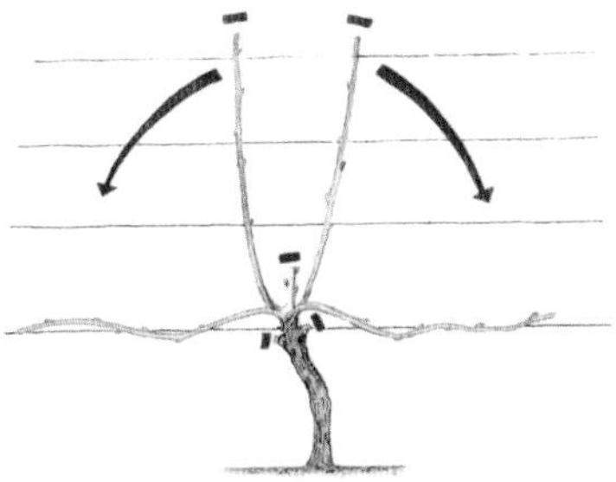

Established double guyot, winter pruning *Each year remove the horizontal branches that carry fruiting stems, leaving three vertical central shoots. Pull two of these down on each side of the central shoot, so they are horizontal, and tie in place on the wire. The third shoot should be cut back to leave three strong buds, which will form the three verticals for the following year. Mulch the plants with a generous layer of well-rotted compost.*

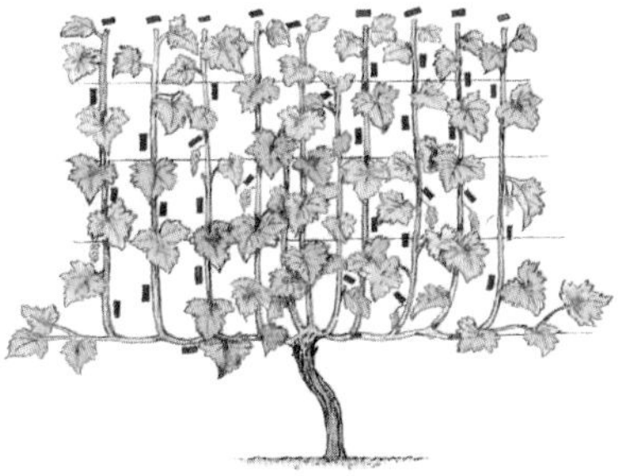

Established double guyot, summer pruning *Train the new shoots from these buds vertically, removing any side shoots that develop on them to one leaf. Allow the vertical fruiting shoots to grow on the horizontal branches, removing any side shoots that appear. Cut back above the top wire to three leaves. After fruiting, remove the horizontal branches and train the remaining three central shoots as described above.*

PRUNING

Plants grown outdoors can be grown as cordons, espaliers, fans or bushes. The bush method is the simplest, although the straggly habit of the bush form makes it a nuisance in the allotment and trailing on the ground may spoil the berries. The cordon consists of a rod trained to a wire framework about 1.2m (4ft) high. The laterals from the rod are cut back each winter to one bud. Espaliers are grown by developing pairs of branches 30cm (12in) apart from the main stem.

HARVESTING AND STORAGE

The fruit is ready for picking when the stems turn brown. Cut the stem on either side of the bunch to leave a small 'T'-shaped handle.

PESTS AND DISEASES

There are a multitude of pests and diseases that can affect grape vines. The main diseases in domestic settings are botrytis and mildew. Pests are few, but include red spider mites, wasps and birds. Use netting to protect against bird damage.

PLANT HEALTH

The main concern for allotment-growers is that their plants will be attacked by pests and diseases. There is an array of techniques to control these undesirables, although the successful gardener must first learn to recognize signs of distress. However, you are unlikely to experience more than a handful of the problems described, all of which are relatively easy to solve. Pests, for example, are eaten by creatures known as beneficials and so the ecology of the allotment, once stabilized, will be enough to keep most problems at bay. There is always a technique to control more persistent problems and so ensure the health of your plants.

Left: *Companion plants such as these French marigolds can provide welcome colour in the allotment vegetable plot.*

Above: *Ladybirds provide a natural form of pest control in allotments because when their eggs hatch, the larvae eat aphids.*

Above: *Netting crops, such as brassicas, can help protect them from attack by flying pests, which cannot permeate the nets.*

Above: *Different types of netting provide a barrier between vegetables, such as carrots, and specific pests, such as carrot fly.*

Above: *Temporary netting is a very good way of protecting vulnerable crops from pests and diseases and preventing potential problems.*

WHY PLANTS GET SICK

Plants are prone to numerous ailments, some of which can pose a serious threat to their survival. Pests and diseases are only one of the potential pitfalls that you will meet during a normal growing season though. A basic knowledge of the other main factors that can affect plant health are all you will need to help your allotment to flourish. While the sight of your plants suffering can be alarming, there are, in general, only a few potential health threats that you are likely to encounter.

FROST

This can cause serious problems and is actually more critical than average minimum temperatures. Most harmful are unexpected frosts that can cause severe damage even to hardy subjects, especially when they may have produced 'soft' new growth.

While warm air rises, cold air will settle and collect in hollows and depressions. Cold air is laden with water vapour and is therefore heavier. Any valley or low-lying area is, therefore, a potential frost pocket. Cold air will accumulate in a depression and then back up the sloping sides as the build-up increases. Any barrier, such as a hedge or a wall, will obstruct the passage of the cold air and a frost pocket will form. Any plants growing in the vicinity will be exposed to the frost and may be damaged by it.

When the soil is frozen, water is no longer available to the plant and shallow-rooted plants are not able to access any water to replace that which they are losing through transpiration. The plant will dehydrate and the foliage will brown and shrivel. Ground frosts may also cause the soil to 'heave' and plants will be lifted out of the ground.

Alternate freezing and thawing is often more damaging to the plant than the initial frost itself, especially for tender or half-hardy subjects. A particularly severe frost can split the bark on woody subjects and may also distort leaves.

The damage caused by frost is directly related to its duration. A temperature of -4°C (25°F) for one hour may cause little or no damage, while the same temperature for four hours may be disastrous.

WATERLOGGING AND DROUGHT

The build-up of water in the soil, particularly where this occurs over a prolonged period of time, can be highly detrimental to the health of your plants. This is of greatest concern with plants that are not adapted to such waterlogged conditions. As a result, the roots of the plants will suffer and probably die from asphyxiation.

Water shortage or drought only tends to occur during the summer months when temperatures and light intensity are at their peak. The most obvious sign of the effects of water shortage on a plant is when it wilts and loses its turgidity. Water shortage also causes plant functions to slow down dramatically and prolonged drought can result in permanent cell damage.

WIND

The effects of wind damage to plants, especially woody trees and shrubs, are sometimes only too obvious. Not only can they knock over and break plants, but wind-rock can cause a plant to move about so that it becomes loose in the soil or it can create a hole around the point at which the plant enters the soil. This fills with stagnant water and the plant can rot. A dry or hot wind can remove moisture from leaves, making them wilt. Cold winds create wind-burn, which shrivels leaves.

It is not all bad news, however, as wind can be tamed to some extent by creating windbreaks. The best defence is a hedge, which filters the wind without creating turbulence, but this may not be a viable option on an allotment plot. Plastic netting that is designed to be used as a windbreak is a more practical solution on many sites. While it is not pretty to look at, it is very functional. Make sure the poles supporting it are anchored securely because the netting will act as a sail and exert enormous pressure on the supports. A double row of netting or hedges set a few yards apart is the very best option if possible, as this will reduce any turbulence to an absolute minimum and give greatest protection.

Left: *Frost and snow can have a negative impact on crops such as these leeks, especially if they alternately freeze and thaw.*

Above: *A maximum/minimum thermometer is ideal for keeping track of the temperature in the greenhouse and outdoors.*

Above: *If a frost pocket is caused by a thick hedge, cut a hole in the base so that air can pass through and continue moving.*

LIGHT IMBALANCES

A plant's growth is always directed towards the available light. Plants growing in shade often become drawn and etiolated. Conversely, strong sunlight damages plants by scorching the foliage. To prevent such problems it is best to select plants that will grow well in the prevailing site conditions.

NUTRIENT IMBALANCES

Plants exhibit varying symptoms that point to a nutrient imbalance depending, in general, upon the severity of the problem. Symptoms of deficiency may include stunted growth, discoloured leaves (including mottling and interveinal coloration), the premature death of leaves and parts of the plant, twisted and distorted growth and poor root growth and development.

The symptoms are usually noticed first on the shoot tips, although problems may appear on any part of the plant and in different stages of growth. Determining a cause may involve an analysis of the soil.

Any nutrient can be toxic to the plant if it is present in sufficiently high amounts or is out of balance with other elements in the growing medium.

Right: *It is important to provide plants such as these raspberries with the correct light and temperature conditions so that they flourish.*

POLLUTION

Specific symptoms of pollution may include leaves turning brown at the tips and margins, leaf discoloration or premature leaf fall. Growth may also be stunted. Soil pollutant damage can be very severe and rapid in its effects on a plant and its growth. Common problems that you may encounter include extreme soil acidity or alkalinity, chemical toxicity, salt toxicity or pesticide residues. Of these, only soil acidity is relatively easy to cure. If serious pollution is suspected, then this requires specialist help. Such situations, however, are thankfully rare.

PESTS AND DISEASES

It is important to bear in mind that a certain level of pest and disease invasion is normal even on healthy crops. However, it is also true to say that healthy vigorous plants are more resistant to serious attack than plants that are growing under stress. The best form of pest and disease control is obviously prevention. You will need to be able to find and recognize a range of pests and diseases in order to prevent outbreaks of them in your allotment and, if necessary, take prompt action. This is examined in greater detail later in this chapter.

Below: *This healthy row of carrots on an allotment is a tribute to good plant care and the result of much hard work.*

PROTECTING CROPS

Even the best allotment-grower will lose some plants during a growing season and, for most short-term crops, this is unlikely to be a particular problem. It pays to be vigilant though, as losses can also be an early warning sign of a greater problem in the making. If you notice that a plant is looking sickly, finding out what has caused the problem should be a priority, as it is only once you have identified the cause that you can act in order to stop the problem from worsening.

Above: *Pests such as cabbage whites, whose caterpillars can devastate crops, can easily be prevented with a little forethought.*

WHY IT IS IMPORTANT TO PROTECT YOUR CROPS

Keeping your plants healthy is an extremely important aspect of allotment-growing. Quite simply, an outbreak of pests or diseases or failing to maintain healthy conditions will ultimately be extremely detrimental to plant growth, development and, ultimately, yields. There is however, in most cases, a fine balance, and a small number of potential pests or limited disease occurrence may well be tolerable, provided of course that it is controlled and prevented from spreading.

In other cases, some pests and diseases pose serious threats to your crops, particularly if their effects are sudden and extreme – as would be the case if for example an animal the size of a goat or horse got on to your plot and started to munch its way through your crops! While this case might seem unlikely, many quite small creatures are equally as debilitating if they appear en masse. Even where these are controlled, the injury that the plant suffers may affect its overall productivity and vigour, and can ultimately shorten its lifespan.

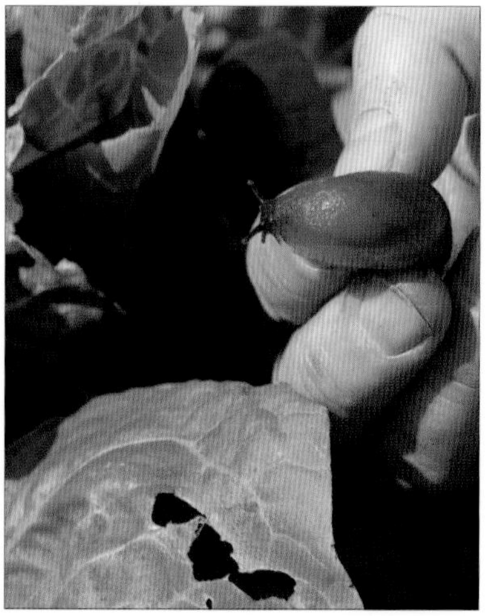

DIAGNOSING THE PROBLEM

Plant health arguably presents the single biggest headache to growers. The sight of a crop suffering under the onslaught of some sudden unexpected ailment can be extremely disheartening, particularly if you don't know what is causing it. Fortunately, the vast majority of conditions that affect your plants are relatively uncommon, and for those remaining ills, the vast majority produce characteristic symptoms that make it possible to successfully diagnose and hopefully treat the problem.

Having said that, even the few conditions that you are likely to encounter on your plot can add up to what seems an extensive list. It is best therefore to familiarize yourself with the basics of a diagnosis. If you can pin the problem down to a general cause, such as a pest, disease or an environmentally related ailment (referred to as a disorder), then you are one step closer to diagnosing the specific cause and choosing the most appropriate treatment. This is vital, as the wrong diagnosis and treatment can waste time and money and ultimately not actually help the plants in question.

It is worth asking your fellow plot-holders for advice once a problem occurs, particularly those who have held plots for some time. They will often know and recognize the commoner ailments, share experiences and help you to control or eradicate the issue.

RECOGNIZING THE CAUSE OF PROBLEMS

Learning how to identify why problems occur can be a complex area, even for very experienced growers, and ultimately you will learn a great deal from experience. It is also important for you to study and understand the life cycles and (in the case of pests) behaviour of the organisms responsible for ill health in the crops that you grow.

Left: *You can often spot some of the more common pests on an allotment, such as slugs, and simply remove them by hand.*

The act of wanting to obliterate anything seen crawling on your plants is a common reaction by allotment-growers dismayed by crop losses. You would do well to remember, however, that only a fraction of these creatures are harmful. You must therefore learn which are pests and which are not.

Vigilance is also a key aspect of crop protection, and usually involves making a regular close-up inspection of all your plants to check for early symptoms of attack. It also means that you need to have a pretty good idea which plants are susceptible to particular pests or diseases and learn what the signs are. In the most obvious cases, the pest or disease will be visibly present, thereby allowing easy diagnosis. In the case of very small or microscopic organisms, however, their presence may only really be apparent once damage has already started.

WHAT IS A PEST?

Essentially a pest is an animal. This can range from almost microscopic invertebrates such as red spider mite, visible pests such as aphids, beetles and molluscs (slugs and snails), to larger more visible creatures such as rabbits, birds and deer. What they all have in common is that they cause harm by directly eating the plant. Some chew, a great many suck juices from the stems and leaves, and others steal fruit or blossom. One of the most disturbing aspects of pest infestations is that they have a tendency to arrive (seemingly quite suddenly) in large numbers and they are often specific to one or a few related plant types. Although most pests are visible, some are very small and can only be viewed through a magnifying glass. Others hide away out of sight and, in these cases, the only evidence you can see is that which is left as a result of their feeding. In essence, nothing beats regularly inspecting plants that you know are susceptible to certain pests and acting quickly as soon as you see the first signs of their presence.

WHAT IS A DISEASE?

Plant diseases are caused by microscopic parasites, which attack plants at the cellular level. As a consequence they cannot be seen with the naked eye, or with a hand lens, meaning that their presence is only usually noticed once harm has occurred. By this point, however, obvious and sometimes extensive symptoms appear, often with an alarming suddenness, and crop losses can be severe as a result.

Having said this, some diseases start as a localized infection on the plant, meaning that prompt action can help save the rest of the plant or the crop as a whole. Knowing which plants are likely to be affected is an important factor in the fight against disease spread, as is using disease-resistant varieties whenever possible.

HOW DO PLANTS BECOME INFECTED OR INFESTED?

Diseases are almost always either already present on the plot or are transported to the plant by a vector such as the wind, water, an insect or other animal. We can also spread them via the soil and organic matter that we bring to the site. Even the soil on your boots – if it comes from elsewhere – can spread diseases and some pests. Good cultural practices and paying heed to plot hygiene and crop rotations will often eliminate much of this human element, but the natural methods of their spread are less easy to prevent.

The relatively large size of most pests means that they usually migrate to suitable host plants by themselves, often in a predictable seasonal pattern or 'outbreak'. Having said this, the wind can often blow small pests over great distances, and these outbreaks are less predictable as a result. Many pests are only active at certain times of the year though, meaning that in most cases knowing when they are likely to appear should engender an added sense of vigilance in plot holders.

Not all plant pests or diseases are able to attack healthy plants, and these tend to concentrate their efforts upon weakened, dying or dead material. This means that they are not normally a problem for a well-maintained crop. Coral spot (a disease of woody plants), botrytis (grey mould) and the majority of slug species are common examples of this. If they are allowed to multiply, however, as a result of poor plot hygiene for instance, they can sometimes become aggressive and start damaging otherwise healthy plants.

WHAT IS A PLANT DISORDER?

A disorder is when a plant experiences a physical change to its normal functions, which is usually brought about by adverse environmental stresses. Disorders differ from temporary stress responses, such as wilting, in that they are irreversible, being the product of a fundamental change in the plant's growth pattern. Ironically, many disorders resemble damage caused by diseases or pests, with physically stressed plants sometimes becoming far sicker than if they actually had been invaded by a pest or disease-causing organism in the first place.

Disorders differ from pests and diseases in that they are, on the whole, an avoidable problem. Don't be disheartened if your plants start to show signs of physical stress and damage though, as this is in effect their way of telling you there is a problem, and many disorders can be rectified if the correct action is taken promptly.

THE CAUSES OF PLANT DISEASES

The science of plant diseases is a complex subject area, although in essence explanations for diseases boil down to three major causes. These are fungi, bacteria and viruses.

Fungi are small either unicellular or colonial masses of cells, the vast majority of which have a beneficial or benign effect on plants. Many have complex life cycles and are only visible at the reproductive phase or after damage has occurred.

Bacteria are primitive single-cell organisms that enter and infect individual plant cells. Once inside the plant they can reproduce rapidly, mostly causing harm as a result of toxins released inside the plant.

Viruses are small life forms that are incapable of independent life outside a particular host plant's cells. Essentially they hijack the cell and cause it to make copies of the virus, often killing the cell and sometimes debilitating or even killing the whole plant.

Right: *Enviromesh is a cheap, easy and temporary way of protecting crops, such as this kale, from pests.*

PREVENTING PROBLEMS

Effective allotment gardening is about working with nature to create an environment in which plants can grow and be productive and withstand attack from pests and diseases. If plants become infested, they may fail to give a good display and crop yields can suffer. Prevention is better than cure, and a keen eye and regular checks will help you to anticipate and prevent the worst of any potential problems.

Above: *A healthy crop, such as these ripe white currants, is more likely if you position the plants in an appropriate site.*

GOOD CULTURAL PRACTICE AND HYGIENE

Many pests and diseases can survive without a susceptible host even under the most unfavourable conditions. Myriad plant diseases survive from one growing season to the next on plant debris, in the soil, on seeds or on alternate hosts (some pests and diseases affect different plant species at different times of the year e.g. peach-potato aphid). This means it is vital to remove and properly dispose of any infected plant materials. It is also important for the allotment-holder to be aware of the diseases that can threaten an individual crop and recognize the conditions in which these potential threats to plant health can thrive.

GROW DISEASE-RESISTANT CULTIVARS

Plant varieties and cultivars were mostly chosen for other reasons than their disease-resistant qualities. Often they become so commonly grown that their diseases become widespread. Many plants have disease-resistant strains or cultivars, but this does not necessarily guarantee that they will be immune to a disease. However, they will be better able to resist the worst of its ravages.

AVOID PLANT STRESS

A plant that is stressed – by drought or an unfavourable temperature, for example – will be predisposed to pest or disease attack. Plants that are not subjected to higher levels of stress than they can cope with will remain healthy and better able to deal with potential attackers.

Stressed plants often show signs of physical disorders (e.g. being tall, drawn and pale due to lack of light). These can be due to the weather, the plant being wrongly sited, nutrient imbalance or the presence of a toxic substance in the air or soil. Physically stressed plants may become sicker than if a pest- or disease-causing organism actually had invaded them. Stress can kill a plant if the problem is not quickly remedied.

RIGHT PLANT, RIGHT PLACE

Plants all have their preferred locations and the occurrence or lack of a particular environmental factor or factors will ultimately determine whether a plant will prosper in the position in which it has been planted. Ferns, for example, need a cool moist site. Placing one in a hot sunny site will lead to its death as it struggles to keep its moisture. Plants that become stressed will neither grow as well, nor be as disease-resistant, as they would otherwise. Choosing an appropriate site in the first place will at least help to ensure the initial health of your plants and will render them more able to resist other potential threats to their health.

RECOGNIZING THE PROBLEM

Allotment-holders who understand pest life-cycles and behaviour are better able to determine when control will be most effective. Insects living in your plot are all part of nature's complex ecosystems and food chains. Less than one per cent of species that you are likely to encounter are considered pests. Since few insects are actually harmful, gardeners must learn which are pests, which are beneficials, and which ones will have no effect on the allotment whatsoever.

Despite the fact that they are not always popular, insects play an important role in our sites. Beneficial insects, such as bees, are necessary in the allotment to pollinate fruit and some vegetable crops. Others,

Far left: *The regular washing down of the glass panes in a greenhouse can reduce the build-up of disease-causing organisms.*

Left: *Regular deadheading of old or damaged blooms will help to reduce the spread of some fungal diseases.*

Above: *Using mesh to prevent the adult carrot fly reaching a carrot crop is an excellent preventative measure.*

Above: *Sturdy wire mesh can help keep out unwanted visitors, such as rabbits and rodents, while allowing light, air and water in.*

Above: *Fine netting is useful for protecting crops from smaller, often flying pests, such as cabbage whites.*

such as springtails, also help to break down dead plant tissue, while wasps and ground beetles capture and eat other pest insects and are called predators. Wasps and midges have larvae that attack pests by living inside their bodies and are called parasitoids. Allotment-holders must learn to cherish this 'willing army' of helpers in their plots.

PEST AND DISEASE CYCLES

Often gardeners believe that their plants have been attacked overnight. This may be true in the case of damping-off disease or with larger pests such as rabbits. More often, however, much has occurred before the symptoms are actually visible.

The pathogen (the pest- or disease-causing organism) must be introduced (inoculated) to the host plant. Most pathogens either move by themselves (as with most pests) or must be carried to the host plant (as with the vast majority of diseases). Rain, wind, insects, birds and people usually spread plant diseases.

Splashing rain carries spores of apple scab fungus from infected apple leaves to uninfected leaves. Wind blows fungal spores from plant to plant, while aphids and whiteflies transmit many common plant diseases. Believe it or not, smokers can transmit tobacco mosaic virus from a cigarette to tomato plants.

Once the pathogen has been transferred to the host plant, it begins to multiply, change or grow into a form that can then enter the host. In many fungal diseases, the pathogen arrives on the plant as a spore, which must germinate before it can begin to grow and invade the plant. Once the fungal spore germinates, it sends out thread-like tubes called hyphae. These penetrate the plant through wounds or natural pores in the outer skin of leaves, stems and roots.

The roots of plants that have been damaged during transplanting are a common entry point for root-rotting fungi. A single aphid that lands on a plant can give birth to a clone every 12 hours and can eventually form a small thriving colony within a few days, leaving the allotment-holder with the impression that it suddenly appeared out of nowhere.

Once established, pests or diseases can grow, spread or increase in number very rapidly and begin damaging plant tissue. As they consume nutrients or plant tissue, evidence of the damage to the plant begins to appear. Symptoms may be seen on any plant parts and include mottling, dwarfing, distortion, discoloration, wilting, shrivelling or holes and notching in the margins of leaves. The first signs of pest infestation may not appear, however, until well after the parent insect has laid its eggs on the plant and disappeared.

Seeds or cuttings from infected plants will also transmit disease. Certified organic seed guarantees that at the time of sale the seeds are free of all diseases. Always try to obtain disease-free stock as this should ensure that the plant is not infected and will not introduce disease into your plot. This is particularly important with crops such as raspberries and other small fruits.

Pest insects and mites may carry diseases that infect plants. Many gardeners use the term 'pest management' rather than pest control or pest eradication. It is impossible to eradicate pests from your allotment completely. The best option is to try to keep pest numbers low in order to minimize the damage that they can cause in your plot.

ADOPT AN INTEGRATED STRATEGY

Allotment-holders should learn how to use a range of pest management techniques, such as introducing beneficial predators into their plots (often referred to as biological controls), making sites less attractive to harmful pests, and encouraging conditions in the plot that favour beneficial predators of all types (cultural controls).

Below: *Companion planting is an environmentally friendly way of deterring pests, and also looks good in your allotment.*

TREATING PROBLEMS

It is essential that you act quickly to safeguard crops as soon as they start to show signs of stress. Knowing what is causing the problem is an important first step, although choosing the most effective treatment is vital if you intend to limit the damage and prevent further losses. A range of strategies is available to the allotment-holder and each of these has its own advantages and disadvantages, meaning that the best approach usually involves a combination of treatments.

Above: *Caterpillars can do a lot of damage in a short amount of time , so it is important to be vigilant and keep an eye on your crops.*

CHEMICAL PESTICIDES

The word 'pesticide' is a broad term, covering a range of products that are used only to control pests and disease-causing agents such as fungi, as well as weed killers, repellents and other chemical agents. Although people usually think of pesticides as purely synthetic (man-made) chemicals, they actually include a huge range of products, some of which are considered to be entirely 'natural' (despite their existence being the result of human endeavour). Examples of these include pyrethrins (a chemical extracted from *Chrysanthemum cinerariaefolium* and *C. coccineum*), plant oils (such as neem, garlic and citronella) or inorganic compounds such as sulphur or copper salts. Yet more are merely slightly altered versions of otherwise 'natural' chemicals.

RISKS OF USING PESTICIDES

While many allotment-holders are quite happy to use pesticides that are of a natural origin, the use of any synthetic chemical as a pesticide is often something they would rather avoid. At first, this would seem to be rather unsurprising, given that concerns over food safety often act as a prime motivation for growing your own food. Although the use of synthetic pesticides does indeed have to be considered with great caution, both for environmental reasons and your own personal health, the simple fact of the matter is that many synthetic products are actually less toxic than their 'natural' (organic) counterparts. It is also worth remembering that just because a poison is derived from a 'natural' source, does not mean that it somehow becomes 'healthier' or less dangerous than synthesized versions.

Before you decide to use any pesticide then, natural or synthetic, you should weigh up the true dangers of using them. Any pesticide is a form of poison or at the very least an irritant. Even if they are specifically targeted, they represent some degree of hazard, albeit slight in many cases. Put simply, hazard is the potential of a substance to cause harm to people. This cannot be

Left: *Slug gel and other pesticides will protect young plants, but you should be aware that they may have an impact further up the food chain.*

Right: *Hand-removal of pests such as snails is more environmentally friendly than using pesticides. Relocate them to a wild area.*

SPRAYERS

Before choosing a garden sprayer, you should consider the use it will get. There are many different types of sprayer on the market, with plenty of shapes and sizes to choose from. Dimensions vary from small hand-held misters to large-capacity backpack or trailer types, so finding a model to suit your needs shouldn't be hard.

Sprayers have many uses beyond simply applying synthetic pesticides. They can be used for applying foliar feeds, misting plants to aid fruit set, and even for applying micro-biological control agents.

Ideally, then, you will need at least two sprayers: one for herbicide and one for pesticide, and if you intend to apply biological agents, then this will need a third separate one. This is because residues from any pesticide can be very difficult to remove completely from inside a sprayer tank and, if used to spray crops afterward, could potentially harm them.

Make sure you label each sprayer according to its use.

changed and a hazardous substance should always be treated with caution. Risk, on the other hand, is the likelihood of a person being harmed by exposure to a hazardous substance. The more hazardous a substance therefore, the greater the risk involved with its use, particularly if it is misused or used in an unsafe manner. Remember also that neither hazard nor risk is the same thing as toxicity. The toxicity of a chemical, whether high or low, cannot be changed by the person applying it.

Having said this, synthetic pesticides do pose significant problems, other than those directly associated with their relative hazard or toxicity. Chief among these are the fact that many pests and diseases have built up tolerances to them, rendering their use ineffective in many cases. In addition to this, the increasing legislative burden upon the manufacturers of pesticides has made their creation and supply less economic and many have been withdrawn from the market as a result.

BIOLOGICAL CONTROL

A living organism that is used to control another specifically targeted pest or disease is called a biological control. This chosen organism might be a predator, parasite or disease and, in effect, it is a way of manipulating nature. In essence it is almost like a 'living pesticide' and, like its namesake, it is not without its problems.

Using a biological control involves careful planning, often taking a good deal of time, patience and sometimes considerable personal research if it is to be effective. The results are not as dramatic or quick as those produced by pesticides, meaning that they are sometimes ineffective in controlling sudden outbreaks. They are also less effective in outdoor settings than the controlled setting of a greenhouse and, in some cases, biological agents (harlequin ladybirds, for example) are inclined to become invasive, even out-competing the native species in areas where they are intentionally or even accidentally released.

PHYSICAL CONTROL

The term 'physical control' often simply means removing the problem entirely or preventing it from reaching the crop in the first place. It is therefore essentially a cultural control and mostly refers to mechanical or hand controls. It often proves most useful in respect of weed control, although cultivation, pruning, burning, and simple removal by hand all have their place in pest control as well. Some insects, for example, may also be destroyed by cultivation, as this can destroy their eggs, overwintering larvae or adults.

Below: *Insecticidal soaps affect only those pests with which they come in contact, meaning they can be targeted at specific areas.*

PESTICIDE SAFETY

Essentially pesticides work in one of three ways:

- Those that kill on **contact**.
- Those that work their way inside the plant – either to kill a weed or provide an internal protection against pests or diseases – called **systemic** or **translocated** pesticides.
- Those that leave a long-lasting barrier on the leaves or in the soil – known as **residual** or **protectant** pesticides.

The mode of action is no guarantee of safety, although protectant and residual types tend to be the least preferable due to their longevity in the environment.

If you do choose to use a pesticide, the following steps should be considered:

- Is there a safer alternative?
- Work out how much pesticide you will need; buying the right amount prevents your having to store leftover product.
- Read the manufacturer's instructions very carefully and make sure you understand how to mix and use the product safely and effectively.
- Ensure you know what safety clothing you will need, and be sure to use it.
- Make sure you know what type of application equipment is needed for the job, and use it properly and accurately.
- Mix just enough of the product to complete the job.
- Once you have finished, clean, store, and maintain the application equipment according to the manufacturer's instructions, ensuring that all chemicals are stored safely and locked away where children and animals can't access them.

Reducing stress factors, such as drought or cold exposure, can also make your crops more resistant to attack from pests or diseases, and practices such as crop rotation or soil sterilization as well as the use of traps and barriers are also essentially physical controls. While physical control does have an important place then, it is essentially preventative, relying upon considered plant selection and correct cultural care in order to avoid problems, and is only rarely a treatment in its own right.

PLANT PESTS

Pests can be described as those creatures that harm your plants and, if left unchecked, they can quickly cause a great deal of damage. There is a huge army of these pests, but most allotment-holders are unlikely to encounter the vast majority of them. A basic knowledge of the commonest types that occur in allotment sites is all that you should need to be familiar with in order to protect your plants and guarantee their health and successful growth.

Above: *Pests may well be present before symptoms appear. Close examination may reveal them before the plants start to suffer.*

HOW CAN YOU TELL IF A PEST IS A PROBLEM OR NOT?

Deciding whether a pest is a problem or not is very much a matter of opinion. Commercial growers assess the importance of a pest in terms of their financial losses. Allotment gardeners, however, tend to grow fewer plants or crops and mainly grow these for the pleasure of eating home-grown produce. The final decision as to the importance of a pest will rely upon the circumstances and experience of individual gardeners. All gardeners must be willing to accept a certain number of pests in their plot as these form part of the intricate food webs that result in natural control. If there are no pests, then the animals that eat them will disappear and open the door to future, potentially serious, pest outbreaks.

RECOGNIZING PESTS

It is important that you are able to accurately identify a pest that has been attacking your plants so that you can take the appropriate action. Just because an insect is seen walking on an affected plant does not mean that it is the one causing the damage. The only real way to control pests involves getting to know them.

Many pests produce characteristic symptoms that make it possible to diagnose the cause with relative certainty. Some have a wide range of host plants, and symptoms may not always be as conspicuous on all affected plants. Close examination – perhaps with a hand lens – may be necessary for the final diagnosis. With careful observation and experience, it is possible to keep one step ahead of the pests in your site.

CONTROL OPTIONS

It is important to control pests before they become a problem. A single black bean aphid (*Aphis fabae*) that lands on a broad (fava) bean at the start of the summer could theoretically give rise to 2,000,000,000,000,000 aphids by the start of the autumn. This would be about a million tons of aphids. Quantities such as those cannot occur as the food supply would run out and a host of predators would move in before this can happen, but it does go to show that early control is essential as, in just a few days, a small number of pests can cause considerable damage to your plants, and this may have irreparable consequences for your harvest.

Effective allotment-holders must employ a full range of control measures to ensure their plants survive this seasonal invasion, including cultural practices (crop rotation, good hygiene and encouraging biodiversity in the surrounding area), physical controls (hand picking, traps, repellents and barriers) and biological control (using other animals that naturally eat pests). These are covered more extensively later in this section but for now it is important to stress that pests can only really be controlled in a responsible and sustained manner by an integrated strategy that uses a variety of techniques.

CAN PESTS BE TOLERATED?

It is worth pointing out that we tend to be unduly concerned with pests damaging our plants. Supermarkets have conditioned us to expect blemish-free produce. We need to judge the overall health of a plant rather than react when we see a pest. If there were no pests in the allotment, then there would be no predators. Step back and look at the whole picture and remember that everything, even pests, has its place in nature. They all add to the interest and diversity that is the most unique quality of a green space.

Above: *Birds can be serious pests in the allotment. Here, large bites have been taken out of a brassica.*

Above: *Rabbits can devastate a plot overnight, leaving nothing but chewed-off stumps as a result of their visit.*

Above: *Although fascinating to watch, squirrels are closely related to rats, and are a pest on the allotment.*

COMMON PESTS

There is a seemingly endless array of creatures that are waiting to devour and attack your allotment plants. The most common pests are almost worldwide in their distribution, but they can be controlled relatively easily.

It can be discouraging to see how many potential pests may attack your plot, but it is important to bear in mind that you will only encounter a handful of these in your allotment-holding career.

PEST		PLANTS AT RISK	TREATMENT
Ants and termites		Ants are not really pests, but they 'farm' aphids for sticky sugar. Termites can attack some woody species.	Few effective treatments, but baits based on borax are useful. Use a herbal spray of essential oil (citronella and lavender) or lukewarm water as a repellent.
Aphids		Most cultivated plants growing in the open, under glass or indoors.	Encourage beneficial insects to feed on them. Insecticidal soap can also be useful, particularly if the aphids are being 'farmed' by ants.
Birds		Some birds will attack fruit and brassicas as well as brightly coloured flowers, including blossom.	Bird scarers may be employed as a deterrent and netting will also provide cover for individual crops and plants.
Cabbage root fly	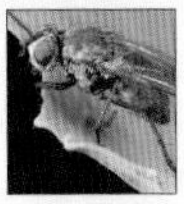	The small maggots grow and develop on and within the roots of the developing cabbage plant.	Place a collar around newly planted seedlings, sinking it into the ground to prevent the newly hatched maggots from reaching the plant roots.
Carrot fly		These root-feeding maggots feed on carrots.	Try companion planting and avoid large monocultures of carrots. Erect plastic or fleece barriers, about 45–50cm (18–20in) high and 2–3m (6½–10ft) apart.
Caterpillars		Many different species of plant, especially those in the cabbage family.	Birds and other predators will reduce populations. Biological control, using a bacterial agent, and pesticides such as derris. Hand-pick off individual plants.
Chafers		Raspberries, strawberries, potatoes, lettuce and young trees.	Keep the ground weed-free and well cultivated in order to reduce the number of bugs. Roll lawns in late spring.
Deer		Browse on many plants. Male deer rub their antlers against trees, causing damage to the bark.	Notoriously difficult to control, often best kept out by fencing. Repellents are available, based upon formulae such as bear or even lion droppings.
Fruit flies		Troublesome on softer fruits in warm conditions, especially tomatoes.	Cover the fruit with a small piece of rag. Paper bags are also good to use, but can be difficult to get around a truss of tomatoes.
Gall mites and wasps		These pests affect a wide range of trees and shrubs.	Generally not problematic or life-threatening. They are a good indicator of healthy biodiversity in an allotment.
Leaf hoppers		There are many different types, affecting a wide range of plant species.	Difficult to control. Remove dead leaves to reduce overwintering eggs and nymphs. Encourage predators such as lacewings.
Leaf miners	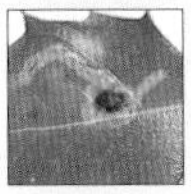	There are many hundreds of species that all have their preferred host species.	Hand-picking of severely affected leaves. Biological controls exist but the problem is rarely serious enough to warrant their artificial introduction.
Leather-jackets		They feed on roots just below the soil surface.	Can be difficult to control. Damp sacking over the soil can lure them up to the surface where they can be hand-picked or left for birds to eat.

PEST		PLANTS AT RISK	TREATMENT
Mealy bugs		Suck the sap of many species and produce a sticky honeydew that supports the growth of sooty moulds.	Biological controls are available. Cultural control is more difficult and involves drenching plants with a soap solution and then rinsing.
Mites		A common pest of many plants, especially those growing in hot dry conditions.	Biological controls are available. For a cultural control, improve humidity around the plant or spray foliage with a soap solution and then rinse.
Moles	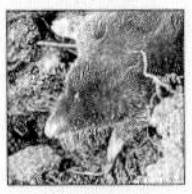	Damage roots by lifting small newly planted trees.	Best controlled by trapping or using repellents. Sonic repellent devices are rarely effective. Removing one mole can simply 'open the door' to another.
Nematodes (eelworms)		A few species cause disease-like symptoms. A problem when the same plants are grown in the same place.	Regular crop rotations can help to reduce damage. If numbers build up or plants become badly affected, avoid growing the affected species.
Rabbits and hares, squirrels, voles and mice		Rabbits gnaw shoots. Mice and voles eat small bulbs and corms in winter. They all ring-bark young trees.	They may be trapped or a variety of repellents are available. Tree and shrub shelters are useful against voles and mice, as is fencing for rabbits and hares.
Sawflies	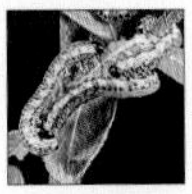	Developing larvae eat plant tissue. Fruit sawflies are notorious. Slugworm sawfly attack ornamentals.	Control slugworm by applying insecticidal soap. Control fruit sawfly larvae with derris. Both these treatments reduce numbers of beneficial insect predators.
Scale insects	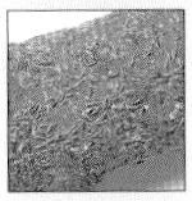	Several species, some of which have specific host plants.	A cultural control consists of swabbing woody stems with a strong organic soap solution or pruning and removing affected parts.
Sciarid fly (fungus gnat)		Tiny flies that feed on soil fungus. The larvae attack the roots of young plants in water-logged compost.	Control by preventing the potting mix becoming too wet, although biological controls of nematodes are also available.
Slugs and snails	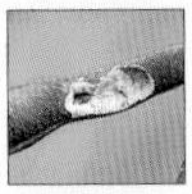	Common pests of a wide variety of plants. Snails, in particular, cause damage and defoliation of plants.	Often difficult to control although they can be caught in traps containing beer. A variety of barriers and deterrents are also available.
Thrips	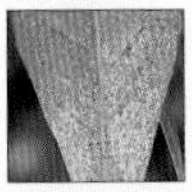	Small insects suck the sap of soft foliage and attack flowers. Rarely a problem outside in cooler climates.	Remove seriously damaged foliage. Several natural predators (usually mites) are available for use against thrips.
Weevils		Larvae attack roots, stems or flowers and fruit of a range of plants. Adults feed on affected plants.	Wet acidic composts favour ground-living types such as vine weevil. Biological control possible with parasitic nematodes if temperatures sufficiently high.
Whiteflies	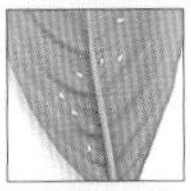	A greenhouse pest in cooler climates that may occur outside in warmer areas.	Biological controls are available but the best option can be to avoid growing susceptible species.
Woodlice (pill bugs)	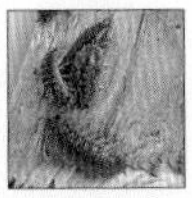	Usually a pest indoors of crops such as cucumbers. May chew through young seedlings.	Often more an indication of poor hygiene than a problem in itself. A sign that you must clean up the greenhouse.

PLANT DISEASES

The early detection of plant disease can help to halt the widespread infestation of your crop. Try to establish a routine of regularly checking your plants and crops. Look closely for any tell-tale signs, using a hand lens if necessary. Remember that the first or most obvious symptom may not always be the only one or even the most important. Always check to see if there are other symptoms to ensure that you get the full picture before making your final diagnosis.

Above: *This raspberry is exhibiting symptoms of damage caused by a virus. Having identified the cause, appropriate action can be taken.*

RECOGNIZING PLANT DISEASES

Vigilance is the key to success in controlling plant disease. Carefully inspect leaves, stems, roots, flowers and fruits for any sign of disease. You may even find it useful to cut open a branch or stem to look for problems such as discoloration of the tissue, which may explain leaf or stem wilting and sudden wilting of a section of or a whole plant.

Stand back and look at the overall picture. Consider the whole environment. This will include the weather, soil, the stage of development of the plant (and any pathogens present), cultural practices and the condition of other plants in the area. All of this information can help to indicate what may be wrong with the plant. Remember that a plant growing in the wrong location may be stressed.

Try to determine when the symptoms became apparent. The onset of a problem may be due to a cultural practice, the seasonal appearance of a disease or insect, or a weather-related event. Remember that long-term stress is slow to appear, taking a year or more at times.

It is important to establish whether the problem is spreading, as this may indicate that it is a disease. Check whether plants of other species have been affected, as diseases are usually (but not always) species-specific. Problems caused by environmental factors do not spread, although the symptoms may become more severe.

You must know what the plant should look like in order to be able to recognize any abnormalities. Reading up a little on `the species that you are growing in your allotment can help you to make a more accurate diagnosis of the problem.

Remember that there is usually no single cause of a disease infestation. The primary cause may be associated with cultural or environmental conditions. And just as there is probably no single cause, there is usually no single symptom.

When you are attempting to diagnose the cause of plant illness, always inspect symptoms that appear on parts that are still alive (or at least partially alive). Dead plants are often invaded by secondary infestations of decomposer fungi, which may hide the original problem. If possible, make an examination of the entire plant, including roots, although this may not be possible for large specimens such as trees.

CONTROL OPTIONS

Ultimately, where a serious disease is suspected, it may be advisable to avoid growing susceptible species altogether, or, in the case of fruit and vegetables, to rotate the crop as part of a regular cycle. Make notes that provide details on disease occurrence (the type of disease and when it appeared), the plants affected, the weather and environmental conditions in your allotment each year. By doing this you can better anticipate what problems are likely to occur in your plot during the growing season.

Finally, remember that even the best gardeners lose plants to disease. This is only serious when large numbers of plants are affected. A diverse allotment site will contain other highlights, and diseases will claim only a fraction of the planting.

Above: *Inspecting plants regularly will help you spot damage and begin the process of assessing what may have caused it.*

Above: *Bacterial problems, such as the leaf spot on this pelargonium, are often most active in moist and warm conditions.*

Above: *Disease-causing organisms can enter a plant each time it is cut or pruned, or when branches break off in strong winds.*

COMMON DISEASES

There are all kinds of diseases that can affect your plants. Most of these are mercifully rare, but every site will suffer from its share of diseases during the growing season. Most of these conditions are relatively easy to deal with, but a correct diagnosis is essential. As always, it is preferable to try to prevent these diseases taking hold and spreading in the first place rather than treating them when they occur.

DISEASE		PLANTS AT RISK AND THE SYMPTOMS	TREATMENT
Apple common scab		A bacterial disease that causes the formation of large (albeit harmless) scabs on the surface of the apples. Commonly encountered in damp weather and on trees with crowded branches.	Rake up and dispose of affected leaves. Prune out cracked or scabby shoots to remove places for the fungus to overwinter.
Bacterial canker	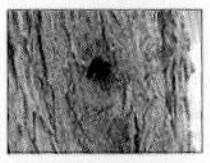	Many different tree fruits. Reduces vigour and the rate of growth of the affected plant. Leaves turn yellow, wither and die. Branches become girdled and die back. A sticky secretion will ooze from cracks or welts in the bark.	Difficult to control once a plant is infected. Cut out and destroy infected material. Confine the problem to one specimen by cleaning pruning tools between cuts and before moving on to another specimen of the same type.
Clubroot		This fungus attacks all plants in the brassica family, including cabbages, radishes and cauliflowers. The spores can live in the soil for up to 20 years. Plants wilt during the day and grow weakly.	Remove and destroy infected plants. Practise crop rotation, lime acidic soils and avoid planting out in waterlogged soils.
Coral spot		A common fungus affecting many woody plant species, including fruit trees and bushes and figs. Appears as pink or bright red, raised pustules on wood that is showing signs of dieback.	Prune out infected tissue and destroy it. Regular 'hygienic pruning' can help to prevent it taking hold in the first place.
Fireblight		Attacks plants of the Rosaceae family, notably apples, pears, plums and cherries. Flowers and leaves turn brown, wither and die. The affected plant dies back rapidly from the branch tip.	Remove and destroy all affected material, cutting back to at least 50cm (20in) below the point of infection. Best to remove diseased plants, replacing them with a non-susceptible fruit tree or shrub.
Fungal canker		Affects many fruit trees. The bark tissue shrinks, cracks and begins to peel and flake away around the affected tissue in concentric rings. The infected area swells up and new growth ceases.	Prune out the affected material, about 15cm (6in) below the point of infection, and burn it. Clean tools with disinfectant between cuts and especially between pruning individual plants.
Honey fungus		A soil-dwelling fungus that parasitizes the roots of woody plants. Leaves tend to discolour and wilt and fail to develop in the spring. Ultimately, this can weaken and kill the plant. Affects tree and bush fruits, rhubarb and strawberries.	Difficult to control. Remove and destroy all infected plants, including the roots.
Mosaic virus		This group of viruses affects a very large number of species, including marrows (large zucchini), pumpkins, cucumbers and aubergines (eggplants), and is characterized by an irregular, angular mottling or streaking of the leaves.	Winged insects that feed on plants, then migrate to another, can rapidly spread the virus. Control the pests themselves where possible. Dig up and destroy infected plants.
Onion neck rot	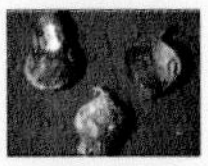	This is a fungus that will cause onions in storage to rot. The bulbs become soft and transparent.	Regular checks must be made on stored crops, and remove any infected material. As the fungus can be soil-borne, rotate crops next year.
Potato blight		This is a fungal disease that is spread by the wind and rain. The leaves turn brown at the tips and can have white mould underneath. Eventually the leaves wither and collapse. The tubers have dark patches and the inside turns slimy and rots.	Spray with Bordeaux mixture as a preventative measure, especially when it is warm and humid. Remove infected material and purchase disease-free seed potatoes next time.
Potato common scab	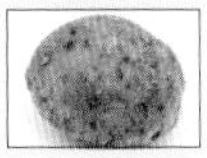	This bacterial disease is found in most soils. It is more prolific in hot, dry years. Brown textured patches are found in the potato skins, but are still safe to eat.	It is best to grow varieties resistant to potato scab. Water regularly to prevent attacks.
Powdery mildew		Affects many plant species. The leaves become covered with white powdery patches that may distort growth or even cause leaf drop in severe cases. Thrives in warm, humid or wet conditions.	Remove and destroy infected leaves. Sulphur and Bordeaux mixture can provide protection, but these are easily washed off in wet conditions. Avoid growing susceptible species if conditions favour the spread of the disease.
Rust		A common fungal disease affecting many species. Characterized by rusty coloured patches or spots, known as pustules, on leaves. Tissue around the pustules yellows and dies, and this, in turn, may distort growth or cause leaf drop in severe cases.	Commonly seen on soils rich in nitrogen. It may have a noticeable effect on seasonal crops or those grown for their leaves. Bordeaux mixture can reduce its spread but it is difficult to control completely. Avoid susceptible crops and varieties if the problem is persistent.
Silverleaf		Affects fruiting and ornamental species of *Prunus*, including cherries, plums, peaches, apples and pears. The leaves on some branches gain a silvery sheen, dying back a year or two later. A purple fungal growth appears on the dead tissue.	The affected wood should be pruned out below the point of infection and disposed of in late summer after fruit has set. Badly infected specimens should be removed completely and disposed of, preferably by burning.
Tomato blight		The leaves have brown patches and curl up, eventually drying out and dying. Stems have brown patches and darken with the fruits turning brown and rotting.	Remove and destroy infected parts of the plant. A Bordeaux mixture will provide protection. Avoid growing tomatoes in the same place next year.

PLANT DISORDERS

Many external factors can affect allotment plants. Weather seldom does what we want it to – there is either too little or too much rain or it is too cold or too hot. If you combine these climatic disappointments with other factors that can affect your plants, such as pollution or nutrient deficiencies, you will see why these difficult conditions can produce a number of disease-like symptoms. They can all put severe stress on a crop and so precipitate attack from living organisms.

Above: *Nutrient deficiencies can cause discoloration of the leaves. This plant is short of magnesium.*

RECOGNIZING DISORDERS

Plants can be susceptible to a long list of outside forces. Extremes of weather, nutrient deficiencies and physical damage can take their toll on the health and vigour of a plant. Other environmental factors, such as too much or too little water, or pollutants in the soil, can also encourage disease-like symptoms.

Soil pollution can be caused by nutrient deficiency, misapplied fertilizer (resulting in too much nutrient and, therefore, toxicity) `or buried inert material. Airborne pollution can be more insidious and more difficult to determine or detect.

Weather events such as high winds or frost may go unnoticed if you are not there to witness them. A huge storm will leave evidence in its wake. The effect of a sharp early morning frost, however, or a steady drying wind on a sunny afternoon may not show the damage caused until several days have passed.

Disease can result from a combination of factors, affecting growing conditions and actual disease-causing organisms. Plants may initially be placed under stress, making them vulnerable to attack by living agents. For instance, drought may damage roots, which in turn renders them more liable to infection by fungal diseases.

It is important to determine whether the problem is the result of a pathogen or due to a problem in the environment. Look to see if the occurrence of ill health is random or uniform in terms of its distribution. As a general rule, randomly distributed symptoms on injured plants are usually caused by a living factor, such as diseases or a pest. In addition to this, infestations, particularly those caused by diseases, tend to radiate out from central points. Uniform patterns are generally associated with non-living or non-infectious agents such as poisons, fertilizers, environmental stress or mechanical damage.

Above: *While rain is essential for a plant's growth, excessive water and waterlogging can kill a vulnerable, young plant.*

CONTROL OPTIONS

If the cause of the problem is physical, you will need to find out whether it is due to a recurring environmental factor inherent in the site, such as constant buffeting by strong winds, or whether it is caused by 'one-off' events such as unseasonable frosts or contamination from a careless neighbour's weedkiller spray. Some factors can often be removed, such as polluted soil, and windbreaks can be planted and fleece draped over tender specimens on cold nights. If plants continue to be affected, it could be that the plant is in the wrong place and you may have to try relocating it elsewhere.

Left: *Weather can have a big impact on an allotment, with sudden sharp frosts and high winds being particularly damaging.*

COMMON DISORDERS

Disorders are the result of either an imbalance of essential nutrients or of a range of stresses that are caused by adverse or difficult environmental conditions. Many of the disorders and conditions described here can resemble diseases. This means that is very important for you to diagnose the cause of the distress in the plant before taking any remedial action. A plant disorder will call for a different response to a plant disease.

CONDITION		PROBABLE CAUSE	TREATMENT
Bare patches or areas of poor plant establishment		The patchy establishment of cover crops or turf can be due to soil compaction or underground obstructions. Soil can easily become compacted if it is walked on a lot, particularly when it is wet. Buried obstructions such as rubble can also cause similar growth distortions.	Remove all buried rubble prior to planting or replanting. Relieve compaction by cultivating and replant if required. If treating turf on an allotment, aerate and scarify to relieve compaction and improve drainage.
Blackening of leaf tips	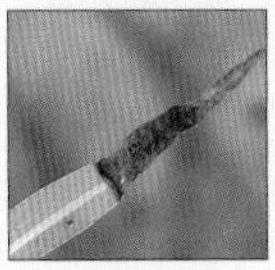	Usually the result of overwatering, particularly with container- grown plants. The waterlogged soil or potting mix forces oxygen out of the soil, thereby suffocating the roots, which suffer a form of drought-stress.	Plants that are waterlogged are best left to dry out. Do not water until the potting mix is dried out, not only on the surface but throughout the pot. Always check to see if plants need watering before doing so.
Etiolation		Sun-loving plants kept in low light conditions quickly become starved and will be significantly weakened. If kept in these conditions for any length of time, the plant will eventually die.	Choose specimens that are appropriate for the light levels in the allotment. If growing in a greenhouse, ensure that correct light levels are achieved. Remove shading and clean glass in winter to increase the levels.
Leaf blackening		Frost damage on buds and leaves in early spring, even to hardy specimens, is usually noticed on new growth that has not yet become acclimatized. It is the sudden shock that often causes the problem, not the actual temperature itself.	Cover slightly tender plants with fleece in the winter. Lightly spray plants with water in the evening to help protect against late frosts. Crops grown in the greenhouse prior to planting out need to be properly hardened off before being planted outside.
Leaf scorch		High winds and bright sunlight, especially on shade-loving species. Some plants can also be damaged by watering in bright sunlight, by providing too little or too much water, or by applying too much fertilizer to the soil. Hail can also cause leaf spotting or holes.	It is best to water first thing in the morning or in the evening to prevent leaf scorch from water that has splashed on to the leaves.
Mechanical or physical damage		High winds, which are especially damaging to deciduous woody plants in full leaf. Tall vegetables can easily break if not adequately staked, as may newly planted fruit trees and shrubs. Animals visiting the allotment, for example foxes, can also flatten or snap plants.	Stake plants firmly and ensure that animals are excluded from areas where plants could be damaged. Stakes used to support newly planted fruit trees should be kept in for at least one year.
Nutrient deficiency		A lack of or too much of a particular nutrient. Nutrients can also become in short supply if other nutrients are present in large amounts. Nitrogen deficiency (shown left) is extremely common. The leaves turn pale green or yellow and the plants become stunted.	Deficiencies are best treated with the application of fertilizer, or choose plants that are adapted to deal with the site conditions. To prevent deficiencies, ensure that the soil is properly prepared before planting and add generous amounts of organic matter if needed.
Poisoned ground		Leaked fuel or lubricants used in construction work can leave the ground contaminated. This is usually more of a problem in allotments near building sites. Underground gas pipes can leak, flooding the ground with gas that is lethal to plant roots. Other chemical spillages could come from machinery such as a strimmers or rotavators.	Remove all affected soil and replace with fresh topsoil. If pipes are leaking, make sure that they are fixed before replacing soil. Fill lawnmowers with fuel over a plastic sheet.
Root girdling		This can cause instability and the collapse of fruit trees and shrubs. Tree and shrub roots become woody following the first year's growth and, if these are constrained in round pots, they tend to grow in spirals.	At the establishment phase, try to use bare-rooted stock whenever possible if using pot-grown trees. Tease out roots from the root-ball immediately prior to planting, even cutting out older woody roots. This will ensure that the root system grows out into the soil instead of spiralling.
Wilting		A normal response in many plants to either a lack of water or high temperatures, and not necessarily a cause for great concern. Squashes habitually wilt on hot summer afternoons, therefore mulching the crop with generous amounts of organic matter aids in reducing stress.	Water if required. A good preventative measure is to mulch, even around vegetables. Use sieved (strained) garden compost or leaf mould as manure can hold too much moisture and this can cause problems with rotting. Choose wind-resistant species, if appropriate. Apply fertilizer at recommended rates. Do not over- or under-water plants.

BENEFICIAL PREDATORS

A thriving population of natural predators and parasites can significantly help to keep pest populations down. The allotment-holder should strive to create and maintain an environment in which these welcome visitors to the allotment or greenhouse can prosper. This usually means avoiding using pesticides, which can wipe out beneficial predators and so upset the natural balance in the allotment or greenhouse.

Above: *Biological controls are a successful way to fight pests. The control insects are released, here from a sachet, to attract pests.*

BIOLOGICAL PEST CONTROL

Nearly every species of plant-feeding insect has another insect that is its predator or parasite. Some pests, such as aphids, are eaten by ladybirds (ladybugs), hoverflies and midge larvae, parasitized by wasps and infested by fungal diseases. Large pest populations are a food larder for many 'natural enemies', including carnivorous animals, parasites and diseases.

Biological methods of control use these natural enemies of pest insects to keep their populations under control. It is like having an army of insects and other creatures doing the work for you. Biological controls can be encouraged into the allotment by creating a suitable habitat. Ironically, this means that the pests must be present first. They must also be present in sufficient numbers to support a viable population of the beneficial predator. This can be a complex area and the easiest way is to encourage the conditions that will favour a balanced food web to develop. Purchasing beneficials is only generally recommended for use in greenhouses, although a few (particularly microbes) are suitable for use outdoors.

CREATING SUITABLE HABITATS

The greater the variety of habitats your plot has, the more biodiversity it will support. Ponds (if these are allowed), long grass, log piles, and food plants for animals with varied tastes all encourage a stable ecosystem where pests are kept at relatively low levels.

Many birds and bats eat insects. Bats need a roosting site, so place a purpose-made bat box on the shady side of a tree. Position the box at least 3m (10ft) high with a clear airspace in front. Night-scented flowers encourage the moths that bats feed upon. This is the key. The predators must be able to live in your site or they will go and find a more suitable habitat elsewhere.

The longer you use this approach, the more balance will appear in your allotment. This is simply because the ecosystem begins to stabilize and diversify over time.

BENEFICIAL INSECTS

Predators (those that devour pests directly) and parasitic insects (those whose young hatch inside and devour pests) are often termed 'beneficials'. Predators include lacewings and wasps. Parasitic insects (more correctly termed parasitoids) are less well known than predators, but equally effective. They lay their eggs in a pest species. When the eggs hatch, the larvae feed on the pest insect, killing it. The majority of these insects are tiny wasps, although some flies and mites also fall under this category. Learning to recognize beneficial insects is crucial if you want to avoid killing your army of allotment helpers.

Above: *Log piles encourage beneficial predators such as beetles to colonize and take shelter in your allotment site.*

Above: *Parasitic nematodes can be used in specific cases to attack pests that live in the soil. Here they are watered into the area.*

BENEFICIAL PREDATORS IN THE ALLOTMENT

There are many beneficial predators that will willingly take up residence in your allotment and help to control populations of pests in a natural way.

- Anthocorid bugs or red kneed capsids
- Bats
- Birds (robin, blue tit and thrush)
- Centipedes
- Earwigs
- Frogs, toads and newts
- Ground beetles
- Harvestmen
- Hedgehogs
- Hoverflies
- Lacewings (adult or larva)
- Ladybirds (ladybugs)
- Mites, e.g. *Phytoseiulus*
- Nematodes, e.g. *Heterorhabditis*
- Parasitic wasps (*Encarsia* or *Aphidoletes*)
- Slow worms
- Spiders on web or wolf spiders
- Tachinid flies
- Wasps (solitary and social)

BIOLOGICAL CONTROLS IN THE GREENHOUSE OR ALLOTMENT

The application of biological controls in the greenhouse or allotment involves using predatory insects or other beneficial animals to control commonly occurring pests. Many pests are only a problem because their natural predators are missing from the allotment. Introducing a biological control usually results in the rapid control of the pest.

PREDATOR SPECIES	PREFERRED TEMPERATURE RANGE	PEST SPECIES THAT THEY CONTROL
Amblyseus cucumeris (predatory mite)	25°C (77°F)	The nymphal forms and adults consume large quantities of immature thrips.
Aphidoletes aphidimyza (predatory midge larva)	21°C (70°F); needs 80%+ humidity	Tiny mosquito-like midge larvae that control substantial populations of more than 60 species of aphids.
Cryptolaemus montrouzieri (predatory beetle)	20–25°C (68–77°F); needs 70%+ humidity	This ladybird is effective in controlling mealybugs on houseplants and in greenhouses.
Encarsia formosa (parasitic wasp)	18–25°C (64–77°F)	Minute, flying parasitic wasps, which lay their eggs inside whitefly scales (the pupa stage) and eat them in two to four weeks
Heterorhabditis megidis (parasitic nematode)	Minimum soil temperature of 14°C (57°F); if temperature drops below 20°C (68°F), they become less effective	Patrol the soil to a depth of about 18cm (7in) and quickly take care of the slow-moving grubs, such as vine weevil grubs and chafers. Very effective in pots and containers. Soil must be moist.
Metaphycus helvolus (parasitic wasp)	20–30°C (68–86°F)	These tiny, black and yellow wasps are effective against several soft-scale species, including brown scale. The females lay their eggs under the body of first- and second-stage scales. The grubs feed on scales and develop into adults within two weeks. Adults also provide control by feeding on non-parasitized scales. *Metaphycus* are most effective in semi-tropical conditions.
Phasmarhabditis hermaphrodita (parasitic nematode)	Minimum soil temperature of 5°C (40°F)	Useful for slug control. Should be applied during the early growing stages of vulnerable plants. Needs moist soil.
Phytoseiulus persimilis (predatory mite)	Use once temperature is regularly above 15°C (60°F). Best at 18–25°C (64–77°F); needs 60%+ humidity	Predator mites, slightly larger than the two-spotted mites (also known as red spider mites) upon which they feed.
Steinernema feltiae (parasitic nematode)	Minimum temperature of 10°C (50°F), although they remain effective when the soil temperature drops below this	Aggressive predators used to control fungus gnats, mushroom flies and leatherjackets. They can be used in flower and vegetable plots and greenhouses.

Above: *Ladybirds are just one of the many beneficial insects that will help to keep the unwanted pests of your allotment in check.*

MICROBES

Bacteria, fungi, viruses, protozoans and parasitic nematodes are microorganisms that attack insects. These microscopic hordes are generally effective against very specific pests and present little risk to humans and the environment. Many experienced gardeners may well be familiar with a popularly known, microbial-based insecticide known as Bt or *Bacillus thuringiensis*. This commonly available product, which is used to kill many different kinds of moth and butterfly larvae, is a bacterium. It produces a toxin that kills specific caterpillars. The larval pest usually dies within four to seven days. There are many strains of Bt, each type controlling specific pests.

Parasitic nematodes are also very effective against certain pests that live in the soil. However, the nematodes require moist conditions in order to survive and their temperature requirements further limit their use to greenhouses in many cases.

Despite their potential, very few fungi, viruses and protozoa are commercially available because these living organisms are difficult to raise, store and apply. The best way to encourage these willing and tiny helpers into your plot is to maintain a healthy soil that is rich and diverse in terms of the life it contains.

Above: *Providing convenient shelter, such as this lacewing hotel, for beneficial insects can help to increase their numbers.*

OTHER CONTROL METHODS

There are many ways of dealing with the different pests that appear in the allotment. Some of these methods have been tried and tested for generations, others are individual to the gardener and are often the result of a happy accident. As an allotment-holder, it is useful to learn and experimenet with as many different tricks as possible to manage the pests in your plot and to protect your plants.

Above: *Companion plants such as these marigolds confuse or deter pests that would otherwise attack plants.*

GOOD GARDENING PRACTICE

The selection and culture of plants can reduce the potential for pests and diseases. Cultural practices are methods the gardener can use to change environmental factors that affect plants and their pest populations. It is essential, therefore, that you know the cultural or growing requirements of each plant. Providing the correct conditions results in a vigorous plant that is less likely to be attacked by pests and diseases and can tolerate some damage.

ASSESSING THE DAMAGE

When problems do arise, you must decide whether a pest is causing enough damage to warrant control. In other words, you will need to assess how far the problem can be tolerated before action is necessary. Some form of pest damage is inevitable with any crop, but you will need to establish limits. To do this, you will need to take into consideration the amount of damage that can be tolerated, the numbers of an individual pest that can cause significant damage and the plants' stage of development. The health and vigour of the plant can also have a direct bearing on when or if you need to take action. A few holes on a leaf may not require control, but, if most of the leaf has been eaten, the plant may die.

Above: *Compact discs are an unusual and amusing way of scaring away marauding birds from your allotment crops.*

TAKING ACTION

Monitor your plants to determine when action is necessary. A thorough inspection of the plant allows you to identify a problem before major damage occurs. You should also inspect the plant's entire environment for clues to the problem. Observing and keeping records of weather conditions, for example, can help provide clues to growth patterns and problems.

Above: *Slugs and snails are notorious allotment pests that are easily kept at bay using a water trap around vulnerable crops.*

TYPES OF CONTROL

Control options can be arranged by their mode of action and their impact on the environment. These methods of control can be grouped from least to highest impact: cultural and mechanical controls and 'permitted' chemical controls (soaps, oils and botanical insecticides).

Cultural control includes hand removal of larger pests, the use of screens, barriers, and traps, freezing and crushing. These methods generally have little or no negative effect on the environment.

COMPANION PLANTING

This is commonly used to protect plants from pest attack. The theory is that the companion plants – flowers growing next to a food crop, for example – disrupt the searching pattern of the pests looking for host plants. They literally smell these hosts but become confused with the more diverse planting style. Separating rows of cabbages, broccoli or other brassicas with rows of onions has always been a popular combination, possibly because the onion's strong scent confuses cabbage pests. Tomato plants also grow well next to cabbages and seem to deter caterpillars, while growing leeks near carrots repels carrot flies.

SCREENS AND BARRIERS

Any material that is fine enough to keep pests out can be used as a barrier. A variety of screens of different mesh sizes can keep out large insects, birds and rabbits, but they can also prevent pollinating insects from reaching a plant, resulting in lack of fruit. Cardboard and metal collars will prevent cutworms from reaching young transplants. Sticky bands placed on tree trunks trap beetles and soil-hibernating pests. Copper strips are available for slug control. These supposedly react with the slugs' slime to shock them. Sharp particles, such as crushed eggshells, are also used to control slugs.

TRAPS

Certain insect pests can be monitored by using traps. Sticky coloured traps, pheromone traps and pitfall traps can all be used to monitor the occurrence of some pests. Whiteflies and aphids are attracted to bright yellow, and this colour is used for sticky cards upon which they become trapped.

You may want to apply a control and then enclose the plants in netting to keep further infestation from occurring – perhaps putting up netting and then releasing predators.

Right: *Garden birds can be dissuaded from attacking your allotment plants if you stretch string and shiny foil over the crops.*

Traps usually serve as a monitoring system, warning of the presence or increase in undesirable pest numbers. Traps can also be useful in timing control measures by showing the presence of migrating or emerging adults. The control measure can then be introduced at the best time to control the particular pest. Codling moth traps for use around fruit trees are a good example of this. They are sometimes used to control numbers, but most types are limited in their real effectiveness. Yellow, sticky traps attract whiteflies, aphids, thrips, leafhoppers and other small flying insects.

Traps that use pheromones or attractive scents to tantalize adult insects are best used as a way to check presence and numbers. Pitfall traps can be cups or jars dug into the ground then filled with yeast and water or beer to attract and trap slugs.

WATER

A jet of water from a hose washes aphids, spider mites and other small insects from plant foliage. This must be done frequently as it does not kill insects or eggs and it does not prevent some insects from crawling back on to plants.

INSECTICIDAL SOAPS

These are made from the salts of fatty acids. Fatty acids are components of the fats and oils found in plants and animals. These soaps should not be confused with ordinary cleaning soaps. Insecticidal soaps kill only what they touch and are effective against soft-bodied pests such as aphids, thrips, crawler stage scales, whiteflies, leafhoppers and mites. Insecticidal soaps may cause burning on some plants, particularly those with hairy leaves. Test insecticidal soap on a single leaf if you are unsure – burning will usually occur within 24 hours.

BOTANICAL INSECTICIDES

Derived from plants, botanical insecticides include pyrethrum, citrus oil extracts and the extract of the neem tree. They act rapidly to stop feeding by insects, although they may not kill the pest for hours or days. There are also disadvantages to the use of botanicals. They must be applied frequently, may be difficult to obtain, and, although generally less toxic than many pesticides, they are still toxic and may harm other beneficial allotment residents.

Above: *Sticky traps are another form of pest control in greenhouses. Here, pheromones attract pests to the trap, where they get stuck. Other traps consist of sheets of plastic covered with a non-drying glue.*

Above: *Sheets of horticultural fleece, which can be stretched over developing young plants, provide an effective physical barrier against some of the smaller types of allotment pests, such as flying insects.*

TRAPS, BARRIERS AND DETERRENTS

The prevention of pest and disease attacks is an essential part of allotment gardening. Plants that are infected by pests or diseases are weaker specimens that are difficult to treat and never quite recover their former vigour. Many allotment pests can be trapped or kept at bay using relatively inexpensive materials and sometimes recycled household items. Put the barriers in place when the plants are young and always ensure that pests are not trapped inside the barrier.

CONTROL METHOD	HOW IT WORKS
Beer traps and deterrents (granules, copper strips and greasebands)	Traps are effective ways of both controlling pests, such as slugs, and finding out which ones you actually have. Deterrents are physical barriers over which the pest cannot or will not pass. There are many types and their effectiveness can vary.
Bird scarers (e.g. scarecrows)	Bird scarers have the drawback of a limited lifespan before the birds learn that they are not a real threat. They can, of course, be changed and most bird scarers are only needed on a seasonal basis.
Bug nets in the greenhouse	Greenhouse vents are problematic in terms of pest control in that they allow both pests in and purchased biological controls out. Bug nets are put in place to avoid this happening.
Fleece on frames	Frames covered in horticultural fleece can be used over outdoor crops to help keep pests out and control the temperature.
Fleece stretched over a crop	Fleece can be used to create a favourable microclimate around young plants. It also acts as a barrier to airborne pests. On the downside, however, it can also keep out airborne predators from pests that overwinter in the soil.
Fruit nets over fruit	Fruit nets are especially useful for summer soft fruit crops that can quickly be devastated by birds.
Individual cloches	Cloches can act as barriers to a wide variety of airborne pests. Any pests that are sealed into this environment may, however, find the perfect environment within which to thrive.
Mesh cages for trees	Mesh cages are usually used to keep rabbits and hares at bay. They are usually simple constructions formed from three or more stakes driven into the ground with chicken wire (or similar) attached to them.
Rabbit fencing	A continuous barrier to prevent rabbits entering areas where plants are growing. The base of the wire should be buried below ground level to prevent the rabbits burrowing a passage beneath it.
String or wire netting stretched over seedlings (e.g. peas)	Aerial barriers can protect against bird attack. They may only be needed for the duration of the crop's life or even less.
Traps (pheromone)	Pheromone traps are used to detect the presence of insects. The pheromones attract members of the opposite sex and the appearance of the target species allows you to begin looking for and controlling the young that cause the damage.
Traps (sticky, coloured traps used in the greenhouse)	Sticky traps can provide a certain degree of control against the flying adults of insect pests. However, they are not as effective as they are sometimes thought to be and are, in fact, of more use for showing whether a particular pest is present or not, thereby allowing appropriate control measures to be put in place.
Tree guards (spiral)	Spiral guards are useful for protecting the bark of newly planted trees from rabbits and hares, especially in winter and early spring. These guards expand as the tree develops, but they are best removed completely after about a year.
Tree shelter	These protect newly planted trees from vertebrate pests and from the worst rigours of the environment by providing a favourable microclimate around them. They naturally degrade under the action of sunlight, but are best removed after two to three years.
Twiggy branches over plants	Arched over young plants, these can be an effective deterrent to pests such as birds and cats. They do not prevent the migration of beneficial predators to the plants.

Above: *Slugs and snails can be caught in a trap that is filled with stale beer, or water that has been mixed with yeast.*

Above: *Ring tunnels that are covered in a fine mesh will prevent flying insects from attacking your allotment vegetables.*

Above: *Plastic netting, stretched over the crop and carefully secured, provides an effective barrier against birds.*

Above: *Old plastic bottles make an ideal barrier to protect young plants from pests. These are cheaper than traditional cloches.*

Above: *Chicken wire, stretched over young plants, will prevent garden birds from reaching and eating them.*

ORGANIC PESTICIDES

Although you can use conventional pesticides, it may well be worth considering some naturally occurring substances to protect your plants from pests and diseases. As with standard pesticides, these should only be applied when and where absolutely necessary and not on a regular basis.

ORGANIC PESTICIDE	HOW IT WORKS
Bacillus thuringiensis	These are bacterial spores that produce a toxic protein that is useful against caterpillars but will not cause any harm to beneficials. *Bacillus thuringiensis* works quickly, paralyzing the caterpillar and so preventing any further damage, although it quickly degrades in sunlight and needs frequent re-application throughout the growing season.
Bordeaux mixture	A compound containing copper and sulphur used to control various fungal diseases including apple scab and potato blight. It is harmful to fish and livestock, and frequent use can lead to a build-up of copper in the soil that can be harmful to worms.
Derris	A chemical extracted from the roots of the derris and longocarpus plants. It is useful against a variety of insects including aphids, caterpillars, sawflies and plant-eating beetles. It can prove harmful to beneficials, although it is not a threat to bees.
Insecticidal soap	This is not soap, like the domestic washing soap, but is made from the salts of fatty acids, extracted from plant material. It can be effective against a wide variety of insect pests, although it can damage sensitive plant species.
Plant oils	Their effectiveness varies but most depend upon coming into contact with the pest itself and suffocating it, although some, such as neem tree oil, do appear to have insecticidal properties.
Pyrethrum	This organic pesticide is extracted from the flower-heads of *Chrysanthemum cinerariifolium* and is especially effective in controlling aphids. However, it does not persist for long and can also cause harm to beneficial insects.
Sulphur	An effective fungicide against a variety of plant fungi, including powdery mildew, grey mould and blackspot. Sulphur can also prove harmful to predatory mites and can cause damage to certain sensitive species.

Above: *Twigs and willow can be used to make a barrier to protect plants from rabbits and other unwelcome larger animals.*

Above: *Scarecrows are an attractive method of deterring birds and occasionally large pests away from your vegetable plot. They should be moved around the allotment and redressed occasionally so that the birds do not get too accustomed to them.*

WEED CONTROL

Even the most successful allotment-holder must fight a constant battle against weeds, which if left unchecked for just a couple of weeks will begin to reassert themselves. Weeds take vital nutrients, compete for light and water and, if not controlled, will overrun, spoil or even kill all but the most vigorous crops. As if this wasn't enough, weeds can also harbour pests or diseases. You needn't be disheartened though as, if they are dealt with early, a short time spent each week is enough to control them.

Above: *From clearing a plot when you first take it on to keeping the site clear when growing crops, weeds are a common problem.*

WHAT MAKES A PLANT A WEED?

A plant that we describe as a weed is one that without help or encouragement establishes itself on your plot, and competes with those that you have planted. They do this by robbing cultivated specimens of nutrients, light and (arguably) most important of all, water. They are able to do this because they are species that have evolved to colonize, compete and become dominant. Most of them are specialists in establishing on disturbed ground – which is often found on a cultivated plot – and usually have rapid growth rates when compared to cultivated specimens.
In natural habitats this competitive capability is often held in check by established neighbouring plants, but natural stability is very rare on the average allotment as cropping means that the vegetation is constantly cleared and the soil disturbed by the regular cycle of cultivation.

Below: *Hand-removal of weeds using a small hand fork is fast and effective, so long as you remove all traces of the weed.*

While many common weeds are native plants and owe their competitive edge to this alone, many others are introduced species that have become weeds because they do not have the constraints of the habitats from whence they came. These are often the most serious weeds in an allotment and can become so troublesome that they assume a national importance.

The term weed is a relative one, however, and any plant that is able to propagate itself and spread freely can become a weed. Weeds may also be the remnants of a previous crop, called 'volunteer' weeds. Although many of these can easily be dealt with, some can interfere with the crop rotation as they can act as a host for diseases in the intervening time between cropping cycles. Equally, some 'wild' weeds also host plant diseases that can subsequently spread to cultivated crops. Charlock (*Sinapis arvensis*) and shepherd's purse (*Capsella bursa-patoris*) for example, can host clubroot, while eelworm can be harboured by chickweed, fat hen and shepherd's purse. Cucumber mosaic virus, a potentially devastating disease affecting not only cucumbers, but also melons, courgettes (zucchini), marrows (large zucchini) etc., is carried by a range of weeds including chickweed and groundsel (*Senecio vulgaris*).

Below: *Annual weeds, such as chickweed, are adept at exploiting opportunities to grow and spread very quickly.*

Most weeds are easily dealt with, although there are always a few that seem to resist all efforts to eradicate them. No weed is completely invincible, however, and the only really successful strategy for weed control is persistence.

WEED TYPES

The weeds that may plague your plot share some attributes with the crops they compete with and, as such, they can be divided into three groups.

Annual weeds are those that germinate, grow, flower and set seed within one growing season. Among these are some species known as ephemerals, which are extremely fast-growing and complete their lifecycle well within a growing season, allowing them to produce several successive generations over a year. This strategy means that they can exploit brief windows of opportunity – during mild winter spells, or between crops – in order to grow and set seed. Many of these are known then as winter annuals, due to their habit of germinating in late summer or autumn, overwintering and setting seed the following summer. A few hardier examples, such as chickweed (*Stellaria media*), can actually germinate under snow cover, meaning they commence their growth at the first sign of spring, often before the surrounding crops appear.

Biennial weeds are actually short-lived perennials that grow from seed during one growing season, overwintering as a rosette of leaves close to the soil surface, before flowering, setting seed and dying the following growing season. This strategy means they are rarer on allotments due to the cropping cycle, although a few such as spear thistle (*Cirsium vulgare*), can occasionally prove problematic.

Perennial weeds live for more than two years and can become established either by seed or by vegetative parts, such as roots or rhizomes being moved around during cultivation, or contained in imported topsoil or compost. Seedling perennials are usually no more difficult to control than any other weed seedlings, although once established, they can be difficult to control and often prove very competitive among vegetable crops. Examples of perennial weeds include blackberry (*Rubus fruticosus*), nettle (*Urtica dioica*), dandelion (*Taraxacum officinalis*) and dock (*Rumex obtusifolius*).

WAYS TO CONTROL WEEDS

Physical control of weeds usually involves hand-weeding, hoeing and forking over and, despite the effort they involve, in most cases it is a perfectly viable strategy if done regularly. It also represents the least environmentally detrimental method of weed control. The real trick is to be able to recognize weeds when they are very young, preferably when they are just seedlings, as it is then that they are most vulnerable and your efforts at weeding can be most effective. In the case of shallow-rooted crops such as brassicas and onions, any control needs to be limited to shallow hoeing as any digging can cause root disturbance to your crops. Perennial weeds may be difficult to control by hand weeding alone, especially those with extensive root systems or which spread by rhizomes in the soil, such as couch grass (*Elymus repens*), bindweed (*Convolvulus arvensis*) and horsetail (*Equisetum arvense*).

Machinery has a limited use on the allotment, although rotavators can be used to destroy seedlings on vacant areas, and strimmers are useful for clearing overgrown areas.

Mulch is a layer of a material that is laid over the surface of a soil or other growing medium, often to suppress growth or prevent germination of weed seed. To be effective, mulches must be laid on a bare surface, as they will not inhibit established weeds. They should also be laid on soil that is warm and moist, in either autumn or spring, depending upon the crop involved.

DIFFERENT TYPES OF WEEDS

Annual meadow grass (*Poa annua*)
A very common annual weed that thrives in just about every situation on an allotment plot. Very variable and adaptable, and able to grow and set seed all year round.

Bindweed (*Convolvulus arvensis*)
Common perennial in well-drained soils that is difficult to control on account of the very deep roots from which the stems arise directly. Seeds prolifically.

Bittercress (*Cardamine hirsuta*)
A diminutive annual plant that often grows in mild periods in the winter. Sheds many seeds and can become invasive if not controlled.

Blackberry (*Rubus fruticosus*)
A highly persistent woody perennial, meaning that hand removal of young seedlings as soon as they are seen will save a lot of hard work later.

Charlock (*Sinapis arvensis*)
An annual plant that occasionally becomes problematic due to its ability to act as a host for clubroot in between normal crop rotations.

Chickweed (*Stellaria media*)
A common annual found on soil that is well cultivated and rich in organic matter. Spreads to make a large mat and seeds prolifically.

Couch grass (*Elymus repens*)
Spreads via perennial underground rhizomes to form thick masses in the soil over time. Can be difficult to eradicate but it will not stand constant cutting.

Dandelion (*Taraxacum officinalis*)
A common yellow-flowering perennial with long, strong tap roots that readily regenerate unless the whole plant is dug up and removed. Seeds prolifically if left in the ground.

Dock (*Rumex obtusifolius*)
A persistent perennial that is difficult to dig out and can regenerate from even a small section of root. Seeds prolifically if not controlled.

Groundsel (*Senecio vulgaris*)
Extremely common annual, often unnoticed beneath crops. It can tolerate very harsh conditions and varies greatly in size depending on site and soil.

Horsetail (*Equisetum arvense*)
Non-flowering perennial spreading via thin black roots to cover large areas. Difficult to dig out as the brittle stems and roots break easily when pulled.

Nettle (*Urtica dioica*)
An extremely common perennial in rich, fertile, frequently cultivated ground. Relatively easy to control but hated because of its stinging ability.

Shepherd's purse (*Capsella bursa-patoris*)
A very short-lived, prolifically seeding annual weed that often completes a whole life cycle in a mild winter period. Can also harbour clubroot.

Spear thistle (*Cirsium vulgare*)
One of a few biennial weeds, which can occasionally become a problem if it establishes between crops. Usually best controlled by cultivation.

Herbicides can give quick results when used correctly and these are split into two groups. 'Contact herbicides' are usually applied as a spray and kill only those parts with which they come into contact. 'Systemic (translocated) herbicides' are also applied as a spray, but are absorbed by the foliage and translocated to all parts of the plant. A few among these are selective, meaning that they target only one group of plants, and thereby leave the crop unharmed.

DO I NEED TO USE HERBICIDES?

This is occasionally a debateable point and, as a rule of thumb, the answer is likely to be no. The majority of herbicides (weed-killers) are toxic compounds that can kill other crops or persist in the environment, so should generally be avoided. The exception to this might be where highly persistent weeds cannot be effectively controlled by hand-weeding or mulches, but try these methods first.

GARDENER'S CALENDAR OF CARE

Understanding the yearly growing cycle is an important part of successful allotment gardening. Plants are acutely sensitive to the changing climate through the year and often require action to be taken within a narrow window of opportunity if the plot is to be fully productive. In order to do this, it is essential that you plan everything on paper in advance, foreseeing potential mistakes or opportunities, avoiding problems and allowing you to budget not only expense but also time. The following pages offer guidance, but over time you should develop your own seasonal planner.

Left: *Mangetouts are ready to harvest when the pods are plump but not fully grown, from late spring until late autumn.*

Above: *Late summer onions signal the start of the harvest which, whilst a busy time, represents the fulfilment of your labours.*

Above: *Squashes and pumpkins are a real sign that autumn has arrived, and mark the impending end of the growing season.*

Above: *Allotments need tending even in the depths of winter, when a layer of snow may be covering the ground.*

EARLY SPRING

Marking the traditional start of the gardening season, early spring is the point in the year when the weather starts to warm up, days become longer and the strength of the sun becomes noticeable. Although frosts begin to subside now, winter can be reluctant to give way to spring, and allotment gardeners still need to keep an eye on weather forecasts and be prepared to protect crops at short notice. Many will still require protection for several more weeks.

Above: *The beautiful stems of Swiss chard add colour and interest to the winter and spring vegetable patch.*

OVERVIEW

Spring is a magical time for allotment-holders, although the longer days and the strengthening sun can easily lull you into a false sense of security. It is the time when outdoor seed sowing really starts, although these first spring-like days are notoriously erratic. If the allotment is in a frost-prone area, delay sowing and planting outdoors, or warm the ground up well with cloches, fleece or black plastic for a couple of weeks before sowing, rather than risking damage to vulnerable seedlings.

Winter rains often have the dual effect of compacting the soil surface while depleting nutrient reserves in the soil. An easy way to give over-wintering crops a boost is to apply a general-purpose, compound fertilizer. Gently fork this into the surface of the soil, being careful not to damage any roots around established crops. Take particular care around plants such as asparagus, whose crowns are still lying dormant below the surface.

VEGETABLES

Sowing outdoors now:

- Broad (fava) beans
- Brussels sprouts
- Calabrese (early)
- Cauliflowers (early)
- Leeks
- Parsnips
- Peas
- Radishes
- Summer cabbages

Sowing under cover now:

On a heated bench or propagator:

- Aubergines (eggplants)
- Celeriac
- Courgettes (zucchini)
- Cucumbers
- Self-blanching celery
- Sweet (bell) peppers
- Tomatoes (early indoor)

Above: *Sow early tomato seeds indoors.*

Under cloches:

- Beetroot (beets)
- Broad beans
- Brussels sprouts
- Carrots (early)
- Lettuces
- Parsnips
- Peas (early)
- Radishes
- Salad leaves
- Spinach
- Spring onions (scallions)
- Turnips

In module trays:

- Lettuces, sown at two-weekly intervals

Planting outdoors now:

- Asparagus
- Broad beans
- Garlic
- Horseradish
- Jerusalem, globe and Chinese artichokes
- Leeks
- Onions (sets and autumn-sown)
- Potatoes (early, once chitted)
- Sea kale
- Shallots

Planting under cover now:

- Cauliflowers
- Peas (second early)

Harvesting now:

- Beetroot
- Brussels sprouts
- Cabbages (Savoy and winter)
- Calabrese
- Cauliflowers (winter- and spring-heading)
- Chicory and endives
- Chinese and Jerusalem artichokes
- Kale and sea kale
- Leeks
- Lettuces (winter-protected)
- Parsnips
- Radishes
- Salsify and scorzonera
- Spinach (winter)
- Spring greens
- Spring onions
- Sprouting broccoli
- Swiss chard

General:

- Remove any remaining covers from forced rhubarb.
- Apply a nitrogen-rich fertilizer to spring cabbage at 30g (1oz) per lm (1yard) row.
- Clean and weed existing asparagus beds before growth commences.

Last chance to:

- Sow celeriac, early peas and onions.
- Plant garlic, onions (sets), shallots and asparagus.

FRUIT

Planting now:
- Drought-prone fruit trees and bushes that need watering in their first season
- Outdoor vines, such as grapes
- Strawberry runners

Prune:
- Blackcurrants to within 5cm (2in) of the ground.
- Complete the pruning of cobnuts and filberts.
- Cut out older wood from acid cherries on established trees.
- Newly planted redcurrant and gooseberry bushes hard, by about half their length.

Harvesting now:
- Rhubarb

General:
- Apply nitrogen-rich fertilizer to blackcurrants and give a second application of nitrogen to fruit trees if growing in grass.
- Apply a potassium-rich fertilizer to cane fruits.
- Check for wind damage, especially following high winds.
- Inspect stakes and ties of newly planted trees.
- Remove any weeds from around the bases of young trees, bushes and cane fruit, then mulch the area.
- Untie and retrain canes of blackberries and related fruits, which have been bundled together against winter damage, and train on wires before bud burst.

Last chance to:
- Plant rhubarb, fruit trees and bushes.

Above: *Train blackberries on wires.*

HERBS

Sowing outdoors now:
- Chervil
- Coriander (cilantro)
- Parsley

Sowing indoors now:
- Basil
- Curled parsley
- Marjoram

Harvesting now:
- Parsley

General:
- Divide overcrowded perennial herbs, such as chives.

Above: *Divide chives, as necessary.*

PLANT HEALTH

Pests and diseases:

▷ Look out for signs of all pests from now on. Aphids are usually the first to appear.

▷ Pinch out the top of broad (fava) beans when in flower to reduce attack from black fly.

▷ Slugs can strip young plants of new growth, doing irreparable damage. These become more active now as the temperatures rises, so keep an eye out for them.

▷ Peaches and nectarines can be sprayed to protect against peach leaf curl. Apply sticky bands to apple trees.

Soil and climate:

▷ Hoe frequently for weed control and soil aeration.

▷ Complete all digging and manuring, adding fertilizer in final soil preparations.

▷ Apply a good general fertilizer to all open ground.

▷ Use nets for frost protection on early blooms and young fruitlets on fruit trees, on still cold nights.

Above: *The hazy, weak sunshine of early spring heralds the arrival of a new season.*

MID-SPRING

Mid-spring brings the real promise of the main growing season to come. Lengthening days combined with steadily increasing temperatures and light levels mean that crops start to grow in earnest as the summer approaches. The effect of the longer daylight hours is extremely important for us too, meaning that we now have the opportunity to get out into our precious patches in the evenings for an hour or two while it is still light. Just as well as it is all go on the allotment from now on!

Above: *The first young stems of asparagus are a very welcome sight; make the most of them as the season is short.*

OVERVIEW

While the risk of a hard frost is generally slight by mid-spring, plants can still be damaged by wide fluctuations in temperature and will either need to be grown under protection or their sowing and planting delayed. Despite this, this is the time where sowing vegetable seed really gets under way.

Mid-spring also marks the start of the pretty blossom period, which reaches a crescendo toward the start of late spring. The buzzing of bees eagerly pollinating these blooms is a welcome sight, but remember that with it come some less welcome guests: the insects and other pests that can ruin a crop if left unchecked.

To survive the coming season, your plants will need a good start. It is most important, then, that they are given proper care and attention now, ensuring they have enough food and being vigilant about pests and diseases. This will mean that they begin their lives in the best possible condition and you will reap the rewards later.

VEGETABLES

Sowing outdoors now:

- Asparagus peas
- Beetroot (beet)
- Brussels sprouts
- Cabbages
- Calabrese
- Carrots (early and maincrop)
- Cauliflowers
- Kale
- Kohlrabi
- Leeks
- Lettuces
- Onions (bulb and spring),
- Oriental greens (seedling crops and bolt-resistant types)
- Parsnips (in situ)
- Peas
- Red chicory (Belgian endive)
- Salsify
- Scorzonera
- Spinach
- Sprouting broccoli
- Swiss chard
- Turnips (early)

Sowing under cover now:

- Aubergines (eggplants)
- Capsicums (sweet and chilli)
- Courgettes (zucchini)
- Cucumbers (indoor)
- Dwarf French (green) beans
- Marrows (large zucchini)

Above: *Sow courgette seeds indoors.*

- Pumpkins
- Runner (green) beans
- Self-blanching celery and celeriac
- Squashes
- Sweetcorn (corn)
- Tomatoes (outdoor)

Under cloches:

- Lettuces
- Mixed salad leaves
- Spring onions (scallions)

Planting outdoors now:

- Potatoes (second early)

Harvest now:

- Asparagus (early)
- Cauliflowers (spring-heading)
- Celeriac
- Chicory (Belgian endive)
- Endives
- Jerusalem artichokes
- Leeks
- Oriental greens (seedling crops)
- Radishes (summer and winter)
- Salad plants
- Salsify
- Scorzonera
- Sea kale
- Spinach (winter)
- Spring cabbages
- Spring onions
- Sprouting broccoli
- Swiss chard

General:

- Start hardening off seedlings of brassicas, leeks and onions from prior sowings in the greenhouse in a cold frame.
- Transplant cabbages, cauliflowers, leeks or broad (fava) beans sown earlier to their final positions.
- Plant up a new asparagus bed.

Last chance to:

- Sow spring varieties of broad bean, Brussels sprouts, cabbage (summer/autumn), cauliflower and celery (under cover).
- Force chicory or sea kale.
- Plant maincrop potatoes, Chinese artichoke, globe artichoke and sea kale.

Above: *Harvest forced rhubarb.*

FRUIT

Sowing undercover now:
- Melons

Planting outdoors now:
- Raspberries
- Strawberries

Prune:
- Figs (before the buds break)
- Gooseberries
- Newly planted raspberry canes to encourage good root establishment and strong new shoots
- Red and white currants if left unpruned through the winter, to reduce bird damage
- Young pyramid plums

Harvesting now:
- Rhubarb (forced)

General:
- Apply nitrogen (light dressing) to established strawberry plants if growth is poor and apply a foliar feed at least every two weeks.
- Hand-pollinate wall-trained peach and nectarine flowers and mist spray at midday to help setting in dry weather.
- Ventilate plants under cloches and add straw mulch as flowering commences.
- Water all newly planted trees, bushes and canes if necessary.

Last chance to:
- Plant blackberry plants.

HERBS

Sowing outdoors now:
- Borage
- Coriander (cilantro)
- Dill
- Feverfew
- Marjoram
- Pot marigold

Sowing indoors now:
- Basil
- Parsley

Planting outdoors now:
- Bay
- Mint
- Oregano
- Parsley
- Rosemary
- Sage
- Tarragon (all types)
- Thyme

Harvesting now:
- Bay
- Parsley
- Russian tarragon
- Sage

Above: *Pick sage (tricolour sage shown).*

General:
- Check that mint clumps haven't grown outside their allotted area as they can grow rampantly if unchecked. Use a spade to dig out unwanted shoots and runners.
- Trim sage, cotton lavender, bay and rue, to keep plants neat and to encourage fresh, tender shoots.

PLANT HEALTH

Pests and diseases:

▷ Uproot and dispose of old brassica stumps by burning them to avoid a build-up of clubroot. Never compost brassica roots as this can spread it around the garden and seriously reduce the efficacy of rotations.

▷ Check the state of fruit netting and supports and repair if necessary.

▷ Try to avoid using any insect control sprays during flowering as this may affect pollinating insects.

▷ Keep an eye out for pests generally throughout the garden.

Soil and climate:

▷ Early flowering fruits may need protection against frost on cold evenings as this can damage the blossom and result in major crop losses. Drape hessian (burlap) or fleece over the plants in late evening but remove this in the morning to enable pollination to take place.

▷ Give some extra protection to lettuces and outdoor tomatoes on colder nights and don't be tempted to remove cloches prematurely. Drape a bit of extra fleece over them on especially cold nights, but ensure you remove cloches or ventilate freely on warm spring days to prevent scorch.

▷ Hoe to remove all weeds from crops, especially in dry weather, when the sun will aid the weeding process by making the soil looser.

Above: *Drape fleece over vulnerable plants.*

LATE SPRING

The arrival of warmer weather and longer daylight hours, often combined with plenty of gentle late spring showers, can create some of the best growing conditions of the year. This is the time to carry out the essential groundwork to ensure a bumper crop on the allotment in the months to come. Make sure that you get your priorities straight and don't try and be too ambitious; it is better to grow fewer crops properly than too many and not be able to give them proper attention.

Above: *Tart green gooseberries are one of the treats of late spring, and signal the arrival of the soft fruit season in the allotment.*

OVERVIEW

Despite the need to get sowing and planting, late spring still gives us a lot of leeway to work out what we need to do for the rest of the year as the plants are still growing and tend to present few problems compared to what could happen in the months to come.

The warm days may distract us from the fact that there may still be an occasional frost, and these can have devastating results on more tender plants or those not properly hardened off before they were hastily planted out. Where there is even a slight chance of frost you should delay putting tender specimens out until early summer.

Late spring is also the time when the army of pests hell bent upon 'sharing' your crop will start to appear in earnest. Vigilance is the key aspect in your defence against these and you should make regular health checks of the crops to ensure that they are in peak condition. Take swift action if you do spot any pests or diseases.

VEGETABLES

Sowing outdoors now:

- Asparagus peas
- Beetroot (beets) (maincrop)
- Calabrese
- Carrots
- Cauliflowers
- Chicory
- Courgettes (zucchini)
- Endives
- Florence fennel
- French (green) beans
- Kale
- Kohlrabi
- Leeks
- Lettuces (short rows in succession)
- Marrows (large zucchini)
- Parsnips
- Peas (maincrop)
- Pumpkins
- Purple sprouting broccoli
- Radishes
- Runner (green) beans
- Salad onions
- Salsify
- Scorzonera
- Sea kale
- Spinach (ordinary and New Zealand)
- Spring cabbages
- Squashes
- Swedes (rutabagas)
- Turnips
- Winter cabbages (early maturing)

Sowing under cover now:

- Cucumbers
- French beans
- Marrows
- Runner beans
- Sweetcorn (corn)

Planting outdoors now:

- Aubergines (eggplants)
- Brussels sprouts
- Cauliflowers (summer)
- Celeriac
- Celery
- Courgettes
- Jerusalem artichokes
- Peppers
- Pumpkins
- Summer and winter cabbages
- Sweetcorn
- Tomatoes

Harvesting now:

- Broad (fava) beans
- Cauliflowers (spring-heading)
- Celeriac
- Chicory
- Early asparagus
- Endives
- Kohlrabi
- Over-wintered carrots
- Peas (early)
- Radishes
- Salad onions
- Salsify
- Scorzonera
- Spinach (summer and winter)
- Spring cabbages
- Spring lettuces
- Sprouting broccoli (late forms)
- Swiss chard
- Texsel greens
- Turnips

General:

- Apply dilute liquid manure to cauliflowers and celery.
- Harden off plants that are to be planted out in early summer.
- Keep greenhouses ventilated. Check cold frames, ventilating when necessary. By the end of the month, the frame covers will only be needed if there is a chilly evening.
- Remove side shoots from vine tomatoes growing under glass.
- Water crops as needed.

Last chance to:

- Plant out early potatoes and Jerusalem artichokes.
- Sow sprouting broccoli, winter cabbage, autumn cauliflower, kale, carrots, parsnips, salsify, scorzonera, asparagus peas, broad beans, leeks, and New Zealand spinach.

FRUIT

Harvesting now:

- Green gooseberries
- Rhubarb
- Strawberries (under cloches)

General:

- Apply nitrogen such as hoof and horn to strawberries if growth is poor as this will promote improved growth over several weeks. Commence foliar feeding with seaweed extract at least every two weeks.
- Protect blossoms of late-flowering fruit from frosts. Remove blossom from newly planted trees.
- De-shoot wall-trained peaches and nectarines and remove shoots from wall-trained plums and damsons growing towards or away from a wall.
- Hoe off or pull out raspberry suckers appearing between rows.
- Mow grass around fruit trees.
- On indoor vines, allow only one flower truss to develop on each lateral shoot and remove the others. Pinch out the tips of fruiting laterals two leaves past a flower truss and non-fruiting laterals after five leaves. Stop side-shoots after one leaf.
- Open one side of fruit cage to allow entry for pollinating insects.
- Remove unwanted shoots from raspberries, leaving only strong healthy growth.
- Shorten back leaders and side-shoots on over-vigorous restricted forms of apples and pears (such as cordons, espalier fans etc.).
- Start netting all fruit at the first sign of ripening.
- Water all bushes and trees well (especially stone fruits and those trained against walls) after flowering.

Above: *Net bushes as fruit ripens.*

Above: *Harvest rosemary.*

HERBS

Sowing outdoors now:

- Basil
- Borage
- Chervil
- Coriander (cilantro)
- Dill
- Fennel
- Florence fennel (bolt-resistant)
- Nasturtium

Harvesting now:

- Bay
- Rosemary
- Sage

General:

- Top-dress container-grown herbs with garden compost.
- Lift and divide chives, hyssop, rosemary and sorrel. Replant with a little added compost.

PLANT HEALTH

Pests and diseases:

▷ Ensure good air circulation in the greenhouse to reduce risk of botrytis and downy mildew on grapes and, if needed, start to apply shading to the greenhouse to prevent overheating.

▷ Control slugs and snails and check all plants for pests, diseases and dieback. Be ready to spray against pests as soon as they are noticed, using natural products. Watch for the tell-tale holes of flea beetle attacks on brassica seedlings. Water well to help them grow out of the pest damage.

▷ Pests can be kept off a wide range of crops by covering with a fine woven plastic mesh, such as Enviromesh. Just make sure that the corners are tucked in or buried to prevent the pests breaching this defence.

▷ Put up pheromone traps in the orchard to help reduce codling moth numbers. Biological control (such as *Bacillus thruingiensis*) may be needed if numbers are high.

▷ Set out companion plants (annuals) around all trees and bushes to encourage beneficial predators.

▷ If using spray of natural products, such as neem, citronella or garlic oil against pests, delay applying this until flowering is complete.

▷ Do not be too worried if the leaves on a pear tree start to come up in small pale blisters. This is probably due to the pear leaf blister mite and, although there are currently no effective organic controls for this, the damage is not as severe as the plant's appearance may suggest and infested trees can still go on to produce a good crop of pears.

Above: *Put straw around strawberries.*

▷ Put dry straw around strawberry plants in order to deter slugs and keep fruit clean. Remove blossom from spring-planted runners of summer-fruiting strawberries.

▷ Weed control is very important at this time of year as they can easily compete with your crops for moisture and nutrients. Hoe between rows during dry weather to maximize the effect of this treatment.

Soil and climate:

▷ Be prepared to drape some fleece over more tender crops if cold weather threatens.

Above: *The flavour of home-grown cherries, far surpasses that of store-bought ones as they should be eaten as fresh as possible.*

EARLY SUMMER

Early summer is the time that sees the longest day of the year, and the associated extra light and warmth encourages the garden to put on an exuberant burst of growth. As a result, the allotment really starts to become productive around now. Prolonged warm spells will also accelerate the rate at which the soil dries out, however, so new plants must also be watered and greenhouses, frames and cloches will need good ventilation during the daytime to prevent inside temperatures soaring.

OVERVIEW

The ever-strengthening sunshine during the early part of the summer means that gardeners need to keep on top of weeds from now on. Hoe annual weeds off and dig out any persistent perennial ones regularly. Mulching when the ground is wet can help suppress weeds as well as conserving moisture.

Early summer is the prime time to plant out tender crops that have been lovingly raised under cover. If you hardened them off properly in late spring then they should be fine, but be prepared to place a covering of fleece over them if cold nights threaten. This will reward you with stronger plants, which in turn helps improve yields.

Although weeding and watering will be the two most important tasks of the month, pests and diseases can become a real problem. Be vigilant and look out for them, as you will need to act quickly once, and if, you find them. Time spent now is a real investment for ensuring the best results at harvest time.

VEGETABLES

Sowing outdoors now:

- Beetroot (beets)
- Cabbages (Chinese)
- Calabrese
- Carrots
- Chicory (Belgian endive)
- Chinese broccoli
- Courgettes (zucchini)
- Endives
- French and runner (green) beans
- Kohlrabi
- Lettuces
- Marrows (large zucchini)
- Oriental greens
- Peas (maincrop)
- Pumpkins and squashes
- Radishes
- Spring onions (scallions)
- Swedes (rutabagas)
- Turnips

Planting outdoors now:

- Courgettes
- Runner (green) beans
- Sweetcorn (corn)
- Tomatoes (outdoor)

Transplant:

- Broccoli
- Brussels sprouts
- Kale
- Leeks

Above: *Harvest Swiss chard.*

Harvesting now:

- Asparagus
- Beetroot
- Broad (fava) beans
- Calabrese
- Carrots
- Cauliflowers (spring-heading and early summer)
- Chicory
- Cucumbers (indoor)
- Endives
- French beans
- Kohlrabi
- Lettuces
- Onions (bulb – autumn-sown)
- Peas (early and maincrop)
- Potatoes (early)
- Radishes
- Spring cabbages
- Spring onions
- Spinach (summer)
- Swiss chard
- Turnips

General:

- Earth up late potatoes.
- Pinch out the top of broad beans once the lowest flowers have set.
- Set up an irrigation system.
- Support climbing French and runner beans with canes.
- Thin rows of vegetables when they become overcrowded.

Last chance to:

- Harvest the last asparagus.
- Plant celery and outdoor tomatoes.
- Sow calabrese, swede, courgette, marrow, squash, pumpkin and summer spinach.

Above: *Uproot fresh young carrots.*

FRUIT

Planting now:

- Melons

Prune now:

- Begin summer pruning of apples and pears.
- Carefully tie fragile new growths of climbing fruit plants.
- Continue disbudding wall-trained peaches or nectarines and tie-in selected shoots.
- Pinch out the top buds on the young shoots of figs at five leaves.
- Prune out old canes on newly planted raspberries.
- Red and white currants will need to be summer pruned before mid-summer.
- Thin and summer prune gooseberries as mid-summer approaches.

General:

- Apply nitrogen such as hoof and horn to strawberries if not already done and apply a dilute foliar feed of seaweed extract at least every two weeks.
- Loosely tie in new shoots of raspberries and train in new shoots of blackberries and hybrid berries.
- Mulch raspberries and currants.
- Peg down runners of strawberries for new plants. Transplant these once they have rooted.
- Put straw, black polythene or mats down for strawberries, and remove unwanted runners.
- Remove any fruits from fan-trained cherries and plums that are growing towards a wall or fence.

Above: *Harvest raspberries.*

- Thin apples lightly if fruit set is heavy, waiting until after mid-summer drop for a final thinning.
- Thin fruits on plums in the early part of the month and again toward the end of the month.
- Thin gooseberries toward the end of the month.
- Thin pears if heavily set.
- Ventilate protected strawberry plants and remove cloches when fruiting has finished.
- Water fruit when necessary and spray foliage in evening during hot weather if possible.

Harvesting now:

- Cherries
- Gooseberries
- Raspberries
- Red and white currants
- Rhubarb
- Strawberries

Last chance to:

- Prune gooseberries, red and white currants.

HERBS

Sowing outdoors now:

- Basil
- Borage
- Chives
- Coriander (cilantro)
- Fennel
- Parsley
- Rocket (arugula)
- Savory (summer and winter)

Harvesting now:

- Bay
- Borage flowers
- Chives
- Nasturtium (leaves and flowers)
- Parsley
- Rosemary
- Sage
- Tarragon
- Thyme

General:

- Hoe and remove weeds regularly.
- Plant out pots of basil or other tender herbs raised under cover.
- Take softwood cuttings of shrubby herbs.
- Trim shrubby herbs after flowering.

PLANT HEALTH

Pests and diseases:

▷ Hang sticky straps in greenhouses to monitor flying pest numbers, treating all pest outbreaks as they are detected.

▷ Continue to protect fruit against birds and regularly check nets for deterioration or damage.

▷ Check for signs of damage on raspberry canes from raspberry beetle, spraying with derris if it is found.

▷ Continue to watch for the tell-tale holes of flea beetle attacks on brassica seedlings.

▷ Keep alert for gooseberry sawfly damage and the raised red blisters of currant blister aphid.

▷ Keep an eye out for asparagus beetles, which are black, red and yellow, and their creamy-black larvae. Pick them off stems and foliage by hand.

▷ Check for signs of apple and pear canker, bacterial canker, and blossom wilt, removing affected material and burning it immediately.

Soil and climate:

▷ Improve ventilation and shade greenhouses or frames if necessary.

▷ Ventilate greenhouses and conservatories every day, but remember to close the vents on chilly nights to prevent a sudden temperature drop.

▷ Remove cloches from all outdoor crops as the risk of frost disappears.

▷ Hoe between rows during dry weather to remove weeds, which can compete with your crops for moisture and nutrients.

Above: *Shade greenhouses.*

MID-SUMMER

Traditionally the warm mid-summer period is a time when you start to gain a real sense of the harvest to come. These long, balmy summer days also offer a chance to sit back and enjoy the work of the previous months, as the long days and summer evenings ensure that there is time to do this after you have tended your crops. There is still plenty to be done though, and hot, dry days can mean that you will spend much of your time making sure everything is kept fed and watered.

Above: *Runner beans (pictured) and French beans are prolific, and provide a bountiful and reliable crop for relatively little effort.*

OVERVIEW

Mid-summer is usually the hottest and driest part of the year. While it can still be prone to showers and unsettled periods, rain is often a bonus and you should try and save water when you can. Frost is rare now, but not impossible, and gardeners in cold areas still need to keep an eye on the local forecasts.

Weeds grow at a phenomenal rate at this time of year, meaning that plots should be regularly hoed off, preferably weekly or even more frequently to ensure control. Pests and diseases also thrive in the warmth, meaning that you will inevitably need to treat these with chemical or biological controls in order to protect your crops from harm.

A lot of crops will be ready for harvesting this month and many of these will need to be gathered quickly as they can soon be past their best if left out. Even if you have a glut, never leave crops to rot as they can quickly spread disease to their neighbours. Share and swap excess produce with neighbouring plot holders, if you like.

VEGETABLES

Sowing outdoors now:

- Beetroot (beets)
- Carrots
- Calabrese
- Chicory (sugar-loaf and red)
- Endives
- Florence fennel
- Kohlrabi
- Lettuces
- Oriental greens
- Peas (maincrop)
- Spring cabbages
- Swiss chard
- Turnips
- Winter radishes

Planting outdoors now:

- Broccoli
- Kale
- Leeks
- Sprouts
- Winter cabbages

Harvesting now:

- Asparagus peas
- Beetroot
- Cabbages (summer)
- Calabrese
- Capsicums (protected)
- Carrots
- Cauliflowers (early summer)
- Celery (self-blanching)
- Chicory
- Courgettes (zucchini)
- Cucumbers
- Endives
- Florence fennel
- French (green) beans
- Globe artichokes
- Kohlrabi
- Lettuces
- Marrows (large zucchini)
- Onions (bulb and spring)
- Peas
- Potatoes (early)
- Pumpkins
- Radishes (summer)
- Runner (green) beans
- Salad leaves
- Shallots
- Spinach (New Zealand and summer)
- Squashes
- Sweetcorn (corn)
- Swiss chard
- Tomatoes (protected)
- Turnips

General:

- Apply regular doses of liquid manure to heavy feeders.
- As cauliflowers start to form their curds, break a few leaves over the curd to protect them from the sun and keep them white.
- Dry shallots ready for storing.
- Earth up and stake brassicas.
- Earth up sweetcorn and celery.
- Feed plants when necessary, usually once every 1–2 weeks with a liquid feed.
- Hand-pollinate the female flowers of marrows and courgettes if fruit is failing to set.
- Mulch runner beans after watering.
- Pinch out any remaining side shoots of cordon tomatoes (not bush types).
- Spray the flowers of outdoor tomatoes and runner beans with water to ensure a good set of fruit.
- Thin carrots and beetroot as they start to fill out.
- Water outdoor cucumbers, marrows, courgettes and beans regularly.

Last chance to:

- Sow beetroot, Florence fennel, beans (French and runner), maincrop and early peas and lettuces (main outdoor crop).

Above: *Harvest young potatoes.*

FRUIT

PLANTING NOW:

- Continue to peg down strawberry runners if new plants are needed.

PRUNE:

- As soon as raspberries have finished cropping, prune out old canes and tie in new ones.
- Complete the summer pruning of all trained fruit trees and bushes by the end of the month but delay if wet as this can encourage water sprouts near the cut branch tips.
- Protect the surface of wounds on plum trees with an antifungal control.
- Prune fan-trained plum and cherry trees.
- Spur prune gooseberries.

HARVESTING NOW:

- Blackberries
- Blackcurrants
- Blueberries
- Cherries
- Gooseberries
- Loganberries
- Melons
- Peaches
- Raspberries
- Rhubarb
- Strawberries

GENERAL:

- Check tree ties for constriction and loosen appropriately.
- Complete any remaining thinning on apples and plums and support heavily laden branches.
- If you have fruit bushes such as citrus growing under cover, these can go outside until the autumn.
- Train in new canes of blackberries, keeping a couple of longer ones so that tip layering for new plants can be done at the end of the month.
- Water all fruit-laden plants when necessary and protect all remaining fruits against birds. Spray foliage in evenings during hot weather.

LAST CHANCE TO:

- Summer-prune wall-trained fruit trees.

HERBS

SOWING OUTDOORS NOW:

- Basil
- Borage
- Coriander (cilantro)
- Chervil
- Parsley

HARVESTING NOW

- Basil
- Dill
- Hyssop
- Lemon balm
- Marjoram
- Mint
- Parsley
- Sage
- Summer savory
- Tarragon
- Thyme

GENERAL:

- Begin gathering seed of caraway and angelica.
- Dead-head where flowers have faded, unless seed is to be collected.
- Dry any excess pickings for later use.
- Feed plants when necessary, usually once every one to two weeks.
- Hoe and remove weeds regularly.
- Most other herbs can also be sown now, and constant picking will help keep young shoots coming throughout the summer.
- Mulch around the bases of moisture-loving herbs such as mint or parsley.
- Take softwood cuttings.
- Thin seedlings sown outdoors.
- Water any plants that show signs of stress.

Above: *Tarragon is at its best in summer.*

Above: *Hoe weeds regularly.*

PLANT HEALTH

Pests and diseases:

▷ Continue to check plants regularly for pests and diseases and treat them accordingly.

▷ Watch out for potato blight, which can be a problem at this time of year, particularly when damp. Remember that it often also attacks tomatoes. Lift potatoes and harvest tomatoes as soon as it is seen. Burn affected plants.

▷ Remove mouldy or damaged strawberries to prevent the spread of botrytis (grey mould) and, immediately after they have finished cropping, remove foliage, straw, surplus runners and all weeds. Dispose of debris, preferably by burning.

▷ Remove any fallen plant debris, such as leaves or old flowers, as this will prevent potential pest and disease problems later in the year.

▷ Keep an early eye out for the sunken brown patches of blossom end rot on tomatoes, especially if the weather has been dry. It can be a sign of irregular watering.

Soil and climate:

▷ Ventilate glasshouses to their maximum to prevent scorch damage to remaining plants and water crops freely in early morning or late evening to avoid the risk of leaf scorch on hot days.

▷ Damp down greenhouses on very hot days.

▷ Continue to hoe off weeds regularly in dry weather.

LATE SUMMER

Late summer is generally the last of the truly hot months and is often dry and sunny, especially at its start. In some places, however, the late summer can be prone to thunderstorms, and as a consequence it may tend to be humid and dull, providing the perfect conditions for pests and diseases to thrive in. Weeds continue to grow apace and as days begin to shorten, the burdens of weeding, watering, and the increasing numbers of plants ready for harvest can make this one of the busiest times on the allotment.

Above: *Choose a sunny day in late summer to dry onions on the surface of the soil, ready for autumn storage.*

OVERVIEW

Many vegetables are ready for harvesting this month and it is important that this is done promptly, as they can soon be past their best. Never leave crops to rot as they can spread disease to their neighbours. Always ensure that rows of crops do not become overcrowded.

Despite the fact that the days are often still hot, evenings are starting to draw in by the end of the summer and it is wise to start to make plans for the coming months. This is a good time to sow and raise seeds for autumn-planted crops. Prepare vacant ground for these future crops by digging deeply, removing any trace of weeds and crop the residue as you go. Work in plenty of garden compost or well-rotted manure as you do this.

You will also need to prepare a plan for how to deal with the crops to be harvested. Ensure your storage areas are clear and clean, and make a timetable for preparing preserves, pickles or for freezing your produce.

VEGETABLES

Sowing outdoors now:

- Chicory (sugar-loaf and red)
- Chinese cabbages
- Corn salad
- Endives
- Florence fennel
- Kohlrabi
- Land cress
- Lettuces
- Onions (bulb)
- Oriental greens
- Radishes (summer and winter)
- Scorzonera
- Spring cabbages
- Spring onions (winter scallions)
- Swiss chard
- Turnips
- Winter radishes

Planting outdoors now

- Cauliflowers
- Late cabbages
- Leeks

Harvesting now:

- Asparagus peas
- Aubergines (eggplants)
- Beetroot (beets)
- Broad (fava) beans
- Cabbages (summer, autumn, Chinese)
- Carrots
- Cauliflowers (summer and early autumn)
- Celery (self-blanching)
- Chicory (sugar-loaf and red)
- Courgettes (zucchini)
- Endives
- Florence fennel
- French (green) beans
- Garlic
- Globe artichokes
- Kohlrabi
- Leeks
- Lettuces
- Marrows (large zucchini)
- Onions (bulbs)
- Oriental greens
- Potatoes (maincrop)
- Pumpkins
- Radishes (summer)
- Runner (green) beans
- Shallots
- Spinach (New Zealand)
- Spring onions
- Squashes
- Sweetcorn (corn)
- Swiss chard
- Tomatoes (outdoor)
- Turnips

General:

- Earth up and stake brassicas that are to be kept for late autumn, winter or spring cropping.
- Feed plants when necessary, usually once every one to two weeks, with a liquid feed.
- Green manure or winter cover crops.
- Hoe weeds during hot weather.
- If the weather is dry, apply water directly to the soil in mornings or late evening, rather than watering little and often, to prevent leaf scorch.
- Lift and dry onions, preferably in the sun, to fully develop their flavour.
- Pinch out runner beans that have reached the end of their support.
- Remove any foliage from pumpkins and winter squashes and lift them on to a straw mat or a couple of bricks.
- Stake outdoor tomatoes and pinch the growing tip out at four or five trusses.

Last chance to:

- Sow Chinese cabbage, spring cabbage, autumn cauliflower, kohlrabi, radish (summer), turnip, onions (autumn-sown) and Swiss chard.

Above: *Raise squashes up on straw.*

FRUIT

PLANTING NOW:
- Rooted runners of summer-fruiting strawberry varieties if beds were prepared last month.

PRUNE:
- Continue pruning restricted forms of apples and pears as well as any over-vigorous trees.
- Prune plums, gages and damsons after fruiting. Cover large wounds with a suitable wound treatment.
- Summer prune cobnuts and filberts by breaking strong lateral growths by hand to about 6–8 leaves from the base and leaving them to hang.
- As soon as wall-trained peaches and nectarines have fruited, cut out the shoots that have borne fruit as well as any dead wood, and tie in replacement shoots.
- Remove dead wood from fan-trained plums, shorten pinched-back shoots and tie in.
- Continue pruning and tying-in new canes of raspberries, blackberries and hybrid berries, cutting out old canes that have finished fruiting.
- Hoe regularly and mulch around the bases of trees and bushes with compost or grass clippings, leaving a gap around the stem to allow air circulation.

HARVESTING NOW:
- Apples (early varieties)
- Apricots
- Blackberries
- Blackcurrants (2nd half of month)
- Currants (last part of month)
- Loganberries

Above: *Harvest blackberries.*

- Peaches
- Pears
- Plums
- Raspberries
- Strawberries (perpetual types)

GENERAL:
- Continue to protect all fruits against birds and water fruit-laden bushes as and when necessary.
- Feed plants when necessary, usually once every one to two weeks with a liquid feed.
- Prepare ground for planting a new rhubarb bed.
- Prepare ground before the end of the summer for summer-fruiting strawberry beds.
- Prepare ground for planting currants, blackberries, peach trees, apricot trees and gooseberries.
- Spray foliage of all fruit in the evening during hot weather.

LAST CHANCE TO:
- Prepare beds for planting summer-fruiting strawberries.

HERBS

SOWING OUTDOORS NOW:
- Parsley (warmer regions)

SOWING UNDER COVER NOW:
- Chives
- Coriander (cilantro)
- Dill
- Parsley (cooler regions)

HARVESTING NOW
- Basil
- Bay
- Chives
- Dill
- Marjoram
- Mint
- Oregano
- Parsley
- Rosemary
- Sage
- Tarragon
- Thyme

GENERAL:
- Take cuttings of rosemary, bay and hyssop.
- Cut back flowered herbs such as marjoram to encourage a second flush of growth.
- Water any plants that may be showing signs of stress and mulch moisture-loving herbs such as mint to prevent them drying out.
- Thin seedlings that have been sown direct in the garden.
- Dead-head herbs with faded flowers, unless seed is to be collected from them.
- Gather seed from angelica, caraway, coriander, cumin, chervil, dill and fennel.

PLANT HEALTH

Pests and diseases:

▷ Remove any fallen plant debris, as this will prevent potential pest and disease problems later in the year.

▷ Check plants for signs of pests, treating these accordingly with a suitable control.

▷ Look out for the caterpillars on peas and brassicas, and spray immediately with derris or the biological control *Bacillus thruingiensis*.

▷ Remove apples, pears and plums affected with brown rot to prevent the disease from spreading and gather scabby leaves from diseased apples and pears. Do not compost any of this.

▷ Remove and burn any outdoor tomatoes and potatoes affected by blight to prevent further infection of the crop. Cut off stems from blighted potatoes and burn them, although the potato tubers can still be harvested.

Soil and climate:

▷ Ventilate greenhouses to their maximum to prevent soaring temperatures. Use shading if necessary.

▷ Water all crops freely when they are in growth and damp down greenhouses on hot days.

▷ Spread mulches over ground that has recently received rain. Rotted-down compost is ideal and will free up space in the heap for next month's waste.

EARLY AUTUMN

The start of autumn is usually a continuation of warm summer weather although inevitably, this gives way to cooler, damper and often rather windier conditions over the ensuing weeks. The other change, which becomes especially noticeable now, is the shortening days. Although conditions remain mostly mild in the day, frosts can occur anytime from now on, meaning you should protect or gather in the last of your tender, summer crops as cold conditions threaten.

Above: *Leeks keep much better in the ground than in storage, so it is best to eat them straight after harvesting.*

OVERVIEW

Despite the advent of cooler, shorter days, the growing season can be extended well into the early autumn, especially in warmer locations, simply by applying a mulch to crops in late summer to help keep the warmth in the soil for longer. Occasional night frosts become common as mid-autumn approaches, particularly in exposed areas, on high ground, and in frost pockets, so have some horticultural fleece handy for the odd nights when it is needed.

Early autumn is the time to reflect upon the success of your labours by reaping the rewards of your hard work, particularly in the vegetable patch. You are likely to have a glut of many crops and so you will need to set about storing it for the winter ahead, when the pickings from your plot can be quite meagre. Towards the end of the month the inevitable clear out must commence as you embark upon the autumn cultivations and soil treatments that will help nourish next year's crop.

VEGETABLES

Sowing outdoors now:

- Cauliflowers (for transplanting to a frame in mid-autumn)
- Lettuces
- Spinach

Sowing under cover now:

- Chicory (sugar-loaf)
- Lettuces
- Pak choi
- Salad leaves

Under cloches:

- Broad (fava) beans
- Carrots
- Lettuces
- Spring cabbages

Planting outdoors now

- Japanese onions (sets)

Harvesting now:

- Aubergines (eggplants)
- Beetroot (beets)
- Brussels sprouts
- Cabbages (autumn)
- Calabrese
- Carrots
- Cauliflowers (summer, early autumn and autumn)
- Celery (self-blanching)
- Chicory (sugar-loaf and red)
- Courgettes (zucchini)
- Cucumbers (outdoor)
- Endives
- Florence fennel
- French (green) beans
- Garlic
- Globe artichokes
- Kohlrabi
- Leeks
- Lettuces
- Marrows (large zucchini)
- Onions (spring and bulb)
- Oriental greens
- Parsnips
- Peas (maincrop)
- Potatoes
- Radishes (summer)
- Runner (green) beans
- Salad leaves
- Spinach (summer and New Zealand)
- Squashes and pumpkins
- Sweetcorn (corn)
- Swiss chard
- Tomatoes (outdoor)
- Turnips

General:

- Cover leafy vegetable crops with bird-proof netting.
- Cut down asparagus foliage and add to compost heap.
- Earth up celery, leeks and winter greens.
- Give Brussels sprouts a liquid feed.
- Keep up with watering winter squash and pumpkins.
- Leave the roots of pea and bean plants in the soil to increase fertility.
- Lift main crop carrots and cut off the tops. Put aside any with split roots. Store the remainder in layers of sand in seed boxes. Keep in a frost-free shed.
- Lift maincrop potatoes and leave to dry before storing them.
- Lift beetroot when they are the size of cricket balls and store in the same way as carrots.
- Sow a quick-growing green manure such as mustard, on land cleared of crops and dig in before it flowers.
- Stake plants of Brussels sprouts and sprouting broccoli exposed to wind.
- Start new compost heaps. Spread the compost you made this year over vacant ground.

Above: *Pick lettuces and salad leaves.*

FRUIT

Planting now:
- Strawberries

Prune:
- Complete any remaining summer pruning of apples and pears.
- Cut off old canes of blackberries and hybrid berries after fruiting and tie in the new ones ready for next year.
- Finish pruning and tying in summer fruiting gooseberries, cutting off any mildewed tips and burning them.
- Finish pruning wall-trained peaches, and nectarines.
- Prune blackcurrants and take cuttings from healthy plants.
- Prune plums and damsons straight after they finish cropping.
- Remove dead wood from wall-trained cherries. Tie down or cut out strong vertical shoots and complete tying-in.

Harvesting now:
- Blackberries
- Blueberries
- Apples (early and mid-season)
- Apricots
- Cobnuts and filberts
- Damsons
- Figs
- Grapes
- Pears (early and mid-season)
- Plums
- Raspberries (autumn-fruiting)
- Strawberries (perpetual)

General:
- Clear weeds around fruit bushes and trees as these may seed.
- Cover perpetual varieties of strawberry with cloches.
- Order new fruit trees and bushes.
- Prepare for storage by obtaining or cleaning wooden trays and boxes.
- Protect ripening fruit on outdoor vines by covering them with netting. Fold back leaves away from the fruit trusses. Remove damaged or mouldy grapes.
- Remove mulches from around fruit bushes and trees.

Last chance to:
- Plant strawberries.

HERBS

Sowing outdoors now:
- Angelica
- Chives
- Coriander (cilantro)

Sowing under cover:
- Chervil
- Parsley

Harvesting now
- Angelica
- Basil
- Bay
- Borage
- Caraway
- Chervil
- Chives
- Coriander
- Dill
- Fennel
- Horseradish
- Hyssop
- Liquorice
- Marjoram
- Mint
- Parsley
- Rosemary
- Sage
- Sweet cicely
- Thyme
- Winter savory

Above: *Transplant sage seedlings.*

General:
- Trim parsley to encourage fresh shoots and cut back herbs that have flowered, such as marjoram or oregano, to encourage a second flush.
- Take cuttings of rosemary, lavender, bay and hyssop and divide herbs before they die back in the cold, in order to keep clumps potted up in the greenhouse for use over the winter.
- Plant out spring sown seedlings of sage.

PLANT HEALTH

Pests and diseases:

▷ When bringing tender, pot grown plants under cover, check carefully for any pests and diseases they may have picked up outside, in particular red spider mite, mealybug and scale insect, treating these as they are seen.

▷ Remove nets from soft fruit to allow the birds to clear up pests over the winter. Hoeing around fruit trees and bushes will also expose pests to birds and other predators.

▷ Begin painting or applying grease bands to trunks of fruit trees to protect against pests next spring.

▷ Cut out gooseberry, apple and pear shoots infected with powdery mildew and destroy infected shoots by burning. Never compost them as this will spread the spores around the plot.

▷ Place slug traps around new sowings and plantings, ideally doing this a week or two before sowing or planting.

Soil and climate:

▷ Ventilate greenhouses and frames during the remaining warmer days to prevent soaring temperatures, but reduce ventilation once the cooler autumn weather sets in. Damping down usually becomes unnecessary as the month progresses.

▷ Reduce watering under cover and try to do this in the earlier part of the day, so that conditions are dry by evening.

▷ Make a note of what was growing where for your crop rotation before harvesting.

Above: *Apply grease bands to trees.*

MID-AUTUMN

Mid-autumn sees a distinct chill setting in as days become much shorter. The growing season is all but over and the winter feel is further enhanced at the end of the month as vegetation dies back and trees and bushes lose their leaves. There is much to be done on the allotment, though, in order to prepare for the new season to come, and the ever-shortening days from now until mid-winter mean that time spent on the allotment becomes all the more action-packed as a result.

Above: *It is time to pick apples when the first fruits have begun to fall and the stems separate easily from the branches.*

OVERVIEW

Despite occasional warm days, frosts become increasingly likely as winter approaches. Gales and rain are both to be expected from now on. Having said this, if the summer and autumn have been warm, sheltered locations can still expect reasonable conditions.

Prepare for frost by moving tender plants into the greenhouse. Outdoors, slightly tender specimens will need a covering of fleece, straw, bracken, paper or some other packing material to protect them from the ravages of the winter. A thick layer of mulch over dormant crowns of tender crops will ensure they return strongly next spring.

The wise should remember that it is easy to be tricked by the first mild days of mid-autumn, as with early spring. Warm days are frequently punctuated by sharp, night time frost, particularly under clear skies, and it is these sudden fluctuations in temperature that wreak havoc on any crops that have not yet been harvested.

VEGETABLES

Sowing outdoors now:

- Broad (fava) beans (mild areas)
- Carrots
- Garlic
- Peas (early round-seeded types in mild areas)
- Spinach (summer and winter in mild areas)
- Winter lettuce (mild areas)

Sowing under cover now:

Under cloches or cold frames:

- Broad beans
- Carrots
- Cauliflowers (early summer)
- Peas (early)
- Radishes (indoor)
- Salad leaves
- Spinach
- Winter lettuces

Planting outdoors now

- New potatoes (plant early cultivars in sacks of compost to harvest in early winter)
- Onion sets (winter)
- Spring cabbages
- Winter lettuces (mild areas)

Harvesting now:

- Beetroot (beets)
- Brussels sprouts

Above: *Harvest Florence fennel.*

- Cabbages
- Carrots
- Cauliflowers (autumn)
- Celeriac
- Celery (self-blanching),
- Chicory (red and sugarloaf)
- Chinese artichokes
- Endives
- Florence fennel
- French (green) beans
- Kohlrabi
- Leeks
- Lettuces
- Onions (spring and bulb)
- Oriental greens
- Parsnips
- Peas (maincrop)
- Peppers
- Potatoes (maincrop)
- Pumpkins and squashes
- Radishes (summer)
- Runner (green) beans
- Salsify
- Scorzonera
- Spinach (summer)
- Swedes (rutabagas)
- Swiss chard
- Sweetcorn (corn)
- Turnips

General:

- Continue to earth up celery and leeks.
- Protect cauliflowers by bending leaves over the white curds.
- Cut down tall stems of Jerusalem artichokes as they yellow and place on the compost heap.

Last chance to:

- Plant winter onion sets.

Above: *Harvest runner beans.*

FRUIT

Planting now:

- Strawberries

Prune:

- Finish pruning blackberries and hybrid berries.
- Prune blackcurrants if not already done, but delay the pruning of gooseberries, red and white currants until leaf fall. If bird damage is likely then delay this until spring.
- Remove any broken branches from stone fruit trees and treat the resultant wounds to protect them from fungal infection.
- Root prune excessively vigorous bushes or small trees, waiting a week or so after leaf fall.

Harvesting now:

- Apples
- Cranberries
- Grapes
- Melons
- Pears
- Raspberries

General:

- Commence planting fruit trees and bushes as soon as leaves fall.
- Do not mix late apples in the store with earlier cultivars.
- Keep apples and pears separate.
- Lift and divide old rhubarb crowns.
- Order new fruit trees early (in advance of the coming planting season) to make sure you get the varieties you want.
- Prepare the ground for planting new fruit bushes and trees from late autumn onward. Give a dressing of rock phosphate a couple of days before planting new stock.
- Provide winter protection for wall-trained outdoor figs to help embryonic green figs overwinter
- Take hardwood cuttings from this year's growth on healthy berry plants.
- Tidy strawberry beds, removing leaves from perpetual types.

Last chance to:

- Plant out strawberry plants before spring.

HERBS

Sowing outdoors now:

- Angelica
- Lovage
- Scatter the seed of annuals and second year biennials that have finished flowering.

Sowing under cover:

- Chervil
- Parsley

Harvesting now

- Bay
- Marjoram
- Parsley
- Rosemary
- Sage
- Thyme

General:

- Lift and divide sections of selected herbs, which can be potted up and transferred to the greenhouse for use as winter crops.
- Parsley and herbs sown outside for late season crops will need to be covered with cloches before the winter.
- Plant evergreen hedge plants such as box if these are to be used to divide your herb plot.
- Plant hardy perennial herbs such as rosemary and sage.
- Tender herbs such as basil will not survive outside during the winter, so bring them under cover.
- Start planning a new herb garden or think about changes you want to make to an existing one.

Above: *Cover outdoor crops with cloches.*

PLANT HEALTH

Pests and diseases:

- ▷ Put up sticky grease bands on fruit trees to protect them from female winter moths. Tree stakes will also need banding if they provide a route up into the branches.
- ▷ Collect fallen apples and pears affected with brown rot. Pick off any affected fruit that remains on the tree otherwise the fruits become mummified and form a source of infection for next year.
- ▷ Remove mulches from around fruit bushes and trees so that overwintering pests will be exposed to birds and other predators.

Above: *Lift all potatoes and dry off.*

- ▷ Take care not to spread compost used for tomato growing over your potato beds, as these crops can share many pests and diseases.
- ▷ Always ensure that you do not compost any diseased material.
- ▷ Always check for slug damage and disease whilst hoeing between rows.

Soil and climate:

- ▷ Dig the plot over as soon as you have cleared crops, removing all residues except for the roots of peas or beans.
- ▷ Draw up plans for next year's cropping, paying close attention to crop rotation.
- ▷ Ground to be left vacant until the spring will benefit from having a green manure sown, such as field beans, winter tares and Italian ryegrass to prevent autumn weeds establishing and to act as a soil improver.
- ▷ Lift any remaining potatoes before late autumn arrives, as keel slugs become a problem by then and can cause considerable losses. Allow them to dry off and store in hessian or paper sacks to prevent storage rots.

LATE AUTUMN

Winter is drawing ever closer: a fact to which the leaves, which by now are falling rapidly everywhere, will attest. Long, colder nights and frequent rain tend to be the norm, but mild spells are possible and a few crops continue to grow and produce a harvest. The gardener's work is far from over, though, as late autumn sees the commencement of a great deal of pruning and planting, tidying and preparation, not only in readiness for the winter cold and wet that lies ahead, but also for the coming spring.

Above: *To harvest Swiss chard, cut the leaves from the base as they mature. Trim off any older leaves and discard them.*

OVERVIEW

Cold snaps are likely, particularly in the last few days of autumn, and frost, gales, freezing rain or even some early snow can become a distinct possibility, depending on where you live. It is important, therefore, that you and your allotment are prepared in advance for cold weather.

Once leaves have fallen from deciduous (not evergreen) shrubs and trees, these can now be collected and either put on the compost heap, or into plastic sacks with several holes poked into them. These will rot down and make leaf-mould – one of the finest soil conditioners there is. It is important that you use plastic sacks only for leaves, however, as any other plant material is likely to yield little more than a smelly, slimey, useless mess.

As long as the ground is not waterlogged or frozen, continue digging, especially on clay soils, so frosts can help make them crumbly and easy to work. Sandy soils can be left as late as early spring.

VEGETABLES

Sowing outdoors now:

- Broad (fava) beans (mild areas)
- Peas (mild areas on free-draining ground)

N.B. Keep both peas and beans under cloches if a hard winter threatens.

Sowing under cover now:

- Broad beans (in pots in an unheated greenhouse)
- Peas (in pots in an unheated greenhouse)
- Dig up chicory roots to be forced, pot them up and position them in a dark warm place.

Above: *Harvest leafy greens.*

Under cloches:

- Broad beans
- Peas

Planting outdoors now

- Garlic

Harvesting now:

- Beetroot (beets)
- Brussels sprouts
- Cabbages (winter)
- Carrots
- Cauliflowers
- Celeriac
- Chicory (red and sugar-loaf)
- Endives
- Jerusalem and Chinese artichokes
- Kohlrabi
- Leeks
- Lettuces (protected winter)
- Oriental greens
- Spinach (summer and winter)
- Swedes
- Swiss chard
- Salad plants
- Turnips

General:

- Cover endive and sea kale with bins or large flower pots to blanch them.
- Cut down any dead asparagus (if not already done) and cover beds or rows with crumbly compost or well-rotted manure.

Above: *Plant garlic cloves outdoors.*

- Give protection to globe artichokes in very cold areas.
- Order seed catalogues for next year, if you have not already done so.
- Place cloches over perpetual spinach to protect it.
- Place orders for seed potatoes now to ensure you get the varieties you want, as some are always in short supply due to popular demand.
- Remove yellow and decaying leaves from Brussels sprouts and other brassicas. Place these on the compost heap.

Last chance to:

- Plant garlic.
- Sow spinach (winter).

Above: *Finish picking pears.*

FRUIT

PLANTING OUTDOORS NOW:

- Cane, bush and top fruit trees, pruning these immediately after planting.
- Rhubarb crowns

PRUNE:

- All currants and berries not already done in mid-autumn.
- Begin pruning grape vines, immediately after the leaves have fallen. Cut all fruited shoots back to one or two buds from the main stem.
- Continue formative pruning of dwarf pyramid, espalier, fans and other restricted forms.
- Prune established apples and pears immediately after leaf fall, but do not prune plum trees.
- Root prune over-vigorous trees only after leaf fall.
- Summer-pruned trees should be pruned back to mature wood where secondary shoots have been produced.

HARVESTING NOW:

- Complete picking of all but the very late apples and pears.

GENERAL:

- If the plot is not ready when bare-root plants arrive, heel them into a spare piece of ground to keep the roots from drying out.
- Regularly check stored fruits, removing any rotting or mouldy specimens promptly so the rot doesn't spread.
- Take hardwood cuttings of gooseberries, redcurrants, white currants and blackcurrants.
- Check supports and wires for raspberries and blackberries and ensure that canes are securely tied. Loosely bundle new canes together and tie to a wire for winter protection.
- Check tree ties, stakes and rabbit guards on young fruit trees before any winter gales.
- Order any new fruit trees and bushes, if you didn't do this last month.

LAST CHANCE TO:

- Plant cane fruits (before early spring) on wet or heavy soils.
- Repair fruit cages to protect buds from birds during the winter.

HERBS

SOWING OUTDOORS NOW:

- Angelica
- Sweet cicely

SOWING UNDER COVER:

- Chervil
- Chives
- Parsley

HARVESTING NOW:

- Bay
- Chives (under cover)
- Hyssop
- Mint (under cover)
- Parsley (under cover)
- Rosemary
- Sage

GENERAL:

- Place cloches over tender herbs or those sensitive to excess rain, to protect them against winter wet and cold.
- Divide and pot up plants of chive or mint, and grow them under cover for winter use.
- In wet areas, apply gravel mulch and/or a well ventillated cloche to help prevent botrytis (grey mould) and fungal leaf spots on Mediterranean herbs, such as rosemary, sage and thyme.

PLANT HEALTH

Pests and diseases:

- ▷ Cover all brassicas with netting if pigeons are a problem.
- ▷ Watch out for pests, such as aphids, on over-wintering plants or glasshouse crops.
- ▷ Ventilate glasshouses, frames and cloches well on mild days and remove any yellow or dead leaves and plant debris to reduce the chances of fungal spread.
- ▷ As the days shorten, reduce watering to a minimum for specimens growing under cover in pots, in order to keep roots healthy and reduce the spread of soil-borne pests.
- ▷ Collect and dispose of any apples and pears affected with brown rot.
- ▷ Ensure fruit cages are closed and netting is in good order, as this will help prevent bud damage from birds.
- ▷ Trap winter moths by placing grease bands around fruit trees.

Soil and climate:

- ▷ Late autumn is a good time to check soil pH and to add lime if needed to bring it to the ideal conditions for next year's crop.
- ▷ Remove or clean off shading in glasshouses or frames and wash down glass.
- ▷ Remove all remaining plant debris from the allotment. Do not compost any diseased material; burn or bin it.

Above: *Remove greenhouse shading.*

EARLY WINTER

Although a few mild days are still likely, early winter marks the time where it begins to get much colder. The approach of the shortest day is enhanced by increasingly cloudy conditions, meaning that light levels are significantly reduced. This, combined with cold winds and the ever-present risk of snow or icy conditions, eventually brings crop growth to a virtual standstill. It is not a period of total rest though, and you should use the time wisely to make plans for the growing season to come.

Above: *You should try to lift any turnips by the beginning of winter or they may become woody and inedible.*

OVERVIEW

In all but the very mildest areas, or those within the shelter and stored heat of cities, night frosts should be expected from now until spring. Even in relatively mild spells, gales, wind and rain can make it feel colder than temperatures would suggest and it can be a tough time for any remaining winter crops.

Frosts are not all bad news, however, as they improve the flavour of winter vegetables. Sprouts, winter cabbages and parsnips are all considerably sweetened by frost, meaning that they are at their best from now until spring. Frost also helps to improve the crumb structure of previously dug soil, and may kill off some pests and diseases.

The hiatus in growth can be a welcome break, and one in which you can do plenty of planning for the growing season ahead. Review what you grew over the last season and spend some time reading the seed and plant catalogues you ordered in the autumn to see what is on offer and perhaps plan to grow something different.

VEGETABLES

Sowing outdoors now:

- Nothing

Sowing under cover now:

- Carrots (round varieties)
- Cauliflowers
- Lettuces
- Onions
- Salad onions
- Spinach
- Summer cabbages
- Turnips

Above: *Cover rhubarb with a plastic bin.*

Under cloches:

- Onions (if they can be kept frost free)

Planting outdoors now:

- Shallots (the shortest day of the year is the traditional time to plant them)

Harvesting now:

- Beetroot (beets)
- Brussels sprouts
- Cabbages (winter)
- Carrots
- Kale
- Leeks
- Lettuces (protected)
- Salad leaves (protected)
- Parsnips
- Perpetual spinach (protected)
- Swedes (rutabagas)
- Turnips

General:

- Dig up chicory roots to be forced, potting them up and positioning them in a dark warm place.
- Firm the roots of all winter brassica crops that may have been lifted by frosts and net them against pigeons.
- Force sea kale outside using a light-proof upturned pot.
- Lift a few leeks at a time and heel them in to freshly dug soil, which will not freeze solid, to make harvesting easier.

Above: Dig a slit trench for beans.

- Lift winter root crops such as parsnips and swedes before the ground becomes frozen, in very cold areas.
- Mature rhubarb crowns can be covered with a large forcing pot or an upturned, tall, plastic bin.
- Prepare a bean trench.
- Stake tall Brussels sprouts by placing a short stake on the windward side and tying the plant to it.

Last chance to:

- Harvest late trench-grown celery that has been protected from frost.
- Harvest the last of the kohl rabi before the end of the month.

FRUIT

Planting now:

- Apples
- Pears
- Soft fruit

Prune:

- Apples (in frost-free periods)
- Autumn-fruiting raspberries (to ground level)
- Finish any root pruning
- Gooseberries
- Pears (in frost-free periods)
- Redcurrants
- White currants

Harvesting now:

- Gather any very late-maturing apples.

General:

- Feed all fruit trees with slow-release fertilizers and apply a thick layer of compost or well-rotted manure.
- Lift and divide overgrown crowns of rhubarb, bringing small sections into a cool greenhouse for forcing.
- Take hardwood cuttings of soft fruit gooseberries, redcurrants, white currants and black currants.
- Trees that cannot be planted directly should be heeled in at a 45° degree angle.

Above: *Prune pear trees.*

HERBS

Sowing outdoors now:

- None

Sowing under cover now:

- None

Harvesting now:

- Bay
- Chervil
- Marjoram
- Parsley (protected)
- Rosemary
- Sage
- Thyme

General:

- Place cloches over tender herbs or those sensitive to excess rain (if not done already), and protect them from the winter wet and cold.
- Mulch the crowns of herbs that have died down for the winter – this will improve drainage and provide some frost protection.
- In cold areas, either bring bay trees under cover for the winter, or place them in a sheltered position.
- Bring mint, chives and other herbs into a greenhouse or sheltered frame to 'force' them for winter use.

Above: *Leeks and brassicas such as cabbages are winter mainstays on the allotment.*

PLANT HEALTH

Pests and diseases:

▷ Apply fatty acid-based winter washes to dormant fruit trees to control over-wintering pest problems, such as aphids, apple suckers and scale insects.

▷ Ensure that crops remaining in the ground, such as Brussels sprouts, cabbage and other brassicas as well as new sowings under cloches, are protected with adequate netting from pests such as mice and pigeons.

Soil and climate:

▷ Even at this time of year, a little winter sun can raise the heat in cold frames to quite high levels, so give ventilation when required.

▷ Reduce watering and feeding of all indoor crops as the days shorten.

▷ Clear leaves and twigs from greenhouse and shed gutters.

▷ Check all stakes and ties on fruit trees and bushes, 'firming in' any loose plants and loosening ties if constricted.

▷ Do not apply fertilizer to freshly dug ground, left rough to allow the frost to break the soil down, as without any crops, it will leach away quickly.

▷ Cover part of the vegetable plot with polythene to warm up the soil if you want to make early sowings in late winter.

▷ Top up compost and leafmould bins.

MID-WINTER

Mid-winter remains cold, and although the days gradually begin to lengthen, much of your plot will remain dormant. This makes it the perfect time to finalize plans for your allotment and firm your resolve in preparation for the coming season. Long winter nights present an ideal opportunity to brush up your garden knowledge by giving your gardening books a really good read and, on any fine days, you can catch up on a whole host of jobs before crops start to grow in earnest.

Above: *Brussels sprouts are plentiful in mid-winter. Their distinctive flavour often improves following a frost.*

OVERVIEW

As mid-winter progresses, it's soon time to make the first sowings of seeds under cover. As late winter approaches, take the opportunity to clean out your frames and greenhouses. Good hygiene will be important over the coming season as it will help to prevent fungal diseases that may devastate seedlings and tender plants later in the spring. Clear out all of the old plant debris and wash down the glass to increase the light transmission.

Take some time to thoroughly clean and oil all your garden tools to ensure that they are fit for action in the season ahead. Start by giving them a good wash, preferably with hot soapy water, but do not soak wooden handles as this can lift the grain. Leave them to dry thoroughly before wiping over with an oily rag to stop them going rusty.

If you did not finish your winter digging before Christmas all is not lost as heavy soils can still benefit from frost action in the cold of mid-winter.

VEGETABLES

SOWING OUTDOORS NOW:

- None

SOWING UNDER COVER NOW:

- Broad (fava) beans
- Cabbages (summer)
- Carrots (round varieties)
- Cauliflowers (summer)
- Leeks
- Lettuce
- Onions (early)
- Peas (early)
- Radishes
- Salad onions
- Spinach
- Turnips
- Winter salad leaves

On a heated bench or propagator:

- Aubergines (eggplants)
- Chillies
- Peppers
- Tomatoes

Under cloches:

- Broad beans
- Garlic
- Lettuces
- Peas (early)

PLANTING OUTDOORS NOW:

- None

Above: *Work from a plank of wood.*

HARVESTING NOW:

- Beetroot (beets)
- Brussels sprouts
- Cabbages (winter)
- Cauliflowers (protected)
- Carrots
- Chinese and Jerusalem artichokes
- Celeriac
- Endive
- Jerusalem artichokes
- Kale
- Leeks
- Lettuces (protected)
- Salad leaves (protected)
- Salsify
- Scorzonera
- Parsnips
- Perpetual spinach (protected)
- Radishes (winter)
- Sprouting broccoli
- Swedes
- Swiss chard
- Turnips

GENERAL:

- Continue preparing ground as long as it is not waterlogged or frozen. When working on wet soils, try to do so from a plank of wood, rather than treading directly on a bed, to avoid soil compaction.
- Force sea kale and chicory outside in milder areas. Chicory can also be forced indoors.
- Start the sprouts on early seed potatoes. Set the tubers to chit (produce shoots) as soon as they arrive.

LAST CHANCE TO:

- Order seed potatoes if not already done.

Above: *Sow early onion seed under cover.*

Above: *Mulch fruit trees.*

FRUIT

PLANTING NOW:

- Apples
- Pears
- Soft fruits

PRUNE:

- Apples
- Established and newly planted bush fruit
- Pears
- Raspberries (summer-fruiting)

HARVESTING NOW:

- None

GENERAL:

- Apply a balanced fertilizer such as fish blood and bone to cobnuts and filberts.
- Apply a potassium-rich fertilizer such as wood ash to strawberries, gooseberries, red and white currants to help them through cold spells.
- Mulch fruit trees, bushes and canes with organic matter.
- Place cloches over existing rows of strawberries to ensure an early crop. Remove covers on fine days to allow pollinators in.
- Prepare a bed for strawberries. Ensure that this is done at least one month before planting.
- Rhubarb can be divided and crown sections brought indoors for forcing.
- Sow alpine strawberry seeds under cover.
- Trees that arrive and cannot be planted directly should be heeled in, in a sheltered spot at a 45° degree angle away from the wind.

LAST CHANCE TO:

- Order bare-root trees and bushes for winter planting.

HERBS

SOWING OUTDOORS NOW:

- None

SOWING UNDER COVER:

- Chervil (glasshouse or frame)
- Chives (glasshouse or frame)
- Parsley (glasshouse or frame)
- Summer savory (heated propagator)

HARVESTING NOW:

- Bay
- Chervil
- Marjoram
- Parsley (protected)
- Rosemary
- Sage
- Thyme

GENERAL:

- As late winter approaches some undercover sowings of herbs can commence. Prepare the ground by placing cloches over the soil to warm it up before planting them out under these in early spring.

Above: *Make a plan for next year.*

- In mild spells, some plants will make new growth. Protect these with cloches to enable an early harvest.
- Review what has done well this year and spend some time planning new ideas and plantings for next year.
- There is relatively little to do in the herb patch at this time of the year. Most plants are dormant, surviving the winter on stored energy made during the growing season.
- Tidy the patch and prepare the ground where new plants are to be planted by digging well-rotted organic matter into the soil.

PLANT HEALTH

Pests and diseases:

▷ Remove big buds on blackcurrants and burn them to control the mite that causes this condition.

▷ Inspect apples and pears for canker, removing infected material and destroying by burning if possible.

Soil and climate:

▷ Check all tree stakes and ties on newly planted specimens for firmness, especially after gales.

▷ Move any stacks of pots, bundles of old canes, etc, outside to sit in the frost for a couple of weeks as this will help to kill off any over-wintering pests.

▷ Watch out for winter germinating ephemeral weeds such as chickweed or bitter-cress, which can soon overwhelm winter salads and other plants, particularly on rich soils.

▷ Avoid pruning fruit trees and bushes during periods of hard frost as the newly cut wound may be damaged by this.

▷ Net crops if not already done so to reduce pigeon damage.

▷ Regularly check stored fruit and vegetables and remove any rotting or mouldy specimens.

▷ Wash canes and supports in storage.

▷ Ventilate cold frames when possible to help prevent build-ups of mildew. Leave them open on mild days but remember to close them at night or if the weather changes.

▷ Continue turning compost heaps to increase decomposition. Leave freshly dug ground for frost to break down, as this will make final cultivation easier in the spring.

▷ When digging soils that are on the acidic side, apply lime to the surface at 70g/m^2 (2oz/yd^2). This is especially important if brassicas were grown in the plot the year before.

▷ Clear spent crop residue and compost. Burn items such as cabbage roots that could spread clubroot.

▷ Make a cropping plan of the plot and set out a rotation system for vegetable plots to ensure the same ones are not grown in the same beds year after year. This will help prevent disease build up.

Above: *Kale is a fabulous winter vegetable, packed with flavour and beneficial nutrients, so it is well worth growing on an allotment.*

LATE WINTER

Despite gradually lengthening days and the promise of spring to come, late winter often gives us the coldest conditions of the year, and this can limit the work you can do, particularly when frost or a covering of snow keeps you off the land. Despite this, however, it is also a time of promise as the new green shoots of spring begin to appear above the soil. It's a time to start raising new stock, and often represents the last chance you will get to finish planning and preparing for the coming season.

OVERVIEW

Despite the cold, late winter is a time to get out and check over-wintering crops. Although the winter takes its toll on the allotment, at the first sign of any warmth, those gradually lengthening days soon start to bring a return to growth for some crops and, with this, a fresh harvest.

It is still a little early for outdoor sowing, although seeds can now be sown under cover and it is time to plant some hardier varieties of crops as spring approaches. The real urgency now, however, is that late winter is the last chance to finish off all of those important jobs that help to pave the way for the season ahead.

Ground preparation can continue apace, as you begin to break down the rough dug earth that you left for the winter frosts to work on. Late winter is also the perfect time to apply a dressing of bonemeal to perennial or over-wintering crops. It takes a few weeks before it starts to break down in the soil, providing a ready source of plant food.

VEGETABLES

Sowing outdoors now:

- Cabbages (summer)
- Carrots (early)
- Fennel
- Parsnips

Sowing under cover now:

- Brussels sprouts (for early picking)
- Bulb onions
- Cabbages (summer)
- Cauliflowers
- Celery
- Celeriac
- Kohlrabi
- Leeks
- Lettuces
- Spring onions (scallions)

On a heated bench or propagator:

- Aubergines (eggplants)
- Cucumbers
- French (green) beans
- Peppers
- Tomatoes

Under cloches:

- Beetroot (beets) (early)
- Bulb onions
- Carrots
- Parsnips
- Peas (mangetouts or sugar snaps)
- Potatoes (compact early varieties)
- Radishes
- Spinach
- Spring onions (scallions)
- Turnips

Planting outdoors now:

- Broad (fava) beans
- Early potatoes
- Garlic
- Jerusalem artichokes
- Lettuces (autumn-sown)
- Onions (sets)
- Peas (early and snap)
- Shallots
- Spinach

Harvesting now:

- Celery
- Celeriac
- Chicory
- Chinese and Jerusalem artichokes
- Early purple sprouting broccoli
- Endives
- Kale
- Leeks
- Oriental greens
- Parsnips
- Radishes
- Salad plants (protected)
- Salsify (forced)
- Scorzonera
- Sea kale
- Swiss chard
- Winter brassicas
- Winter spinach

General:

- Draw up earth to the hearts of young spring cabbages and apply a fertilizer such as bone-meal.
- Dress asparagus beds with a general fertilizer such as fish blood and bone.
- Salsify and sea kale can be forced outdoors in mild areas.
- Start potatoes into growth now (if not already done), in trays in a cool frost-free place with plenty of light for around four weeks before planting.
- Start to dig in over-wintered green manures prior to planting.

Last chance to:

- Dig, lime or manure beds in time for spring planting.

Above: *Plant out early potatoes.*

FRUIT

Planting outdoors now:

- Rhubarb
- Strawberries
- Trees and bushes

Prune:

- Apple and pear trees
- Blackcurrants
- Cobnuts and filberts (if weather is mild)
- Gooseberries
- Newly planted and established stone fruits as growth begins
- Outdoor and indoor vines
- Raspberries (autumn-fruiting, to 15cm (6in) from ground
- Raspberries (tip-pruned, summer-fruiting)

Above: *Prune apple trees.*

Harvesting now:

- Rhubarb (forced)

General:

- Apply nitrogen-rich fertilizer and mulch to young trees, bushes and cane fruit with manure or compost as early spring approaches.
- Apply potassium-rich fertilizer to apples, pears and plums.
- Check all stored fruit and remove any that show signs of rotting or shrivelling.
- Check all tree stakes and ties on newly planted specimens for firmness, especially after gales. Do not let bush fruit or fruit trees crop in the first year.
- Cover wall-trained trees with draped hessian or the equivalent.
- Divide rhubarb crowns into sections, replanting some and forcing the remainder under cover.
- Place cloches over strawberries early in the month for an early crop.
- Sow melon seeds under cover in a heated propagator to extend the cropping season.

Last chance to:

- Plant bare-rooted trees and shrubs.
- Prune apple and pear trees.

PLANT HEALTH

Pests and diseases:

▷ Peaches and nectarines can be protected against peach leaf curl if not sheeted over by spraying them with Bordeaux mixture.

▷ Apply sticky bands to apple trees.

▷ Check apples and pears for canker and treat if necessary, pruning out infection if possible.

Above: *Tidy up plant debris.*

▷ Net cabbages and other crops to reduce pigeon damage.

▷ Dig up any 'volunteer' potato plants growing from tubers left in last year, as soon as you see them. They could be carrying potato blight.

▷ Clear up any plant debris, and remove diseased leaves from overwintered crops; put them on the compost heap.

Soil and climate:

▷ Ground left rough for winter frosts to penetrate can now be broken down if not too wet.

▷ Place protective covering over soil in areas where you are going to plant or sow seeds to warm up of the earth so that sowing can take place earlier.

▷ Elsewhere, complete all digging, liming and manuring by the end of the winter, if possible, as time is now running out for this.

Above: *Harvest hyssop.*

HERBS

Sowing outdoors now:

- Chervil (under cloches in mild areas)
- Chives (under cloches in mild areas)
- Dill (under cloches in mild areas)
- Parsley (under cloches in mild areas)
- Sage (under cloches in mild areas)

Sowing under cover:

- Chervil
- Chives
- Dill
- Parsley
- Rocket (arugula)
- Sage

Harvesting now:

- Horseradish
- Hyssop
- Parsley
- Sage
- Thyme
- Winter savory

General:

- Clear away any dead twigs and remains of fallen leaves from perennial herbs, especially if they are lying on top of the plants, and mulch them with a 2–5cm (1–2in) thick layer of garden compost.
- Lift, divide and pot up plants of chives for growing indoors.
- Protect tender shoots that have emerged during mild spells against hard frosts with fleece or hessian. Remove the protection on warmer days to allow air to circulate around the plants.
- Repair any paths and bed edgings as necessary before growth recommences.

SUPPLIERS

AUSTRALIA

Pest Control Tools, Sundries, Plants and Seeds
Flemings Nurseries
Web: www.flemings.com.au/

Garden Express Online Nursery
(Suppliers of a range of plants and accessories across Australia)
Web: www.gardenexpress.com.au/

Garden worms.com
Web: www.wholesaleworms.com/

Greenhouses, Sheds and Frames
ABSCO Delivered Sheds
Web: www.abscodelivered.com.au/

Greenhouses Online
Web: www.greenhousesonline.com.au/

Organizations
Australian City Farms and Community Gardens Network
Web: http://communitygarden.org.au/
(See websites for state contact details)

Sustainable Gardening Australia
Web: www.sgaonline.org.au/contact.html

CANADA

Pest Control Tools, Sundries, Plants and Seeds
Contech Enterprises Inc.
Web: www.contechenterprises.com/

Stokes Seeds Ltd
Web: www.stokeseeds.com/
Email: stokes@stokeseeds.com

Thompson & Morgan
Web: www.thompson-morgan.com

Greenhouses, Sheds and Frames
Cedarshed Industries
Web: www.cedarshed.com/
Email: sales@cedarshed.com

Rion Canada Greenhouse Kits
Web: www.greenhousescanada.com

NEW ZEALAND

Pest Control Tools, Sundries, Plants and Seeds
Edible Garden Ltd
Web: www.ediblegarden.co.nz

Kiwicare Home & Garden Pest Control
Web: www.kiwicare.co.nz

Waimea Nurseries Ltd
Web: www.waimeanurseries.co.nz

Yates
Web: www.yates.co.nz

Greenhouses, Sheds and Frames

Gary's Garden Sheds
Web: www.garysgardensheds.co.nz
Email: gary@garysgardensheds.co.nz

Winter Gardenz Greenhouses
Web: www.wintergardenz.co.nz
Email: grow@wintergardenz.co.nz

UNITED KINGDOM

Pest Control Tools and Sundries
Harrod Horticultural
Web: www.harrodhorticultural.com

Greenhouses, Sheds and Frames
A1 Sheds
Web: www.a1sheds.com

Plants and Seeds
Ken Muir Ltd
Web: www.kenmuir.co.uk

Thompson & Morgan
Web: www.thompson-morgan.com

Organizations
National Society of Allotment and Leisure Gardeners
Web: www.nsalg.org.uk/
Email: natsoc@nsalg.org.uk

UNITED STATES

Pest Control Tools, Sundries, Plants and Seeds
Planet Natural
Web: www.planetnatural.com

Stokes Seeds Ltd
Web: www.stokeseeds.com
Email: stokes@stokeseeds.com

Thompson & Morgan Seedsmen, Inc.
Web: www.thompson-morgan.com

Greenhouses and Frames
Frostproof.com
Web: www.frostproof.com
Email: questions@frostproof.com

Gothic Arch Greenhouses
Web: www.gothicarchgreenhouses.com

Sheds USA
Web: www.shedsusa.com

Organizations
American Community Garden Association
Web: www.communitygarden.org
Email: info@communitygarden.org
(Also covers Canada)

Green Guerillas
Web: www.greenguerillas.org

INDEX

Figures in *italics* indicate captions; directory entries are indicated in bold.

ABOUT THE AUTHORS

Christine Lavelle is a lecturer in horticulture and plant ecology at Writtle University College, Chelmsford, UK. She trained at the National Trust for Scotland's Threave School of Practical Gardening and the Royal Botanic Gardens, Kew, where she was awarded the Sir Joseph Hooker Prize by David Attenborough and the Kew travel scholarship by Professor David Bellamy to study plant conservation in the Galapagos Islands. Christine was assistant Head Gardener at Levens Hall topiary gardens in Kendal, and Hardy Ornamentals team leader at Askham Bryan College in York. Christine's main area of work is teaching practical and applied horticulture on a variety of Royal Horticultural Society qualifications.

Mick Lavelle has been a keen observer of nature since his early childhood. He studied horticulture at Askham Bryan College in York, England, and environmental management at Wye College in Kent. He worked as a landscaper before becoming a horticultural lecturer in the 1990s. Michael has designed and constructed several educational exhibits at the prestigious Chelsea Flower Show on the subject of plants and their uses, achieving gold and silver medals. He is a book author and magazine writer on the subjects of plants and gardens as well as a broadcaster on local radio. He is also a senior lecturer in landscape management at Writtle University College, Chelmsford, UK.

To our gorgeous daughter, Anne

This edition is published by Lorenz Books
an imprint of Anness Publishing Limited
info@anness.com
www.annesspublishing.com
www.lorenzbooks.com

If you like the images in this book and would like to investigate using them for publishing, promotions or advertising, please visit our website www.practicalpictures.com for more information.

Publisher: Joanna Lorenz
Senior Editors: Lucy Doncaster and Felicity Forster
Designer: Lisa Tai
Illustrator: Liz Pepperell
Photographers: Peter Anderson and Colin Leftley
Indexer: Diana LeCore
Production Controller: Ben Worley

Previously published, in part, as *Organic Gardening*.

ACKNOWLEDGEMENTS

The authors would like to thank Colchester Borough Council and all the wonderful gardeners at Colchester's Drury Road, Irvine Road and Bergholt Road allotment sites, especially Iva Sallis.

The authors would also like to thank the following people who worked as models for photography: Graham Thompstone, Jon, Hen and Oscar Marcar, and Sarah and Thomas Wiechamp.

The publisher would like to thank the following picture libraries for allowing their photographs to be reproduced in the book (t=top, b=bottom, l=left, r=right, m=middle): **Corbis:** 10b. **Felicity Forster:** 27tl, 225m, 226t, 234t, 248t. **Garden Picture Library:** 35tr, 135t, 135m, 135bl, 211 (moles), 213 (mosaic virus, onion neck rot, potato blight), 214b, 227br. **Holt Studios International:** 211 (cabbage root fly, leatherjacket, nematodes, sciarid fly), 213 (fireblight, phytophthora). **iStockphoto:** 18b, 25b, 35tm, 91b, 93br, 99tr, 198tl, 221br, 242t, 242b, 244t, 245b, 246t. **Joanna Lorenz:** 9r, 12t, 240b. **NHPA:** 210br, 211 (ants, chafers, deer, fruit fly, gall mite, mites, rabbit, sawflies), 213 (bracket fungus). **Science Photo Library:** 213 (clubroot, onion neck rot, potato common scab). **Helen Sudell:** 11b.